The Hopefuls

The Hopefuls

Chasing a Rock 'n' Roll Dream in the Minnesota Music Scene

Paul V. Allen

McFarland & Company, Inc., Publishers
Jefferson, North Carolina

LIBRARY OF CONGRESS CATALOGUING-IN-PUBLICATION DATA

Names: Allen, Paul V. author.
Title: The Hopefuls : chasing a rock 'n' roll dream in the Minnesota music scene / Paul V. Allen.
Description: Jefferson, North Carolina : McFarland & Company, 2018. |
Includes bibliographical references and index.
Identifiers: LCCN 2018042645 | ISBN 9781476675640 (softcover : acid free paper) ∞
Subjects: LCSH: Hopefuls (Musical group) | Olympic Hopefuls (Musical group) | Rock musicians—Minnesota—Biography.
Classification: LCC ML421.H666 A6 2018 | DDC 782.42166092/2 [B] —dc23
LC record available at https://lccn.loc.gov/2018042645

BRITISH LIBRARY CATALOGUING DATA ARE AVAILABLE

ISBN (print) 978-1-4766-7564-0
ISBN (ebook) 978-1-4766-3456-2

© 2018 Paul V. Allen. All rights reserved

No part of this book may be reproduced or transmitted in any form or by any means, electronic or mechanical, including photocopying or recording, or by any information storage and retrieval system, without permission in writing from the publisher.

Front cover: (left to right) Erik Appelwick, Eric Fawcett, John Hermanson and Darren Jackson (photographs by and courtesy of Stacy Schwartz)

Printed in the United States of America

McFarland & Company, Inc., Publishers
  Box 611, Jefferson, North Carolina 28640
    www.mcfarlandpub.com

In memory of Shalini Dhuria Van Hoek,
who introduced me to Minnesota music.

Acknowledgments

Great thanks to everyone I interviewed for trusting me with their stories: Peter Anderson, Erik Appelwick, Kii Arens, David Campbell, Andy Carlson, Joe Christenson, Chris Cunningham, Bill DeVille, Eric Fawcett, Todd Hansen, Heath Henjum, John Hermanson, Jay Hurley, Darren Jackson, JMatt Keil, Jim Kowitz, Ben Krueger, Ryan Kuper, Alex Oana, Matt O'Laughlin, John Ostby, Dennis Pelowski, Ian Prince, Chris Riemenschneider, Doan Roessler, Nathan Roise, Dave Scarbrough, William Schaff, Justin Seim, Johnny Solomon, Rob Stefaniak, Leo Vondracek, and David Weeks.

Appreciation to those who assisted me in one way or another: Darin Back, Scott Comstock, Kendra Focken, Dave Halvorson, Jennifer Halko, Jon Hunt, Dmitry Iyudin, Lindsay Kimball, Andrew Klein, Sean McPherson, Erik Ritland, Michelle Santos, Mark Schwandt, Stacy Schwartz, Andrea Swensson, Andrew Turman, and Andrew Zilch, as well as all of the Twin Cities music writers who worked the local beat between 2000 and 2014 and captured so many great quotes.

I literally could not have done my research without the Internet Archive and its wonderful Wayback Machine, which allowed me to extract valuable nuggets of information from 15-year-old defunct websites. The Coffeehouse in Normal, Illinois, provided a cozy spot to spend what felt like endless hours transcribing interviews.

Thank you to Layla Milholen, and everyone at McFarland & Company for believing in me and the book.

Love to my mom, Donna Grovesteen; my dad, Les Allen; and my grandpa, Leslie Allen, each of whom passed on a love of music in their own unique way. And of course deepest thanks and love to Wendy, Peter, and Theo for supporting my time-consuming second career.

Table of Contents

Acknowledgments   vi

Introduction   1

Part I: It Was Once Upon a Time (1969–2000)

1. Hi, Kids!   7
2. Different Waters   17
3. Half the Time with You   27
4. Somewhere in Between   38
5. Instead of a Habit You Should Have a Hobby   49
6. Stand Up and Win   57

Part II: Let's Go! (2001–2005)

7. Things Are Getting Better   69
8. Two Fronts   85
9. A Holiday Until Tomorrow   101
10. Everyone Needs a New Soundtrack   113
11. Before They Interfere with a Beautiful Thing Somehow   122
12. Don't Look So Surprised   133

Part III: Love Without a Future (2006–2012)

13. Blazing Out of Sight   142
14. Hold Your Own   158

15. Caught in a Mess	169
16. Seven Shades of Blue	178
Epilogue: Enjoy the Ride (2013–2018)	188
Discography	197
Bibliography	205
Index	211

Introduction

Showtime was supposed to be 20 minutes ago. We've watched the band carry in their gear and set it up on the tiny stage, but then they disappear for awhile. When they walk back on stage one by one, it's with no ado. The lights don't dim; the overhead music doesn't even turn off.

Despite the lack of usual ceremony—this is a slightly upscale bar on the edge of Loring Park, after all, not a club—they seem like trickster gods taking the tiny stage, resplendent in their matching red and orange tracksuits. They're visually striking, Appelwick tall and lanky with a lopsided sly smile; Darren short, bespectacled, and poker-faced; Johnny tucking his long brown hair almost shyly behind one ear while focused intently on his keyboard; Heath smiling widely; and Matt fresh faced and blond behind the kit. Darren asks politely that the overhead music be turned off, and his request goes unheeded. The band look at each other and shrug.

The feeling that we're seeing something special isn't solidified until they start playing, an insistent double guitar attack, rumbling bass, marching drumbeat, and whirling keys. "I don't think your mother likes me," Darren croons. "Your dad says my head is filled with rocks and sand." Patron conversations slowly fall away, though the overhead music is still audible in quiet moments (it won't be until the third song that someone behind the bar finally heeds the band's polite requests to turn it off).

The songs add up. They're energetic, harmony-laden, funny, emotionally piercing. The audience starts to buzz a bit more after each one: "Did you hear that one?" "These guys are local?" "How come I haven't heard of them?"

That was the first time I saw the Olympic Hopefuls, just before they took over the Minneapolis music scene.

* * *

If you paid any sort of attention to local music in Minneapolis-Saint Paul between 2000 and 2010, you bought a CD, heard a song on 89.3 the Current, or went to at least one show featuring Erik Appelwick, Eric Fawcett, John Hermanson, and/or Darren Jackson. As performers and producers their influence reached into nearly every corner of the Twin Cities music scene. Six degrees of separation? These guys only need one or two degrees to get to every big musical name in the Cities (Prince, the Replacements, Hüsker Dü) and to dozens more outside of it (Todd Rundgren, Flaming Lips, Dave Matthews Band).

Their accomplishments, collectively, are mighty. As songwriters and/or primary band members they've released more than sixty separate albums. Their work as producers and session players easily adds another sixty. They've sold in the tens of thousands of records without the help of any major label. Their music has appeared in films and TV shows, and they've performed on *Saturday Night Live*, *The Late Show with David Letterman*, and *A Prairie Home Companion*. They've brushed elbows with celebrities, shared bills and stages with their musical heroes, and toured the world.

Along the way, they were part of the revitalization of a proud Twin Cities scene that had fallen into disrepair. In the early 2000s, there was hardly any evidence left of the heyday of the '80s when Prince, Hüsker Dü, the Replacements, and Jam and Lewis made Minneapolis an hotbed of nationally recognized talent. Twenty years later, Prince had become the Artist Formerly Known as Prince and was wandering in a noncommercial musical wilderness. Paul Westerberg was a stay-at-home dad, Tommy Stinson was in Guns 'n' Roses, Chris Mars had given up music for painting, and Bob Stinson was dead. Hüsker Dü had been defunct over for a decade. Soul Asylum's hitmaking days were through. Jimmy Jam and Terry Lewis' Flyte Tyme Productions was soon to leave for California. Even the local bands that had populated a wild scene in the late '70s and early '80s—the Suburbs, Suicide Commandos, the Flamin' Ohs—were dormant.

There were still plenty of talented musicians, but both 400 Bar and First Avenue were struggling in the late 1990s and early 2000s to draw crowds to local bands, something both Johnny and Fawcett experienced firsthand. The Uptown Bar even stopped booking live music for a time in the late '90s. And the musicians themselves weren't banding together to build one another up. "It's amazing how scattered everything and everyone is," Semisonic bassist John Munson told the *Star Tribune* in an article about how to revive the scene.

When the Olympic Hopefuls came along, followed not long after by the debut of a groundbreaking public radio station, 89.3 the Current, and the concurrent rise of hip-hop labels Rhymesayers and Doomtree, the local scene became markedly more robust. And though that didn't necessarily mean the rest of the country and world started noticing them again, the Cities once again became a place where on any given night there were a ton of fantastic homegrown bands playing great venues to enthusiastic crowds.

That summer night in 2004 at Bar Lurcat I found the first here-and-now local band that I truly loved. It helped greatly that their brand of smart pop rock was exactly in my listening wheelhouse, right in line with favorites like Sloan, Matthew Sweet, and XTC. I had been slow to embrace the Twin Cities music scene upon moving to Minneapolis in 1999, partly out of not knowing where to start, but largely because it didn't really feel like there *was* a scene. Once OH came along, however, I was all in. I would end up seeing them 13 times over the next four years, and even now I regret that that number isn't much larger. Beyond the fact that I connected so thoroughly to their music and lyrics, a big part of their appeal to me was the band's configuration. I knew from articles in the local press that the band was comprised of members of other acts—a local supergroup, if you will—but at the time I barely had an inkling of where they had come from.

Part of the fun, then, of becoming a fan was discovering the everything else those guys were involved in, and just how vastly dissimilar those other projects were from OH and from one another. There was the dark indie rock of Kid Dakota, the groovy R & B of Vicious Vicious, the earnest power-pop of Alva Star, and the harmony-driven folk of Storyhill. Getting to know each of these groups only deepened my interest and affection. When Eric Fawcett joined OH after the demise of Spymob—a band I already adored—it just seemed meant to be.

Introduction

For a while there the guys were unstoppable. Appelwick's production work on Tapes 'n Tapes' record *The Loon* helped shoot that band into the indie rock stratosphere. Storyhill signed to Red House Records. The Olympic Hopefuls somehow got prominent enough to attract the attention of the United States Olympic Committee (and not in a good way). Rupert Pederson III, a dancing hype-man, started appearing onstage with OH, taking the energy levels to crazy new heights. They were heady times.

I loved the music, but the men behind it fascinated me just as much. What were they like as people? What inspired their music? How had they met? How did they get along? What was the division of labor in the band? How did they know which song fit with which project? And later, after OH dissipated, and life had taken me in other directions (marriage, mortgage, fatherhood), I started to wonder what exactly had happened to bring it all to an end.

It was all of those questions that prompted me, in the late summer of 2015, to get in touch with Eric Fawcett and have the first of many conversations that led to this book. During our first chat Eric warned me that I didn't have an easy road ahead, largely because "there are contingents of the band not speaking to one another." As a fan, this was disheartening news. As a writer, nothing could have been more intriguing or terrifying. I charged forward and found that to be one of the more minor revelations I'd uncover in my interviews and research.

When every interview was done and every article, interview, and old MySpace page had been scoured, I found myself with a very different story than the one I'd expected. When I first started researching, I jokingly told a friend that my template for the book was the bullshit line William Miller feeds his *Rolling Stone* editor in the film *Almost Famous*: "It's a think piece about a mid-level band struggling with their own limitations in the harsh face of stardom."

What really happened was that, like any good researcher, I let the research lead me. And that led me to a series of discoveries I couldn't have anticipated.

I discovered that the Olympic Hopefuls were only a part of a much deeper, richer, more complicated story. I found the real story was the improbably intertwined musical lives of Appelwick, Fawcett, Darren, Johnny, and decades of friendship, musical collaboration, and creative searching. These are four remarkable, and remarkably different, individuals. None of them originated from the Minneapolis-Saint Paul area, or even Minnesota, instead hailing from Montana, South Dakota, Michigan, and Iowa. Musically they came from different traditions that rarely cross over: folk, alt-country, jazz-pop, lo-fi. Their influences range from KISS to John Cage to Rush to John Denver. They have drastically contrasting philosophies and personalities—the joker, the talker, the searcher, the philosopher.

They each took their own distinctive path to becoming working independent musicians, their stories intersecting and co-joining in places along the way, wildly diverging in others.

But they shared several traits that likely brought them together and drove them forward: intelligence, versatility, work ethic, and above all the desire to be their best creative selves in a system that doesn't offer rewards based on merit.

I discovered that creative collaboration is an incredibly complex process. One of, if not *the*, most unique aspects of these four guys' work is how so much of it was the result of the musical collective they formed upon converging in Minneapolis. The first time one starts poring through all the liner notes and realizes just how much they all worked on each other's records and played in each other's bands, it's almost dizzying. And this was a huge part of their local success. They propped each other up, promoted one another, and worked together to achieve more than any of them could have alone. The Olympic Hopefuls were the culmination of that collaboration, the place where they all finally came together in one band. So it's very fitting that that's the place—at least locally—where they received the most love and acclaim. And maybe it's also fitting that it's the place where their collective fell apart.

Collaborative music-making is often a paradox. Bassist Brian Roessler calls it "an idealized version of how we should be with each other, you're listening to them and they're listening to you, cooperating with each other." And yet the most thrilling music is often made by people who despise one another or end up despising one another (for examples, start with Lennon and McCartney and Jagger and Richards and work forward from there).

Eric Fawcett explains this pardox as the result of two (or more) people in a band holding very different ideas of perfection. "Those two frequencies resonating together," he says, "sometimes in consonance, sometimes in dissonance, sometimes both, is what brings out the greatness in a band." He likens this tension within a band to counterweights on a balance scale. Things sway back and forth, but the scale doesn't tip over unless one set of weights is completely removed. When communication stopped and relationships frayed between Appelwick, Fawcett, Darren, and Johnny, the scale crashed.

I discovered that success is a spectrum. When I met with *Star Tribune* music writer Chris Riemenschneider, who covered all of these musicians in all of their iterations, he said, "The big question for the book is, are these guys happy with the way things have gone for them?" Success in the realm of rock music is often exclusively tied to fame and fortune, and at one point or another that was definitely the goal for Appelwick, Fawcett, Darren, and Johnny. Because that didn't happen for them—at least it hasn't as of this writing—the question of whether or not they could have or should have made the big time is one that nags their musical careers.

There were a few who believed that, had the guys lived in New York or Los Angeles, they would have become stars (Andy Carlson, co-founder of Peppermint CDs, says, "I still firmly believe that if Kid Dakota was based in Brooklyn in 1999, 2000, 2001 instead of Minneapolis, and some hip writer for the *New York Times* would have seen the peak Kid Dakota, that they would likely have become a well-known indie act as big as TV on the Radio or Interpol"). Some said that it was only a matter of timing (Riemenschneider said of the Hopefuls: "I fully believe that in the late '90s they were a band that would have gotten a big record deal"). Others saw the Olympic Hopefuls as a cautionary tale of hubris overtaking any chance of lasting success. While it's highly debatable if the OH had a realistic chance at any sort of sustained career as a major label band, the question of what might have been still lingers.

But that's all looking at things from a very narrow measure of achievement. If nothing else, these four musicians' stories illustrate that there are many other definitions of "making it."

Taking what you do as creative and emotional and personal expression and putting a dollar value on it, relying on it for your car insurance and mortgage or rent and groceries is an extremely untenable situation. Being an independent musician takes extreme sacrifice and requires a lot of luck and help, and even then the odds and economics are against you. Giving yourself over to a label often requires unpleasant artistic compromise, and the economics are only slightly less against you. And that was under the old model, before downloads and streaming changed nearly everything. Caught between the death of the golden ticket major label deal and Internet-driven acclaim, Appelwick, Fawcett, Darren, and Johnny all found ways to get their music to a receptive audience and make a living off of it. They were each able build up an impressive body of work under those harsh conditions.

Perhaps the truest way to measure the effectiveness of a creative endeavor is by what it inspires in others. Odd Future rapper Tyler, the Creator was asked by the *Austin Chronicle* in 2015 to name his ideal live backing band, dead or alive, defunct or active. His first choice was "Spymob from 2002 when they used to tour with N.E.R.D."

89.3 the Current DJ Bill DeVille describes himself as a superfan of the Olympic Hopefuls: "I didn't miss shows. I'd go see them wherever they played. Their shows were fun and eclectic. I miss 'em. I'd go see them again tomorrow."

When Grace Pettis appeared at the 2014 Storyhill Fest, she told Chris and Johnny, "Your fans are like a cult." As Garrison Keillor so humorously put it, they were "prisoners of popular acclaim," their devotees simply not allowing them to go away.

Communist Daughter bandleader Johnny Solomon credits Johnny for teaching him how to write songs and adds, "All those guys taught me how to be a musician, each one of them was hugely influential to my music. That core group of guys was basically my whole world. I wouldn't have the career I have now without that."

Musician and artist William Schaff says of Darren and Kid Dakota, "I'm blown away by his songwriting and his use of the studio. His voice is one of my top three voices in modern music."

Music manager and label owner Ryan Kuper said, "Of all the bands I've had anything to do with, more than anyone else, my friends, family, and industry people reference Vicious Vicious more, or bring up song titles and lyrics, or send me a picture of the album they stumble across, or a picture of the digital track playing on their car or their phone."

"You know, the reward is intrinsic," Alex Oana says. "The reward is in creating something together and getting to work with these awesome people. Building something that you couldn't have built by yourself. But for us also there was a dream attached to it." The dream wasn't simply to "make it big," but to have the prolonged career in music that comes along with that. When Olympic Hopefuls were forced to become the Hopefuls (a story told in Chapter 12), their name became a deeper expression of their experience. To be hopeful is to be optimistic, but to be *a* hopeful is to aspire to something, and at some point your ambition is either fulfilled or not. You can't be a hopeful forever.

Or can you?

Who Was in Which Band?

	Alva Star	The Blue Turks	Camaro	Communist Daughter	Friends Like These	The Harvesters	The Hopefuls	INTL Falls	Kentucky Air	Kid Dakota	Round Trip	Spymob	Storyhill	Tread Water	Vicious Vicious	Violet
Erik Appelwick	x		x		x	x	x			x					x	
Eric Fawcett	x			x		x	x	x				x	x			
John Hermanson	x			x		x	x	x				x	x			
Darren Jackson	x	x	x	x			x			x	x				x	
Peter Anderson	x						x									
Martin Dosh										x					x	
Heath Henjum							x			x					x	x
jMatt Keil		x			x		x									
Christopher McGuire	x		x							x						
Matt O'Laughlin					x		x									
Alex Oana	x						x			x	x	x	x		x	
John Ostby									x			x				
Ian Prince	x		x							x						
Doan (Brian) Roessler	x						x			x		x	x	x		
Dave Scarbrough					x											x
Justin Seim		x			x											x
Christian Twigg									x			x				

Note: Individuals were given an "x" for being a primary member, playing in the live line-up, or doing behind-the-board work (producing/engineering/mixing/mastering).

PART I: IT WAS ONCE UPON A TIME (1969–2000)

1

Hi, Kids!

In which we meet the cast of young hopefuls and learn their origin stories.

Darren Jackson was born in October 1971 in Bison, South Dakota. Located in the northwestern corner of the state, and boasting a population of 333, Bison has the distinction of being farther away from a McDonalds than any other town in the lower 48. It's not a typical origin point for an indie rock jack-of-all-trades, but music played a part in Darren's life from the beginning. His mother, Gladys, boasted a large record collection, and started Darren on piano lessons young. He never enjoyed it, nor did he find a knack for it. "When I stopped [taking lessons] I think I was just about a little better than I was at age five," he jokes.

But guitar was a different story. At 14 Darren first picked up the instrument, and a deep love was ignited. He became obsessed, and started a band not long after, recruiting classmates Justin Seim and Erik Hulm. The Blue Turks, as they were called, learned songs by a wide array of artists: Tom Petty, Ozzy Osborne, the Clash, Lynyrd Skynyrd, the Beatles, Guns N' Roses, and Johnny Cash. Their repertoire eventually grew to include 70 tunes, enough to fill four to five hours if needed. Soon they started getting gigs, playing proms, parties, and street dances all over western South Dakota. The band also went through a few name changes, an evolution that reflects the eclectisim of their setlists: the Turks, Blitzkrieg, the Beatniks.

Justin Seim says the band served as a vital connection between Bison and the other surrounding small towns. He claims that sports rivalries were often the source of great animosity between the teens of the various towns, but the Beatniks would play everyone's parties and engender goodwill that way. Darren was an athlete himself, starting for the Bison basketball team despite his modest height.

He also was in the school band and honor choir, and his musical tastes were ranging ever outward. Despite being a couple of hours away from the nearest record store, new music filtered back to Darren and Justin through mixtapes from friends who'd gone off to college, or magazines like the skater-culture touchstone *Thrasher*. That was how Darren discovered artists such as Suicidal Tendencies and Dead Kennedys. His favorites were the Replacements, R.E.M., the Cure, and U2, but he was also into Frank Sinatra, Harry Connick, Jr., Bill Evans, and Vince Guaraldi.

"We definitely had different tastes in music than your average western town of [less

Darren's high school band in 1988 when they were known as Blitzkrieg. From left to right: Warren Veal, Eric Clark, Darren Jackson, Erik Hulm, Justin Seim. Courtesy Darren Jackson.

than] 500 people," Justin says. "Kids thought we were weird because of what we were listening to."

The Beatnicks lasted through Darren's senior year, during which he decided he would attend Saint Olaf College in Northfield, Minnesota. Saint Olaf is a private liberal arts school known internationally for its choir, band, and orchestra. Since Darren planned to be a music major, with the goal of becoming a music teacher, the school seemed a perfect fit.

* * *

Erik Appelwick was born in November 1972 in Yankton, South Dakota. Yankton is located in the southeastern corner of the state, diagonally opposite from Bison. Erik's father, James, was a surgeon in the Army, and that kept the family on the move. When Erik was three or four the family moved to Fort Hood, Texas, and then a couple years later back to South Dakota, to Madison, about 95 miles north of Yankton. Madison is home to Dakota State University and a population of 6,474. This is where Erik started kindergarten, and where his rock star dreams were born.

When he was four years old, Appelwick asked his parents for KISS's live double album *Alive!*, which had come out the year before. They bought it, but Erik remembers that there was some debate between his parents about whether or not to let him have it, so the record sat on a shelf for awhile. It finally got into Erik's hands on his fifth birthday.

Erik imagines wryly that his parents said to themselves, "Well, he's five now, he's all grown up."

He recalls, "I played the shit out of it" on a portable plastic record player with a picture of a bowtie-sporting Mickey Mouse exclaiming, "Hi, kids!" from a text bubble. Appelwick's bed serving as a stage, rock star fantasies exploded in his head. "I wanted to play guitar like Ace Frehley," he says. Instead, like Darren, he endured unwanted piano lessons. It wasn't until he was 14, also like Darren, that he got a guitar.

That momentous occasion coincided with another family move, this time to Essexville, Michigan. Known as the "gateway to Saginaw Bay" on Lake Huron, Essexville has less than 4,000 people, but is close enough to Bay City to have the amenities of a larger city. Here Appelwick started high school, and music continued to be a lifeline. He says it was "the main thing that held my attention throughout my formative years." At 16 he got a 4-track recorder and started putting his musical ideas to tape. He also played percussion in his high school orchestra (he was first chair).

He was in a couple of bands. The first—the Beg—arose out of a high school talent show (its name came from its founding members' first names, Ben, Erik, and Greg—Erik fell in under the second "e"). His second band, Sacred Money, played R.E.M. covers and was inspired by the then-burgeoning grunge sound.

Appelwick's musical tastes ranged. In his early teens he reveled in the mainstream pop of Duran Duran, Michael Jackson, Prince, and Cyndi Lauper. In high school he gravitiated toward acts with more of an outsider perspective, artists like the Smiths and the Cure. During college he diversified a bit more, adding Pavement, Radiohead, and '70s R & B to the mix. He claims that his tastes didn't follow any particular logic save that he liked what he liked, but there's a definite common thread of strong melodies and lush productions.

Post-graduation, Appelwick enrolled in community college, but he lost interest quickly. His parents made it clear they would no longer support him financially if he wasn't seeking higher education, so he moved in with his girlfriend at the time, and made his living at the Great American Cookie Company in the Bay City Mall. He'd also hooked up with a band called the Rugby Mothers, formed by two brothers—Bryan and John Curry—who needed a bass player. And so, though he wanted to be Ace Frehley, Erik settled for being Gene Simmons without the lead vocal duties. Because of his almost innate sense of rhythm, honed as a percussionist, he had a gift for the bass. The Rugby Mothers were a "skate rock power trio" who played gigs as far away as Kalamazoo, Michigan, but mostly stuck to playing around their home base.

Around this time Appelwick lost both his girlfriend and his job in quick succession, and quickly decided to enter what he calls "the soft, warm blanket of parent-funded college living." For the conservative James and Linda, who never regarded music as a serious career choice, it was likely a relief when Erik headed off to the University of South Dakota, in Vermillion, to study English literature. Little did they know.

* * *

When Darren arrived at Saint Olaf he learned that not only does the school have its choir, band, orchestra, and ensembles, but also a fifth musical dimension: Saint Olaf had its own rock scene. Being a school that attracts the musically-inclined, it's natural that those whose tastes run beyond classical and jazz would need another outlet. And while the school doesn't formally facilitate the forming of rock bands, it definitely nurtures the conditions. This comes mostly in the form of the Lion's Pause, an on-campus concert venue and rehearsal space run by the Student Government Association. The Pause was already a campus institution by the time Darren arrived in the fall of 1990, and had been for a while. A 1979 LP, *Live from the Lion's Pause* documents original songs by students of the time.

Two of the bands Darren probably couldn't help but notice making waves on campus in 1991 were the whimsical piano-and-horns combo Shark Sandwich and the earnest acoustic harmony duo Chris & Johnny. Both groups were highly popular, and both, as it happens, were led by men that would figure prominently in Darren's musical future.

Shark Sandwich's drummer was Eric Fawcett, whose surfer blond hair and jovial loquaciousness make him seem more like he hails from California instead of Ames, Iowa. Eric was born in that college town in May 1969 to Kennedy and Audrey Fawcett. He was the youngest child. His four older sisters provided the soundrack to his early years, sharing their Joni Mitchell, Bread, Seals and Crofts, Styx, and Kansas records. When Eric was seven years old he discovered KISS, and the first record of his collection was the band's 1976 opus *Destroyer*. As it was for Appelwick, listening to KISS was a transformative experience for Eric. Peter Criss, the band's drummer, seemed like a "magical superhuman" to young Eric's eyes and ears. Though he admits now that Criss is not an especially technically-gifted drummer, the drum solo on the song "100,000 Years" (on *Alive!*) flipped a switch in his mind. Previous to this road to Damascus moment, Eric had been known to do the requisite banging on pots and pans, but now he wanted real drums. He singled out a blue sparkle set featured in the 1978 JC Penny catalog, and his parents obliged.

Eric Fawcett and childhood friends indulge their KISS obsession, circa 1977. Eric (second from right) sports the make-up of his drum hero Peter Criss. Courtesy Eric Fawcett

Fawcett's first band, Outrage, circa 1984. From left to right: Robb Vallier, Eric Fawcett, Jeff Vallier. Courtesy Eric Fawcett.

Fawcett started a band with two friends, brothers Robb and Jeff Vallier, in the summer of 1982. He had just finished 6th grade and his musical crush on KISS had been superseded by Rush and the Police, both power trios with iconoclastic drummers that Eric admired greatly. Those two groups served as the blueprint for Outrage, a cover band that would remain together for the next six years and play all over Iowa. The band used their 1969 VW Westfalia camper bus to travel to youth leadership conferences, proms, Christmas dances, Iowa Dairy Queen beauty contests, bar mitzvahs, fundraisers, and homecomings. Eric served a de facto band manager, lining up gigs and making connections.

Outrage's song choices through those years reflected their interest in quirky, progressive bands such as Rush and XTC, but also more mainstream stuff like Billy Idol's "Mony Mony" and Corey Hart's "I Wear My Sunglasses at Night."

Fawcett says now that being in a cover band—and this is likely true for Darren Jackson and the Beatniks as well—was the "greatest school for learning how music works, for learning how a song works." He goes on: "You have to really mindfully see how an artist is creating this thing that makes you feel a certain way, to really dive in and see, 'Oh I see what that chord change does,' or 'I see what happens in the chorus to make you wanna move your ass.'"

When it came time to choose a college, Fawcett initially planned to go to the University of Iowa in Des Moines, his father's alma mater. But a patient of his father's had suggested that Eric look at Saint Olaf. A liberal arts college was a draw because Eric didn't know yet what he wanted to do for a career. When he was a kid he'd wanted to be a meteorologist—his mom would even take him to the ABC affiliate station so he could see the weather man in action—but now he was directionless. "I was a driven kid who didn't know where I was driving," he says. One thing he knew at the time was that he wouldn't study music. He loved being in Outrage, but he didn't see a future for himself as a musician.

So fate had a twinkle in her eye in the fall of 1988 when she randomly assigned Fawcett to be roommates with John Ostby, a pianist and songwriter from Palo Alto, California by way of Annandale, Virginia (his family had moved west when he was 13). Having taken piano lessons since the age of seven—his first teacher was his grandmother, Borgny—John was already performing regularly by his early teens. He formed his first band for a middle school talent show, doing covers of keyboard-driven classic rock hits "Light My Fire" and "Baba O'Reilly." He had an affinity for pop, and grew up a huge Beatles fan, but it was jazz that initially inspired his own playing. While still attending Palo Alto High School, he studied jazz at Stanford and performed in both big bands and combos. Eventually he would circle back to pop, getting into what he calls "harmonically advanced" songwriters such as Paul Simon, Stevie Wonder, Joni Mitchell, and Steely Dan.

He'd started writing songs when he was a freshman at Palo Alto High School and was driven forward by a competitive peer group. "I had a lot of really talented kids around me. It helped me, even as an 8th and 9th grader, to have really high standards for what kids could do in songwriting."

Fawcett and John connected immediately. During their first conversation they discovered a mutual love of XTC's 1986 pop masterpiece *Skylarking*. This led Eric to introduce John to the music of Todd Rundgren, who had produced the record. With that kind of beginning, it was inevitable that the two would start playing music together. On the weekends they'd hook up with whoever was around and jam on original songs. Though they never performed for an audience or had a steady line-up during that first year, they did come up with a name: Nectar of Devotion. Eric says nothing expecially memorable grew from the band, "probably a bunch of wanking," he says, but it was a start.

Sophmore year, however, the two upped their ambition. They joined with Gary Rice, Jr. (a counselor in their dorm who played guitar), Joe Kutchera (saxophone), and Scotty Jones (bass) to form Shark Sandwich. The group's name was a reference to *This Is Spinal Tap* (in the film, Shark Sandwich is the name of one of the band's albums; it's mentioned that one critic gave it a two-word review: "Shit sandwich.") The band began to play gigs around campus almost immediately.

The main influence on John's songwriting for Shark Sandwich was a late '80s funk-rock revival that took over the Bay Area in the late '80s, typified by bands such as O Mighty Isis, the Freaky Executives, and Red Hot Chili Peppers. What those groups had in common, John says, was a recasting of supposedly cheesy elements of '70s culture as being cool. This became the model for Shark Sandwich, funk rock with a hint of jazz, and a horn section to keep things lively (Nathan Anderson had joined on trumpet). As Fawcett put it, the primary goal of the band was to get the kids to dance.

* * *

Chris & Johnny were contemporaries of Shark Sandwich, but the two didn't interact much. Besides a shared dedication to songcraft, the two groups couldn't have been more different. Where Shark Sandwich's songs were lyrically wry and musically fun, Chris & Johnny's were thoughtful and soul-searching. Where Shark Sandwich had horns, drums, and bass to beef up their sound, Chris & Johnny were stripped back to only two voices and two acoustic guitars. On a typical weekend night in the early '90s Chris & Johnny would play at Larson Coffeehouse in the early evening and Shark Sandwich would play later in their underwear at the Hockey House. And though the two groups knew some key people in common, they ran in very different circles.

Johnny was John Hermanson, from Bozeman, Montana. He was born in November 1970, the third child and only boy, to John and Pat Hermanson. His family was heavily into music. His father, a physicist, had harbored dreams of being a professional musician, and played multiple instruments, mainly the piano. His two older sisters played violin and cello respectively, and Johnny picked up the violin as well. The family performed together regularly. The first album Johnny bought with his own money was Hall & Oates' *Private Eyes* when he was 11 or 12 years old, but he says the first record that really made an impact on him was Queen's *The Game*, the 1980 opus featuring "Another One Bites the Dust" and "Crazy Little Thing Called Love."

In a 7th grade world geography class, Johnny's teacher had instructed the class to pair off for a project. He and Chris Cunningham were the only two left without a partner once the dust settled. They teamed up to research the Bermuda Triangle, and a friendship was born. The two were opposites in many ways. Johnny was confident and involved in many school acitivites. Chris was more introverted, and tended to keep to himself. Chris says of Johnny, "He was really kind of an exciting personality for me. I always liked his gung-ho, his enthusiasm for things. It was kind of captivating for me; it pulled me out of my shell, 'cause I was pretty shy." This led Chris to try activities he might never have otherwise, including tennis and choir.

When Johnny was a sophomore in high school he got an acoustic guitar at a garage sale, and this created another point of connection between he and Chris. Chris's parents were fans of singer-songwriters of the '70s, artists such as Gordon Lightfoot, Joni Mitchell, Jim Croce, and John Denver, and so he grew up with that kind of music constantly in the background. His family had an old upright piano that Chris used to play along to his favorite records, or just make something up. He also played trumpet in the school band, and took it very seriously, even springing for private lessons on top of those he was getting at school.

He and Johnny naturally began playing together. Typically they'd go to Johnny's house after school, and Chris would sit down at the upright and bang out songs by the Beatles, U2, or R.E.M., while Johnny played guitar. Other friends tagged along as word began to spread about these little jam sessions, but Johnny and Chris were always at the core. Eventually both teens started writing their own songs. Johnny's early compositions were lyrically informed by his involvement in his church youth

John Hermanson and Chris Cunningham at Chris's parents' house in eighth grade. They'd known each other for about a year. Circa 1985. **Courtesy Storyhill.**

group and an ELCA Lutheran wilderness/backpacking camp where he eventually became a leader, Christikon. According to Chris, getting involved in the camp served to both ground and give a sense of identity to Johnny, who had been popular in high school from the beginning. This had led him to grow his hair out, get involved in the underground music scene, and date older girls. The cool guy persona was balanced out by the church camp leader/religious persona, and these two identities would continue to run parallel for Johnny for many years ensuing.

Musically, the songs Johnny wrote were in the folk tradition, but that didn't necessarily represent the range of his musical interests. He had continued to play violin, and was a member of the orchestra and choir. He had also gotten an electric guitar and learned to play Pink Floyd and Def Leppard songs. His listening went in phases, from classic rock (the Beatles, Neil Young), to indie rock (the Smiths, Hüsker Dü,) to minimalist composers (Phillip Glass, Steve Reich).

Johnny was also a member of two bands in high school. One was a punk group called Shock Treatment Vacation. Johnny played guitar and sang in the group, but he didn't write songs; the lyrics, which John describes as "incredibly dark and offensive," were written by the band's drummer. Their one claim to fame was an opening slot for Green River—the band whose members eventually split into Mudhoney (Mark Arm and Steve Turner) and Pearl Jam (Jeff Ament and Stone Gossard)—at the Molly Brown in Bozeman. John also joined a talented local cover band called Taxxi, whose calling card read: "If you want a ride, call a cab. If you want to rock, call Taxxi."

The playing that Johnny and Chris had done together had been strictly for their own enjoyment, but that would change when they got a chance to perform together in public. Their choir director, Marco Ferro, had begun hosting candlelight dessert concerts where choir members could perform a solo or duet, and the guys signed up. Chris says, "Almost everybody chose 'Hey Jude' or some song that was popular, but Johnny and I decided to do an original." With Chris on piano and Johnny on guitar they did one of Chris' songs, "Broken Is the Word." When the two boys started harmonizing, the audience began spotaneously applauding the perfect blend of Chris's baritone and Johnny's tenor.

The enthusiastic response was galvanizing. Johnny started carving out more time for them to get together and practice, and encouraged Chris to keep writing. He also had a vision of dual guitars, so he basically told Chris to switch instruments. "I don't know what he said," Chris says, trying to remember Johnny's pitch. "Something like, 'Girls love 'em. They're portable.'" So Chris began playing guitar, and the two-voices-two-guitars formula really took hold. It didn't hurt that the two of them looked great together, both with soulful blue eyes, Johnny's long brown hair and angular cheekbones contrasting perfectly with Chris' short fair hair and ruddy complexion. Eventually they booked their first concerts, a two-night stand at a restaurant called Deville's, where they played both originals and covers. The first night was plagued by sound problems, but friends and family came back the next night anyway.

The musical chemistry between the two was undeniable, but their partnership was nearly undone before it could go anywhere. A classmate, we'll call her "Beth," had become involved with Johnny, but she'd also caught Chris's eye. Beth was somewhat shy and insecure, but she held a deep and infectious passion for music and poetry and art. Chris says eventually both he and Johnny fell in love with her, and that she likewise had feelings for both of them, oscillating back and forth. At some point, Johnny moved on from the

The marquee advertising Chris & Johnny's first public performance, at a restaurant called Deville's. Courtesy Storyhill.

situation, but not before "a lot of drama, a lot of tears, and a lot of songs." By senior year, Beth and Chris were an item. He took her to senior prom, where Johnny was crowned king, and sang Richard Marx's "Hold on to the Nights" while Beth and Chris danced. "God, it was so trippy," Chris reminisces.

Having survived what might have derailed two friends with a weaker bond, Chris and Johnny continuing to perform together, most notably at their senior baccalaureate service, where Johnny was named "most likely to succeed." For graduation, Chris and Johnny's parents gifted them $200 each, which the boys parleyed into four hours of time at a recently opened studio in Bozemen, Peak Recording, to properly capture the songs they'd accumulated. They recorded nine songs to quarter inch tape, and then they had to decide how many copies they wanted and, more significantly, what to call themselves. Chris recalls, "I remember us somehow getting up to Kinko's and he's like, 'What should we call it?' 'How about our names?' 'Okay Johnny and Chris.' I was like, 'Well, it doesn't quite sound like … Chris and Johnny has more of a ring to it.' So it ended up being Chris and Johnny."

Johnny hand-drew a logo with their names half framed by the outline of a guitar, and they had 100 copies made on cassette. As one would expect, the songs represent a very early draft of the sound the two would eventually develop. They're very traditionally folky, in some places almost baroque. The harmonies are there, but not quite at the transcendent levels they'd later achieve. And each of Johnny's songs is concerned with religious matters in one way or another, from the hymn "My Father" to the false-idol chastising "Yellow Sun" to the I'm-a-sinner lamentation "Help Me Lord."

There are also many ways in which the songs show the duo to be mature beyond their years, primarily in the sophistication of the playing and the depth of expression.

The chorus of his peace anthem "Common Ground," is probably the purest distillation of who Chris and Johnny were and would be: melodic, soaring, two voices almost becoming one. Chris's romantic travelogue "Fear of Far Forgotten" particularly seems like the work of a much older artist. And both writers take turns at inhabiting other viewpoints. Chris's "And Her Eyes" tells of an Old World romance from the perspective of an aged man looking back. Johnny's "Surrender to a Wheelchair" features a paraplegic addressing God. The narrator tells how he has dreams of dancing in the fields and climbing in the mountains, and asks why it had to be him. He ends with a chilling plea: "Take me to your meadow/I'm dying to be free."

The recording was meant as a souvenir, since the two were going their separate ways after graduation. Chris, after feeling academically directionless for most of high school, had decided to indulge a travel bug he'd picked up on a summer trip to Ecuador when he was 16. He was going to spend a year studying in Spain at the University of Salamanca. John had at first planned to attend Montana State, but in the summer before senior year had encountered 12 Oles (as Saint Olaf students and alumni often call themselves) at Christikon. The students sang the school's praises and encouraged John to apply. John liked Saint Olaf's musical pedigree, so he applied and was accepted. He planned to be a classical violin performance major.

2

Different Waters

In which the guys go to college and start making noise.

When John Hermanson arrived at Saint Olaf in the fall of 1989 he played a couple of solo acoustic shows at the Kildahl Lounge and the Pause, and immediately sold out of the nearly 100 *Chris & Johnny* cassettes he'd brought with him. He wrote a letter to Chris saying, "You know I'm playing these things solo and selling these duo cassettes, maybe you should come to Saint Olaf when you're done." Chris was unsure, he didn't like the idea of being confined, but he didn't have a better plan. He agreed to visit campus for a tour—and a concert Johnny had arranged for them to perform—with his parents in spring 1990. Chris, after nearly a year in Spain, experienced culture shock at suddenly being in the middle of what he calls a "little microcosm on the hill." However, he liked the idea of continuing his musical partnership with Johnny, And most of his credits from Spain would transfer, so he'd only be a semester behind. He decided to enroll, telling himself that if he didn't like it he wouldn't stick around.

Johnny hadn't stayed with his violin performance major long; he quickly discovered it wasn't what he wanted for his life or his music. For one, it was a solitary and stressful life, and for another, it was all about interpreting someone else's compositions. He was more interested in writing and creating his own lyrics and music. Around this time he saw the folk singer L.J. Booth in concert, and it was there that Johnny made the decision to follow that path instead. He recalls, "Just the way [Booth] communicated with the audience with music was appealing to me. I kind of jumped off my current course of study and focused on music at that point." John started studying world religions, and via Saint Olaf's Paracollege progam—which allowed students to design their own course of study—explored the idea of interfaith dialogue via art, poetry, and music between Zen Buddhism, Christianity, and Islam. But all of his free time went to nurturing his musical ambitions.

* * *

As one might guess by Shark Sandwich's name, the band had a sense of humor. Their lyrics were often funny or wry, taking on topics not typically covered by pop songs. There were tunes like "Big Wheels," an ode to the low-riding plastic tricycles; "Bald," in which the narrator fears he's losing his follicles; and "My Sense of Manhood," about a chauvinist having an identity crisis.

But the group itself, and their performances, were not fatuous. Fawcett and John wanted their music to be fun, but not sloppy. They prided themselves on technical proficiency. They rehearsed obsessively, and developed a potent chemistry. Alex Oana, a classmate who recorded a nine-song live demo for the band at the Pause, said of the group, "One of the amazing things about Shark Sandwich is that what came out of their instruments, right off the stage, was already magical. Together they concocted a magical arrangement of sound."

The band performed their own original songs exclusively. John and Gary wrote the tunes (the latter responsible for "Bald" and "Alan G.'s America") while the whole band contributed to arrangements. Despite its funk-rock origins, the band's music didn't have an easily-defined style. In a 1990 profile in the *Carletonian* (the student newspaper of Carleton College, also in Northfield) they listed Earth, Wind and Fire and XTC as influences, while the piece's author compared them to Sly and the Family Stone and early Chicago. In their small body of recorded work, one can also hear echoes of the Police, Duran Duran, and most prominently, Oingo Boingo. As Fawcett put it at the time, "We throw little bits of everything into the metaphorical sandwich, and each bite (or song) is a little bit different."

They proved to be popular both on campus (playing at the Hockey House and a steady stream of parties) and off (doing gigs at the likes of a ski resort called Welch Village and a bar/restaurant in downtown Northfield called the Rueb'n'stein, a.k.a "The Rueb"). During spring break of their sophomore year, Shark Sandwich recorded a four-song cassette at Salmagundi Studios in downtown Northfield with owner/engineer/producer Steve McKinstry. The EP opens with "Green-Striped Shirt," the tale of a "sophisticated piece of apparel" that was stolen by an ex-girlfriend. The song's narrator details

Shark Sandwich circa 1990. From left to right: Scotty Jones, Nathan Anderson, Gary Rice, Jr., Joe Kutchera, Eric Fawcett, and John Ostby. Courtesy Eric Fawcett.

the shirt's virtues while lamenting its loss, even going so far as to conclude that the girl only dated him in the first place so she could purloin it (this premise should sound familiar to any Ben Folds Five fan, as their "Song for the Dumped" covers very similar territory; Shark Sandwich's song predates it by seven years). Musically the song is driven by Scotty Jones' melodic bass and a punchy horn hook. When performed live, the song ended with John commanding his ex to "gimmie the god-damn motherfuckin' shirt back," but the EP version keeps it clean.

"Clueless" sounds very '80s, but in the best way possible, with John's vocal evoking a New Romantic style and Gary's guitar giving off a dreamy tone. "Alan G.'s America" could be a condemnation of the corporate-friendly economic policies of then Federal Reserve chairman Alan Greenspan and their effect on the working class. In the song, an out-of-work narrator says, "America, why don't you act your age/Hey Uncle Sam/don't say that I'm insane." But the real inspiration—despite the misspelling of his name in the song's title—was poet Allen Ginsberg, whose work often addressed the crippling effects of materialism and comformity. A funky guitar figure moves the song along, and there's even a brief spoken (or more accurately, shouted) section that sounds almost like hip-hop.

The EP is rounded out by "Freewheeling," in which a carefree dude invites others to be spontaneous with him. This is where John's jazz background is most evident. His vocal is almost loungey, the horns sound like they're from a TV theme, and there's a noodly guitar solo. The EP was both slick and professional sounding, and the band even picked up some airplay in the Minneapolis/Saint Paul area on the respective local music shows on Cities 97 (then hosted by local radio legend Bill DeVille) and KJ104.

However, their momentum was stymied somewhat by the fact that Fawcett had decided to spend his junior year at studying astronomy at Oxford. The band replaced him for that one year with Nate Moir, who hailed from a royal Minneapolis family; he was the second cousin of Monte Moir, keyboardist in the Time and writer/producer of Janet Jackson's hit "The Pleasure Principle." That year they started doing more club gigs, appearing in Minneapolis at the 7th Street Entry and the 400 Bar.

Fawcett returned to the drum kit for his senior year, and though the band had built the beginnings of a career, there were zero plans to continue Shark Sandwich beyond college. John was on his way to L.A. to pursue composing music for films. Still without a clear career direction, Eric planned to take time off from school to follow a girlfriend to Washington state.

* * *

Similar to Johnny, Darren decided to drop his academic pursuit of music not long after arriving on campus. First semester freshman year, he took a music theory class that met at 7 a.m. The content didn't help overcome the early-morning bleariness. He summarizes his reaction to the class as "Screw this music stuff. I don't really want to learn to compose in accordance with classical rules." That, paired with an inspiring philosophy course on Frederick Nietzsche, inspired him to change his major. He didn't give up on music, though. He soon found his way into a campus ska band called … wait for it … Skaboom.

Skaboom's singer was the tall, thin, angular-featured Alex Oana, who had engineered live sound for both Shark Sandwich and Chris & Johnny. A junior when Darren was a freshman, Alex had previously lived down the hall from Shark Sandwich's Eric Fawcett

Cover of Shark Sandwich's self-titled EP, released on cassette in 1990. Author's collection.

and John Ostby, and roomed with Nathan Anderson, the band's trumpet player. Hailing from Mount Pleasant, Michigan, Alex was possessed by sound from an early age. One of his earliest memories is of being four or five years old and listening to a "Let's Pretend" record on his dad's hi-fi system. As a steam train rumbled by the immensity of the sound at once frightened and excited little Alex. He fled behind the floor-standing speaker only to realize that it was louder back there, the bass powerfully reverberating through his body.

A couple of years later, he was playing with a plastic bike reflector he'd gotten from a Frosted Flakes box while listening to music on his portable record player, and he had the idea to lower the pointed edge of that relfector onto the spinning record. "Because of the size of it and the lightness of it, it vibrated with the groove of the record and it actually amplified the sound of that record," he says. "It was some kind of association I made right there with sound vibration and recording."

He pursued that association doggedly throughout his childhood, crawling under the organ at church while his mother—the organist—worked the pedals with her feet, taking piano lessons (eventually abandoned because "all I really wanted to do was have someone teach me 'Iron Man' by Black Sabbath"), and playing alto sax.

He also became a hi-fi enthusiast, and a regular loiterer at local stereo shops, along with his best friend Russ Herron. He read magazines like *Stereo Reivew*, and began to connect the idea of a great-sounding record and the fact that there was a person whose job it was to make "the production" happen. "That's when a light bulb went on," he says, "and it was like, 'Oh, I want to be that guy!'" It was Russ's older brother Jim who facilitated Alex's first transcendent experience with a sound system, and secured his desire to be involved in audio engineering. "I don't know how he came into this money, but one summer all of a sudden he had a $10,000 stereo system." There were DCM Time Frame speakers and a high-end Carver CD player and amp. Jim put on a Peter Gabriel track, from his 1986 album *So*. It was the first time Alex had heard a Peter Gabriel song, and simultaneously the first time he'd ever heard a recording sound so good. *So* producer Daniel Lanois became Alex's producing and recording ideal, and that ideal sound experience was something he would constantly chase. "I became the guy who if I showed up at your party I would find your stereo and I would start tweaking it. I would tweak the bass and the treble. I might reposition your speakers. I would put my head in between the speakers and find out if they were in phase or out of phase and then rewire them if necessary."

This fascination with sound and recording continued at Saint Olaf, though after getting involved in choir and music theater in high school, Alex also had his sights on being a lead singer. That's how he ended up in Skaboom. He knew almost nothing about ska, but the opportunity to be a lead singer was too good to pass up. "When I saw people like John Ostby and all the attention he got, and I was like 'Whoa, I want that!'" Darren wasn't particularly a skankin' to the beat type either, so it's no surprise that the two soon decamped from Skaboom with a desire to explore musical territory that better fit their interests.

For Darren, that was the avant garde composers he'd gravitated toward: John Cage, Iannis Xenakis, Phillip Glass, Charles Ives. For Alex it was the idea of creating a concept album along the lines of Queensryche's 1988 rock opera *Operation: Mindcrime*. He and Darren shared an admiration for Pink Floyd and their thematic albums. Together, those influences drove the formation of Round Trip. The band's primary work, and raison d'etre, was a 60-minute, ten-movement conceptual piece about a journey of self-discovery brought on by an acid trip. It was called "The Round Trip." In general Darren came up with the basic ideas, and the rest of the band—Alex, Chris Chelgren, Brad Bath, and Andy Rath—fleshed them out, attempting to create the piece not thinking of it as melody, chord changes, rhythm, and lyrics, but instead as a complete unit unto itself. In Chris's case, he not only contributed compositional ideas, but also, Alex says, "five minute organ solos, which helped us extend our magnum opus to the one hour mark."

The band rehearsed for months, and when they finally began to perform shows they endeavored to make them a complete experience, putting together a slideshow and interpretive dancers to accompany the music. Alex served as the band's lead singer, dominating the stage with a shirtless, emotive Jim Morrison-esque presence. The band recorded "The Round Trip" in a 24-hour session at Nu Music Studios in downtown Northfield in the winter of 1992, but never released it. Alex had found the experience equally frustrating and exhilarating. He was very hard on his vocal performances, and tended to get easily discouraged that his pitch wasn't perfect on every take, which he later would come to

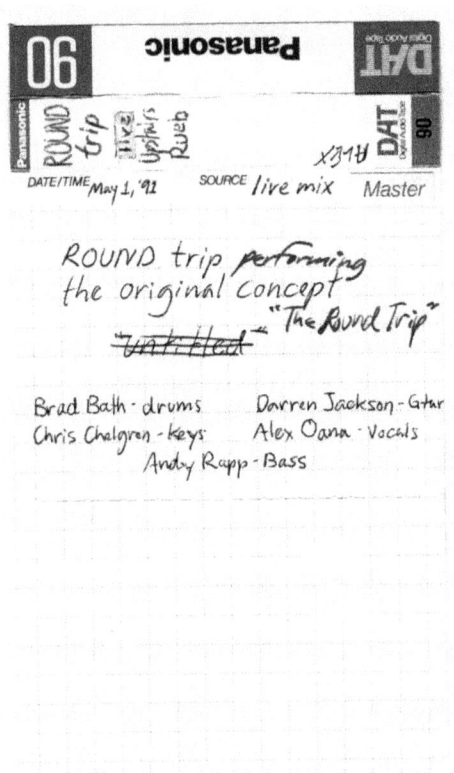

Label for the DAT recording of Round Trip's live performance at the Upstairs Rueb in Northfield. Courtesy Alex Oana.

realize was a common occurance for most singers in the studio. At the same time, he was thrilled by the idea of being a producer on the album, working out arrangements, bringing in members of the Saint Olaf Choir to sing, and making musical decisions. Between singing and production, it was clear which one he would pursue.

Darren says Round Trip had plenty of off-the-wall ideas they never implemented, such as having three bands perform simultaneously in the same space. The main goal of the band was to push against boundaries and be unique, and by all reports they succeeded. The group did some shows with Shark Sandwich, in what must have been a fascinating bill. They also played now and again with a band called Tread Water, which featured none other than John Hermanson.

* * *

That Johnny had a band at Saint Olaf besides Chris & Johnny is not a widely-known fact, but Tread Water's under-the-radar status wasn't due to lack of musical pedigree. The rock quartet was rounded out by guitarist Jake Evans, bassist Brian Roessler, and "a rotating cast of drummers." Jake, now a well-known guitarist in the Twin Cities improvisational jazz scene under the name Park Evans, spearheaded the group. Tread Water arose from hangout sessions between he, John, and Roessler when they were freshman. Early on, Roessler had seen Johnny perform solo and says, "It knocked me off my feet." They talked about forming a band but they had one guitar too many. Roessler wanted so badly to be in the band, he sacrificed his own deadly seriousness about playing guitar, and lied and said he knew how to play bass. As it turns out, his lie was the precursor to a lifelong pursuit.

Roessler had come to Saint Olaf by way of New Jersey. He'd been drawn to the college by a desire to return to the Midwest (his family had lived in Chicago until he was 10 years old), and by the Paracollege program, putting him in the company of not only Johnny, but Fawcett, Alex, and Chris as well. The deal had been sealed by a snowy weekend campus visit during his senior year of high school. His hosts were none other than Eric Fawcett and John Ostby. As Eric tells it, "The year we were freshman, John and I, Brian visited campus and he stayed as a prospective student. He had long dreads, this scrawny kid, and he brought his electric guitar. One night we all stole trays from the cafeteria and went traying." Brian also met Alex Oana that weekend.

Tread Water served a couple of functions for Johnny. For one, when the band started, Chris wasn't there, so it was a way to perform something other than solo gigs. For another, it gave Johnny an outlet for his musical restlessness. "I've always been in all kinds of different genres," Johnny says, "I've never been able to just settle in one. I'm just so excited about all kinds of music." Roessler was similar, having gone through obsessions with Yes, the Grateful Dead, Led Zeppelin, and Miles Davis. Jake was going through a ska phase, so Tread Water really was a mélange of styles. They played songs they liked, including covers of Rush's "Tom Sawyer" and Zeppelin's "Achilles' Last Stand," and originals by both Jake and Johnny. Ultimately, it didn't last much beyond their freshman year, as everyone moved on to different musical pursuits. Johnny says, "That was a funny band. We all think it's kind of funny now."

Once Chris Cunningham arrived on the Saint Olaf campus in the fall of 1990, Chris & Johnny started playing shows. Almost immediately, they sounded and looked like they were headed for stardom. Their musical chemistry had not diminished in the year apart, and they immediately began writing new songs. They realized they'd need more to offer their listeners than their now two-year-old *Chris & Johnny* cassette with half of its songs about God. So in early 1991 they spent a weekend at Nu Music Studios making what they consider their first true album, *Shapeshifting*.

The set was recorded by Andy Carlson, a then-recent graduate of Carleton College—the other liberal arts school in Northfield. Nu Music was far from a professional studio. Its main business was recording music for local ads, using the at-the-time-new computer workstation technology. It was a suite of offices with some acoustic treatments, an 8-track ½-inch reel-to-reel recorder, and some nice mics, but it was "not a place you could make a nice top-notch album" according to Andy. Andy himself was only a year out of college, working at the studio for next to nothing. He says Nu Music would take anyone who came through the door with a project, but he found Chris & Johnny to have something special: "Their songwriting style was really original, and the blend of their voices is one of those really rare awesome beautiful musical things that you can't explain, but it just works."

Over the course of a few days, they spent about eight hours recording the album. There were no effects or overdubs, just Chris and Johnny playing live. Andy says none of them quite knew what they were doing when it came to the recording process. "Even though it was the blind leading the blind, I still think very fondly of that project. I love that album in a way you might love a ceramic pot you made in kindergarten; I know that everything about it how it was recorded is wrong, I still love it."

The sound of the record is immediate and intimate. The songs themselves are a definite progression from the ones on the pair's self-titled cassette, but the guys' style was still not completely defined. Most songs feature both men sining in unison throughout, with only their guitars as accompaniment (there's occasional harmonica and violin, and a female backing vocalist—classmate Krista Dryer, now a nationally successful mezzo soprano opera singer known as Krista River—on two songs). As Andy puts it, the album is "kind of a like a photograph of Chris & Johnny before they keyed into their thing."

Some of that "thing" is definitely there, such as on "I Am a Lover" and "Shapeshifter," both featuring delicate finger-picking and rich harmonies, or the hooky "The Things I Love." Though it wasn't as developed as it would become, Chris and Johnny's songwriting process was already cemented by this point. They each wrote songs separately, and would then came together to work out harmonies and guitar parts. Chris estimates that "at least half" of his songs would be reworked in some way by Johnny, a process Johnny describes as "I tend to be more of the editor, and Chris tends to be more of a generator of ideas." Chris says a main contrast between their writing styles is that he usually writes from a personal place, where Johnny does more third-person perspective. As a result, a lot of Johnny's lyrical changes were to make individual details feel more universal.

Andy digitally mastered the album, and Chris and Johnny made the artwork by hand. Together, they got both cassettes and CDs manufactured. It was a big deal for a local band to have a CD in 1991, and that helped *Shapeshifting* sell nearly 500 copies that first year.

The following spring, Chris and Johnny returned to Nu Music and teamed with Andy on a set of songs that would form their next record, *Different Waters*. "This time we thought we knew what we were doing," Andy says. There are more effects and overdubs, and more players. A drummer named Dave Steidtman played percussion on four songs, and the Tread Water guys got involved. Brian Roessler played bass on "She Holds My Heart Out in the Wind," and Jake Evans performed the off-kilter electric guitar solo on "Inside Emotion."

Different Waters is the album where Chris and Johnny's songwriting begins to blossom. The promise of "Shapeshifter" and "The Things I Love" is fulfilled with a collection of songs that are more hooky, melodic and straightforwardly arranged. Chris's songs, especially, are more playful and bluesy than they'd ever been, as in the jaunty drinking song "Pancho and Lefty" (a tale straight out of his experience in Spain). Johnny's songs tend to be more delicate, both in sound and in content: the beautiful "Within" features a repeated finger-picked hook and chill-inducing harmonies on the chorus, and "Holding On" is almost a lullaby. However, he also contributes the light-hearted and robust "Missouri River," which ends with the brief music lesson ("This chord's a D/and this one's a G/And this one here is an A/Yes, we know that it's basic/The most common arrangement/But we're using it anyway").

One of the reasons Chris and Johnny's songs connected so well with college students was that they were college students themselves, and wrote about topics that weighed on thoughtful college students' minds. These included, naturally, the intensity and complexity of relationships, but also the difficulty of finding and holding on to one's identity in the face of unprecedented freedom. And they did this in an eloquent way that gave dignity and depth to the struggle. Johnny's "Inside Emotion" is a perfect example of this, encapsulating both themes in a tune that builds as it goes. The song starts with the narrator intensely examining his own beliefs about himself and the world around him: "I've changed my answers/And I've changed my plans/ And I'm living for the feelings/That I can't understand." In the end we find out that the turmoil isn't just internal, and that a break-up is exacerbating matters. "Love has a way of making everything easy/And with this new-found freedom, I have never been so lonely." Things end on a hopeful note, with the narrator convinced he sees things more clearly now than he ever has before. The details are left vague, so the listener can interpret and apply the lyrics how he or she wishes.

Andy Carlson did the artwork for the CD on a Mac. A friend they'd met through Paracollege, David Weeks, took the cover photograph on the Waterford Iron Bridge, just outside of Northfield. On the inside of the CD booklet, Andy took three or four lines from each of the album's songs, and arranged them into what he calls an "impressionistic story" that he's especially proud of.

Chris & Johnny played constantly, both in Northfield and in Bozeman on breaks and during the summer. In Northfield, they played most often the Rueb. Their gigs didn't always go well or attract a big audience, but every show was a learning experience. As Andy put it, "Playing hours and hours and hours of those kinds of gigs is what makes people good. Learning how to please crowds, and sort of having that physical mind meld where Johnny can do something and Chris can sort of read his mind and just join in and vice versa. I think that's where that solidified and they went from being gifted amateurs to pros."

Bars like the Rueb were not a great fit. People might be there just to drink or socialize, not see a sensitive acoustic duo, and the environment didn't necessarily suit the people who had come specifically to see them. As David Weeks said, "Frankly the bars are not

Chris & Johnny perform at Saint Olaf circa 1991. Courtesy Storyhill.

that excited to having a Chris & Johnny audience. It's like 'Where are the chairs? Where can we get chairs to sit down?'"

Eventually the guys moved to the friendlier, larger Grand Theater, a turn-of-the-century opera house that served as a movie theater into the mid-'80s before being retooled as an event and concert venue. It was here in November 1992 that Chris & Johnny performed and recorded a set of sold out shows. Because the Grand shared a wall with Salmagundi (where Shark Sandwich had recorded their EP), the guys were able to record their performances directly into the studio, with Steve McKinstry manning the board. They would release highlights from the shows as their album *Live at the Grand* in 1993. More than the first two studio records, *Live at the Grand* shows the chemistry and power of Chris and Johnny's partnership. And while there's not yet an approving roar to greet the audience's favorite songs, the enthusiastic clapping along with "Pancho & Lefty" showed that Chris & Johnny were on their way up.

* * *

By Johnny's senior year, the musical landscape at Saint Olaf had shifted. John Ostby and Eric Fawcett graduated in spring of 1992 and struck out for the frontier. Alex Oana had graduated as well, moving into an apartment above Brent Day's house and working for Day Productions, including engineering Chris & Johnny's live performances. Johnny and Roessler were due to graduate in the spring of 1993, with Chris following close behind that winter. Other Saint Olaf groups were coming up to take their place, such as the soon-to-be-mega-popular jam band the Big Wu. Chris & Johnny were already looking beyond Northfield, having decided to continue their DIY, grassroots musical movement into their post-college lives.

3

Half the Time with You

In which Reno and the Harvesters are born, Chris & Johnny hit the road, and Darren finds and loses his way.

Eric Fawcett had been in Olympia, Washington, for less than a year after graduation when the relationship he was in—the one he'd moved there for—ended. He left the northwest and decided to enroll in graduate school closer to home. His Shark Sandwich bandmate John Ostby had moved to Los Angeles with the aim to study composition at the Dick Grove School of Music. First he had to earn some money, so he moved to Hermosa Beach and worked taking phone orders for his uncle's furniture components company. He lived rent-free in a beachside apartment also owned by his uncle. At night he'd go home and write songs on the piano. The songs were the only part of his life that was working.

The former roommates and bandmates hadn't spoken much in the 9 months since graduating, but that February 1993 Fawcett and Ostby reconnected. Eric was at the University of Wisconsin in Madison doing a final round of interviews for entrance into a PhD program in the history of science when John called him. John played some of his new songs, and Eric says the tunes were earnest and sweet, long and strange. He was intrigued. Over several nights of calls the two began to discuss the logistics of forming a new band together.

They each had their reasons. For Ostby, it was the realization that the lifestyle of a film composer wasn't something that he wanted. He didn't want to be a studio rat; he enjoyed rehearsing, writing, and performing too much, so it felt natural to pursue that. For Fawcett, it was a more drastic decision. It was literally a choice between deep study of a subject he loved in the small, safe environs of a university campus, or throwing himself out into the mercies of the wide world to pursue an unlikely goal. In the end he knew he couldn't pass up the potential reward of pursing music, even if it was a much bigger risk. He was anxious about telling his parents, fearful that they'd upbraid him for being irresponsible. Instead, they were completely supportive, and Eric realized that all the pressure he'd felt had been self-imposed.

Fawcett and Ostby's new band needed a homebase. Eric was open to doing it anywhere, including L.A., but John wanted it to be Minneapolis. This was partly because he'd lived in L.A. for almost a year and had learned enough to know it wasn't going to be the best place to try to break in. The Twin Cities, however, had a lot going for it. John's parents were both from Minnesota originally, so he'd spent a lot of time there growing up. He and Eric had already had some experience with the diverse and supportive music scene in their Shark Sandwich days. And Alex Oana was there too, along with many other friends from Saint Olaf, including Johnny, when he was not on the road, and Darren, who was planning to attend grad school at the University of Minnesota.

So Ostby abandoned L.A., and Fawcett left Madison for his hometown of Ames, Iowa, where he worked for a couple of months tiling bathrooms to fund another move. They settled in Minneapolis in the spring of '93, and once again became roommates. To pay the bills, John got an office job doing data entry, and Eric was hired on at French Meadow, a bakery/café in Uptown Minneapolis but the band was the main thing.

Fawcett had decided that if he was going to pursue drumming, it was his job to become the best drummer he could possibly be. Even deciding to label himself a drummer was what he calls "big, courageous" step. He applied that same sense of focus and obsession that he would have to his PhD studies to his drumming, practicing six to eight hours a day. He began studying privately with jazz drummer Phil Hay, who had a long, distinguished list of credits.

Fawcett closely examined the styles of the drummers he loved and was learning to love, guys like Elvin Jones (who played with John Coltrane), John Bonham, Zigaboo (from the Meters), Clyde Stubblefield (who played with James Brown), and Stevie Wonder, whose drumming on his own songs, such as "Superstition," Eric calls "beautifully simple."

Fawcett and Ostby were calling themselves Reno, after one of the songs John had written. They had convinced Scotty Jones, the bass player from Shark Sandwich, to join them, but it would be a couple of months before he'd arrive in town. In the meantime, they needed to find a guitarist, so they began the audition process. They asked Brian Roessler, who had just graduated from Saint Olaf that spring, to fill in on bass during the auditions.

Fawcett estimates that they auditioned 25 guitarists that summer looking for the exact right player to complete their sound. Matt Kirkwold, a Musictech College student (the school later became the McNally Smith College of Music), was one of the last to audition, and he said to them, "Listen guys, I would love to be in this band, but if I'm not the right player, you have to audition Brent Pashcke. He's tighter than a frog's ass." Brent grew up in Grand Forks, North Dakota, a mid-sized city about five hours northwest from the Twin Cities. He described his youth and teen years as "Go-carts, off road motorcycles, and muscle cars in the summer, snowmobiles in the winter," and, from his early teens on, "guitar playing year-round." After graduation, he had moved to Minneapolis in 1991 to attend Musictech.

They brought Brent in, and Fawcett recalls, "he was just amazing. By the end of the audition it wasn't even an audition." Brent was offering ideas for arrangements like he was already a member of the band, and his funk-rock style was an unconventional but effective match for the songs John had written. Even so, they brought Brent back for two follow-ups, partly because they were such a careful group, but also because they couldn't quite believe they'd found someone so right. During the third audition, Brent asked bluntly, "So am I in this band or what?"

Scotty Jones arrived in the fall of 1993, and the band started rehearsing and arranging John's songs. It wasn't long before they got together with Alex and recorded a 3-song cassette to serve as a calling card. Alex says the recording conditions and process were quite similar to the first time they recorded Shark Sandwich at the Pause, "A quiet Sunday afternoon at a momentarily dormant live music venue." Titled *Reno*, the EP makes a very clear distinction between the new band and Shark Sandwich, despite having the same rhythm section, singer, and songwriter. The glib way to describe the songs would be the Beatles go jazz. "A Week from Today" is an impressionistic reminiscence of a lovely day spent by the ocean. The melodic bass, clean guitar, and harmonies (provided by Fawcett) give the song a classic pop feel.

The boppy "Half the Time with You" is next, in which the song's narrator prepares a meal for his love, cuts his thumb, and bleeds into the pineapple. It's all a metaphor for the shaky ground the relationship stands on (spoiler: he ends up eating the fruit by himself). Finally, "Sunbelt" is a slow-burning jazz number about a retired couple rediscovering their love for one another after a move to Florida. The most affecting detail comes in the middle: "Talking of old times/When the kids were all young/Do you remember how we used to sing to them?" John's lyrics are like this throughout, almost literary, evocative, giving just enough detail to paint a vivid picture without giving it all away. And taken in tandem the three songs explore different facets of romance—the exciting potential, the confusion of mismatched levels of affection, and the ups and downs of decades spent together—all told in unconventional ways.

Not long after they put out the EP, Fawcett, Ostby and Brent decided to cut ties with Scotty, at least partly because they felt he wasn't as willing to work for the band's success as the other three were. And so Roessler was brought in full time, though not completely willingly. Since the Tread Water days he'd gotten more into jazz and improv, and had formed a band called Fly Manifesto with Jake Evans (Eric occasionally played drums for the group). He was also playing with Chris & Johnny off-and-on, and wasn't sure if he was ready to make the kind of commitment he knew Reno was going to be. But he agreed to become the band's permanent temporary bassist.

* * *

One of the reasons Ostby and Fawcett had chosen to settle in Minneapolis was because that's where Alex Oana was. After nearly a year living in Northfield and working for Day Productions after graduation, he headed north and began working for Southern Thunder, at that time the Twin Cities' biggest live sound company (Alex got the job by impressing the company's owner, Loren Wiklander, with a board tape of the Patsy Cline cover band in in which Loren played drums and his wife sang). Southern Thunder had the contract for installing, maintaining, and operating the sound system at the Fine Line Music Café's a mid-sized venue in downtown Minneapolis that hosted shows by local, regional, and national acts. For Alex, doing sound engineering at the Fine Line was a signifier that he'd "made it." "In college, I was visiting the Twin Cities with my girlfriend and we walked past the Fine Line. I was like a kid looking into a toy store, I pressed my face up against the glass and through the window I could see the LED level meters going up and down on the huge console as the sound engineer in there was mixng the show. I remember turning to my girlfriend, I said, 'Someday. Someday, I'm gonna mix on that board in that room.'"

Someday came, and when the Fine Line decided to buy out Southern Thunder's contract and hire their own house sound engineer, Alex got the job. As the audio engineer, he prided himself on giving artists the best customer service he possibly could. He says: "I was not the typical live sound guy. The stereotype is that he's a curmudgeon, he's got a bad attitude, he's resistant to whatever you say, no matter how many times you say please or thank you it's going to be a fight to get what you want. I was the opposite and it freaked people out. Bands would come and they'd be all tiptoeing around me expecting me to be resistant, and I'd be like, 'Sounds great! Is there anything else I can do for you?'; 'No problem.'"

As a result, he would build a rapport with the bands that came through, perhaps having an eye on the fact that it could benefit him down the road. And indeed, local bands who typically traveled with their own sound engineer would start giving their regular guy the night off because they wanted Alex to take care of their sound.

In the midst of living his dream at the Fine Line, Alex took a major step toward his other goal: Becoming a record producer. In 1994, he purchased a recording studio that played an outsized part in Minnesota rock music history. How does a sound engineer in his early twenties working for cash afford to buy a recording studio? Alex had become friendly with the weekend bouncer at the Fine Line, who was also a real estate agent and had heard Alex share his fantasy of owning a recording studio in a barn in the country. One day he came up to Alex and told him he had a property he needed to see. It wasn't a barn (it was a 1918 Craftsman house), and it wasn't in the country (it was situated in the bustling Dinkytown neighborhood in Minneapolis), but it did have a studio. The fates were definitely conspiring to bring that house to Alex's attention. Dave Weeks had noticed the listing, and passed in on to Johnny. Johnny wasn't interested, but passed it on to Alex. The house in question had was the former Blackberry Way, where Hüsker Dü recorded their first single, and the Replacements cut their early albums, including the classic *Let it Be* (1984). It was also where influential label Twin/Tone Records was born. Label co-founder Paul Stark had bought the house in the early '70s and converted the first floor into a studio

Twenty years later, not a whole lot had changed in terms of aesthetic. Alex says the house was in no way impressive on first sight. "It was like walking into someone's makeshift Halloween haunted house, dark draperies, you kind of had to push things aside, and things smelled a little off." The house had three bedrooms, one bathroom, a kitchen, dining room, and an unfinished basement. Two-thirds of the main floor had been converted into a recording studio, with cedar-lined walls, a built-on control room and a rickety-looking glass separating them. "The overall squalor and weirdness of that house cannot be overstated," Andy Carlson says. There were rodents in the basement ceiling, holes in the floor, one of the rooms had black carpet on the walls, and several of the doors in the basement had non-functioning electronic panels mounted on them."

As the seller's agent showed them around, he pointed to a section of the living room and said, "Paul Westerberg sat there at a grand piano and played that song 'Adrogynous,'" though this bit of history was lost on Alex, who at the time didn't know anything about the Replacements or Twin/Tone.

Given its condition and odd configuration, and despite its historical significance, the house was cheap, around $80,000. "On the real estate market nobody really got it," Alex says, "But for me it was absolutely perfect." He qualified for an FHA loan, got a $4000 loan from his mom for a down payment, and became the proud owner of 606 13th Avenue Southeast.

Alex renamed the place CityCabin, since the cedar planks on the walls made it feel like an urban cabin. It became both his home and his workspace, as well a halfway house for wayward musicians. Dinkytown sits along the north side of the Univeristy of Minnesota campus on the east bank. With a musical equipment, rehearsal and recording space in the house, noise-apathetic college students living all around, and record stores, live music venues, bars and restaurants all within walking distance, it was an ideal location for a starving singer-songwriter. As such, it would serve as ground zero for the music scene that eventually developed around Johnny, Fawcett, Appelwick, and Darren.

* * *

Aside from rehearsing, recording, and playing together, Chris and Johnny led very separate lives at Saint Olaf. Chris says he made a conscious decision to do the opposite of whatever Johnny was doing academically, so while Johnny took art and religion classes, Chris studied Spanish and used his Paracollege experience to go deep on Argentine political history. He didn't have a clear career path to follow. So when Johnny asked him to commit to making a go of Chris & Johnny when Chris graduated in winter of 1994, Chris was up for it, though unlike Johnny, he didn't have any aims at making a career in music. For Chris, continuing the duo was a way to indulge his travel bug and to take advantage of being young and not ready to settle. Another factor was that, by this time, Chris and Johnny were already basically full time professional musicians. With the *Live at the Grand* album they had hired managers, Brent and Meleia Day, who both worked as flight attendants and were heavily involved in the local music scene in their free time. He rented out equipment and did sound for shows, and she booked acts for the National Association of College Activities (NACA). The guys had initially rented equipment from Brent for gigs at the Rueb, and then connected with Meleia to arrange gigs on the college circuit.

The NACA circuit was, according to Chris "a pretty good bread and butter way to go." They could get a lot of bookings at once and put together a tour. Chris and Johnny and their music were of the exact right appeal to the college audience, and they provided some diversity in the typical NACA offerings of jugglers, comedians, and a capella groups. CD sales were also a boon. The mid–1990s were the peak time for CDs, and Chris and Johnny's combination of charisma and accessibility (and great tunes) led to an unusually high percentage of show-goers walking away with a CD. It got to the point where on a good night Chris and Johnny might sell 100 albums, pocketing $1000. Though it didn't make them rich, this income allowed the guys to make music their full-time job. It also gave them incentive to continually have new product to offer.

As such, they had already recorded and released their third album by the time Chris graduated, this time at Salmagundi with Steve McKinstry. *Miles and Means* found Chris & Johnny continuing to expand their sound by using additional musicians. Brian Roessler plays bass on almost half the songs. Guitarist Dan Neale plays on three songs, and Marc Anderson offers percussion on four of them. Eric Fawcett also drums on two tracks, a significant first that didn't come about smoothly. According to Roessler, during the sessions for the album they needed a drummer, and he suggested Eric. Eric was resistant at first, as he was no Chris & Johnny fan. "That is so corny," was his exact assessment of their music. Wisely, Roessler advised him to go to a show before making a final decision. So Eric and Brian went to see Chis & Johnny at the Loring Bar, and Eric came away impressed. He would end up drumming on nearly every subsequent record Chris and John made together.

The songs on *Miles and Means* feature both Chris and Johnny's strongest writing and playing yet, and would provide them with some of their most enduring live staples. Those included Chris' catchy traveling tune "I-90" (with its crowd-pleasing line "a Minnesota gal to be my friend") and contemplative "Parallel Lives." John's sweet devotional "If I Could" and his twisty "Schoolbus" also became frequently-played fan favorites.

"Schoolbus" is lyrically emblematic of Johnny's songs on the album, its narrator battling with "so many thoughts inside my head" and "so many people in there" while at the same time bemoaning a lost love. The song was inspired by the woman both Chris and Johnny had been involved with in high school, "Beth." When she was with Chris after the break-up with Johnny things were understandably awkward and somewhat unresolved, so Chris encouraged the two to hash things out. The verse in "Schoolbus" that includes the lines "We didn't talk too much 'cause we had too much to say/She wore her sunglasses so I wore mine" came directly from that meeting, which, as you might guess, ended with things still unresolved. Beth and Chris's relationship, by the way, hadn't survived his year in Spain. At first they'd vowed to continue their commitment long-distance, but her initial zealotry about it (she wanted to come visit basically right away) dissipated when she fell for her boss's son. Chris says she continued to inspire songs for both him and Johnny.

"If I Could," in contrast with "Schoolbus," is what Johnny called a "complete fabrication" that he wrote in the back of his Volkswagen Westphalia camper while Chris drove them back to Montana on a break from school. Johnny was single at the time, so it wasn't about a specific person. Instead, it was an attempt, he says, to write a positive love song to balance things out. It was a good instinct, since the album has more than its share of heartbreak, such as the pretty-but-bleak tandem of "Boulder River" and "Hide in the Rain." And then there's Chris's aching "Parallel Lives," a love song for a person he can never truly be with. The details in the story are sparse, making way for multiple interpretations, but the deep emotions are painfully clear.

Once the guys were firmly ensconced in the NACA circuit, they found it to be lucrative (they were able to pay off their traveling vehicle, a Dodge Caravan, and their sound system) if tiring. To make everything work, they had to do near constant shows, nearly 200 a year. The plus side of that was their repeated appearances at many colleges in places like Wisconsin, Iowa, Washington, and Oregon helped them build the beginnings of a solid fanbase.

With growing CD sales and a mailing list of nearly 6,000 fans, soon it became apparent that the day-to-day operations of the group were too much for the guys to handle on their own, especially since most of their time was spent traveling. Brent and Meleia had been managing things together, but Brent wasn't able to keep up his side of things. Andy Carlson, who after recording Chris & Johnny's first two CDs had started sporadically going on the road with the guys selling merchandise and doing live sound, had relocated to Minneapolis after a stint working with Steve McKinstry at Salmagundi. He moved into an apartment in with David Weeks, got a job at Rykodisc, and was looking for a way to make a career in music. In the past, he'd been a great help to Chris and Johnny in various business-related matters, so they brought him on as manager. His duties included things like making sure their CDs and t-shirts stayed in stock, handling the finances and copyrights, and coordinating the touring schedule with Meleia. There was no shortage of work for him to do.

* * *

Darren's former bandmates in the Beatniks, Justin Seim and Erik Hulm, had graduated high school in 1991 and both moved on to the University of South Dakota in Vermillion. They brought their gear but didn't have much intention of starting a band. Eventually, though, Justin got together with one of his Lamda Chi Alpha fraternity brothers, a drummer named George Gongopoulos, and some other players, and they formed Pastor Dean. The group recorded a demo, but then their guitarist split. While looking for a replacement, George thought of a guy he knew from his job at the mall, a musician he thought might get along well with Justin. His name was Erik Appelwick.

After being introduced in the spring of 1994, Appelwick and Justin quickly found themselves to be musically simpatico. Erik was writing songs, which inspired Justin to write more, and with George on drums, they set out to form a band. They asked Dave Scarbrough, a Sioux Falls singer/songwriter who had mixed the Pastor Dean recordings, to join on guitar and vocals. That meant that Erik had to move over to bass once again, something he says he did only grudgingly. Despite that, it worked. Dave says, "Everything just clicked. The four of us just had a similar vibe, a similar taste, that kind of Americana, Uncle Tupelo/Johnny Cash kind of thing ... we had three writers, all slightly different, but it all kind of meshed together well." And thus were born the Harvesters.

By bringing in Dave, Justin and Appelwick were allying themselves with a small-but-surprisingly-vital Sioux Falls music scene. Dave was a Sioux Falls native who had been playing in bands since high school. The original music scene there had begun there in the early '80s with an ultra-popular rock outfit called Wakefield, who opened for both Head East and ZZ Top before disbanding in 1987, and politically-charged punk band called No Direction, who self-released three albums between 1983 and 1988. The members of that band were Rich Show, Rick Smith, and Charles Luden. By the time he joined the Harvesters, Dave had worked with both Charles (on a recording-only project called the Habitual Groove of It) and Rich.

Rich Show had run through a couple of bands after No Direction broke up in 1989. The first was the Midwestern country-rock-flavored Flag with Hank, a group he formed with guitarist Ralph Mills, drummer Lance Beier, and bassist Heath Henjum. This line-up recorded an album in Minneapolis, titled *Weaselroni*, in 1991, and then moved to Austin, Texas to try to make a go of it. The band stayed there for a couple of years, but when stardom didn't beckon, they made their way back to Sioux Falls. They swapped out Mills for guitarists Mark Romanowski and Mark Bombara, and changed their name to Violet. Violet were a huge influence on Justin. He says now, "That was one of the main reasons I started writing songs, listening to Violet and Rich. They were my heroes."

Violet had done some localized touring, and even recorded an album at Prince's Paisley Park Studios (*Global Village*, recorded and released in 1993). They garnered some interest from labels, and did several showcases, though nothing came of it. Other bands, such as Janitor Bob & the Armchair Cowboys and Crash Alley, rounded out the scene. It was a time when people in Sioux Falls were regularly going out to see original live music, and that was nothing to take for granted. The center of the Sioux Falls scene was the Pomp Room, a club/music venue downtown that had played host to the likes of Cheap Trick, Fugazi, Gov't Mule, and a surprise four-song set by Aerosmith in 1993, which was featured in a report by Kurt Loder on MTV. The Harvesters and Violet played there constantly, often together, and sometimes drew crowds of 800 plus people.

The Harvesters played in Vermillion, too, often at Lambda Chi parties, but also at Leo's Sports Bar & Grill and the Press Box. Dave Scarbrough says gigs there were usually packed, but attributes that to them having a "captive audience" of fraternity and sorority members. The band opened for Minneapolis acts such as singer-songwriter Marlee MacLeod and former Replacement Slim Dunlap. They also played Okoboji, a live music mecca in northern Iowa. With so many well-attended, well-paying gigs, the band started to build up quite a significant bank account, enough to buy studio time to make a record. So they took a trip to Minneapolis, to Third Ear Recording, a studio in the warehouse district downtown run by Tom Herbers. Third Ear was an institution in the Minnesota music scene, hosting sessions by local luminaries such as Low, the Hang Ups, and Replacement Slim Dunlap, among many others.

Rich Show's bands No Direction, Flag With Hank, and Violet helped kickstart a vibrant local scene in Sioux Falls in the '90s. Courtesy Rich Show.

At that time the studio was still analog, a 24-track reel-to-reel that used 2-inch tape. The Harvesters had set aside enough money for five days' in the studio, so they spent four days recording, went home, and then Dave came back on a weekend and used the fifth day to mix it. He did it fast, as he says, "a whole album's worth of stuff in 8 hours." The final product was the band's self-titled debut. There were fifteen songs, with each songwriter—Appelwick, Justin, and Dave—contributing five.

The album, which the band self-released in September 1995, is pretty impossible to find. Justin says they made about 500 copies, "and they just sold so quick." Its rarity is unfortunate, because it's a very good record, a uniformly uptempo mix of pop, country, and rock. It also contains the first of Appelwick's songs ever committed to physical form. Not surprisingly, they're clever and catchy, with a genuine emotion that manages to bleed through a top layer of cool detachment. Each of his five songs explore the ups and downs of romance. "Sense of Style" is an edgy paean to a fantastic lady, featuring a rough, countrified vocal. "Feel So Bad" ("I used to keep your picture by my bed/But now I just throw darts at your head") is a relationship post-mortem. The narrators in "I Can Only Say Too Much" and "Everything's Cool" are trying hard—likely in vain—to hold on to romances that have seen better days. And "Skid Row" finds the singer musing upon what attributes he'd need to win over a girl he admires: "If I could learn to sing like Morrissey/If I could move my pelvis like Elvis/If I could paint like Van Gogh/If I could rock like Skid Row/Would you let me take you to a show?" It's the funniest song on the album, put over the top by Appelwick's vocal imitation of the Smiths' singer after the Morrissey line.

Dave's songs included the jangly, heartfelt "Memory to Eight" and "Wachet Auf," which could be easily mistaken for a lost Smithereens single. Highlights from Justin are the bitter "Hate Between Us" and atmospheric album closer "Rattlesnake."

The Harvesters happened to put out their CD in what was, arguably, the watershed year for the alt-country genre. The Jayhawks' *Tomorrow the Green Grass*, the Bottle Rockets' *The Brooklyn Side*, Vic Chestnutt's *Is the Actor Happy?*, Old 97's *Wreck Your Life*, and debuts from Whiskeytown, Son Volt, and Wilco, all came out in 1995, and every one of them is an alt-country classic. According to Dave Scarbrough, the Harvesters weren't consciously bandwagoning. It just happened that they were all listening to and digging the same stuff at the same time. And the mix of songwriters, Justin being a "true, real, honest cowboy" well-versed in classic country like Merle Haggard and Waylon Jennings, Appelwick's "Jon Spencer Blues Explosion kind of edginess," and Dave's own melodic "guitar pop nerd" sensibilities happened to be the same combination of elements that defined alt-country.

They were in the right place at the right time, which is a rare and enviable position for a young band. And people around them recognized that. Justin's sister lived in Houston at the time and suggested they try to get into South by Southwest (SXSW), Austin, Texas' annual music festival that serves as an industry showcase. They got an application, and were both amused and dismayed at the the eighteen or so check boxes on the form asking if the band had a manager, producer, sound man, record deal, etc. The only one they could check was "none of the above." Despite that, in January of 1996 the Harvesters got

The cover and credits for The Harvesters' 1996 CD. Courtesy Dave Scarbrough.

word that they'd been accepted. Dave says, upon hearing the news, the guys "just kind of flipped out." They would be the first South Dakota band to play the festival.

Bands playing SXSW are required to pay their own way, so the band once again dipped into their joint account, practically exhausting it. They played a set to a respectably-sized crowd on March 14 at the Driskill, a 19th-century luxury hotel. Right outside the hotel was one of the big SXSW stages, and Iggy Pop was one of its performers that night. He was staying at the hotel, so when his set was over, he and his entourage walked right past the stage where the Harvesters were playing. Dave says he Iggy looked up at him and gave him a thumbs-up and a smile. "I was like, 'Aw, man, now I'm good.'"

Everyone had a blast, though Appelwick quickly tired of hearing "You don't sound like you're from South Dakota." Backhanded compliments aside, the band did garner some label interest, and a lawyer/manager from New York was especially enamored, and requested some new recordings he could shop around. They demoed about ten new tracks in April, recording live to ADAT on a Sunday night at the Pomp Room's main stage, and finishing up vocals at a small long-lived Sioux Falls studio called Earsay that was "just as grungy and old and smelly as the Pomp," Dave recalls. The new tunes were a mixed bag, but Dave says the gem of the session was the last one recorded during the Pomp session as it stretched past 2 a.m., a sloppy, impromptu tune called "Waltz Across Texas" with, as Dave describes it, "Justin singing and doing a great feedback solo and making up all the words; pure genius."

Unfortunately, the demos didn't work their magic on the potential manger, and not long after that bad news, George quit the band. He'd just gotten married and had good job prospects in front of him. Their momentum was halted, but the Harvesters weren't quite done yet. Violet had recently broken up when bassist Heath Henjum moved to Minneapolis and guitarist Mark Bombara left for Seattle, so drummer Lance Beier and guitarist Mark Romanowski joined up with Appelwick, Justin, and Dave, essentially creating a Frankenstein's monster of two of Sioux Falls' most popular bands. But by then Dave had gotten married and was expecting his first child, so he decided to move to Sioux City to live the grown-up life. His last gigs with the band were in late October 1996. The Harvesters carried on for a bit after that, but without Dave it wasn't right. They were, as Lance put it, little more than a Harvesters cover band. It was time for something different.

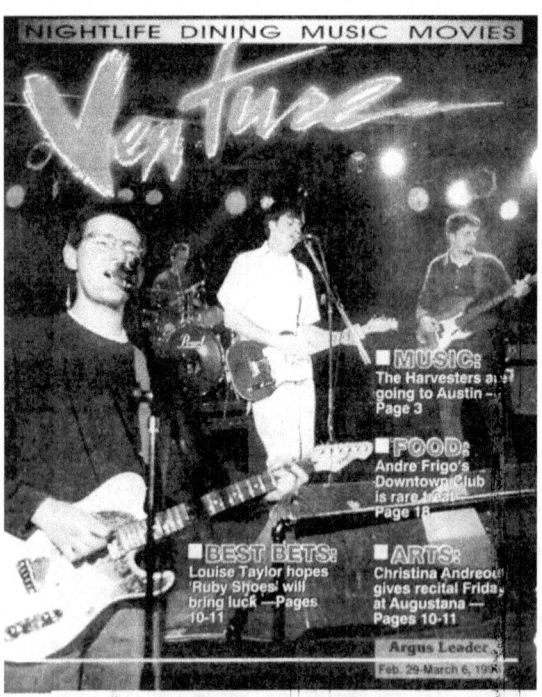

The Harvesters' get some local press in the Sioux Falls Argus Leader, February 29, 1996. Left to right: Dave Scarbrough, George Gongopoulos (background), Justin Seim, Erik Appelwick. Courtesy Argus Leader.

* * *

Darren Jackson graduated in spring 1994. Unlike Fawcett and Johnny and

Appelwick, he hadn't spearheaded any popular campus band. His own relationship with pop music had become strained, to the point that he wasn't writing songs, and, further, didn't really feel there was much left of interest to be accomplished in the field. He certainly wasn't thinking of it as a career option. His plan was to go to grad school to get his master's degree in philosophy, but he ended up moving to Minneapolis instead, landing at CityCabin, where Johnny was also living.

It was a fateful move. He met a singer and artist named Pamela Valfer, who was in a popular local group called Saucer (bassist Howard Hamilton, guitarist Ted Kersten, and drummer Peter Anderson rounded out the lineup). She introduced Darren to lo-fi indie music such as Smog, Sebadoh, and post-rock bands like Stereolab and Slint. Artists like these were the true alternative music in the early to mid–'90s when the bands that had previously been underground took over the mainstream. These groups' use of dissonance, rhythm, and atypical song structures helped Darren realize that "rock 'n' roll could be interesting again" and inspired him to think about writing songs again.

It wasn't long before he got ahold of a 4-track cassette recorder and started laying down his new compositions. The technology, he says, wasn't as much a means to record songs he'd written as it was a part of the composing process and him learning to hone his craft. Darren wrote and recorded many songs during this time without any real intent of releasing them or perfroming them in public. Eventually though, after about a year in Minneapolis, he formed a band—his first since Round Trip. They called themselves Headache, and not long after forming moved to Boston. They recorded some songs and released five of them ("Of Age," "Come on Nurse," "Pointing to Your Head," "Alternababe," and "Bathroom") on a self-titled cassette. Headache played a few shows, but the band didn't last. Part of the reason was that Darren had fallen into drug addiction.

This is a hazy and gap-filled part of his story. It's not something Darren has talks about in much detail except in songs, and even then its masked and ellipitical. He admits he had experimented with several different drugs, and eventually this led to him becoming hooked on heroin. Though heroin addiction conjures up notions of Sid Vicious and Nancy Spungen wasting away in a hotel room, much of Darren's time, it seems was spent traveling from city to city, trying and failing to kick the habit. He traveled light, with little but his guitar, amp, 4 track, and a few select books.

He often returned home to Bison when things got too serious. During one of those stints, crica 1996, he got tired of his hometown and ended up staying for a stretch in Justin Seim's basement in Vermillion. At that time, the Harvesters were still an ongoing concern, and in fact Justin was living with Appelwick. And that's how Darren Jackson met Erik Appelwick.

Even through his years of addiction Darren continued to write and self-recording on four-track, often documenting what he was going through. Ever the perfectionist, he would often record several versions of the same song, altering lyrics and arrangements subtly from take to take. The treasure trove of recordings he made between 1995 and 1999 would end up serving as the basis for a lot of his future work, but he didn't know that at the time. He just wrote and recorded, and even sporadically booked gigs, but, he says, "I could never really get my shit together to form a band." Eventually, he would make his way to Providence, Rhode Island, with his demons following close behind.

4

Somewhere in Betweeen

In which Spymob make their first record, and Chris and Johnny call it quits.

Not long after releasing *Miles and Means*, Chris and Johnny were back in the studio to make a new record. There was definite benefit in having something fresh to sell the fans, and a new CD was a direct injection of cash that was like "a financial drug" according to David Weeks, especially because most of the time everyone was operating hand-to-mouth. It also happened that the guys were prolific enough to make that happen on a yearly basis without sacrificing quality.

For the new album, they had decided to record at CityCabin, which meant that after years of working on Chris and John's live shows, Alex finally got a chance to work on one of their studio albums, though making that happen was no small feat. A major catch of his purchase of CityCabin was that the recording studio was completely devoid of equipment. The opportunity to do Chris and Johnny's new record had come so soon after Alex closed on the house that he had to scramble to get the place ready.

He had negotiatied a $100 per day fee for all of his services (producing, engineering, mixing), which on a 30-day project would net him $3000. But to get the place ready, he had to buy a mixing board (a 32-channel Mackie), stands, cables, and microphones. Everything else he had to rent. "So at the end of the day, either I was breaking even or I was literally paying for Chris and Johnny to record at my studio," Alex says (because Alex got rent money from some of the guys and then in turn sometimes hired them for gigs and odd jobs, Andy Carlson says there was a running joke that they should just laminate a dollar bill and pass it around in a circle).

But for Alex it was a dream come true. He says, "I just remember that feeling of, 'Oh my God, this is what we've always talked about.' There we were at CityCabin, laying down the opening track, 'Absaroka Air,' and Brian Roessler's standing there with his upright bass, Fawcett's on drums, Johnny's in the corner, and Chris is on the other side of the glass, standing in my dining room, and I was in the control room hitting record, man. It was kind of surreal."

For Chris, working at CityCabin wasn't as transcendant. The spartan conditions, especially after having recorded at other professional studios, took some adjustment. He says, "It was slightly flophouse. At different times different people would be crashing in different rooms. I was always slightly on edge, who's going to show up, who's going to be here?" Cleanliness was not a priority in either the house's single bathroom or kitchen. Alex worked on his own idiosyncratic schedule, with seeming disregard for anyone else's. But Chris really liked being in the control room, listening back, and organizing the tracking, an opportunity he hadn't gotten previously. He also had full trust in Alex's ears and recording skills, and the microphones in the studio were great. He says that several of the full band performances with Roessler and Eric were "pretty powerful." That shows on the record, which would be titled *Clearing*.

Released in 1995, *Clearing*—featuring an impressionistic cover photo taken by Andy Carlson in the studio—is the first Chris & Johnny "band" record. Half the songs feature Roessler on bass and Fawcett on drums, with highly respected Minneapolis-based fiddle and mandolin player Peter Ostroushko (and a regular on Garrison Keillor's A Praire Home Companion) on five tunes. Cello and pedal steel also find their way into the mix. In concert, for the most part, it was still just Chris and Johnny performing with their guitars, harmonies, and an occasional harmonica, but on record they were interested in a more expansive sound. This, combined with Alex's meticulous attention to sonic details led to the album being the most polished Chris & Johnny record yet (Paul Frantzich of the Twin Cities band Ride Ruby Ride to tell Alex that Clearing "sounded like a $100,000 record").

Despite, or maybe because of, the sonic changes, the CD would be another hit with fans. Johnny's "Absaroka Air," "Stillwater," and "Somewhere in Between" and Chris's "Loose Summer Clothes" would become concert staples. And then there's "Steady On," Chris's inspirational pep talk of a song that many fans came to consider the duo's signature tune (a humorous list published on Scott Comstock's now defunct fan site listed "You have 'Steady On' tattooed on your body" as one of the 26 signs of being a superfan of the band). That devotion was likely in part due to the anthemic, motivational lyrics, but also in the way the song builds into a dual lead with countermelodies, leading to the thrilling moment when the guys' voices combine into one again.

Thanks to Ostroushko's contributions and Kenny Wilson's pedal steel, the sound of the album is decidedly more country-leaning than any of its predecessors. "Absaroka Air," one of Johnny's most affecting songs, exemplifies this. The title refers to the Absaroka mountain range, the northern edge of which is just south of Bozeman. As in many songs from this period, Johnny is feeling lost. "I've had a hard time believing/In all the things that give me life," he sings. But returning home provides a tiny affirmation and glimmer of hope: "But I believe in that Absaroka air/because it takes my breath away." Unlike "Steady On," though, this is no statement of purpose. The song ends with two questions, one of which is "Can you ever go back home again/And find who you were back then?"

"Back Home" and "Happiness Runs" both reveal a weariness about the life of a working musician. In the deceptively-titled latter, Chris details the joy and pain of songwriting: "Happiness runs through the middle of a revelation/The thrill of a moment when we're feeling inspired/ But then the downdraft comes/And in the wake of your own elation/ You lay your head down and admit you're tired." The song itself is gentle and hushed, with the harmonies sharing the spotlight with Wilson's pedal steel. Johnny's "Back Home" finds him returning to his apartment from being on tour and feeling disoriented. "Back home again," he sings over a hushed guitar, "I guess that's what I call this place I'm in/But it doesn't feel familiar anymore." He discovers that he left the radio on for the whole week while he was gone, and it was playing for no one. In the end he relishes being alone, but realizes it can't last because his calling requires a partner and an audience: "But if a song is sung/and there is no one there to hear/does it even make a sound?"

Indeed, by the time *Clearing* was released, the guys were getting worn down with the high volume of shows and the undending cycle of writing and recording new music. The shows themselves weren't always the most satisfying creatively or artistically. For some gigs, the guys were just collecting a paycheck, playing a student union at lunchtime while people ate and walked through. Eventually they began getting into local coffee shops as well, and those gigs would begin to equal or surpass the NACA ones. But even that required Chris and Johnny to be out on the road constantly.

Clearing is not attributed to "Chris & Johnny." Instead they used their first and last names with no "and" between them: Chris Cunningham Johnny Hermanson. This was the first step in a process. They had firmly decided they didn't want to be called Chris & Johnny anymore, for a host of reasons. For one, they thought it had a dated '70s ring to it, like Sonny & Cher or Loggins & Messina. More than that, the guys had become increasingly uncomfortable, as their fanbase grew, with the informality of using their first names. In their experience having their names so tied to their performing identity gave the fans too much license to treat them as if they knew them personally, especially since the songs themselves were already intimate. On top of that, they were recording and performing more as a band with Roessler and Fawcett, so "Chris & Johnny" made less sense in that context. So, though it was risky to surrender the brand they'd been building for four years, they both agreed it was time for a change. The problem was they couldn't decide on a replacement. Adding their last names was a transitional compromise until they could find something they both liked.

* * *

Reno was going through a similar crisis regarding their name. They now had a solid line-up and tunes, but no one really liked "Reno." Ostby filled notebooks full of words and phrases he that might serve as band names, and periodically ran them by the other guys, who always shot them down. But during one of these sessions John said, "What about Spymob?" It didn't have any meaning, Ostby just liked how it sounded. For once, so did the other guys. Thus they became Spymob.

While the band was very much his priority in 1994 and 1995, Eric Fawcett was a man going many directions all at once. He was manager at French Meadow, a recording member and sometime-live member of the artists formerly known as Chris & Johnny, he was studying with Phil Hay, and he was

Poster for a mid-'90s Chris & Johnny show at the University of Missouri. Courtesy Storyhill.

playing in Fly Manifesto. He also become involved in the dance community when he started dating choreographer, performer, and teacher Sarah Hauss in 1993. Once Eric and Roessler began collaborating with Sarah it led to lots of other connections in the dance community. Eric says, "That's where my drumming took a huge leap forward, because I would just have to keep really steady pulse and beats going for a half hour sometimes. It was such a high, such an incredible musical experience collaborating with dancers, watching them and responding to them. It was such a lesson in that sometimes in order to go forwards you have to go sideways."

Spymob, meanwhile, were doing shows and preparing to record their first album. They took their time. John says, "We spent so much time writing and arranging and rehearsing ... [for] some bands the central thing to drive them is performing. I think the central thing that drove our band was just playing in a room together." When they were finally ready, Eric reluctantly sold his beloved '66 Mustang to his 7th grade biology teacher, Harold Dorr, for $5,000 to help fund his portion of the expensive studio time. Recording on the set of songs that became *Townhouse Stereo* commenced in July 1995 and would take 6 months and three studios—Salmagundi, CityCabin, and Wild Sound in Minneapolis—to complete. Alex Oana was behind the board.

Roessler played bass on all but two songs, with Jeffrey Bailey playing on "Paul Harvey" and John "Strawberry" Fields sitting in on "Seventeen New Recipes" (Fields was everywhere in the Twin Cities music scene, working with Soul Asylum, the Rembrandts, and Greazy Meal before going national with the likes of the Jonas Brothers, Jimmy Eat World, and Miley Cyrus). But, as evidence of his permanent temporary status, Roessler is not listed as part of the band in the liner notes, nor is he in the accompanying photo.

Townhouse Stereo is difficult to describe. Musically it belongs in its own category. Fawcett has labeled it as "prog-pop" but that doesn't quite encompass the jazz influences and the psychedelic guitar solos that are present throughout. The use of the word "pop" also makes it seem like it's catchier than it really is. Many of the songs are long, and the tempos are in no hurry. So maybe "psych jazz rock"? Eric says, "It's a weird record. You know, you'd think that we're all big stoners, I don't think that any of us smoked weed at all. But it has that patient, being in the moment feeling."

On the lyrical front, Ostby was reading a lot of Earnest Hemingway around that time, and began to adopt the writer's "Iceberg Theory," in which the details the writer omits are more important than the ones he provides. This is most evident on a tune like "Bleachers" where we learn enough to know that the narrator is both driving home and thinking about attending a high school or college football game. Is he remembering his early courtship with his wife as he drives home to her? Maybe. The full details are absent, so the story becomes what you want to put into it. The pretty "Kissing the Neighborhood Houses Goodbye" is similar. It's about the aftermath of a death, told in sparse images: A burial by the sea, the news coming while family members are watching TV, going through his letters and tapes. We don't know who died, yet we still mourn right along with the narrator.

The lyrics are part of what makes *Townhouse Stereo* strange; they ask you to do some work to appreciate them. So does the music. More than half of the songs are five minutes or longer, with a couple pushing six, and the title track going over seven. "Uncontrollably" has an egregious title-to-musical style mismatch, as everything about the song's arrangement and performance is completely controlled. John even sings "I wanna thank you for being patient with me" as if speaking directly to the listener.

Townhouse Stereo has a few songs that are more lyrically straightforward and musically accessible. "Half the Time with You" from the *Reno* EP appears again in a slightly different version, with less wah-wah guitar and more pots and pans, but still just as catchy. "Seventeen New Recipes" is a slow burn; while the band creates a groove, John lets his story unfold slowly, with the lyrics taking center stage. The song's narrator has found himself obsessed with a show called *Cooking in the '90s with Mary Steen*, clearly developing a crush on the host. When the show gets cancelled after 17 episodes, he's heartbroken, but consoles himself with all of the new recipies he's learned.

And then there's "Reno," a song that might have joined the ranks of great band theme songs had the group not changed its name. Spymob often cited Steely Dan as an influence, and this is the tune where that comparison is most apt. It's a melodic love story about a race car driver who falls hard for a woman named Reno. Fawcett and Brent are the MVPs, with the former holding everything together through the tricky time changes, and the latter reeling off an extended lyrical guitar solo over a jazzy breakdown.

When the band self-released *Townhouse Stereo* in 1996, it got some positive reviews (Jim Mayer wrote in the *Star Tribune* that the album "incorporates a lot of classy influences with impressive originality" and called John a "wordsmith that who paints unusual views of ordinary life") but was not a sales success. Eric reports sardonically that it sold "dozens and dozens" of copies. Compared to Chris and John, whose own 1996 CD—*This Side of Lost*—would sell nearly 2,000 copies on release, this was a disappointment. That disappointment was perhaps even more stinging because there was no one to blame. There was no meddling by the label, because there was no label (though it did get picked up and promoted by local label Oar Fin Records). Creatively, the band had made the record they wanted to make, and Eric is proud of that fact now. He says: "The band went for it. Alex went for it. It's an album of real instruments. I don't think there's a synthesizer on that record. We just ignored all electronics, as far as I can remember. And everything that is floaty or synthy is a human voice. On 'Capital Buildings' there's this weird percussion thing where I'm breathing into a mic and sweeping my hands down a pipe."

Ostby, at the time, felt like they were making something everyone would love. But in hindsight he has some regrets about the songwriting: "When I listen back it's so funny to me that I would go that far with a song or lyrical idea, because who would care about it other than me and just a few other people? I think if I were doing it all over again, I would be more interested in how you communicate to a wider audience [and] speak to more universal themes." Writers are typically harsh critics of themselves, but they don't always have the clearest perspective the success of their work, either. Drummer jMatt Keil offers an alternate take: "[Spymob] wrote a record ahead of their time in *Townhouse Stereo*, which I didn't get at the time, but now I listen to it and it just blows my mind." It's a testament to the care with which the album was created, but also to the necessity of giving it the attention and time it needs to fully reveal its pleasures, though Fawcett says, "I don't think the time for *Townhouse Stereo* ever came, unless it's still coming."

It seems that Fawcett and Ostby's perceptions of the album now are still intertwined with how its underwhelming reception. At the time it was pure frustration that they'd put all this effort and energy and money into something that wasn't going to advance the band. They'd reached a point where they could play anywhere in the Twin Cities, and had a fanbase enough to get a couple hundred people to come to a show, but what they really wanted was to move to the next level. The problem was they didn't know how to do that.

4. Somewhere in Between

This led to a period of uncertainty for Spymob. Not only was their music not connecting with a large audience, the band weren't getting along. It didn't help that the Twin Cities were suffering a string of brutally cold winters that had started in 1994 and would stretch into 1997. Fawcett says, "Everyone individually was thinking, 'Shit, I just gotta get the hell out of here,' and then everyone's next thought was, 'I can't because this incredible goldmine of friendships, relationships, and talent are right here.' We literally got together at Alex's house and sat in a circle and discussed, 'How do we do this? How do we get out?'"

The idea was to get everyone to Los Angeles, but when it came down to specifics and logistics, they couldn't make it work. "It just fell apart," says Fawcett. "We kind of fucked ourselves and got stuck in a place with really cold winters. We definitely stuck together for that community." He jokes now, referring to his long blond locks: "I have this surfer hair because I want to look in the mirror and think, 'I'm in Santa Cruz.'"

To properly combat the cold weather and the chilly relations between the members of Spymob, Eric decided he needed a change of setting and perspective. He applied for a Jerome travel study grant to go to Rio de Janeiro for six weeks to study dance accompaniment and learn Portuguese. He was awarded the grant, and was set to go to Brazil in January of 1998.

* * *

When Chris and Johnny's manager, Andy Carlson, decided to enroll in law school and reduce his role with the band, David Weeks came on to co-manage the duo. One of Dave's first tasks was to navigate the guys through the selection of a band name. A name that made it fairly far in the selection process was Once Eleven, a play on words since "once" in Spanish is the number eleven, but also an acknowledgment of the role childhood nostalgia played in their songwriting. When that one fizzled, the guys were set to call themselves AM, as in AM radio. But Chris didn't like it, plus Wilco had just put out their debut album, *AM*. Every other suggestion met a similar fate, being dismissed for one reason or another in what Dave calls "endless discussion leading nowhere." It got to the point where Dave pled with them to "pick something and stick with it." He tasked the guys to ask themselves if they could live with any of the options for more than a single day.

One day, Johnny and Alex were discussing the name conundrum over a meal at their favorite restaurant Vietnamese restaurant, Bona, located in in Stadium Village on the University of Minnesota campus. Alex said something like, "It should be something you from your roots that you and Chris are both connected to," and Johnny thought of the Story Hills. The Story Hills are the ones that surround their native Bozeman and are home to meadows, pastures, and breathtaking views of the city. "The Things I Love," from their first album, featured the line "When I'm old I'd like to rest in the Story Hills/Telling tales of all my life's been through." Calling themselves the Story Hills, Johnny realized, would tie into their shared past—both personal and professional—while also providing a fresh start. Later that night, when he told Dave Weeks his idea, Dave suggested a one-word version: Storyhill.

Chris loved the name: "It was the perfect blend of tying us to our roots, our home, and encapsulating our style of music." Dave says, "I think that was a good choice. At the time it was just like, 'Thank god it's done.'"

Chris and John had vacillated before, so once Storyhill was seemingly decided upon, Dave rushed to get the CDs of their next album pressed so they couldn't easily change their minds again. That next album was *This Side of Lost*, the seventh CD by Chris and Johnny and the first by Storyhill. It completed their transition from a duo to a full band. All but one song (fittingly, Chris's "Standing on my Own") was recorded live in the studio with Fawcett on drums and Roessler on bass. As if having half of Spymob wasn't enough, John Ostby came in to play piano on some tracks. They recorded, with Alex Oana once again serving as producer, engineer, and mixer, at Third Ear Recording, not long after Appelwick and the Harvesters had made their CD there.

This Side of Lost came out in September 1996 with CD release shows at the Emerson Cultural Center in Bozeman and the Great American History Theater in Saint Paul. Johnny has described his songs on *This Side of Lost* as "odd" and rebelling against the "whole mountain acoustic thing" while Chris's songs—such as the touching metaphorical tribute to his grandfather, "Old Sea Captain"—remained as folky and traditional as ever. There's definitely some truth to that, but Johnny's idea of odd is still quite catchy and relatable. What he was likely referring to was the darkness of his songs on the record.

None of Chris and Johnny's previous albums were exactly light-hearted, but they had moments of levity in music or lyrics or both, your "Pancho and Lefty" here, your "Loose Summer Clothes" there. *Lost* doesn't have anything comparable outside of the musically buoyant but emotionally murky "White Roses," and there's good reason for that. The weariness brought on by their lifestyle—first glimpsed on *Clearing*—had worsened.

On *Lost*, it shows up on the first two songs, the one-two punch of Johnny's "Great Divide" and "Hard Wind." The former refers to the Continental Divide which bisects the U.S. along western Montana and down through Wyoming, Colorado, and New Mexico. This line had a special significance for Chris and John because they'd crossed it countless times in their travels from the Pacific Northwest to the Midwest. Fittingly, the song is about the toll endless travel can take, the inability to form any lasting connections and or feel grounded. At the same time, Johnny trades in double meaning and metaphor. The great divide for Storyhill, and more specifically for Johnny, was the same as it was for Spymob: how to make the leap from semi-professionals with a small fanbase to professionals with national recognition. Or at least to continue to be profitable without travelling constantly. The song's chorus seems to refer to this, with the prospects dimming: "The great divide you're waiting for/And praying you can cross/You can't deny you're straying from it/To find another way around from this side of lost."

John Hermanson (standing) and Alex Oana at Third Ear working on *This Side of Lost* circa 1996. Courtesy Storyhill.

The fast-paced "Hard Wind" refers to the same conundrum, the realization that five years of toil had not moved the needle as much as he'd have liked. "A hard wind pressed against the windshield," he sings. "But I'd always thought myself a part of the weather/Waiting with the heat, release with the rain/But I'm sorry to say it's fighting me now." Later, he mentions "every race that I've run that's beating me down." Though Storyhill's career to that point was on a steady upward trajectory, as former contemporaries Semisonic and the Jayhawks signed major label deals and scored hits, Johnny started to feel left behind. He'd often felt out of place in Minneapolis, especially musically.

In "Gone Away," Johnny admits to not being able to keep the pace of touring. It's less about the struggle for more success than it is about not being able to sustain relationships because he's never in one place long enough. Johnny wrote the lyrics after spending an especially nice evening with friends and then realizing it wouldn't be easily repeated: "But tomorrow I'll be somewhere else," he sings, "Walking on someone else's feet/I'm always only a ghost of myself." This was a time before tablets and smart phones, so staying in touch took much more effort, and that effort was almost impossible for Chris and Johnny to make. Chris's song "Another Time" is a variation on that theme, with a nostalgic visit to a childhood friend turning melancholy. In addition to the fleeting nature of it all, the song also contemplates the sharp contrast between the direction the friends' lives have taken. To Chris, it seems as though his friend's future is "so bright that it burns his eyes" with a wife and baby and a steady job. And this has the travel-bug-bitten singer—who at that point didn't have a city to call home—thinking about sticking in one place: "Someday I'll settle and I'll bring you to mine."

As if fatigue and disillusionment weren't enough, Chris and Johnny were also having trouble with each other. Tensions had built up steadily over the years, largely due to their very different personalities and approaches to nearly everything (for one, they didn't share the same vision for Storyhill, which Johnny constantly wanting to push them to a commercial breakthrough and Chris not sharing that goal). Their divergent personalities didn't blend as easily in friendship as they did in song, and their grudges and annoyances built up. They had rarely been apart for five years, and they were tired of each other. As Dave puts it: "They were like an old married couple at 25 years old." It certainly didn't help that their identities had been inextricably tied together almost their whole adult lives.

So "Spaces" finds Johnny musing on his need for freedom. He might be singing to a girl, but he could just as well be speaking to Chris when he says, "And I know I need the spaces/The uncertain places in between" (Ironically, the guys' harmonies on this song are as strong as they'd ever been). Similarly, Chris's "Standing on My Own," which he says is about "that inner yearning to know myself without being so tied to Johnny." Accordingly, he performs the song completely solo. "Continents Collide" is less about the need for identity than it is an attempt to address the tension between the two. Chris says when he started writing the song it was about his relationship with his uncle, but it morphed into a song about Johnny. The chorus goes, "Continents collide in their clumsy dance/They make mountains and drift out to sea/And I imagine the same thing could happen/If left to chance, to you and me."

Though it ends on a hopeful note—"And at least for now, there's no doubt that we can begin again"—the song has a funereal air.

Even the album artwork points to tension and disconnectedness. The CD cover has two images. On the right third we see a tiny Chris and Johnny all but obscured by a blurry red truck rushing by. They're facing each other, but not really looking at each other. On the inside of the booklet, with an image of a field and sky interrupted by Chris and Johnny in a tunnel somewhere in downtown Minneapolis, the former in the foreground standing still and gazing into the distance while the latter runs almost frantically. Even their clothes are in contrast, with Chris sporting jeans and a windbreaker and Johnny dressed like a hipster professor. On the back of the CD, it's just Chris and John in the middle of an insanely busy street, again looking in different directions.

It should be no surprise, then, that sometime around the release of *This Side of Lost*, Chris and Johnny decided to call it quits. As Chris tells it, they were on a plane to their umpteenth appearance at a NACA conference (they performed there to encourage various college representatives to book them) and it hit him that he'd reached the end. He turned to Johnny and said, "I can't do this anymore." Johnny, who'd known deep down the day was coming, accepted it with grace. Though he'd felt that same constriction of being only a half of something, Johnny also had a musical wanderlust that Chris didn't, a desire to bring the wider range of his personal tastes into his songwriting and performing. So though it meant starting over in building a fanbase and searching for that elusive level of success he wanted to reach, it also meant freedom.

After deciding to split, the guys quickly realized they needed an exit plan. For one, they were in debt after recording *This Side of Lost*, but they also had a whole tour lined up to promote the album. They also felt an obligation to their fanbase, which was ever expanding. They were now a good five years older than the college audiences they were playing for, lending them an elevated stature, and they had a solid show able to draw the best from their growing discography. This also coincided with the wider availability of the Internet, and so 1995–1996 seems to be when the fans were at their most fevered. Scott Comstock, a Storyhill devotee who attended Graceland University in Lamoni, Iowa, started an unofficial website and that helped to focus the fan community.

Scott posted lyrics and news updates and maintained a guest book that would serve as a meeting place. The fans embraced the new album and new name, and with them had adopted their own label: Hill Heads. Hill Heads liked the band's songs and recordings but the real draw for most seemed to be the live show. One fan, writing on the website, wrote about seeing Storyhill perform: "I get the feeling that the music I'm hearing isn't actually coming from Chris and Johnny, but rather from somewhere else—somewhere higher or farther away somehow—and they are merely channeling this sound." None of these admirers knew at the time that Storyhill had decided to break up.

Also, ironically, *This Side of Lost* got the duo some of their first significant press in the Twin Cities. Vickie Gilmer of the Saint Paul *Pioneer Press* wrote a review of the album in the October 20, 1996, paper, praising the duo's "ability to create refined folk-pop tunes that cascade gently" and comparing them to Simon & Garfunkel (of course) and Harry Chapin. She also incorrectly stated that they only had two previous albums, which showed how little attention the local scene had afforded the guys.

To Chris and Johnny's great surprise, the decision to break up had completely cleared the air between them. John says, "It was like the best times that we had because all the tension between us was gone." Chris adds: "There was clarity again, this emotional relief, and it was back to being fun. It was like, 'Oh, I don't have to worry about anything, just got a bunch of fun shows ahead.'" With a light at the end of the tunnel, they were free to enjoy one last trip to some of their favorite colleges and coffeehouses, admire what they'd created together, and to be easier on one another. John's girlfriend, and soon-to-befiancée, Bettine Hoff—a Norwegian immigrant he'd met at Saint Olaf—came along, as did Fawcett and Roessler for a few shows. Alex was there too, recording several shows for the group's second live album.

That CD, simply titled *Storyhill Live*, would be released in early 1997. Featuring performances from five different concerts across five different states, it showcases a mix of old favorites, songs from *This Side of Lost*, and a cover of Nanci Griffith's anti-racism anthem "It's a Hard Life Wherever You Go." There are three new songs, and two of them are performed as solo pieces. The first of those is a fantastic version of "Letter of the Law," which would appear on Johnny's next album. Chris's solo turn comes on "Elizabeth Page" a sweet tune about the depth of feeling that comes with being a new parent (Chris was writing from observation, as he wouldn't become a father until much later). In Johnny's galloping "Let the Wind Come In," the duo sing in unison once more. The song was inspired by a friend of Johnny's who struggled with substance abuse, but as with many songs of this period, carries a double meaning. Lines like "You've opened the windows, you've opened the doors/You let the wind come and and blow where it wants to" seem to speak to the joy of newfound freedom, of a letting-go of something that was pulling you down. It was the last new original song by Storyhill before their parting of ways.

It was in April 23, 1997, that the guys broke the news to their fans, via a website posting and in their print newsletter. Chris and Johnny each wrote a statement explaining the decision, and they are inadvertently coordinated-sounding, one last harmonious release. Both speak of the complexity of their professional relationship and how that fed their creativity while essentially leading them to split. That established dynamic, of Johnny playing the part of cheerleader and coach to Chris is made clear. Chris says Johnny's talent and enthusiasm "inspires and compels me to sing out," while Johnny says, "I have always encouraged Chris to write from his heart, to sing in his voice, to go his way." Both are exceedingly thankful for their travels and experiences, and both are surprisingly prescient about the long-term prospects for their music. Chris says, "It's my hope and suspicion that the songs we've known and sung so freely for so long will continue to echo and ring long after dark." And Johnny writes, "I'm sure these songs and stories will only sound better and mean more as years go by." And neither is quite sure what the immediate future holds, though, tellingly, Johnny promises to continue making music while Chris doesn't. At the time, Chris was pretty sure he was done with recording and performing.

Storyhill financially maximized their farewell tour as much as possible. Fans came in droves to see one of their favorite acts for what they thought was the last time. Many essentially followed the band around to the extent that it was possible. Chris, John, and Dave were all amazed at how they were forced to add additional shows in some places, or to come back around a few months later and still sell out. Chris says, "We were trying to hit all of our hot spots and do what we could to serve the fans, and it just kept culminating." Dave admits that there were even a couple of instances where they billed a show as the last one, knowing full well they'd be returning. They also played some significant gigs in that stretch, including opening for one of their heroes, singer-songwriter David Wilcox, at Bethel College. They also did several full band shows, and Chris says one of the most fun was at Matter's Ballroom in Decorah, Iowa. The legendary venue had hosted the likes of Lawrence Welk, Johnny Cash, Wanda Jackson, and Buddy Holly in its decades-long history.

They did 26 shows in May of 1997 in Iowa, Wisconsin, Minnesota, and Montana, all leading up to the final Minnesota shows at the Great American History Theater on May 23 and 24, and a final final show at the Emerson Cultural Center in Bozeman on June 3. Many fans made their best effort to be there, including nearly 40 from Minnesota alone. Packed with friends and family and Hill Heads, the concert was recorded by Alex for posterity and later released as *Echoes: The Final Show*.

Listening to the recording, one is immediately struck by the fact that the between song banter has been left intact, unlike the previous two live albums. And while it may not make the best experience for repeated listens (and served as a bit of an embarrassment to both Chris and Johnny), it's a fascinating document for a couple of reasons. One is that it presents a more accurate picture of the live Storyhill experience, where the guys' easy back-and-forth, dry humor, and sometimes-rambling song intros are part of the fun. The other is how clearly both are overcome by the emotion of the moment. Chris almost skips a verse on "I-90" and later admits, "I'm a little nervous tonight." Before the final song ("Steady On"), he thanks everyone and Johnny, and then begins to choke up. Johnny plays it a bit cooler, but has gets a definite catch in his throat when recognizing the music teachers that nurtured them in his introduction to "Boulder River."

The setlist for that night was a good mix of their entire oeuvre, featuring a number of their earliest tunes from *Shapeshifting* and *Different Waters*. The only song that hadn't appeared elsewhere was a faithful cover of the Paul Simon song "American Tune" (it was a solo Paul song, but there's a Simon & Garfunkel version on *The Concert in Central Park*) and a full band "White Roses" that segues into the Beatles' "I'm Looking Through You" replete with Eric Fawcett providing harmonies.

After the show Chris and Johnny and a group of friends and fans went to Chris's parents' house for a barbeque and volleyball. From there they went camping at Hyalite Lake. The next morning they took some photos and came back down the mountain. They headed literally in opposite directions. Chris, after briefly considering moving to Santa Fe, was off to Seattle in the Caravan he got in the break-up (Johnny got the sound system). Johnny loaded into his VW van and headed to Minnesota.

5

Instead of a Habit You Should Have a Hobby

In which Appelwick and Darren finally end their wanderings, but not before wandering some more.

"Dark days," Darren calls the period (late 1997 and early 1998) in which he lived in Providence, Rhode Island. Darren got a job as a security guard at the Rhode Island School of Design museum, and found his way into the local community of musicians, which included William Schaff, Alex K. Redfearn, and Margie Wienk (all members of the genre-defying ensemble the Eyesores). He connected especially well with Schaff, who played both guitar and drums, and the two began rehearsing together on a semi-regular basis. Out of that a new musical persona emerged: Kid Dakota and the Tumble Weeds. The first part of the name was a tongue-in-cheek play on "Kid Rock"—who had recently risen to fame that on the back of his songs "Cowboy" and "Bawitdaba"—but also acknowledged Darren's roots. Recruiting some members of the Eyesores, Will and Darren did a couple of gigs.

At this point, though, doing shows was not as important to Darren as honing his craft. He was still writing songs and recording 4-track demos obsessively. Inspiration for the songs he wrote during this time came largely from an intense romance, the ending of which had left Darren shattered. He was also back to using heroin regularly, and his habit was getting the best of him. During one bender, he says, he fell face first on a gravel road. When the cops came, they found a needle on him, and so Darren woke up in jail. His elbow was broken and he'd lost some teeth. His forehead, nose, cheekbone, upper lip, and chin were scraped raw. He says he spent three days in jail before friends bailed him out.

This was a wake-up call, the figurative and the literal rock bottom. He went back home and sought help at an outpatient treatment center some three hours from Bison. It was cold turkey. Upon getting cleaned up, Darren returned home again to his parents' house. There he demoed more songs in the basement, and he hooked up again with Justin Seim to do some recording in Justin's dad's barn. As 1998 turned into 1999, Darren decided he needed direction. He applied and was accepted to graduate school at the University of Illinois–Chicago for the fall. His plan was to continue his study of philosophy, with the goal of becoming a professor. With the time he had before returning to academia, he decided to go to Minneapolis with his suitcase of songs to get some of them properly recorded.

Alex Oana, unsurprisingly, was the catalyst. He had become a fixture in the Twin

Cities music scene, his time at the Fine Line had introduced him to both local and national artists, leading to a steady stream of recording projects at CityCabin. He also worked as an engineer at Seedy Underbelly, a studio on Washington Avenue in Minneapolis (in the warehouse district) started in 1996 by John Kuker. Kuker was a gearhead and collector who had amassed a formidable array of vintage microphones, amplifiers, effects pedals, and instruments impressive enough to attract local royalty such blues wunderkind Jonny Lang and Semisonic (who recorded their number one hit "Closing Time" there), and national acts like Girls Against Boys. Alex worked on all of those records and many more.

CityCabin thus far had only seen lower-profile local acts, but it offered Darren free studio time, and a place to crash while he and Alex worked. It was the ideal laboratory in which to perfect a sound. Darren didn't want a full band, instead envisioning his guitar and vocals paired only with drums. He liked the idea of a minimalist approach that emphasized space as a vital part of the songs. "Like a good poem, I think the responsibility of a song is to create a space where a story can unfold," is how he described his vision to the *Minnesota Daily*. "I think a message will be delivered regardless of how the story is communicated, but I think it's important to let the story show itself." He needed a drummer who could provide space, but at the same time hit hard and strong when necessary. When he conveyed this to Alex, the producer had one name in mind: "Fucking Christopher McGuire," he said. McGuire played in the popular local art rock band 12 Rods. His drumming style was idiosycncratic and powerful, with a punch that Alex thought would suit Darren's songs perfectly.

Flyer for the very first Kid Dakota gig, billed as Kid Dakota & the Tumble Weeds. Courtesy Darren Jackson.

McGuire and his 12 Rods bandmates had grown up in Oxford, Ohio and through various iterations of the group ended up in Minneapolis in the mid-'90s. Their first release, the 1996 EP *Gay?* got a rare-as-a-unicorn perfect 10.0 on the nascent (and initially-Twin Cities–based) Pitchfork, and led to 12 Rods securing a major label deal with V2. Their debut album, *Separation Anxieties* (1998), hadn't been a hit, but V2 was excited about the songs they had demoed for the follow-up. It was at this point that Christopher and Darren first met.

On a couple of days' rehearsal, Darren, and Christopher laid down eight songs with Alex at CityCabin (Darren had recorded an additional song, "Pairin' Off," on his own, with just voice and guitar). He took the recordings back with him to South Dakota that spring, and upon listening back decided that though the songs sounded really fresh, the drums were "way too busy" and robbed the tunes of their open space. A few months later he headed back to Minneapolis and they tried it again. Christopher had had more time to think through the arrangements, Darren had more clarity about what he wanted, and everyone was happy with the results this time around. A comparison of the final versions of the songs to their demos shows that Darren had the arrangements figured out early on, but that McGuire provided an elevated sense of drama. It was an effective combination.

The duo had chemistry, but Darren was headed to school soon, and Christopher was off to Hawaii to record the next 12 Rods record with Todd Rundgren as producer, so for now they'd just have to be happy with having created some cool recordings. If there was going to be a Kid Dakota, it would have to wait. Or so they thought.

It wasn't long before fate intervened in a couple of major ways. First, Christopher's already-tense relationship with his 12 Rods bandmates—largely thanks to them tiring of Christopher's in-your-face persona—snapped completely in Hawaii, and they sent him home three weeks in. Not only was he out of the recording process, he was out of the band. Meanwhile, Darren's time in graduate school had an inauspicious start. He fell off the wagon, and began doing heroin again.

So it was back to Minnesota, or "the land of 10,000 treatment centers" as Darren put it. This time it was full-fledged rehab at a state hospital, residential, with drugs to help him taper, and both group and individual therapy sessions designed to help him get at the root of his addiction. This latter bit, perhaps not surprisingly given his personality, was what Darren found the most difficult. As he describes it the therapy involved "the incessant owning of consequences, the making of amends, the taking of steps, the intellectualizing (of which I was always accused), the blatant stupidity, and the retarded sayings ('works if you work it, sucks if you don't,' 'keep it simple stupid,' etc.). Whenever I wasn't in one group I was in another—big group, small group, relationship group, sitting group, standing group, crouching group, leaning-slightly-forward group, sitting-on-the-edge-of-our-chairs group, etc., ad infinitum, ad naseum."

Despite his cynicism about the process, it worked. The Darren that came out of treatment in December 1999 was not only drug-free, but also more focused on his health. In one interview, he jokingly described himself as leading "rigidly ascetic lifestyle" with no alcohol, nicotine, or sex. In truth, he just tried to eat better and exercise more (he began long distance running) to keep himself healthy. He'd made the decision to not return to grad school, but would instead settle in Minneapolis, live in CityCabin, get a job (he ended up working in the office of the registrar at the University of Minnesota) and pursue Kid Dakota. With Christopher now free, there were few obstacles in the way, at least in terms of time. Christopher had left a band he'd been in for seven years and broken up with the girlfriend he'd been seeing for three, and Darren was still learning to function without drugs. "Needless to say," Darren says wryly, "We were an intensely happy, well-adjusted pair."

They played their first show at the cramped Foxfire Coffee Lounge in downtown Minneapolis in February of 2000. The Foxfire was one of the few Twin Cities venues at the time to offer all-ages shows and consistently affordable cover charge, and had a devoted audience of emo kids and local musicians (many of whom worked as baristas in the coffee shop out front). Upon its closing just a few months after Kid Dakota's debut, *City Pages* eulogized the Foxfire by noting that it was "widely recognized as having revitalized the local rock scene."

Alex spent weeks tinkering over the final mixes of Darren's songs, leading Darren to joke that Alex was "probably more familiar with the music than we are" after spending so much time with the songs. They self-released *So Pretty* as a 5-song EP on self-burned CD-Rs. The cover art featured a close-up photo of Darren not long after his fall, his arm in a sling, his face still splattered with fresh red wounds. It's an arresting, disturbing, almost stomach-churning image. The songs behind the cover inspire a similar feeling. With few exceptions, the lyrics are dark and squirm-inducing, and the music has an air of menace.

What's interesting is that these songs were created in a place of hope. In a 2001 *Pulse Magazine* interview, the following exchange occurred:

Pulse: And having been down those dark alleys, it's nice to realize there's light at the end of the tunnel, you know. And that's what I get from So Pretty. It has that crackling back to life quality. I mean, is that accurate?

Jackson: Yeah, I think that's accurate. I man, those songs were all kind of written when I was sober and excited about being sober.

The fact that Darren fell off the wagon again after recording them doesn't dull the fact that the songs came from a place of clarity. Later, Darren said that when he wrote the *So Pretty* tunes, "those were really powerful times from me when everything was right at the surface." Darren wasn't particularly interested in trading on his addiction, but he couldn't deny what it had inspired in him creatively, something he'd admit when he told the *Minnesota Daily* about arguing with his mother over whether or not his addiction had been a good thing on the balance. His side of the argument was that he wouldn't have written so many great songs without being able to draw on that experience.

The *So Pretty* EP is proof of that, and no song is more emblematic than the title track. The song is a harrowing look at the desperation of a junkie. We learn in the first verse that the narrator and his friend Jesse are hard up ("We ran out of cash and they ran out of pity"). In the second verse he's "double-boilin' cottons," which is a method where the cloth used to filter the heroin is bascally harvested of its residue. In the third verse he contemplates his rig, which is dull and bent, but "nevertheless it's my friend." This leads to the wordless chorus, the repeated klaaack-click-click of a metal ice cube tray which soars into "ah-ahs," perhaps replicating the high. The ice cube tray came into use when Darren was demoing the song in his parents' basement and found the best thing he could to provide percussion. In concert, the band began handing out ice cube trays so fans could play along.

The next verse finds the narrator musing on Niki, a fellow addict who the narrator feels is too young for this: "Instead of a habit, you should have a hobby/Like Barbie or bubblegum cards," he notes dryly. Perhaps Niki gives them the money to score, we're not told for sure, but in the final verse, all instrumentation drops out to emphasize the harmonized lines, "What good are the Make-Up and what good are the Makers, if nothing can make you feel good?" and then Jesse heads to "the bad neighborhood" to get what they need. The music once again responds, going into a repeated guitar figure that becomes more wobbly and distorted as it goes. It's a remarkable amount of detail and feeling and storytelling packed into five minutes.

The only other song to address Darren's addiction directly was "Smokestack," which tells of a couple's trip to Cape Cod in the off season. There, they witness "the smokestack we adored" billowing dark puffs and producing acid rain. Whether this is a metaphor or an actual event is unclear, as the song mellows to drone and then comes roaring back with a lyrical guitar part and the revelation that things have gone wrong. "And when I came back it had wasted away/By it I mean most of the best part of the day." Did he sneak away to shoot up? Maybe. The next line is "I promised to quit if you promised to stay." But it doesn't work. Next, he tells us, "You packed up your shit/My life remained the same." The song is one of the many inspired by the monumental relationship Darren had when he was in Providence. The sense of space that Darren mentioned giving his songs is definitely present on the second half of this tune as it starts and stops many times.

"Coalminer" and "Summer Cold" share the same sense of dread and stark hopelessness as "So Pretty" and "Smokestack." "Summer Cold" is an enigmatic tune that features some very pretty guitar passages paired with storming drums and crunchy guitars. The reverby "Coalminer" is a harsh look at Appalachia, inspired by the 1931 James Faulkner novel *Sancutary*, where moonshine-fueled debauchery takes place in the hills of Tennessee. It's centered on an assault, rape (and murder?) of a woman who "looks a little like Loretta, just like a coalminer's daughter." The lyrics are full of threat, and so is the music with drums cracking and intruding, the background vocals literally screaming in your ear. Easy listening it ain't. Which makes "Pairin' Off" such a relief (on the EP it followed directly after "Coalminer"). It's brief acoustic love song which also concerns sex, but in a consensual and sensual way—the line "Come on girl, girl cum with me" shows why it pays to read lyrics in the liner notes. The song is as light and breezy as "Coalminer" is dark and heavy, featuring only Darren and his guitar and some lightly overdubbed harmonies.

So Pretty and Kid Dakota were like catnip for the local music press. There was the two-man set-up, which loudly proclaimed itself as different from the usual four-to-five member bands (the most famous two-person indie band, the White Stripes, were a couple years away from being nationally known). There was the live show, which was always a spectacle thanks to Christopher's unorthodox, theatrical playing style. He seemed like a man possessed, if not by the music than by OCD tendencies, alternating standing and sitting, and doing all sorts of machinations with his cymbal, removing and replacing it, licking it suggestively, and playing it with his nipple rings. Darren says of Christopher, "He definitely brought a level of drama to the whole thing that I hadn't anticipated. Christopher is very much a showman. He was very serious about performing. And he was very serious about making an impression."

Early Kid Dakota promo photo by Jayson Wold. Darren Jackson (left) and Christopher McGuire. Courtesy Darren Jackson.

But what insured attention from the media was the story behind the songs. Journalists love a good hook, and a musician who comes back from the depths of addiction and chronicles the journey doesn't get much hookier. None of that would have mattered much, though, if the writers hadn't liked the music. But they did. *The Minnesota Daily* wrote, "Kid Dakota sounds like a cross between Shellac's start and stop arrangements and the utter beauty of Will Oldham and The Cure." *Pulse Magazine* opined: "In an almost processional and mock grandiosity, these waltzes sweep and swell to fill both vast, arched chambers, but also the tight crawl-spaces between the stations of the mind." *City Pages* called the EP "gorgeous and sprawling" and named it the number five local release of the year. The Current 89.3 host Bill DeVille says "The first time I heard Kid Dakota, it blew me away." At that time he hosted the local show at Cities 97, and spun the *So Pretty* songs regularly.

Darren and Christopher continued to play shows and work on new material throughout the summer, building buzz around town. They tried to get the EP into the hands of the contacts Christopher had made during his time in 12 Rods. They sent it to Radio K, the student radio station for the University of Minnesota, and a local tastemaker, and eventually started getting play there. But it was a chance encounter that would prove to have largest impact on the band's long-term prospects. Christopher McGuire told the story to the website *30Music*: "I've been a Low fan since '93, before I moved to Minneapolis and people were playing Low for me and I was very affected by it. So I moved to Minneapolis, listened to all the Low records, and was at the Fine Line shortly after *So Pretty* had been finished. In the middle of the line for the bathroom I see none other than Zak Sally from Low. I go up to him. I get down on one knee. I present the *So Pretty* EP. I begged Zak Sally. I said, 'Look, I've bought every one of your records, your music means a lot to me, it would me a lot to me if you would just listen to the first track of this record before you go to bed tonight.' And he said, 'Alright, I will do that.' He called me the next day and said, 'Impressive shit.' I'll never forget that." Sally would end up playing with the group, and Low's leader, Alan Sparhawk, would eventually take Kid Dakota under his wing. By all indications, Darren was on his way.

* * *

With the Harvesters officially defunct, a new band had arisen from their final incarnation. Keeping the same Violet/Harvesters hybrid line-up (Justin Seim on guitar and vocals, Appelwick on bass and vocals, Mark Romanowski on guitar, and Lance Beier on drums), the new group dubbed themselves the Lefty Devils. With Appelwick and Justin providing fresh material, they started playing shows in Vermillion and Sioux Falls, and self-recorded an album's worth of songs. They were a strong combo. Justin says now, "I thought that was the best band that we had." The rest of the band was living in Sioux Falls while Appelwick finished up his senior year of college at USD, and he planned to join them and make a go of it.

So when Appelwick graduated with a degree in English in the spring of 1998, he and Justin got a tiny apartment to share. To pay the bills, Justin was working as a carpenter. Appelwick got hired on as a manager at Bagel Boy, which required him to report to work at 5am every morning. It wasn't an ideal situation, but making it as a rock star takes sacrifice. Unfortunately, as good as the Lefty Devils may have been or could have been, no one else in the band was as serious as Appelwick was about making a career in music. Their album remained unmixed and unreleased, their practices and gigs were sporadic.

In short order Appelwick lost it. He came home from work one day only a couple months after moving to Sioux Falls and announced to Justin that he was leaving. Erik says he packed up two garbage bags full of clothes, a "Sam's Club size" jar of peanut butter, a lap steel, and a road atlas into his car. He headed west without a destination in mind. He made his way to the northwest and visited friends here and there, and spent up the money he had left. His car broke down three weeks later in Montana, where Erik got a job as a bartender at a "swank place in the Gallatin Valley beneath Big Sky." He had become stranded in Storyhill country.

Appelwick eventually made his way north to Bozeman and settled there. He played guitar at the Haufbrau, a bar near the Montana State University campus and wrote song after song without a way to record them. He would stay in Bozeman until September 1999. He wrote in an online bio, "After reclaiming my grip on reality (at least as much as I ever had to begin with) I opted to return to Vermillion."

Back in South Dakota he settled in a place on High Street (just east of the USD campus). There, surrounded by family and friends, Appelwick had more resources available to start making recordings of the songs he'd been writing. His first order of business was to take the five Lefty Devils songs he'd written and get them mixed. Though not particularly happy with the end result, he burned some copies and handed them around to friends. The EP is a fascinating document of what might have been, as well as a glimpse into Erik's post-college mindset.

Though the songs were written and recorded before he lit out for the west like Huckleberry Finn, their themes clearly presage what would happen. The songs' narrators are almost uniformly dealing with trouble (both internal and external) by running away to somewhere else. There's even a literal predictor. The opening rocker "Route 191" is named after the north-south highway that runs through Montana, Wyoming, Utah, and Arizona to the Mexican border, and of course the Montana stretch of the road is where Appelwick ended up stranded. The tune extolls the pleasures and virtues of escaping to god-knows-where, but there's a dark edge behind it, as the song's narrator speaks of leaving footprints in the sand that "might be the last of me they'll ever find." This is followed by the chorus: "All I want is to lose myself/All I want is to disappear/Either way we'll find our place in the sun/Down Route 191."

Conversely, the closing ballad "Neon Lights" talks about running away being an ineffectual way to escape problems, a la Paul Varjack's blistering final speech to Holly Golightly in *Breakfast at Tiffany's*: "No matter where you run, you just end up running into yourself." The song's narrator has realized it's time to go back the place one left behind, predicting Appelwick's eventual return to Vermillion.

The three songs in between deal with ill-advised and doomed romance, wicked women and weak men, culminating in the honky-tonk ballad "Even You Can't Save Me Now," wherein the narrator tells his virtuous girl "baby, baby, don't try to change me/I've been this way for far too long." Clever turns of phrase throughout all five songs show Appelwick's English degree wasn't a complete waste: "Neon Lights" has "the road is riding you." In "Replacement" he sings, "You chipped my heart of stone," and "Even You Can't Save Me Now" contains the likes: "My musical tastes don't include God's word/Because there ain't single line I haven't already heard/So I'm runnin' with these devils to chase my demons away"

Musically, the Lefty Devils sound like a more confident band than the Harvesters. The songs feature great guitar work throughout, and well-placed harmonies. Without Dave Scarbrough's pop leanings, the band were left with a purer and more traditional country sound than that of their predecessor.

Releasing his Lefty Devils songs definitely served as evidence of Appelick's talent, but didn't have much more purpose than that since Erik wasn't writing songs in that vein anymore. His new stuff, which he began recording upon resettling in Vermillion, showed a new range of influences and styles. They were also decidedly less slick in their presentation than the clean, straightforward Lefty Devils songs. Partly out of a change in aesthetic but mostly out of necessity, Erik went lo-fi. He recorded on a four-track to Maxell tapes, using instruments that had accumulated around him. He humorously listed them his Independent Underground Music Archive page as "dried up broken gourd (invaluable), drums that Charles left at my house for a week, Wurlitzer electronic piano that Sam left, fretless bass guitar (also Sam's), my own acoustic guitar, there was an Epiphone electric too, Casio sk-1 (sweet drum beats, yo!), harmonica (key of D), telecaster that Alex M__ gave me because he was such a drunken ass during D-Days, handclaps, the piano at my parents' house (badly needs a good tuning), various drinking glasses, pots and pans, tambourine, large three gallon kettle, small xylophone, and the 'scratchy fish.'"

The resulting collection of songs, which Appelwick dubbed *Cellophane*, are a bridge from his Americana roots to something much less defined. There are still the country leaning songs: "Kitchen," "Roll Away," "Holiday," and "Heartache Tonic," but there are other influences creeping in, such as the Eels-like whimsical-instrumentation-paired-with-morose-sentiments indie pop of "Adjacent to Me" and "Everything." The latter feels like the most timeless thing on the album, a beautifully simple tune based around the trio of acoustic guitar-piano-xylophone. There's a '70s feel in places, too, especially in the wah-wah guitar solo on "Pretty Bigmouth" and the soulful organ on "Ring Finger."

The most significant track in terms of Appelwick's musical evolution is album opener "The Same." It starts with a Casio drumbeat, a hummed line, a funky guitar, a repeated keyboard horn figure, and clinking glasses all layered on top of one another, creating an irresistibly danceable effect. This is where Erik was headed: Uncategorizably dense music that makes you want to move.

The whole album is much less lyrically focused than Appelwick's Harvesters or Lefty Devils work, with the most notable exception being "Imaginary" (which we'll talk about at length later, as it's one of two songs on *Cellophane* to get a higher-profile second life). The point of *Cellophane* seems almost to be less about songwriting than it was about learning to use the materials at hand to make a recording, to bring something to life. Erik says, "I lived in a small town and there really was no threat of anyone in the world hearing it, so I didn't really give any fucks about whether it was any good or not. I was simply a dude having fun trying to make something without any formal training of any kind in recording. Not being afraid to make some shitty stuff is a great vehicle for getting better at something."

Appelwick got a bunch of CD copies of *Cellophane* pressed but mainly just handed them out to friends, family, and acquaintances. The cover featured a grainy black and white photo of a rotary telephone with a lit cigarette hanging from one of the number dials. Upon returning to South Dakota, Erik had reconnected with Justin Siem, who had begun playing in a revived version of Violet with Mark, Lance, and Rich Show. Though Justin wasn't writing songs anymore, he was instrumental in motivating Erik to be ambitious in his own music. He had also reintroduced Erik to Darren, in whom he saw the same talent and drive. The two had started a correspondence as Darren settled in Minneapolis. Darren sent Erik the *So Pretty* songs and Erik sent feedback, both constructive (he suggested adding a chorus to "Smokestack") and not ("this stuff's kinda weird"). Darren was aggravated and ignored Erik's suggestions altogether. But the two musicians had enough common ground for Erik to decide to follow Darren to Minneapolis.

In September 2000, he packed up and headed east. Having been a small-to-mid-size-town kid all the way to his mid–20s, the idea of a larger city was intimidating, but Appelwick knew that if he was serious about his rock star dreams, Minneapolis was the next step along the way.

6

Stand Up and Win

In which Spymob breaks through, Darren and Appelwick team up, and Johnny goes indie pop.

Eric Fawcett returned from Brazil in early March 1998 fully expecting to find himself without a band. Before he left, things had looked dire, both artistically and interpersonally, for Spymob. Eric had gone to Rio to immerse himself in "escola de samba" of Brazillian music, but equally because he needed to get the hell out of a dysfunctional situation and to recharge from the creative exhaustion coming out of *Townhouse Stereo*. When he came back he was amazed to find that Ostby, Roessler, and Brent were all getting along again.

For his part, Ostby never believed Spymob's future to be in jeopardy. He was disappointed by the reception to *Townhouse Stereo*, but his commitment to the band and their collective vision never wavered. He attributes that, at least in part, to being "necessarily delusional." He says that no one trying to make it in an artistic field can be totally logical. "If you were being really rational about it, you'd be just too daunted by the odds stacked up against you." He credits his alliance with Eric and their complementary skill sets for that irrational confidence. "Both of us felt very empowered and confident from our partnership ... we didn't have any illusions about how hard it is to make it as a rock band, yet we also really very much expected to be successful."

Upon Fawcett's return, the group almost immediately got back to work, first providing accompaniment to Sarah's multimedia dance piece "Image Control" which was inspired by '60s girl groups. During the winter, John had written a couple of songs—"Thinking of Someone Else" and "Half Steering, Half Eating Ice Cream"—that were unlike anything the band had done before, certainly more pop-oriented than the challenging tunes on *Townhouse Stereo*. This wasn't by accident. Ostby cites Roessler as being the one who challenged him to write material that was more commercial. "I remember him laying down the gauntlet saying, 'Okay, the writing has got to be more accessible. We have to make music that's appealing to people' and everybody, including me, being very receptive to that."

Meanwhile, Fawcett was pulling triple duty. In addition to his dance accompaniment and Spymob commitments, he'd started playing with singer/songwriter Matt Wilson. At that point, Wilson was trying to jumpstart a solo career after a stint playing with Ed Ackerson's band Polara. He was most known, however, for founding Trip Shakespeare, a quirky pop group who'd built up a small-but-fierce following over their decade long career. Trip Shakespeare consisted of Matt on guitar and vocals, bassist John Munson, drummer Elaine Harris, and Matt's older brother Dan on guitar and vocals. They had put out two albums on their own in 1986 and 1988, respectively, and then signed with A

& M Records, releasing two more records in the early '90s before breaking up in '94. The post-mortem read that that they were too pop to be alternative and too alternative to be pop. Dan Wilson and John Munson learned their lesson and went over to the pop side for their next project, Semisonic.

Matt was a drummer himself—that's what he'd played in Polara—and had recorded all the drums for his first record, *Burnt, White, and Blue*, himself. But as a front man he needed someone to perform drums live, and for nearly three years, Eric was the man. *Burnt, White, and Blue* was released in March, just after Eric got back, and the band went out on a tour where a quite a few of the shows were attended by record-industry types, thanks to Semisonic's "Closing Time" rapidly ascending the charts (the record it came from—*Feeling Strangely Fine*—had also been released that March), though nothing came of that. They returned home in August for a show at the 7th Street Entry. Eric would play with Matt for another year or so beyond that, even as things began heating up for Spymob. Eric says now of working with Matt, "He's just such an amazing songwriter and drummer himself. I learned so much." It was part of his education, but also where he made some long-lasting musical connections in the Twin Cities.

When Spymob got together to work on arrangements for the new songs, they found a new sound emerging, a sound that had potential for mass appeal, but that also felt like a natural evolution of what they'd been doing before. The band worked up four more songs in a similar vein, and they went to Seedy Underbelly with Alex Oana to get them all on tape. The result was a six-track EP simply called *Spymob*. It was the recording that would take the band places they couldn't yet imagine.

Lyrically, the songs that make up that EP are not measurably less quirky than the ones on *Townhouse Stereo*. There's a song about wanting to be doted on by one's mother, another that's from a dog's point of view, and one that details the randomness of biking around aimlessly on a summer day (with a break to watch *Nosferatu*). As on *Townhouse Stereo*, the songs are by turns funny, clever, and affecting. It's in the music and arrangements where things are dramatically different from the band's previous work. The tempos are uniformly faster, the structures are more traditionally verse-chorus-verse-bridge-etc., the instrumental performances are more muscular, and the hooks are more than plentiful. The EP also makes better use of Brent, Fawcett, and Roessler's singing abilities, featuring their backup vocals and harmonies prominently as on the sweet, Beatlesque "Walking Under Green Leaves" and the self-pep-talk "Stand Up and Win."

The band had made all of their sounds organically on *Townhouse Stereo*, but embraced electronics on the new songs, mostly in the keyboard settings. They also let Brent go crazy on guitar, especially on "Sitting Around Keeping Score" and "Half Steering, Half Eating Ice Cream." The latter track features no less than four distinct shifts in direction, but somehow manages to still feel like a pop song. Similarly, "It Gets Me Going," has a ton going on musically—tempo shifts, different instruments dropping in and out—but makes it all work within a pop structure. Spymob had found a true signature sound, and the confidence behind it was self-evident.

Everyone believed strongly in the quality of the EP. As Roessler said, "We knew: This is really good." With the new songs and a "hard sell" from Fawcett, Roessler was convinced to remove his temporary tag. Eric's pitch was that things were about to happen with Spymob and that they needed to be all in. "Eric is very good at convincing people of things," Roessler says.

The band at this point had accepted that it was unlikely that they'd get big in the

Twin Cities, and even more unlikely that getting big there would lead to a record deal, so they decided to direct their focus outward. Fawcett put his drive and ambition into deeply researching how to get a demo in the right hands. He began blanketing the country, both record labels and entertainment firms, with copies of the *Spymob* EP.

It worked. Columbia Records' Chicago arm liked what they heard and immediately offered the band a "demo deal," in which the label would fund them to go in to the studio to record a certain number of songs, and then decide whether or not to sign them. The guys turned it down. They felt they had already made the demo that would get them their deal. It was yet another instance of the band's unwavering self-belief leading them to bet on themselves. And it was a good bet. Another place the EP had landed was in the hands of Tim Mandelbaum and Alan Mintz, of the Los Angeles entertainment law firm Selverne, Mandelbaum, & Mintz, who counted Van Halen and the Black Crowes among their clients. Tim and Alan loved what they heard and came to hear the band play a show at the Double Door in Chicago. From there, they agreed to represent Spymob. This happened often in the music industry at that time, where law firms worked gratis with artists they felt had potential. If they could get their clients a deal, it could mean a healthy payday for all parties. Ever cautious, Spymob conducted interviews with several different firms before finally signing on with Selverne, Mandelbaum, & Mintz.

Mintz in particular was a high-powered ally. He had, at that point, more than a decade of high-level experience in the music business, having provided legal services for Michael Jackson (on the *Bad* tour and in the sale of his music catalog) and had worked as a GM at Epic and a senior vice president at Columbia Records. Mintz used his contacts to arrange showcases in both Chicago and New York. The latter were held at a private studio/rehearsal space. Nearly every major label came to see them, and nearly every one (Epic, RCA, Sony, Hollywood) offered them a deal. Spymob promptly found themselves the object of a bit of a bidding war between RCA and Epic. They were getting personal pleas from A & R reps on their cell phones, and taken out to lavish dinners with $1000 tabs. "It was stupid," says Roessler.

In early summer 1999, they made the decision to sign with Epic. Roessler says they seemed to be the most straightforward. They also had the sweetest offer: a two firm deal (meaning the label guaranteed they'd fund two albums from the band) worth nearly a million dollars. It would turn out to be one of the last big money deals given to an unknown band, as the record industry would soon find itself in the midst of a wholly unanticipated sea change.

Not long after, Spymob would complete their ascent to the big time by signing with Famous Music Publishing and bringing on manager Billy Diggins, who'd repped Steve Winwood, Bjork, Billy Idol, and TLC. After six years of toil, Spymob were an overnight success.

* * *

John Hermanson was free of Storyhill, and his immediate path was set. After joining Storyhill on tour for awhile, Bettine had headed back to her native Norway in the spring of 1997. After the final Storyhill show in early June Johnny joined her. He'd proposed earlier that year, and their wedding was that August. Chris, along with Alex and about thirty other close friends of Johnny's from the Saint Olaf and Christikon days, made the trip. Almost immediately after the wedding, Bettine got pregnant. "Total accident," Johnny says, "Awesome accident." Because of Norway's generous maternity laws (they pay 85 percent of your salary to stay home for a year), the couple decided to remain in Oslo for a year while Johnny laid the groundwork for a solo career.

Johnny was still writing music, but he was also working a "regular" job for the first time in a long time. More accurately, it was a series of regular jobs. He worked at a daycare for while, and for a sprinkler system installer, and even as a truck driver. The latter was a dicey proposition. Johnny says, "I didn't have a driver's license, let alone a commercial license, but I filled in for this guy in the middle of the night I drove from Oslo to Lillehammer and back. They have traffic cameras that take a picture if you're just speeding a little bit, and they see who's driving. They monitor that. I was just terrified the whole time."

In January of 1998, Johnny returned to Minneapolis for a couple of weeks to demo some of the songs he'd been writing. The place to both record and stay, naturally, was CityCabin. In addition to Alex, Johnny had another connection to the place now. Storyhill's managers, David Weeks and Andy Carlson, who had been runnig Storyhill's business affairs from the room with the black carpeting on the walls, and were now starting an endeavor called Peppermint Records.

The idea for Peppermint arose from the fanbase Storyhill had built over the previous six years. After Storyhill's break-up, Dave and Andy found themselves in possession of a 10,000-person mailing list and the infrastructure and knowhow to support independent artists. They began to wonder if they could, while still shepherding the Storyhill catalog, help similar artists find an audience. They thought they could sell Storyhill fans on musicians with a similar aesthetic, namely acoustic-based folk singer-songwriters. Storyhill's music sold very well in independent terms, and Andy and David knew they couldn't expect the same sales levels from their new artists, but figured if it was around 10 percent less, they'd have a thriving business.

Peppermint Records wasn't a label in any traditional definition of the term, instead serving more as, in Andy's words, as a "cross-marketing company." The artists were responsible for their recording costs, and retained full ownership of their music. Dave and Andy would help manufacture, distribute, and market their CDs. With Alex's help, they found three artists to sign on initially, all Twin Cities locals: Peter Mayer, Billy McLaughlin, and Ellis. All were fairly established by the time they hooked up with Peppermint, each having released at least one CD on their own. Ellis also happened to be another Saint Olaf grad, and a member of the band Bobby Llama (more on her in the next chapter). The roster would eventually grow to include Brenda Weiler, Stuart Davis, Justin Roth, and Ericka Luckett, among others.

One of the big things Peppermint offered to artists was an online presence and a way to sell CDs on the Internet, which in the late '90s was not at all common. Dave and Andy tried to build trust in their brand and their stable of artists. Each order was packaged with a catalog and a peppermint candy. They created samplers of their artists that came free with the purchase of two CDs. As a start-up business, they had to suffer through non-ideal conditions, most arising from being housed in CityCabin. Their office was tiny, and they stashed boxes and boxes of CDs wherever they could find space. The house had 15 DSL lines going, and Alex's odd hours and revolving stable of musician squatters made things unpredictable. "It was a pretty funky scene," says Andy. In 1999 they would move to a more conventional office in the Lowertown area of downtown Saint Paul.

After his winter visit to Minneapolis, Johnny went back to Oslo and kept writing songs. That spring Bettine gave birth to a healthy baby boy. When Isak was 6 weeks old the new family came back to the states to settle in Minnesota. Well, "settle" isn't quite the right word. They stayed with Johnny's cousin for a month and a half, then housesat for a while before finding an apartment in Saint Paul. John had gotten a loan from his parents to properly record an album. Like Spymob before him, he chose to work at Seedy Underbelly; John Kuker generously gave him a discounted rate, and Alex came in to record and produce. The Spymob guys (and Storyhill rhythm section)—Fawcett and Roessler—played on several songs, and John Ostby came in to provide back-up vocals on a couple of songs. Six different string players contributed as well.

Released by Peppermint in October of 1998, *John Hermanson* is a combination of the completely unexpected and subversions of the expected. In a lot of ways Johnny's first solo record is akin to Spymob's *Townhouse Stereo*, in that it does exactly what it wants with no consideration of commerciality and, in Johnny's case, an almost willful disregard for what Storyhill fans expected of him. That, in tandem with Alex's love of sonic experimentation, resulted in a wholly unconventional record. Johnny's songs on *This Side of Lost* were a hint of his desire break free from genre constraints, but the ones on *John Hermanson* are stating it unequivocally.

Roughly half the album takes Johnny's singer-songwritery tunes and twists them with dark, inscrutable lyrics ("Needle in your Heart,") and/or off-kilter performances ("Thomas of Twelve," "Weight of Wanting"). Many of the songs in this category expand beyond the guitar/voice foundation, adding dramatic string accompaniment.

The other half of the record is even more eccentric. There are Johnny's first recorded forays into pop rock, "'80s Party" and "Rockstarrin'" The latter is based on a boogie-woogie piano backing, while the former is driven by handclaps and an acoustic strum that becomes electric on the sticky chorus ("You made up your mind to be cool/You decide to let nothin' affect you."). Alex Oana co-wrote the track with Johnny, and provided backing vocals on it as well. "Background Vocals" has a melody that never quite goes where you expect it to, creating an uneasy feeling. The jazzy-bluesy "Ginny and June" is a weird story about two artists who drive across the country running people off the road and documenting it in pictures. After getting in a wreck, they make one last masterpiece out of the remains of their vehicle, and dissolve their partnership in acrimony. It's hard not to see this as analogous to Storyhill ("Ginny and June" could easily be "Johnny and Chris"), especially in lines like "we had shows the size this town's never seen" and "all the things not said, the chances are dead, the open road ahead."

In general, the lyrics on *John Hermanson* survey damaged relationships, missed connections, and wasted opportunities. Not what you'd expect considering all the positive things Johnny had going on in his life when he was writing these songs—settling into the early days of marriage, the anxiety and excitement of impending fatherhood, living and working in another country—though his Norway experience at least did have one definite effect on the songs. Johnny says, "I was completely removed from any influence here and I don't know if that's why it ended up such a strange record." He also revealed in a 2001 interview that the record was "a cleaning of the slate" for him and that he was more concerned with how it sounded ("groove and layers") than anything else. "Some of the songs," he said, "were more music for music's sake than as a vehicle to say something specific."

Johnny says the record had a few vocal ardent supporters, but that "everybody else freaked out." Andy, who had helped to shepherd the album through the recording, design, and release stages, acknowledges that the record was too offbeat for many fans, but that he himself found it "interesting, adventurous, and cool." He also says that it served as an essential step in the process of Johnny "breaking out of his Storyhill persona and moving toward something more edgy and expansive." Roessler says, "For my money, [it's] probably the best record I've been involved in." Despite the mixed reaction to the album, it earned Johnny Minnesota Music Award nominations in 2000 for best songwriter and best male vocalist (he lost to Mason Jennings and Jonny Lang, respectively).

Chris was conflicted about the record, both emotionally and musically. He was impressed, as always, by Johnny's ambition and his seeming fearlessness. Chris admired that, but also felt a degree of jealousy because it made him realize that he hadn't yet found his voice or direction. But there was also the music itself, and he admits that some of it was "too intense for me, too avant garde." He also had a mostly correct hunch that it wouldn't go over well with audiences, especially Storyhill fans, when Johnny took it on the road.

With Spymob busy being courted by their major label suitors, Fawcett and Roessler weren't available for shows, so Johnny recruited drummer Joel Dodson and bassist Arron "Al" Bergstrom to form the John Hermanson Band. The trio went on a 6-week tour, hitting many of the familiar venues and cities he'd played with Chris. Though the month and a half on the road was something Johnny had done plenty of times in Storyhill, this time was different. Isak was not even a year old, and infants at that age are a daily revelation. "When I came back he looked totally different and it just freaked me out," Johnny says. He decided then that he wouldn't be going on any more extended tours. His thoughts turned toward finding ways continue making and playing music closer to home.

* * *

Erik Appelwick arrived in Minneapolis in the fall of 2000 and moved into a room in CityCabin. He got a job at a coffee shop called Espresso Royale that was two blocks away from the house, and where Darren was a regular. It would be the first of many day jobs in Minneapolis Erik would hold while writing, recording, and performing.

First up for him was to self-release another album. The songs that comprised *Lacerate* were recorded at the same time as the ones on *Cellophane*. As such, the two CDs have a lot in common. Like *Cellophane*, *Lacerate* is a mishmash of styles. Opener "My Town," "Uninspired," and "Texas Belle" are all in a country vein. The spooky, static-laden "Transmission" sounds like it belongs in a David Lynch movie and matches well with the almost-industrial "Friday." "Fine Now," "A Dream I Had," and "Ordinary" are all straight-up rockers. And then there's the pure keyboard-driven pop of "Shy" (another song that would get an extended second life).

Like "The Same" on *Cellophane*, "In Your Arms" is a nod in the direction of Appelwick's musical future. With a groovy wah-wah guitar backing, funky bass, and a wailing keyboard lick it grabs the ears immediately and doesn't let go. It even makes some effective use of samples, lending a bit of a hip-hop edge to the '70s nostalgia. Erik didn't do shows to support *Lacerate*, or go out of his way to sell it. It was not as much a proper release as it was a calling card for a musician looking to make his name in his new city.

The fact that Appelwick and Darren were both living in CityCabin and surrounded by instruments and recording equipment made it inevitable that they would begin playing together. This initially took two forms. Darren had been wanting to expand the sonic palate of Kid Dakota by adding more instruments. Christopher McGuire was initially opposed to it, but with Zak Sally coming in on bass the argument was lost, and so Erik came in to provide another guitar (and sometimes bass when Sally wasn't available). Playing with the band would prove to be a steep learning curve for Erik. In one particular rehearsal incident, McGuire strongly chided him for coming in too loud ("like a clodhopper," Erik described it) and ruining the dynamics. Erik was taken aback, but took it as a "kick in the ass" to start paying attention to more than just his part. He'd never been in a band where the other players were more serious and intense than he was, nor where the degree of musicianship was so high. Erik had long been wanting to be around musicians as ambitious as him, and now here he was.

"When I was in college," he says, "you would try to be drunk more often than you would write songs. It's not a very good way to be productive. That's what I ask about the Replacements: How, if they were drunk all the time, did they ever actually get anything done? It boggles my mind."

Applewick and Darren's other collaboration grew directly out of *Lacerate* and *Cellophane*. Among Darren's cache of four-tracks were tunes that clearly didn't fit the Kid Dakota style or aesthetic, being catchier, "happier, more playful" as Darren put it. So songs like "Holiday" and "Trust Fund Junkie" were just sitting around unused. When he heard Erik's songs he recognized that there was something simpatico with his own misfit pop tunes. The guys started playing around with the idea of forming a different band to serve as a vehicle for both of their more mainstream melodic tendencies. They had their own recording set-up in the basement so as not to interfere with Alex's paying clients upstairs. As they began experimenting with recording some of the tunes together, they initially called the project Cellophane after Erik's CD. Once they had settled on an initial repertoire, the next step was getting a full band to play shows and fully arrange the songs. So they recruited jMatt Keil, another CityCabin regular, on drums, and Erik's boss at Espresso Royale, singer-songwriter Jay Hurley, to play bass. The new band began rehearsing regularly, and took on a new name, Camaro.

* * *

After signing their deal Spymob's next major decision was the choice of a producer. Their label A & R reps, Rose Noone and James Dowdall, wanted someone who would be sensitive to the band's pop sensibility but also bring experience in nurturing the R & B side of their sound. So they suggested Steve Lironi, a Scottish multi-instrumentalist who'd once upon a time been in the '80s band Altered Images. Having transitioned into production, he worked with Happy Mondays offshoot Black Grape on their 1995 debut *It's Great When You're Straight... Yeah* and Hanson on their 1997 smash hit "MMMBop." The common thread between the two was that both featured melodic pop songwriting with samples and drum loops integrated into the production. Mixing live drums with loops was something Spymob wanted to do, and so Lironi seemed to be their man. He flew over from Scotland to Minneapolis and got along great with the guys. Together they recorded their Epic debut—titled *On Pilot Mountain*—in the summer of 1999 at Seedy Underbelly.

The album consisted of three of the songs from the EP ("Thinking of Someone Else," "It Gets Me Going," and "Stand Up and Win"), a reworking of "Joe Namath" from *Townhouse Stereo*, and seven new songs. The new "Joe Namath" shows the difference between the old Spymob and the updated one. The earlier "Joe Namath" jarred itself into existence and didn't have a chorus to speak of. The new version smooths out the vocal, and excises the original's jazzy torch song breakdown and extended guitar freak-out.

Ostby put a chorus in place using lyrics from the original ("Back at home my family's watching me/Slapping hands in the middle of a stadium…. She's thinking of me/Waiting to see me") over an affecting new melody. Though he did the rearranging himself, John says Steve was "the George Martin on that one. He was very helpful in trying to stay true to what we were doing, but trying to make it more accessible and palatable."

The newer songs on the album were very much a continuation of the sound established on the *Spymob* EP: Uptempo, harmony-laden, dense with hooks and killer choruses. The funny and prescient *2040* imagines a future where grandkids "have little gadgets to talk to their friends around the world," paper is no longer used, and robots do the housework. The appropriately-titled "German Test Drive" features a Kraftwerkian programmed keyboard line and a tale about taking a luxury car out on some mountain roads (it's also one of a preponderance of Spymob songs that involve driving, along with "Bleachers," "Reno," "Paul Harvey," "Capital Buildings," "Keep Your Speed Up," and "Making a Killing"). "Palo Alto to Grand Forks" uses a similar musical approach to recount a conversation between John and Brent about the differences between their home cities. "Fly Fly Fishing Poles" details a weekend fishing trip.

Then there's "National Holidays," which is told from the perspective of a dad who doesn't have custody of his daughter and only gets to see her on holidays. His relationship with her mother is not at all functional, and that makes everything all the more difficult. The final verse is the heartbreaker: "Years ago you told me how/You could not imagine life without our little baby/Wouldn't it tear you up too, if you could only see her one day out of thirty?" It's a perfect storytelling song, but so ultra-melodic and filled with layered, interlacing hooks that if the lyrics were nonsense, you'd likely still be moved.

When the album finished and turned into an enthusiastic Epic, the label told them to stand by while the label created a release plan, with a tentative May 2000 street date. Cover art was created, promotional photos taken, and then the guys stood by. And stood by. And stood by. The waiting stretched on for months with no definite plan for *On Pilot Mountain*. Then, in April of 2000, Epic announced that it was dropping over 40 bands from their roster. Spymob was one of them.

Everyone was baffled. How do you go from being aggressively courted to dropped in less than a year? The label had spent significant money on Spymob that it now had no chance of recouping. It turns out that there were a mix of factors at play. The band didn't know at the time, but Billy Diggins was feuding with Epic over various issues with some of his other artists, and that didn't engender any goodwill for the other groups he represented. Epic was also doing some internal restructuring and housecleaning around this time, thus the multi-artists massacre. The guys also speculated that the label didn't know how to market them or the album, but as Roessler said, "It doesn't seem like it turned out significantly different from what they bought."

No matter the reason for their rejection, the guys were crushed. Everything they'd worked for and seemed to have achieved was gone in an instant. They remained clear-eyed enough to make an important decision about the band's future. Because their deal had been two firm, and the band hadn't had a chance to make a second record, Spymob were given a choice: take the money they would have been given to make the second album, or receive the full rights to *On Pilot Mountain*, which the label owned otherwise. With an unwavering self-belief and a strong sense of ownership of the songs they'd created, the band chose to take their album back in hopes of landing it with another label, or self-releasing it.

Before any of that could happen, though, there would be another major setback for the beleaguered band. Brian had always felt his musical interests being pulled elsewhere, and had grown increasingly serious about studying double bass and playing improvisational jazz. His wife had recently had a baby, and he felt that, upon getting dropped, the time was right to move on. The other guys were shocked and heartbroken. Ostby says, "I completely drank the Kool Aid. I just had blind faith in what we were doing. When [Brian] quit, I just remember being shocked. I was just completely committed, and really believed we would be successful. I'm not saying this in an arrogant sort of way, I just thought we were an incredible band and I just believed so completely in what we were doing. I was just completely, completely into it. I was the member of the cult that believes until the end."

For Fawcett it was also impossible to react logically. He and Roessler had been through so much together and were not only bandmates in many different iterations, but dear friends. Suddenly he found himself in the awkward position of having to negotiate Roessler's exit in temporal and financial terms. On top of that, it was a delicate time for the band. Being dropped by a label is a scarlet letter on an artist's prospects, and Spymob were working to convince even their lawyers that they were still worth representing. Eric says, "It was at a time when we had just gotten punched in the gut. We wished we could be at full strength at that moment and face what was coming. And then we lose not just a bass player, but a frickin' great bass player."

Roessler played on some new songs the band were recording, did some label showcase shows in L.A., and then made his exit from Spymob. Ostby, Fawcett, and Brent were in the unenviable position of replacing an ultra-talented player who with whom they'd logged hundreds of hours and had nearly perfect musical chemistry. They couldn't even conceive of how they'd be able replace Roessler, so they opened it up to all possibilities.

One of those possibilities was John Hermanson. He had never played bass before, but busted ass learning Spymob's songs. In the end he didn't get the gig. Eric says it was all about fit. "Musically Johnny can do anything. It wasn't for musical reasons. You know it's kind of like asking Paul McCartney to play in the Rolling Stones; that's just kind of weird." Johnny, for his part, was disappointed at the time, but in retrospect, with full knowledge of the strange journey that was ahead for Spymob, he's come to be thankful for not getting it. "I wouldn't have been able to hang, I mean, actually, I shouldn't dis myself, I've gotten to be a better bass player, but I'm no Appelwick."

Another guy who'd come in to audition was Christian Twigg, a friend of Brent's from his days at Musictech. Twigg grew up in the northeast suburb of Maplewood, and had gotten into music in high school when he auditioned to be the singer for a heavy metal band and ended up learning to play bass in the process. He and Brent had kept in touch and had even collaborated for awhile in the mid–'90s on a just-for-fun band that melded rock and hip-hop. As the legend goes, Twigg had coveted being a member of the Spymob for awhile, even learning the bass parts for the *Townhouse Stereo* songs despite not being much of a fan of the record. When Brent called to tell him Spymob were down a bass player, Twigg "expressed his condolences, paused appropriately, and recommended himself as a replacement."

When they brought Twigg in, Fawcett says, "The bass playing was great, but the thing that Twigg brought this band at the time, which was sorely needed and that none of us could provide, was unbridled optimism." The guys loved his enthusiasm and energy.

Spymob, even in a knocked-down position, was a careful band, so Twigg got the gig on a three-month trial basis, July through September. Sometime in October or November, Fawcett recalls, "we were driving somewhere up north and we were just shivering our butts off in the van, and [Twigg] said, 'So, like what's the deal, am I in?'" The band had forgotten to tell him he'd passed the trial period, a fact that still embarrasses Eric. "Normally, we would have been very on top of it, like the good Saint Olaf students we were."

Fawcett says that Twigg "was such a powerful emotional presence that it just became a new era of Spymob with its own new colors." His sense of humor (including a penchant for quoting Jim Carrey movies) and fresh enthusiasm got the band laughing again, and once again hopeful for their musical future. Eric summarizes the renewed ambition and attitude as: "Let's go fuckin' get 'em. There's no moping. It's time to turn your frowns upside down and let's go get 'em." It was a vital injection of energy, as the prospects for another major label deal looked dark, and Spymob were grappling with the reality going back to doing things independently.

Ironically, this is when the local music press finally started paying attention to Spymob. Perhaps it was the schadenfreude of their story, or perhaps their more accessible songs were finally getting to local ears. Maybe it was both. In June of 2000, the *St. Paul Pioneer Press*' Amy Carlson included a brief summary of the band's unfortunate label situation, and the *Pulse of the Twin Cities* wrote a praise-laden profile that labeled them as "Minnesota's best-kept secret" and "four guys whose musical prowess and lyrical witticism pushes the boundaries of genius." The article, written by Dallas Apold, also says that Spymob's style "falls somewhere between that of the Jackson Five and Ben Folds Five."

After losing their deal and Brian Rosseler, Spymob regrouped (pictured here in 2004). Clockwise from top left: Eric Fawcett, John Ostby, Brent Paschke and Christian Twigg. Courtesy Eric Fawcett.

6. Stand Up and Win

With a renewed sense of purpose, Spymob finished out 2000 by playing more gigs around town (the 400 Bar and Fine Line were frequent spots). They pressed their own copies of *On Pilot Mountain* to give out to fans and friends. They also began working on new songs, all the while wondering what the future might hold. They never could have guessed.

* * *

After his Johnny's experiences working in Oslo, he decided to earn money in a way that fit better with his skill set. He began freelancing for Compass Entertainment, who produced the Lifescapes series of relaxation, easy listening, and nature CDs that were featured in end-cap displays and kiosks in Target stores. It paid well, and allowed Johnny to learn-on-the-job about self-recording. Musicians would be given a generous budget and carte blanche for how to manage it. Johnny decided to buy a digital recorder ("with this tiny little LED screen" he says) and figure it out himself. He did two records that way until Eric convinced him to invest in ProTools. Johnny would end up doing 20 instrumental titles in the series, over the next decade, most under the name John August and featuring titles such as "Yoga Flow" and "Sleep, the Wellness Seeker" ("deep strings and dreamlike flutes are combined with calming Delta waves" reads the description). Eric Fawcett would often pair with him to provide drums and other miscellaneous instrumentation on these CDs.

It was around this time that Johnny also started working as a producer. Singer songwriter Brenda Weiler had recently moved from her hometown of Fargo, North Dakota, to the Twin Cities. She'd released two albums on a Fargo indie label, *Trickle Down* in 1997 and *Crazy Happy* in 1999. She signed a deal with Peppermint, and Johnny brought in his usual cast: Alex to co-produce, record, and mix, and Eric on drums and percussion. Brian Roessler and John Ostby even contributed to a couple of tracks each. The resulting album, *Fly Me Back*, won a fair share of local acclaim (*Pioneer Press* music writer Jim Walsh said the record was "as well written and well sung as anything by [Weiler's] more famous soon-to-be-contemporaries") and Johnny had instant credibility as someone who could help shepherd artists' creative visions.

Though he hadn't been chosen as Spymob's bass player, Johnny was still watching them closely. The strength of their demo CD had gotten them a record deal, even if it had fallen through. Johnny wondered if he could make the same thing happen for himself, so he got together with Alex and Eric and cut four songs he'd been working on. He learned his lesson from his debut solo CD and tried for a more focused sound, so "Beautiful," and "Victorian" are both electric guitar driven pop-rock songs with strong choruses. "Ghostlight" and "Sanity" are both moodier and more vibey but still melodically strong. Both feature string accompaniment, as on some of the *John Hermanson* tunes, but "Sanity" adds looped drums to the mix.

The EP didn't ignite any record label bidding wars, but it did lead Johnny to start recruiting a new band to play shows with him and work out more new songs. He knew the guys he'd been playing with previously as a trio weren't the right fit. So he asked Darren—who Johnny had become friendly with again hanging out at CityCabin—to play lead guitar. On bass, he brought in Brian Roessler, an ironic turn given that Johnny had auditioned to replace him in Spymob. Drums were a bit trickier. Initially he'd wanted to play with Fawcett, and since Spymob wasn't currently tied down, that seemed possible. But then, due to events we'll hear about in the next chapter, Eric wasn't an option anymore.

Johnny was bummed: "I remember at the time being like, 'Shit I can't play with Fawcett,' and just dwelling on that." Instead, Darren brought in Christopher McGuire. The result was a line-up that was part Storyhill, a dash of Spymob, and half Kid Dakota. As they were recording, it started to feel like a band.

But that initial quartet didn't last long. In the midst of recording, they were also doing some shows. McGuire called Johnny right before a gig at the Fine Line and said he wasn't going to be able to play that night. "But man," he said, "I got you set up with this guy Peter Anderson." Anderson was one of the most experienced drummers on the local scene, a Robbinsdale native who started out with two classmates in the mid '80s as the Bloods. They started playing together when they were 11 and stayed together for 13 years, releasing a 1987 album on Gark (the same indie label that was home to the Gear Daddies and Trip Shakespeare initially). Peter then moved on to the Willie Wisely Trio, Planetmaker (Matt Wilson's first post–Trip Shakespeare project), Saucer (the same band that Darren's friend Pamela Valfer had been in), and Polara (replacing Matt Wilson). When he got the call to sub for Christopher, Polara were on hiatus, and Peter was mainly picking up gigs wherever he could.

The show at the Fine Line turned out fantastically, and everyone was amazed at the instant chemistry. Peter was affable, experienced, and communicative. Johnny thought Christopher McGuire was an "unbelievable" drummer, but now had a conundrum. Following up with McGuire after the gig, Johnny told him, "Dude, I think Peter might be a better fit for us." Christopher was gracious about it, and thus Peter joined the band. Now with a solid line-up, they went to CityCabin to finish up recording on what had started as Johnny's second solo album but was now the debut album from a new band. Though it was still very much his project and his songs, Johnny had decided not to use his own name again. "I wanted it to be my name but I didn't like my name. My theory with Gerry Rafferty—you know that guy from the '70s—is just that he didn't make it big because of his name. And I felt like 'John Hermanson' was even worse."

While recording they used the name Rialto, but found that name was already taken. Then Johnny realized that the title of one of the songs they were working on—one that was proving to be a thematic centerpiece of the record—would also fit the group. And thus they became Alva Star.

PART II: LET'S GO! (2001–2005)

7

Things Are Getting Better

In which Spymob get an unexpected benefactor, Storyhill make a surprising return, and Alva Star and Camaro enter the scene.

Fully explaining the story of Camaro requires a bit of a sideways journey into the musical lives of the two men Darren and Appelwick had recruited as band members: Jay Hurley and jMatt Keil.

By the time he joined Camaro on bass, Jay was already a veteran of the rock game. He grew up on the east side of Saint Paul, at first being more interested in sports than music. But in high school that changed. He became a regular at a nearby record store called Hot Licks (later it became Northern Lights) in the Hillcrest shopping center, and eventually started working there. He formed a punk band in high school called Dark Circle, in which he was the lead singer. The following year he began teaching himself guitar and writing songs.

When Dark Circle petered out in 1984, Jay combed the ads in *City Pages* looking for new bandmates, and met drummer Steven Nelsen and guitarist David Beckey. The three, along with bassist Dwight Erickson, formed the Sedgwicks, a jangle pop group à la the Byrds and Big Star. The band got some nice local notice, had some personnel changes (Erickson was replaced by Tim Hanson, who was then replaced by Amy McCumber; Beckey was replaced by Krystal MacCay), and recorded a seven-inch single with Ed Ackerson (who at that time was in a Twin/Tone band called The 27 Various) for his Susstones label.

The Sedgwicks dissolved, and wanting a break from the interpersonal dynamics of being in a band, Jay recorded five songs with Ackerson in Tommy Roberts's Underground studio in Minneapolis (Tommy is also known as Zachary Vex, designer of a popular line of effects pedals). Though those songs never got an official release, Jay is still proud of them: "When I'm trying to impress somebody I'll say, 'Hey listen to this.'"

Around this time Jay had gotten into fuzz rock bands like My Bloody Valentine and Dinosaur Jr., and his songwriting followed suit, adding distortion and shoegaze elements while keeping a sharp melodic sense. Eventually he got back in touch with Steven and they brought on bassist Robbie Robello (who played with former Replacement Bob Stinson in the Bleeding Hearts, Stinson's last band before his death in 1995) and formed Hovercraft. With financial help from a friend, they recorded an EP—*Been Brained*—with Ed producing.

Enter engineer and producer Paul Q. Kolderie, a Saint Paul native who had founded Fort Apache Studios in Boston and made his name working with the likes of the Pixies, Morphine, Uncle Tupelo, and Radiohead. While visiting his parents, Kolderie happened to see a *City Pages* article about Hovercraft, and went to see them play a show at the 7th Street Entry. He had just secured an imprint deal with MCA Records and was looking for bands to sign. This was circa 1994, after Nirvana had broken the commercial floodgates on "alternative" music. Jay says, "All the major labels were going, 'Hey let's just sign all the bands we can and see what happens.'" Kolderie invited Hovercraft out to Boston to record a demo, and though it took a year and a half, they got a record deal.

One hitch was their name. A band out of Seattle featuring Eddie Vedder's then-wife, Beth Liebling, was also using the name Hovercraft. Though Jay's band had come first, he agreed to sell the other group the name for roughly the price of a touring van. Hovercraft became Shatterproof.

Shatterproof recorded their debut album, *Slip it Under the Door*, under some duress. Kolderie pressured Jay to replace Steven Nelson with a "better drummer," and Jay caved, crushing his friendship with Steve. Amidst the drama and uncertainty, Ed, who was coproducing with Kolderie, took over the project and added a bunch of overdubs. Jay loved the results, but was depressed that his his "lack of recording experience and musicianship" had prevented him from realizing his own parts on the album. "The record just kind of slipped through my fingers," Jay says now.

With new drummer Jeff Jara, whom Jay had pulled out grad school in Milwaukee, and guitarist Jon Hunt added to the line-up, the band attempted to tour to support *Slip in Under the Door* upon its release in 1995, but they couldn't find a booking agent, even with the head of the label helping them out. So they booked their own shows as much as that was possible. "You had your land line and had to call the club 20 times a day to try to get anything booked," says Jay. *Slip it Under the Door*, which the press release called "a sad chunk of guitar noise," didn't sell well.

But the band soldiered on. They played their highest profile gig ever, opening for Oasis at a 1995 Minneapolis show. Jay started writing songs for a second record and the band proceeded recording in the middle of 1996 in both Boston and Minneapolis. Producer of local indie pop darlings the Hang-Ups, Bryan Hanna, recorded the album, and the bands's A & R rep was encouraged by the new songs. But then Jay Boberg (co-founder of IRS Records) became the new president of MCA. When Boberg listened to the album, he singled out a tune called "Septemberine" that he thought sounded like early R.E.M. (who were the darlings of IRS Records in their early days). He asked for more songs like it, and the band reluctantly obliged. But it was a fruitless endeavor. Boberg didn't like the new songs, and at the same time Fort Apache head Gary Smith was attempting to play hardball with MCA, making several demands for his bands, including bigger marketing budgets. According to Jay, MCA essentially responded with a "fuck off" and dropped the entire Fort Apache roster.

Even worse, they decided to keep the second album's masters, though what use it was to have ownership songs you don't plan to release by a band you don't have under contract is a mystery (that second album, *Splinter Queen*, was eventually released on Catlick Records in 2007, and is worth seeking out. Jay says, "I was writing fantastic songs, though I was super depressed." It was all too much, and by 1997 Shatterproof had, well, shattered.

"I was pretty devastated, but for whatever reason I didn't quit." Jay says. "I took some time and got Landing Gear together." Landing Gear was comprised of Shatterproof

7. Things Are Getting Better

holdovers Robbie Robello, Jon Hunt, and Jay, joined by guitarist Mykl Westbrooks. The group cycled through a couple of drummers before landing on David West. In 2000, right before Appelwick began working at Espresso Royale, Landing Gear had released a five-song EP recorded with both Ed Ackerson and Bryan Hanna, and were gigging around town.

Darren often stopped to get coffee before work and started to get to know Jay. One day he mentioned and Appelwick were looking for a bass player for a new project, and Jay jokingly said, "I'll play bass." Though he'd said it off-handedly, Jay followed through because it offered a couple of rare opportunities: to get better at an instrument he didn't have much experience with, and to not have to be the frontman. For Appelwick and Darren, a bandmate who could sing, write, and who had lots of connections in the local scene was a huge get, one that they might not have appreciated as much as they should have.

Jay Hurley during a Camaro rehearsal. Note the left-handed bass, purchased for him with band funds. Courtesy Darren Jackson.

By 2000, drummer jMatt Keil was well known on the CityCabin scene. He was a fellow Saint Olaf grad, starting there just after everyone else had graduated. Originally hailing from Beaver Dam, Wisconsin, he, like Jay, grew up playing sports. In high school, jMatt was a three sport all-state athlete. But he also came from a musical family—his mom played piano and performed in local theater—and he discovered an affinity for rhythm and dancing at a young age. When he was 13 he became "entranced by the power of drums" watching the pep bands playing during the halftime of his basketball games. He begged his dad for a drum set, and "much to the chagrin of everybody" his father eventually relented. The catch was that he would only be allowed play on Friday nights when everyone else was out of the house for dinner. His athlete friends weren't especially supportive either, derisively nicknaming him "Little Drummer Boy."

But that only served as motivation. He played along with the radio and records. He carried gear for a classmate's father's cover band, just so he could watch the drummer up close. He even took lessons, though he didn't find them fulfilling. "I wanted to learn how to use all four limbs; I didn't want to learn how to paradiddle."

He graduated high school in 1992 and went to Germany to study for a year. There he hooked up with a punk-leaning rock group called Masculine Fragrance and played his first show with them at an elementary school. He was immediately hooked, partly because of the contrast from his sports experiences: "I absolutely loved that everybody won and no one lost," he says. jMatt called his father the next day and said, "Dad, I know what I wanna do. I wanna start a band. I'm going to go to college, but I'm gonna start a band, and we're gonna make it."

In Germany he dated a girl who had him over every day to "drink tea, smoke cigarettes, and listen to music." She introduced him to music beyond the top 40 and albums from his siblings' record collections, artists like New Model Army, Soul Asylum, 24-7 Spyz, early Nirvana, Pearl Jam (via bootlegs), and underground German and American punk bands. He got involved in the punk scene there, and his whole identity turned over. "I had a sweet hoop earring, long hair, cigarettes rolled up in my shirt; it was everything I didn't know I could be." When he got back in the summer of '93, he put together a power trio with a couple of younger guys. They called themselves Sweet Chuck.

jMatt had chosen to attend Saint Olaf starting that that fall because of its "bucolic" setting and proximity to the Minneapolis music scene. His older brother had attended Carleton, so jMatt already knew Northfield well. As with Fawcett and Darren, music didn't draw jMatt to Saint Olaf. He wanted to get into the field of psychology. Once on campus, he felt overwhelmed and baffled by the popularity of the choir and the a capella group (the Limestones). To jMatt, it felt like everything had gone topsy-turvy, where the choir and orchestra were bigger draws than the football team. But he also believes that dynamic is what helped to create a musical counter-movement at the school, and helped the like-minded find each other and form their own community.

jMatt was aware of the bands that had come immediately before him, Shark Sandwich and Chris & Johnny, especially the latter. "Their legacy was ever-present," he says. But he wasn't necessarily a fan at first: "I absolutely despised [Chris & Johnny]. I did not get it. I one hundred percent did not understand why they were selling out the Pause and girls were fawning over them. They're singing about every piece of sand on every shore and every mountain high and I'm like, 'This is bullshit. This isn't cool.'"

JMatt had arrived onto campus with a splash, playing a show with Sweet Chuck in the freshman dorm right away that fall. Since the other guys were still in school in Beaver Dam, regular gigs weren't quite possible. So JMatt's M.O. at Saint Olaf was to make himself available. He would play with "anybody and everybody" he could in order to figure out how to be a better player. He also went to see (and talk to) any band that came to play on campus, whether he liked their music or not. He was a regular at the Pause, which he describes as: "This perfect black box theater...[with] all the makings of a great nightclub that you would play eventually with a band." He says that the Pause is "where we all came out of; we all logged hundreds if not thousands of hours rehearsing, playing, and then performing for our friends in this great incubator."

jMatt's ambition soon got him noticed. Christoph Höft, who was the head of the student concert committee, had noticed jMatt's "hustle and intensity" and thought he'd make a good member of the committee. jMatt was hesitant at first, but Christoph took him to a Toad the Wet Sprocket show the committee had arranged, and jMatt got to meet the band. The members arrived on campus in a four-door car pulling a trailer with their gear, even though by that point "All I Want" and "Walk on the Ocean" had already been hits. Seeing a successful band roughing it didn't give jMatt pause at all. Instead, he realized the committee would be a perfect way to get to know the business he wanted to get into.

He eventually took over the concert committee, managing a nearly $40,000 budget to put on shows. He brought in the likes of the Mighty, Mighty Bosstones and the Violent Femmes, turning a profit for every concert.

Meanwhile, he had met some musicians in his dorm. Jason Rosenbaum, a double bass major from Nebraska lived down the hall. They started jamming with guitarist Peter Hanson and held a fruitless search for a lead singer. Their sophomore year they redoubled their efforts and ended up auditioning a freshman from Minneapolis-by-way-of-Texas named Ellis Bergeron. jMatt knew the moment he heard her sing that she was it: "I was in awe of her voice. I thought, if I can take my ambition and this woman's talent, we can go somewhere." Ellis was already seasoned, having played with a semi-professional band called the Unfinished in high school. She was writing some conversational folk songs, while Jason had some worldbeat style joyful basslines he'd been working on, and they decided to sort of smash the two together. In the vernacular of the time, they were H.O.R.D.E. Festival meets Lilith Fair. They added a horn section of Andy Bast on trumpet and Jess Fox on sax, and Bobby Llama was almost complete. When Peter took a semester abroad, they brought on new guitarist Mike McCrady.

For jMatt, Bobby Llama offered two opportunities. For one, being surrounded by such serious musicians forced him to push himself to keep up and get better. The other opportunity was to use his strong interpersonal skills and drive to serve as the band's manager. He took care of all the scheduling and other logistics for the group. That year they wrote songs together and played their first few shows. In jMatt's junior year they sold out the Pause, which was the campus popularity litmus test, and continued that momentum into the summer by decamping to a barn just outside of Northfield where they wrote the songs for their first record. That same summer Ellis spent three days at Third Ear Studios in Minneapolis to record her debut solo album, *Soft Day*. Alex Oana, whom Ellis had met when Bobby Llama opened for Chris & Johnny at a Saint Olaf show, produced and engineered the album. Jason and JMatt both played on several songs.

Bobby Llama's self-titled debut album was recorded live at Seedy Underbelly with Alex. The band were in fact the first artist to record at the newly opened studio. "They were still painting the walls," jMatt says. The band slept in the studio to save money. When the album came out that fall is when, according to jMatt, they "just took off like a rocket." Like Chris and Johnny they started playing more off campus, at places like the Grand Theater, and like Chris and Johnny, they also began working with Brent and Meleia Day, and the latter helped them get on the NACA circuit. Three of the band members, including jMatt, graduated in 1997 and three more the following year. jMatt and Jason headed to Minneapolis to live at CityCabin and set up Bobby Llama headquarters. It was a heady time, with Johnny working on his solo album, Spymob doing their EP, and Alex working with Semisonic on their second album. "We were all hoping each other would make it," jMatt recalls.

jMatt had even come around on Storhyill. Ellis opened for Storyhill at their CD release show for *This Side of Lost* at the Great American History Theater in Saint Paul and is was at the soundcheck for that show where jMatt became a Storyhill convert. He liked the first song he heard, and then the next, and by the third he was thinking, "Holy shit, these guys are amazing." He felt the need to confess to Chris and Johnny, telling them, "I'm embarrassed to admit, but I didn't like you guys in college. You guys are phenomenal and I hope you go far, far into the universe."

Bobby Llama started a steady diet of touring, topping out at about 150 shows per year, mostly at colleges and clubs, on the same cicuit Storyhill had followed. They bought an RV and toured up and down California a couple of times. They sang the national anthem at a Colorado Rockies game. But it wasn't all great. jMatt reveals there were times, for instance, where they played a bar in Superior, Wisconsin and "literally three people" showed up to watch.

They recorded a second album, the *Dyskonesia* EP, also with Alex. The EP came out in 1999, and shortly after that, jMatt entered them in the "Bandemonium," a contest for unsigned bands sponsored by Sam Goody/Musicland stores. They played regionally against a group called Johnny Clueless at the Cabooze in Minneapolis. jMatt says the fact that they based it on crowd reaction gave Bobby Llama an unfair advantage. "Ellis is magical on stage; she lights people up and makes you feel like she's singing to you." They ended up making the finals, playing in Florida against a Tampa Bay act, Harry Dash. The contest took place during spring break, which brought in a huge contingent of Midwestern fans. They played what jMatt calls a "killer" show, and won the contest. The grand prize included an opening slot for Moby and Marcy Playground in Panama City in front of 7,500 people.

As great of an accomplishment as it was, it was also the beginning of the end for the band. As they started to get record label interest, Ellis was resistant to that path for a host of reasons. There was the record exec who predictably told the short-haired, t-shirt and jeans-wearing singer she should try to look more girly. There were the horror stories of other bands' music being hijacked either creatively or physically. And more than anything she felt that the band should continue to tour independently to both develop musically and grow their fanbase. She was looking to build a solid, lasting career in music, brick by brick.

This was in direct opposition to jMatt and some of the other band members, who felt there was a ticking clock on their time together. jMatt says, "I felt we had to get there sooner than later because it's a six-person band." Mark had already gotten married, and all of them had college degrees in something other than music. The fear was that if they went on too much longer without going to the next level, the band would split. "We were not built for the long haul. [We weren't] willing to be 30 years old and broke. We watched the Black Eyed Peas, we opened for them in 2000 or 1999 at Macalester and they were nowhere. They didn't break until 2003."

Ellis decided to go fully solo in April 2000, and would go on to have an evergreen career as an independent singer-songwriter. Bobby Llama soldiered on for a few more months with a different singer, but by the time jMatt's opportunity to play in Camaro came about, Bobby Llama was on life support. He played on Brenda Weiler's *Crazy Happy*, and started drumming for Peppermint artist Stuart Davis (in fact, jMatt brought Stuart into the Peppermint fold). He'd moved out of CityCabin and was sharing a place with Eric Fawcett while Sarah Hauss (the couple had married in the summer of 1997) was attending graduate school in Colorado. jMatt still had an office in CityCabin when Darren moved in, and that's when the two started to get to know one another.

Camaro offered jMatt a chance to learn to play in a new style. "I was so excited to play that kind of power pop music. It was such a different challenge from what I'd been

jMatt Keil during a Camaro rehearsal circa 2002. Courtesy Darren Jackson.

doing, to hit the drums hard and steady." And the songs themselves were a big draw as well, "I just loved the music they were writing. I was like, 'Oh my god, these are great songs. These are songs I want to hear.' They were just such juicy hooks."

The songs in question were Appelwick's tunes "Shy," "Pretty Bigmouth," "Imaginary," and "Ordinary" from the *Lacerate* and *Cellophane* CDs, and Darren's "Jay's a Wreck," "45s 'til 3," "Trust Fund Junkie," "Whisper," and "Holiday." There had initially been talk of trying out some of Jay's songs as well, though that never quite materialized. As much of a waste of great songwriting talent as that seems, Jay was mostly okay with just playing bass and singing harmonies.

Another interesting aspect of the band's creative dynamic is that, even though they gave each other suggestions for arrangements, Darren and Appelwick did not collaborate. Erik was open to it, but Darren, he says, liked his songs to be his own. They definitely enhanced one another's work, but at the same time kept their unique visions for their compositions. As they worked out a repertoire, a couple of Darren's slower songs ("45s 'til 3" and "Jay's a Wreck") fell away.

The band began rehearsing in Landing Gear's practice space, and fairly quickly worked up arrangements for the tunes. Much as in Kid Dakota, rehearsals were not for goofing around. "When we rehearsed it was business," says jMatt. "You have to play your part well and be proficient on your instrument." He was amazed by both Appelwick's and Darren's chops, Erik's "incredible natural rhythm" and Darren's excellent, practiced guitar work. "I was playing with people better than myself and that brought my level of drumming up," he says. "What I loved was just how raw it was. I would massively blister. I would throw my body into the drums. I would crack cymbals."

Over a weekend circa February 2001, the band went to Seedy Underbelly and John Kuker recorded them playing four of their songs live. Darren was battling a head cold, but fought through it. They played "Whisper," "Holiday," "Pretty Bigmouth," and "Easier" (a reworked version of "Ordinary" from *Lacerate*). They called the results "El Demo" and pressed up some CDs that jMatt could use to book shows. Because of their work schedules and other commitments, the band didn't play too much, but they did manage to do gigs at Sursumcorda, the Dinkeytowner, the 400 Bar, the Fine Line, and the Cave at Carleton over that first year. They played the latter multiple times, and for jMatt those were the highlight. "The students who would show up would just pogo and dance the whole time and just completely go for it." Those gigs were also pretty good money, so much so that Jay convinced the guys to use some of their profits to buy him a left-handed bass.

After that initial burst of activity, however, Camaro would go on the back burner. Landing Gear got their song "Atmosphere" placed on the WB show *Roswell* in May, and it looked like things might take off for them. Kid Dakota was ramping up as a four-piece, leaving little time for the upstart pop rock band. Darren claims that he and Appelwick initially didn't take Camaro completely seriously, largely because they weren't feeling the right chemistry yet.

* * *

John Hermanson started 2001 with two major musical items on his checklist for the year. First was the release of Alva Star's debut album, *Alligators in the Lobby*, and second was a surprising reunion. The latter first.

Since Storyhill's break-up in 1997, Chris Cunningham had tried multiple paths to an unclear destination. His time in Seattle was spent searching for meaning. During his off times from Storyhill he had gone to Pittsburgh and volunteered with a Christian construction organization similar to Habitat for Humanity. He was looking for something to believe in, but even more he was looking for community in which he felt he could belong. He hadn't found it in Pennsylvania, and he didn't find it Seattle, either. He explored some of the more mystical aspects of spirituality that the city offered, and embraced some of the cosmic/psychic/new age concepts, but they still didn't feel like the answer he was looking for. On top of that, Chris found the city to be unfriendly and fast-paced. He became depressed.

When Chris called Johnny to congratulate him on Isak's birth in 1998, Johnny intuited right away that his old friend wasn't well. He mentioned it to his mom, who in turn relayed Johnny's concern to Chris's mom. She booked a visit to Seattle and convinced Chris to come home to Bozeman for a visit. He relented. In Bozeman, he found, things had changed just the right amount in the ten years since he'd graduated high school. It was still familiar enough to feel like home, but different enough that some of the unpleasant aspects (and people) from his youth no longer had power over him. He decided he wouldn't return to Seattle.

Back home again, Chris found the community he'd been searching for. He started getting invitations to play weddings and funerals and other events, and though that become connected to other musicians in the city. Informal rehearsals at his place eventually coalesced into a four-piece acoustic band called Sixth Sense (the name a nod to his mystical explorations in Seattle). The group began playing shows, and then recorded an EP (*The First Snow*, 1998) followed by a studio album (*Full Circle*, 1999). The songs on these releases leaned hard into a country/bluegrass sound that had always been underlying Chris's songs in Storyhill, and the band complemented him well. But it didn't last: "Sixth Sense was only destined for one long-distance tour to the Midwest before the drummer's wife broke up the band," Chris reports.

The net effect of his Sixth Sense experience was that Chris rediscovered his love of writing and performing. He recorded and released his first solo album, *House Concert*, in 2000, but still didn't quite feel confident touring behind it on his own, filling two hours of showtime. So he thought about Justin Roth, another Peppermint artist who'd just put out a record. They'd known each other for many years; Justin had brought Storyhill to the University of Minnesota–Duluth several times while he was a student there. The two had different-but-complementary styles, so Chris proposed they do a joint tour, with each singer doing a 40-minute set, and then teaming up on a few songs. Thus was born the "2 Forms of ID" tour, starting in late summer 2000 and hitting Ohio, Pennsylvania, Illinois, Iowa, Wisconsin, and Minnesota.

When their tour came to Saint Paul in early November, a gig at Scooter's on the University of Saint Thomas campus, Johnny showed up. The two old friends hadn't seen each other in three and a half years. Chris was surprised by Johnny's new haircut (he had chopped his signature long locks around the time of his solo album release) and says, "It made me nervous and excited to see him and I was definitely distracted. [Justin and I] were trying to take ourselves seriously as a duo and what's going on in my brain is, 'Oh, there's my other duo, the duo that I built this duo on.'"

After the show, Johnny came up to Chris and said, "I've been thinking we should play again sometime and do another show." He went on to tell Chris about just how much Storyhill support there continued to be. Sales were still good, and there was constant clamor through the Peppermint website and Scott Comstock's fanpage for them to get back together. Chris was heartened, and gave a noncommittal, "Yeah, sure" to them playing together again, thinking they'd get something together in a year or two.

Johnny had a different idea: "Let's do something in the summer." He wanted to do just one show in the Twin Cities to scratch the old itch, a special event. They booked a July 21 date at the Great American History Theater, and sent out an e-mail to the Peppermint mailing list. The 500-seat venue sold out in five hours. They added a second show on July 20. Both could hardly believe the response, and both felt a mix of caution and curiosity about rehearsing and performing together again.

Meanwhile, Johnny was all-consumed with Alva Star. The primary recording on *Alligators in the Lobby* (the title is a reference to the Jefferson Hotel in Richmond, Virginia, which in the first part of the 20th century kept several alligators in marble pools in the lobby) had been done over 10 days in the fall at CityCabin. Because the band came together as the recording was happening, there are three different drummers on the album. Peter Anderson plays on over half of the songs, but Christopher McGuire appears on "Falling" and "Thing for Me," and Eric Fawcett is on "Adore" and "Revelation." The latter performance was most impressive to Johnny because it was done in a time crunch. Eric had never heard the song, and he only had 15 minutes. Johnny gave him some brief guidance on how he wanted it to start, and they ran through the song three times in quick succession. They ended up using the first take. "It's the most awesome drum performance," says Johnny, "It's just so loud and crazy."

Johnny's template for the album was the Beatles' *Rubber Soul*, where the individual songs can stand alone, but also work together as a whole. "I had made the *John Hermanson* record and every song was so dramatically different," Johnny says, "I was like, I can't even listen to it myself. I wanted to make a cohesive record that you could play when you're in a certain mood."

He also wanted it to sound as live as possible, like four guys in room, and that's what it was for the most part. There are some vocal overdubs and effects here and there, some strings and horns that show up briefly. But the for the most part it's a guitars-bass-drums rock record. More than anything, the album sounds like its taking direct aim at the mainstream. The production is clean and sweet, there're plenty of hooks and the lyrics are straightforward (at least as straightforward as Johnny gets).

The album's songs do stand alone, but also speak to one another, helping to achieve that unified effect Johnny was going for. There are subtle things like the fact that record's first three tunes all use the word "falling," as in "falling apart on you," "falling on yourself," and "I am through falling for you." But there are also shared themes—mainly romantic facturing and deception. While writing songs for the album, Johnny found some inspiration in unlikely place. One afternoon, he caught the 1966 film *This Property is Condemned* which was based on the one-act play by Tennessee Williams. He was struck by the parallels between the lives of actress Natalie Wood and the character she played, Alva Starr, namely that they both met early, untimely deaths. In the film, Alva Starr tries to escape the complications of her life by indulging in a robust fantasy life. The movie got Johnny thinking about the power of fiction to influence reality, and the roles we play to fool ourselves and others. He ended up including some of those themes, and even dialogue, from the movie, into his lyrics.

This is most evident in three songs: "Beautiful" (you're beautiful, as an actress/you're beautiful, forever after/preserved by a happy ending"), "Girlfriend" ("you played the girlfriend brilliantly/I should have written the review"), and, of course, "Alva Star." The latter is a slow-building spectral tune addressed to Alva herself, expressing sympathy and sorrow at her predestined path: "Alva Star, you'll be dead/they let us know from the start that you would be, in the end/and it's all written down/whatever you decide to do between now and then is decided."

Alligators in the Lobby came out officially on February 20, though the band had celebrated with a CD release show four days earlier at the 400 Bar with Brenda Weiler opening. Alva Star paid for radio promotion with Tinderbox, and Peppermint gave the record a big press push. Both paid off. *Alligators* made it onto the College Music Journal (CMJ) charts for college radio play, becoming the #19 add in its debut week, and making it to #158 on the top 200 list. They also earned play on XM satellite radio's "unsigned" channel.

The reviews were overwhelmingly positive. *Star Tribune* critic Jon Bream wrote: "John Hermanson's new group may be the next significant Twin Cities pop band. Smart, catchy, sweet, and timeless." *Amplifier Magazine* called *Alligators* "that rarest of albums that shimmer and sparkle from start to finish." Local DJ and musician Dave Campbell fell for the album too, especially "Unhappily Yours": "That song should have been all over MTV at the time," he says, "That song is incredible." In May 2001, *City Pages* unveiled its annual "Picked to Click" list of the best new local bands. Alva Star came in at number three. The write-up praised the pairing of Johnny's "emotive vocals and plaintive lyrics" with the "lush sonic backdrops" of the band. "Why would longtime singer-songwriter and semi-folkster John Hermanson hook up with a band after gathering such a devoted local following on his own?" writer Adam Hall questions. "Answer: to gain a sound."

Alva Star as photographed by Tony Nelson in early 2001. From left to right: Brian Roessler, John Hermanson, Peter Anderson, Darren Jackson. Courtesy Tony Nelson (www.tonynelson-photo.com).

That same month, Alva Star won the Best New Band honor at the Minnesota Music Awards, beating out Tin Porter, Faux Jean, Sunset Black, the Crush, and Kid Dakota (which means Darren essentially beat himself). After the win, Johnny told the *Minnesota Daily*, "We got the biggest congratulations from bands that were on the ballot with us. It's good to be in a scene that is genuinely excited about each other's success." The award ceremony took place at First Avenue, and were hosted by the Zone 105 morning team of Mary Lucia and Brian Oake. The big name winners that night were the Jayhawks, Dillinger Four, Atmosphere, and Mason Jennings, but the CityCabin crew did their damage as well. In addition to Alva Star's win, Alex Oana won Producer of the Year, and Brenda Weiler won Best Acoustic Artist (Johnny and Brenda both lost out in the Best Songwriter category, as did Christopher McGuire for Best Drummer). As part of the award festivities, Alva Star and Kid Dakota played in the "Best New Band Nominees and Acoustic Showcase" at the 7th Street Entry.

After 10 years, Johnny had finally been fully embraced by his adopted hometown scene, and the general perception was that Alva Star was a star on the rise. Andy Carlson says, "It seemed like it was going places; like maybe Johnny would get signed or something." The band didn't mount a full-scale tour, but they did venture out to Chicago and Madison a couple of times, trying to build some buzz. Peter remembers those as good times, and he was particularly struck by everyone's level of intelligence: "I remember road trips when it would be like, 'When was the last time I was in a band van and there's this huge conversation about Kierkegaard and Nietzsche?'" Alva Star began rehearsing some new songs for a potential EP release, including a tune called "Only Dreaming" that Peter thought might signal a new direction for the band. "It was groovy, heartfelt, and intense in a smoldering way," he says.

They did a ton of Twin Cities shows over the spring and early summer at places like the 7th Street Entry, the Uptown Bar, and the 400 Bar. But in late summer/early fall things began to slow down, and the band lost some of their initial momentum. The main culprit was divided interests. As Peter put it, "These are all really talented people with a lot of ideas and it's hard to keep everyone focused on one thing."

And Johnny said something telling in a 2002 interview with Andrew Ellis at GloryDazeMusicwww: "My hope is just to be able to focus as much energy as possible on making music and as little as possible on marketing it." He'd later tell the *Pioneer Press* that the hardest part of being a musician was the business side of things, scheduling, rehearsing, making it work financially. By summer, Johnny was devoting a lot of his time to the reunion shows with Chris, and Darren was recording new Kid Dakota songs. Roessler always had musical interests outside of pop music, though he and Peter did team up to back Ellis on her second studio album, *Everything That's Real*, recorded in early 2001 at Seedy Underbelly.

During the slowdown, in the fall of 2001, Roessler received an offer from renowned double bass player François Rabbath to study with him in Paris. He told his wife, Kjirsten, of the offer and she was immediately on board. So they sold their house and moved to Paris with their two-year-old son Eli and their two dogs. That meant leaving Alva Star, but it was something he felt he had to do. "It's the best decision I made in my entire life," he says. Roessler's replacement was a familiar face: Erik Appelwick (if you're keeping score, that means Appelwick and Darren were now in three separate bands together).

As things were slowing down with Alva Star, they were gearing back up with Storyhill. The July reunion concerts went very well. The musical chemistry was still there and the audience reaction was just as—if not more—enthusiastic. As Johnny put it, the shows were, "Trippy, but in a good way." They documented the shows by having Alex record them, and Peppermint released a two-CD set called simply *Reunion*. Much like *Echoes*, the set presented the concert in its entirety, though in this case they chose between performances from both nights. The between song patter is there, and reveals an ease of interaction as the old friends riff with one another about "planned spontaneity," old sea cats, and snoring.

The older songs they chose to play are fairly predictable, drawing heavily from *Miles & Means*, *Clearing*, and *This Side of Lost*. The real revelations come in the new and solo songs they chose to perform. They do a surprisingly faithful version of Alva Star's "Thing for Me." There's a sped-up duo version of "Spirit of the Ghost of Nothing" from Johnny's self-tilted album, but their rendition of Sixth Sense's "Full Circle" is the most drastic reinvention. What was a pretty good song becomes a great one with the addition of Johnny's harmonies and the trade off of the line "come full circle" on the chorus. They feel like they were always meant to be there, and the song's message of homecoming takes on even deeper meaning in the context of the reunion, especially on the line "He used to sing out, without a doubt of a harmony."

There are three brand new Storyhill songs on the set: "With You Here," "All I Need," and "What was Wrong," with the latter being most significant. In a long, slightly awkward introduction, Johnny explains that he wrote "What was Wrong" the day after the last Storyhill show: "It's a song about release, like, oh finally, a weight off my shoulders." The lyrics go deeper than that, addressing the way we can live in a dysfunctional situation for so long that we don't even recognize that doesn't have to be that way. It shows that, though it may have been Chris that decided to end their partnership, Johnny hadn't been content in Storyhill either.

It's even more interesting that he didn't include such a strong tune on his solo album, almost as if he knew somewhere in the back of his mind to save it. That the guys chose to rehearse and play new songs at all seems to belie the premise that the reunion shows were a one-time special event. What's more accurate is that that the shows were a testing of the waters, done with on an underlying hope that more would follow.

Sure enough after the summer shows, just to be fair, they decided give some love to their Montana and western fans and do a December appeareance in Bozeman. That one went just as well as the first two. Moving forward, there was no grand plan or agreement. Both men were still hesitant, but they couldn't deny that, thus far, the water had been just fine. For Chris, the act of playing with Johnny was unlike any other. "I get an opportunity dig in musically and get challenged and to rise to the occasion, and try to seek that grace and perfection. I got enough of that with Johnny it was addicting. It was satisfying, it was fun, it made the thing worthwhile." And just as the first time they performed in public, at the candlelight dessert, the rapturous reaction of the audience was what pushed Chris and Johnny forward. As Johnny told an interviewer when asked what the best part of being a musician is for him, "Playing live—there's nothing like having the attention of an audience that just wants to listen to your music."

* * *

Spymob rang in 2001 with a show at the 400 Bar, playing with 12 Rods. What the new year would hold for the band was murky, but they had a determination to move forward. They were working up some new material, but already had enough unreleased

Storyhill managers Andy Carlson (left) and David Weeks kept the Storyhill flame alive during the band's break. Courtesy Storyhill.

tracks lying around to fill another album, so put together a release called *Basement Tapes*, a nod to the Dylan album, but also to the unreleased/unused nature of the tracks. The collection highlights Spymob's eclectic and ever-evolving nature.

There are songs that are very much in line with the funk-meets-AM-Gold sound of the *Spymob* EP and *On Pilot Mountain*, tunes like "John Madden," and "Keep Your Speed Up." There are tunes that recall the *Townhouse Stereo* days, namely the unhurried "Napping Mid-Day" and the hilarious-yet-affecting "I Still Live at Home." The latter is a first-date confessional from a guy who lives in his parent's basement. It contains one of the band's best bridges, both in melody and lyrics: "If we went back to my place/I'd light incense and candles/No one would dare disturb us/We'd feel all alone/And if things did get serious/It would be convenient/To walk right up the stairs and/Have you meet my folks." And there are even a couple of songs that lean in a more country direction. Ostby had been listening to a lot of Johnny Cash and folk music and had become enamored with the directness and simplicity of those kinds of songs. So "Up for a Good Time" and "Wake for the Night" work in that milieu.

The band pressed some CDs of *Basement Tapes* and sold them at shows and via their website. Having new product was a good way to feel like they were looking to the future. They continued to give out copies of *On Pilot Mountain* in hopes of landing it with a label. In April, Fawcett got a call from the band's lawyer, Tim Mandelbaum. He'd just been in a meeting with one of his other clients, a songwriter and producer named Pharrell Williams. Williams, who along with his partner Chad Hugo comprised the duo the Neptunes, were rising stars in the music industry. They'd already scored several hip-hop hits, including Ol' Dirty Bastard's "Got Your Money," Mystikal's "Shake Ya Ass," and Jay-Z's "I Just Wanna Love U (Give it to Me)." By 2000, artists from across genres were lining up to work with them. They had enough clout to get a record deal for their skate-rock/rap outlet, N.E.R.D. and were looking into starting their own imprint built on artists they'd discovered, such as Clipse and Kelis.

Thanks to Mandelbaum, Pharrell had been in possession of the *Spymob* EP since 1998, and he dug it. It reminded him, he would later say, of the music of his childhood. "Like Steely Dan crossed with the Meters and Prince." He'd turned Chad on to the band as well, who said, "The drumming sounds like the old break beats DJs used to play at parties, and I hardly ever hear any live drummers play that funky style. And the guitarist was playing all these jazz licks and all these changes that just blew me away." So when he and Mandelbaum were meeting with Epic Records' head Polly Anthony about the possibility the label hosting a Neptunes imprint, he mentioned how much he liked Spymob and how much he was looking forward to their new record. Anthony was forced to admit that she'd dropped the band, and incorrectly assumed Mandelbaum had engineered the moment to embarrass her.

Unsurprisingly, there was no deal with Epic, but after the meeting, Pharrell told Tim that he wanted to help Spymob get to the next level, possibly even by signing them to his imprint. When Fawcett heard this, he first took it with a grain of salt. He and the rest of the band hadn't heard of Pharrell or the Neptunes, and weren't especially into the hit songs they'd done up to that point. Eric summarizes the band's initial reaction as, "So what?" But an opportunity was an opportunity, so Mandelbaum arranged for Eric to fly to New York City and meet with Pharrell in a Manhattan recording studio. The meeting went went well, and ended with Pharrell telling Eric: "I'm gonna blow Spymob up. Everyone is gonna know who you are."

The first step was to have Ostby sing on a track with Kelis, the New York R & B singer who was featured memorably on "Got Your Money," and who had scored her own minor hit with the furious, Neptunes-written-and-produced "Caught Out There" (chorus: "I hate you so much right now"). Kelis, Pharrell, and Chad were working on her second album, *Wanderland*, and John was brought in to duet on a jaunty track called "Mr. UFO Man." It's not a paltry eight bar appearance. Not only does John sing with Kelis on the chorus and some of her verses, but he gets a whole verse to himself. Kelis had a lot of buzz, so being featured on her new album had great potential to get John and Spymob's name out there in a big way. Unfortunately, the album wouldn't get a U.S. release. Kelis, feeling unsupported and misunderstood at Virgin Records, left the label during the record's rollout. *Wanderland* would only be released in the U.K.

In June, not long after John recorded "Mr. UFO Man" in New York, Spymob flew out to the opposite coast to do some label showcase performances in L.A. that had been arranged by Mintz and Mandelbaum. Though the shows themselves went well, nothing came of them. More than one label rep admitted to being scared off by the fact that the band had already been dropped once. As John would put it in a later interview, record labels and their employees have a fear-based culture. A dropped band, no matter the circumstances, was "damaged goods."

Pharrell and Chad, along with rapper Shay Haley, had already recorded their debut album as N.E.R.D, *In Search Of...*, and were planning to put it out in the U.K. in August with a U.S. release not far behind. As the dates approached, the guys began to have second thoughts about the CD, which they had recorded themselves using their customary drum machines, samples, and synths. There was something lacking. "It sounded restricted to us," Shay explained in an interview. "It lacked progression." The group also realized that

7. Things Are Getting Better

to differentiate themselves from the "Neptunes sound" and achieve their goal of revealing their inner AC/DC, the album needed real rock instruments. Shay added, "As we found out, there's nothing like being able to scream over a real band." So they cancelled the U.S. release date and pulled the U.K. version in order to rerecord the songs with a band. They could have had their choice of any studio players they wanted, but they chose to call Fawcett and ask if Spymob would be willing to play on the album.

That July, Spymob packed up their gear and flew to Virginia Beach. They spent ten days recutting the album's original twelve tracks. Girlfriends and wives flew out to visit, including a 6-months-pregnant Sarah. Everything went great. Pharrell later said that Spymob were almost like musical directors for the recording, and were "integral" to the success of finished album. The guys' vintage gear (Brent's '64 Fender Stratocaster and '57 Telecaster, Twigg's Fender Precision bass, and Eric's old Ludwig drums) gave Chad and Pharrell the warm sound they were looking for, and having real players provided an energy the original recordings lacked. The album was fast-tracked for a November release, though that was eventually pushed back to March 2002 to give Virgin Records time to create a promotional push.

Even more exciting for Ostby, Fawcett, Brent, and Twigg was the fact that Pharrell was serious about signing Spymob to their imprint—called Star Trak—and releasing their album. The latter part of 2001 found him closing a deal with L.A. Reid, the drummer/writer/producer turned record executive, to bring Star Trak to Arista Records (though N.E.R.D. themselves would remain signed to Virgin). Before Spymob put out their own record, however, Pharrell wanted to take them on the road to help turn N.E.R.D. into a live, performing entity. As part of that, the band would be given the chance to open with a set of their own songs to build up buzz.

As if that weren't enough Eric and Sarah welcomed a baby boy, Jackson, in October, and John got married in October to Kristina Halvorson, a fellow Ole. Things were, to paraphrase one of the *In Search of...* songs, definitely and finally getting better in Spymob's life.

* * *

Darren had had a blur of a year. He was working full time, and playing in three separate bands, two of them in which he was songwriter and singer. Together, the three bands' commitments added up to well over 50 shows. It got so crazy, he began to carry a day planner to keep track of all of his obligations. As if his dizzying number of gigs and rehearsals with Kid Dakota, Camaro, and Alva Star, he'd also joined Brenda Weiler at several gigs, including a July 6 concert at the 400 Bar which was recorded and several tracks from which ended up on her album *Brenda Weiler: Live*. His ghostly background vocals on "Trouble" help make the song a standout on the record.

Darren's very full schedule was a function of not turning down opportunities, his ability to network, his talent, and his desire to keep busy and away from the vices that had dragged him down before. The latter was also a big part of why he'd taken up running obsessively, and began training for the Twin Cities Marathon.

Along with all of the accolades for Alva Star, Kid Dakota got their share of attention. They were named the number five "Picked to Click" band by *City Pages*, just a couple of slots below Alva Star. Writer Melissa Maerz declared, "The music is intriguingly ugly, lonely, and self-destructive. In short: it makes Kid Dakota an indie-rock dreamboat." And though they lost to Alva Star at the Minnesota Music Awards, no one else could say they were nominated twice in the same category. Darren had made a name for himself on the Twin Cities scene, and things were only looking up. His playing with Zak Sally led to an offer for Kid Dakota to release a full-length album through Low's indie label, Chairkickers Music, in 2002. With Low being known and respected nationally, it was a chance for Darren to advance his music beyond Minneapolis and out into the world.

8

Two Fronts

In which Kid Dakota and Storyhill rise to prominence, Vicious Vicious emerges, and Camaro and Alva Star fade to the background. Also, Spymob hits the road with Pharrell.

For Appelwick and Darren, 2002 kicked off with a busy Kid Dakota schedule. The band played at First Avenue's "Best New Bands of 2001" showcase that January, the first time either of them had played the Twin Cities' most famous room. They were part of a line-up that included Work of Saws, Andrew Broder (of the Fog), and the Ashtray Hearts. One of Darren's biggest talents was turning out to be creating connections with other musicians, so it's no surprise that Broder ended performing with Kid Dakota on occasion as a turntablist, and that Kid Dakota landed new brooding two songs on a compilation (*Apartment Music*) on the Ashtray Hearts' label.

The first, "Two Fronts," was recorded with John Kuker at Seedy Underbelly. It features Appelwick on bass and lap steel, turntables by Broder, and Electro-Harmonix mini-synth from Alex. The song uses an extended weather metaphor to describe a doomed relationship. "The weatherman was wrong," Darren sings. "He said the storm would pass before too long/But when two fronts like us collide/There's just no telling when or how the storm will ever subside." Broder's turntables offer an underlying staticky beat to Darren's acoustic before building into a whirling coda.

"Get Her Out of My Heart" was recorded with Spymob's Brent Paschke and also features Broder, along with bass from Zak Sally and violins by John Hermanson, a worlds collide sort of line-up that was becoming commonplace. The title is a reference to a Beach Boys lyric from "Help Me, Rhonda," and also name checks that song. As if that weren't enough, Broder repeatedly samples in the "aaha" from the opening line of "Good Vibrations" (as in "Aaah, love the colorful clothes she wears."). The songs have an almost completely different feel from the *So Pretty* tracks, and one of the main differences is down to the absence of Christopher McGuire. He had accepted an offer to tour with singer-songwriter John Vanderslice (Kid Dakota had done a show with Vanderslice at the Entry in September of '01, and this is likely where McGuire got on his radar).

The compilation was released in March, and that same month, Kid Dakota made their first trip to Austin to play South by Southwest. They played outside of the Empanada Parlour and, according to Chris Riemenschneider's report in the *Star Tribune*, managed to draw a crowd away from a more buzzed-about band—pop punks the Movielife—that was playing inside.

Darren was also doing quite a bit of recording. In addition to the two *Apartment Music* songs, he was working on three new tracks for the expanded *So Pretty*. He also did a song—"DJ DJ" (deejay Darren Jackson)—with Andrew Broder's Lateduster bandmate Martin Dosh for the latter's debut album.

* * *

Appelwick, meanwhile was prepping his own album. In the early part of 2001 he had borrowed a four-track recorder from Christopher McGuire and, much like he had with *Cellophane* and *Lacerate*, created an entire album almost by himself. This time, however, he'd done it at the musical playground that was CityCabin, with access to professional microphones and in a space designed for recording. He also had better instruments (the mini-synth provided the bass on many of the songs) and had sound wizard Alex Oana to master it. He'd decided to release the record under the name Vicious Fishes, but discovered it was already taken. A girlfriend suggested that he drop the "Fishes" and double the Vicious. Appelwick thought was the "stupidest fucking idea" but went with it anyway.

Appelwick self-released the first Vicious Vicious album, *Blood and Clover*, in June of 2002. He Erik says his vision for the record was to "take contemporary beats, like hip-hop beats, and put roller-skating music to it." But this only fits a couple of the songs. A more apt description is the one Appelwick gave to *Minnesota Daily*'s Lindsey Thomas: "white guy soul" suitable for "shaking ass and drinking malts, or smoking a bong, listening to headphones and sitting in one of those '70s egg shaped chairs."

Also, and this may be obvious given his method of recording, Appelwick didn't want things to be too polished. "There's the occasional missed note and there's a lot of really loose things in there," he told Marcie Hill of *City Pages*. "It's really human, which is a characteristic that I'm a really big fan of."

Throughout the diverse album, Appelwick's knack for melody serves to hold everything together. Be it the way his voice soulfully handles the "If easy living is wrong, I don't want to be right" line in "Sinister Summer" or the lovely use of xylophone in the extended instrumental ending of "On the Last Day of May." The album's "hit"—it got steady play on Radio K—was the supremely groovy "Shake That Ass on the Dancefloor," in which Erik laconically celebrates an enigmatic lady who's "got a little more back there than the next girl."

The CD also features a reunion. One weekend while Appelwick was working on the album, Erik's Harvesters/Lefty Devils bandmate Justin Seim came to Minneapolis for a visit. He and Erik wrote and performed "That's Not How It's S'pose to Be," a vibey number on which Justin plays mandolin and organ.

The release of *Blood and Clover* gave Appelwick his turn in the spotlight. The local media fell hard for the album, and the comparisons they made to other artists is a testament to the genre hopping nature of Erik's music, which itself was an extension of his own wide range of listening. *City Pages* said "Appelwick's slack, gritty-sounding production creates a light, playful sound, recalling Syd Barrett sans psychedelia." Dan Haguen, of the short-lived *Lost Cause Magazine*, wrote that "*Blood and Clover* melts with ease from laid-back, ironic funk to clever sunburned pop to blusey, heatstroked rock." The *Star Tribune*'s Chris Riemenschneider described Vicious Vicious as "a greasier New Order with two capable guitarists and a record full of great songs." Charles Spano's review in the *All Music Guide* says that *Blood and Clover* is "a feel-good, skewed pop record with the awkward eccentricity and pop smarts of Ween and early Beck" and "absolutely indelible in a lo-fi, accidentally-stumbling-into-brilliance sort of way."

Appelwick put together a live line-up for Vicious Vicious and began doing shows in late summer 2002. On drums he recruited Martin Dosh, and on guitar, who else could it be but Darren (if you're keeping count, this means that they were now in four bands simultaneously)? He also lured Alex out from behind the sound board to perform. It didn't take long for the band to become a draw, and their November show at the 7th Street Entry was packed. When VV placed at number six on *City Pages* "Picked to Click" list, the paper wrote: "Rather than being predictable when he performs, Mr. Vicious (a.k.a. Erik Appelwick) plays shows like emotional swings: One moment he's all high jinks and humor, the next he's just killing you with a lovelorn little tune about a long-awaited reunion. Some cheeky lyrical gags are steeped in his lounge-pop melodies, but those tender little ballads just give him away."

Interviewers also seemed to fall Appelwick himself as well. His playful, is-he-joking manner and knack for a well-turned phrase made him a fascinating interview subject. He'd give choice quotes, such as when he revealed that he'd like to do the soundtrack for a sequel to the 1980 Olivia Newton John-starring fantasy film *Xanadu*: "I don't think anyone wants to make it but if they come knocking, I'm up for it."

City Pages took notice of his charm and gave him a one-off "Dear Abby" style love advice column in the September 18, 2002, issue. He gave cheeky but useful counsel about how to approach a stranger you've been crushing on, how to deal with a boyfriend who's no good at oral sex, and a surefire method for a band's drummer to siphon off groupie attention from the guitarists. To a young man that complained about his girlfriend falling asleep during the movies he picked out, Appelwick offered this: "Movies, schmoovies. It sounds like you and your girl need to find some other way to while away the hours. Try any combination of the following: bike ride, cocktails, sensual massage, long walk around the lake, cocktails, salsa dancing, arm wrestling, pie-eating contest, bird watching, cocktails, sex, fishing … check out a band, for fuck's sake!"

* * *

With Vicious Vicious and Kid Dakota rising to prominence, it left little room for Camaro. Though Appelwick and Darren liked how the songs had developed, and thought the band had done some pretty great shows, they used the break to reconsider both the group's configuration and the recordings they'd done so far. Appelwick once again rewrote "Easier" with the idea of making it more overtly catchy and poppy. The new version, called "Let's Go" had completely different lyrics, a punchier chorus, and felt like the missing piece in the set of songs they were recording.

They started recording drums at CityCabin on Erik's 8-track, but it didn't go well. jMatt's recording experience to that point had all been done live with a full band. In this case, though, all he had was Erik strumming and singing along, and it just didn't work. jMatt says, "It was nearly impossible for me to lay down tracks, and frankly I wasn't that steady when I wasn't playing with a band." So, to everyone's frustration, they scratched two day's worth of drum tracks.

It was a tumultuous time, as Darren and Appelwick had also made the decision to get rid of Jay. They didn't do it gently; as Darren put it, "we unceremoniously dumped him." From Appelwick and Darren's perspective it was simply a matter of needing a more experienced bass player who didn't have another major commitment. For Jay, it was a bummer but he also realized it was probably for the best. Landing Gear were working on a full-length album and really hoping to push beyond the local scene. Camaro had been using, and abusing, Landing Gear's rehearsal space, which was a headache for Jay. And overall, he had grown weary of Appelwick's and Darren's mercurial natures. He liked both men personally, but says, "It was so difficult to tell which one you were going to get on any given day."

After giving up on jMatt's tracks, Appelwick and Darren brought in Peter Anderson to record drums. They got together a couple of times to rehearse, and then spent one night at CityCabin recording to a Tascam 388 eight-track reel-to-reel. "Nine songs: bang, bang, bang!" Peter recalls. He says Darren and Appelwick played in the control room while he played along to a click track. He'd heard earlier versions of the songs and kept a lot of the drum parts jMatt had written, but added his own experience and style into his performance. "That kind of music is right down my alley," he says. "Somewhere between the Replacements and Polara. Balls out modern rock."

jMatt was crushed. He loved the band and the songs wholeheartedly, and had put his all into them, though he says, "It hurt a lot less" to know that Peter used his parts as a basis for the final recordings. "Peter is a phenomenal player; that was a good call from a studio standpoint," he says now.

Appelwick and Darren now had decent recordings of their songs, but they no longer had a full band to play them live. So they put everything—the band and the recordings—aside while focusing on Vicious Vicious and Kid Dakota.

* * *

The expanded *So Pretty* was released on November 5, 2002. Kid Dakota celebrated with a CD release show at the Turf Club's basement Clown Lounge in late October. The three new tunes aren't all that different in songwriting from the original five, but they have a wider sonic scope to them. Since the recording of the EP, which was recorded on 16-track ADAT, Alex had gotten ProTools, giving them way more tracks to work with. When recording the new songs, Darren and Alex had considered going back to the ADAT in order to stay true to the feel of the EP songs, but in the end they decided to not put that limitation on themselves. Sequence-wise, the songs are mixed in with the older tunes, which makes the differences a bit less stark.

The new album opener was "Crossin' Fingers," wherein the jealous, suspicious narrator has raided his girl's diary to discover her infidelity. Finger-picked guitar accompanies the verses and then buzzsaws through the chorus. The most thrilling moment comes when a multi-tracked Darren peels off three part harmonies to lead into the gut-punch line "a million proofs everyday/there's no doubt that you should stay/But you'll do what you wanna do, and I know that you'll go away."

"Bathroom" is a mid-tempo reworking of the old Headache song that breaks open a couple of times to rock out. It features a tremolo effect that makes it sound as if Darren is singing throguh an oscillating fan. The lyrics tell of passing out on a cool toilet seat, waking up the next morning, and heading home. The line "Hello hallucination, it's good to see you once again/'cause sometimes I get lonely and I need a little company," seems like an addict's justification for the drug use, black humor, or both.

Finally, "The Overcoat" is an epic album closer that offers a glimpse into Darren's rehab experience in the Black Hills in the winter of '98, weaning himself off with no scripts or pills and walking in the snow. He's also rereading the short story by Nikolai Gogol that gives the song its title. In the story, a government clerk scrimps and saves to buy himself a nice new coat, only to have it stolen in a mugging. It's the biggest humiliation in a series of them, leading the clerk to utter despair. That Darren chose to name the song after the story is telling, as that same sort of empty hopelessness seems to pervade the lyrics, despite the fact that its narrator is in the middle of conquering his demons. Or is he? In the end of it, during his walk in the snow, he can't tell if he's just going in circles. Fresh snow has filled his old tracks. Musically the song shows off some of Darren's more pop-leaning instincts, especially in the lovely, melodic guitar work and the harmonies. Also, Appelwick's xylophone makes an appearance at the beginning of the tune.

The "new" release on a high profile (at least by indie standards) label generated a fresh round of assessment and praise for Kid Dakota. Besides falling all over themselves to find artists to compare Kid Dakota to, the critics also worked up some interesting descriptions and insights. Some reviews focusd on the way Darren's voice served and created a mood. Paul Morel at *Pulse of the Twin Cities* called the vocals "bone-dry" and "always center stage, with the instruments providing dramatic counterpoint." Music blog Brainwashed wrote "Jackson's voice, like that of an anemic angel, floats between humming guitars and sparkling cymbal crashes. Sweet, lazy, and clear, almost every trembling note is about pain." Others talked focused on the production. *Minnesota Daily*'s Hall opined, "The production work by Alex Oana is gorgeously shiny, with almost every note agonized over at some point or another ... strap on some decent headphones and you can sense every desolate scrap of minutia, every conceivable detail carefully mapped out."

Chris Riemenschneider's *Star Tribune* review called the record "haunted, frayed ... pretty is probably the last word to use in describing their work." Leah Greenblatt, writing for *Time Out New York*, concluded of the album, "It would all be too unremittingly grim if Jackson didn't have such a sure sense of melody."

So Pretty crashed the CMJ charts, entering as the #7 add the week of its debut. It would spend several weeks on the Top 200 list, peaking at #39 in early 2003. Meanwhile, Darren, Christopher, Appelwick, and Zak were at work at Seedy Underbelly, already recording tracks for the next Kid Dakota album, which they were tentatively calling *Pilgrim*.

* * *

Johnny was spinning a lot of different plates as 2002 began. He was continuing to make music for Compass Entertainment as John August, his production work with other bands was picking up, and the dormant giant that was Storyhill was beginning to awaken. One thing that wasn't a concern, at least in the first half of the year, was Alva Star. Peter Anderson had received an offer to go on tour with Iffy, a local group that featured members of early '90s favorites Run Westy Run. Iffy had just signed a deal to release their debut album, *Biota Bondo*, on the California label Foodchain, and to mount a national tour. Peter understandably went with the more steady, predictable, and high profile gig. With Appelwick and Darren gearing up for busy years for Vicious Vicious and Kid Dakota, Alva Star went into limbo.

Meanwhile, Chris and Johnny convened at a cabin in Stillwater, Minnesota and did some preliminary recording of new songs on Chris's Roland VS-1680 digital workstation. The aim was to get enough tunes together for a new Storyhill album. They also plotted out more reunion shows for July and August, one in Minnesota and one in Bozeman. When tickets predictably sold out for the Saint Paul show, they added a second. What had started out as a tentative testing of the waters was turning out to be a few laps in the pool. What didn't seem likely, though, was a full-fledged 100 percent reunion. Both men were now too attached to their individual identities to give them up, and both had developments in their personal lives that tied them to their perspective homes. Chris had met Leslie Rickard, a program director for the county health department, and fallen deeply in love. "Through the course of my whole love life, finding Leslie was the one, the answer," he says. Johnny and Bettine, meanwhile, had welcomed a second son, August.

With his sensitive production of Brenda Weiler's *Fly Me Back*, his extensive recording experience, and growing contacts in the indie rock world, Johnny was starting to become an in-demand producer. And he brought Eric Fawcett along on the ride. The two first worked on the debut CD by a Saint Cloud band called Panoramic Blue. The modern rock group had zoomed onto the scene in early 2000 by winning a best unsigned band contest only a couple of months after their formation, which led to gigs at festivals and several Twin Cities venues. In the summer of 2001 they hooked up with Johnny at Angel Beach studios in Minneapolis to record their debut album, *More Than Just a Lady*. Not only did Johnny produce, engineer, and mix the CD, he also played and/or sang on six of its tracks. Eric played drums throughout.

The other band Johnny worked with during this time period also had Saint Cloud origins, its two primary members—John Solomon and Adam Switlick—having attended Saint John's University. They had connected with jMatt when Bobby Llama did a show there circa 1999 and that eventually led to Solomon spending the summer before his senior year at CityCabin (it had been his room that Appelwick took over) working with Johnny. "Johnny basically taught me how to write a song," he says. Fawcett adds: "Those guys were young. They hadn't done much, but they were clearly talented, and Johnny helped wrangle that."

Solomon kept working with Johnny and eventually moved to Minneapolis after graduation. In the summer of 2002, he and Switlick started playing gigs as Friends Like These, with jMatt on drums. They also started recording their debut at CityCabin, with Johnny playing bass and producing and Eric laying down the drum tracks while at home between N.E.R.D. tour dates. As had happened with Camaro, jMatt had basically written the drum parts, but didn't play on the record because he needed a live band to stay steady. He had other commitments anyway, having joined the power pop group Hi-Test, featuring Saint Olaf grads Jamison and Todd Geisler.

So Friends Like These put an ad in *City Pages* for a drummer, mentioning the Flaming Lips and the Kinks on their list of influences. One of the respondents was a University of Minnesota photography student named Matt O'Laughlin. Matt had grown up in Mankato, a mid-sized town an hour or so southwest of the Twin Cities. He played percussion in jazz band in high school, but his musical life was equally informed by Mankato's surprisingly robust punk scene. The epicenter was Marti's Pizza, a venue started by Jeremy Jenson (a friend of Matt's older brother Kevin) in the early '90s. Black Flag, AFI, Rancid, the Offspring, Jawbreaker, NOFX, and Green Day all played there. Marti's closed in 1997, but the scene lived on in all-ages basement shows and venues like the Fillin' Station Coffeehouse and Slackers. Matt became consumed with the first wave of emo (Promise Ring, Jimmy Eat World, the Get Up Kids) and he became the drummer in a couple of punk bands (Short Changed and Markinside).

Turns out he lived only a few blocks from CityCabin. He wanted to join Friends Like These, but was hesitant about not being part of the writing process, and the songs they were working on weren't his style. But he joined anyway. They started writing together, added bass player Steve Murray, got a nice rehearsal space in the Lowertown area of downtown Saint Paul, and began doing gigs right away amidst the early 2003 release of their album, *I Love You*. The music on the record fell somewhere between power pop and shoegaze. At the time, Solomon described it like this: "We tend to write pretty pop songs and then just throw weird things at them to keep things interesting."

The album made it on the CMJ chart, got some radio play around the country, received a bunch of rave reviews, and was nominated for a 2003 Minnesota Music Award for Best Rock Recording. The guys were doing a lot of local gigs, but started thinking bigger. They had already delved in to recording songs for a second album with Johnny, but abandoned that due to a lack of funds and a desire to take the show on the road in pursuit of a record contract.

John Solomon would end up playing accordion on the new Storyhill album, which Chris and Johnny were recording around this time. Titled *Dovetail*, the record was unveiled in November of 2002 at a CD release show at the Women's Club Theater in Minneapolis. They had gotten got the band back together: Fawcett plays drums, Brian Roessler—back from France—plays bass, and Kenny Wilson is once again on pedal steel. Chris stuck around Minneapolis to do his vocals and guitars, and left the rest to Johnny and the other players. Johnny pushed the songs toward a full, countrified sound similar to *Clearing*, an interesting approach since Chris and John had no intention of touring with a band (nor did they have the ability to, given Roessler and Fawcett's schedules). Chris says the choice was to make sure the album had commercial appeal. They simply didn't feel the two-voices-two-guitars was as saleable on CD.

It's hard to argue with the results. *Dovetail* is a beautiful sounding record, full of strong tunes that are served well by the arrangements and production. Take the two songs that appeared on *Reunion*, "What Was Wrong" and "All I Need." Neither are drastically changed, but both are enhanced by the extra instrumentation. Chris's soaring album opener "Seven Sisters" makes effective use of mandolin, and Solomon's accordion buoys up "Cupid's Dance."

The latter song is the clearest evidence that Chris was deeply in love. "Who knows why the angel in the sky/With his quill and clever eye/Decided to try and aim for us and send us spinning?" Johnny's "Angel," meanwhile, covers a similar feeling of devotion, but in the form of an apology. The song's narrator feels that it's his responsibility to look after the person he's addressing, but that he hasn't done the best job of it so far. The song is a bit of a return to Johnny's Christian songwriting youth, with a line lifted from Psalm 121.

Finally, just as Johnny wrote "What Was Wrong" about Storyhill itself, a couple of Chris's songs seem to do the same. Neither Johnny nor Chris were excited to dive headlong back into Storyhill, and both were fearful of interpersonal issues surfacing again. "Honesty," then, seems to refer to breaking down one's resistance to self-imposed limits. It's framed in terms of a romance that seems to be blossoming again after laying dormant, but with a couple of pronoun changes could just as easily be about John and Chris's partnership. The lyrics talk of second chances, different time zones, and making a blanket from a long thin thread. Both guys had strong justifications for ending their partnership, but both had overcome those and found reasons to go back. The first was the aforementioned establishment of their own separate musical identities, but perhaps more important than that was the realization that nothing was going to be as musically fulfilling and unique for them as Storyhill was. There was the simple fact of having put in more hours together than they possibly could apart or with anyone else, but there was also something nearly magical about the combination of their two particular talents and sensibilities.

Superfan Andrew Klein wrote on his Storyhill website (www.storyhill.info): "When I see Storyhill live, a strange and wonderful illusion seems to occur. I get the feeling that the music I'm hearing isn't actually coming from Chris and Johnny, but rather from somewhere else—somewhere higher or farther away somehow—and they are merely channeling this sound." He goes on to describe their contrasting performing styles, Johnny twitching and twisting, Chris still and understated. "But oddly, the illusion is not diminished in the least by the contrast. Chris is as possessed as Johnny—his head moving side to side, and the perfect harmony line finds its way out the corner of his mouth and matches Johnny's melody note for note, in tone, volume and emotional intensity."

Chris says, "There really isn't anyone else so far in my life that I've played with where that's happened, this kind of third entity, this higher angel thing starts to vibe out. Oftentimes, when Johnny and I are in good emotional spaces and relaxed on stage I'll perceive this extra layer of overtones in our harmonies. It's kind of this creepy, eerie, high pitched kind of ring thing as we're holding out notes. We've been able to get so good at that, we'll be in such synch, people have noted will be breathing at the same time and enunciating all the words together just in time. That whole thing is really kind of the magical zone for us."

Johnny felt the same, admitting in an interview around this time that he and Chris have "a musical chemistry that I haven't felt with anyone else." But the clamor of fans and the clairity that time brings also helped him find his way back to Chris. Johnny had heard a female quartet called Rhubarb Pie, who'd done a record full of Storyhill covers, and thought, 'Hey, we weren't bad.' He recalls, "So, I got to hear somebody else's interpretation of our music, and it was really inspiring. It was like hearing our music for the first time. Hearing what it means to other people—or what they hear in it—is important. It was kind of a revelation, like, 'Wow, I can understand why people want to hear Chris and I play together.'" Then again at the first reunion shows he was touched by the impact he and Chris's songs had had on these fans who were so eager and thankful to see them together again.

By the end of "Honesty," Chris seems convinced he's doing the right thing: "And I'm so tired of resisting/Holding back for fear of what might be missing/And these old fencepost limits/They were put in by me, who's to argue if I should take them out?" As Dave Weeks put it, the second time around it was their choice to go back. "I don't know that they felt it was a choice beforehand. I mean, of course it was, but then it grew and it was like, 'I don't know if I have the choice of stopping this.'"

Now, the plan was for Storyhill to be one of the things on their plate, instead of being the plate itself.

* * *

In January of 2002, Pharrell Williams and Chad Hugo signed a deal with Arista to house their new imprint, Star Trak. The first artist signed to the roster was the rap duo Clipse. The second was Spymob, a deal worth $400,000 to the guys. Plans to release an album went into motion, but the first priority was N.E.R.D. *In Search Of...* was released on March 12, 2002. Because of Pharrell and Chad's growing profile (songs they'd done with Nelly, Usher, No Doubt, Britney Spears, and N*SYNC had all become TRL staples on MTV) and the unusual circumstances behind the album (the fact that the original version had been shelved and rerecorded), there was a lot of media attention. The general consensus in print reviews was that the album was better off for Spymob's presence.

David Browne, writing for *Entertainment Weekly*, said the album has "a crackling vigor missing from the first stab." The *Onion A.V. Club* asserted that "the American version of *In Search Of...* sounds dynamic and alive in a way that would be nearly impossible to imagine without live instrumentation." And *Rolling Stone*'s Barry Walters wrote: "Now played live, those rhythms rattle with even greater complexity and resemble the truly old-school breaks that the original hip-hop DJs cut up decades ago. Credit has got to go to Christian Twigg and Eric Fawcett for supplying *Search* with dexterous, downright joyful bass and drums." Only *Pitchfork*, living up to its cantakarous reputation, wasn't impressed, describing Spymob's contributions as "the despicable addition of rap-metal drumming and distorted guitar posturing."

Listening to the final and original versions of *In Search Of...* back to back reveals Spymobby touches everywhere, from Brent's guitar solo on the outro of "Truth or Dare" to John's distinctive backing vocals on "Am I High" to the loungey, '70s style vibe of "Run to the Sun."

Fawcett, Ostby, Brent, and Twigg were swept up in major label promotion and touring. They shot a Randy Quaid-starring video for the song "Rock Star," in which all of the Spymob guys can be seen rocking out as the band takes over a high school basketball game. On March 20 they appeared on *The Late Show with David Letterman*. Ten days later, they kicked off a summer tour in New York. In June they did a hometown show at the Quest (formerly Prince's club Glam Slam), and then hit the Pacific Northwest and two stops in California. Spymob opened all of these shows with their own sets. From there they did appearances on *Late Night with Conan O'Brien* and *Last Call with Carson Daly*. For the band, these TV appearances with their audiences of millions were nerve-wracking to say the least. For Eric at least, it got easier after the first one: "You do it once and you realize there's life afterwards."

Strange as it sounds, Spymob were the veteran performers despite being the unfamous ones. Pharrell had done most of his music making in the studio, Shay was a rookie, and Chad rarely toured. Fawcett, Ostby, Brent, and Twigg, in contrast, had over a decade of performing experience. Shay said at the time, "The three of us have no idea what we're doing on stage, because we haven't performed much, but those guys are total professionals." The reviews noticed their steadying presence. An MTV.com write up of their Philadelphia show at the Trocodero noted, "Spymob aptly backed all of N.E.R.D.'s musical excursions, pounding a funky rhythmic base on 'Stay Together,' providing a soulful folkie shading on 'Bobby James' and finally rocking the house on the band's hit 'Rock Star.'"

In July they performed in London, Paris, Amsterdam, and opened for David Bowie at a show in Nimes, France. The venue was the Arenas de Nimes, a centuries old Roman amphitheater. Bowie was on tour supporting his album *Heathen*, and took time to meet with the guys before the show. Fawcett says, "It was just incredible. He was just such a sweet, sweet man. His people were very protective, so we didn't get much time, but I just love that there's a photo of him looking at me and smiling."

From there they took a month break before joining up with the Warped Tour for a couple of dates and then on to the Sprite Liquid Mix Tour which featured Talib Qweli, 311, and, most notably, Jay-Z, who would occasionally join N.E.R.D. on stage. Celebrity encounters like this and the one with Bowie were becoming commonplace for the guys. They found themselves in the company of megastars like P. Diddy, Kobe Bryant, and Beyoncé. At a concert in Central Park, Busta Rhymes came out as a special guest, and

Eric remembers the comical image of him crouching behind the drumset waiting to make his surprise appearance.

Janet Jackson attended their show in London, and Fawcett's first glimpse of her was from behind. "I knew it was her because of her booty," he reports. Justin Timberlake was around a lot, too, and Eric even gave drum lessons to the soon-to-be solo star. They were in the middle of a lesson when *People Magazine* called Justin to ask about his very recent break-up with Britney Spears. It was all a bit surreal for a band that just a year before had almost zero prospects. As a *City Pages* profile put it, "They are enjoying the trappings of stardom without being stars."

With the Sprite tour, N.E.R.D. traveled all over the country, playing in nearly 20 cities in nearly every part of the United States well into September. Their audiences were young, diverse, and enthusiastic. In another profile-raising instance,"Stand Up and Win" played over the end credits of the Ryan Reynolds-starring film *National Lampoon's Van Wilder*.When Spymob got back to Minneapolis, they found themselves nominated for Artist of the Year at the Minnesota Music Awards. They didn't win, but performed at the ceremony, held at the ballroom at the then two-year-old Xcel Energy Center, and saw Alex win his second consecutive award for Producer of the Year (Vicious Vicious was nominated for Best New Artist that year, but lost to Iffy).

At first there was hope that a Spymob CD would come out in the fall of 2002, but that quickly proved unrealistic. The guys didn't plan on doing any new recording, but instead put together a sort of "best of" package with tunes drawn from the *Spymob* EP, *On Pilot Mountain*, and *Basement Tapes*. The result was retitled *Sitting Around Keeping Score*, and was set for a July 22, 2003, release on Star Trak/Arista.

Pharrell Williams (left) and Eric Fawcett in Paris in 2002, early in Spymob's tenure backing N.E.R.D. Courtesy Eric Fawcett.

The guys did photo shoots, supervised the creation of the album art, and started doing interviews. In March, they did a couple of rare hometown shows and then headed to South By Southwest. Ahead of their appearance both the *Austin Chronicle* and *Dallas News* singled them out as a group to go see during the event. They played an Arista-sponsored party at Maggie Mae's on 6th Street, where Pharrell was forced to play hype-man when the party-goers wouldn't leave the upstairs patio to go downstairs and see Spymob. "It's going to be a good show," he assured them from a hijacked microphone. Spymob also did a public show at the Iron Cactus. In an interview with MTV2, indie rock queen Liz Phair said Spymob was one of the best acts she'd seen at SXSW.

N.E.R.D. opened for David Bowie in Nimes, France, in 2002, and Spymob got to meet the man himself before the show. From left to right: David Bowie, Eric Fawcett, Brent Paschke, John Ostby. Courtesy Eric Fawcett.

From there it was on to Coachella, the annual two-day festival in southern California. N.E.R.D. played the same stage as headliners the Beastie Boys, and Spymob did a 6-song opening set before their biggest-ever audience of 8,000 people. Going forward, the guys had agreed to once again join the Sprite Liquid Mix Tour with N.E.R.D in August and September, this time with Alex Oana along to help do live mixing. *In Search Of...* still had legs, even more than a year past its release. The album had been nominated for the annual Shortlist Prize for Artistic Achievement in Music (which it would win that October), and was rapidly approaching the 500,000 sales mark, giving it Gold certification. The idea was to hitch Spymob to that star as they promoted *Sitting Around Keeping Score*, so the band would get its own set on the "B" stage of the tour.

The guys traveled to North Carolina for a couple of days to shoot a video for "Walking Under Green Leaves" with Van Neistat (one half of the filmmaking Neistat Brothers, who had their own self-titled HBO show in 2010). The video featured the band converting a pickup truck into a traveling stage, replete with fireworks and their name emblazoned in lights. It opens with the hand-drawn plans, shifts to shots of Ostby, Twigg, Brent, and Fawcett building the stage and rigging the lights, etc., and then performing a nighttime traveling concert on in the stage/bed. The guys did all the construction themselves, and the fireworks were real. So real, Fawcett reports, that the county fire marshall supervised the whole process.

As of early summer, promotional copies of the album were being circulated, and major magazines were giving the band space. Lead single "It Gets Me Going" (which had been released as a promo single) got write-ups in both *Entertainment Weekly* and on *MTV.com*. Jon Caramanica gave the album a B+ in *Spin* ("breezy, spacey, ornately orchestrated soft rock, redolent of late-summer laziness"), *Blender* gave it 3 out of 4 stars ("worthy descendants of disgraced late-'70s chart-toppers like Hall and Oates, Toto and the Doobie Brothers"), and GQ put a nearly-full page profile of the band in its August 2003

Eric Fawcett behind Paul Shaffer's keyboard during an appearance on The Late Show with David Letterman in August 2003. Courtesy Eric Fawcett.

issue ("Modern rock power-pop meets old-school blue-eyed soul," was how they described the band). It was all that an unknown group could ask for from the music press.

Then, at the last minute, Arista boss L.A. Reid made the baffling decision not to release *Sitting Around Keeping Score*. No clear reason was ever provided, but whether Reid personally didn't like the band's music or just thought it wouldn't sell, the end result was that Spymob were left in the lurch. They weren't dropped from Star Trak, but they had no parent label to put out their record and thus no way to capitalize on the momentum they'd been building. At this point, everyone in the band was wondering if they were under some sort of ancient curse

There were two bright spots. One was that Reid, perhaps feeling some modicum of guilt and/or basic decency, let the band have their album back. The other was that Spymob had a song on a Star Trak sampler, *Clones*, which was released in mid–August to brisk sales. The song was "Half Steering Half Eating Ice Cream," which had been on the original EP, but had missed the cut for *Sitting Around Keeping Score*. Spymob still had the support and faith of Pharrell, they just needed a label to make the third time the charm.

But what were the chances? At the time, writers for both the *Star Tribune* and *City Pages* openly wondered about Spymob's commercial appeal. Record sales in general were down 10 percent in the ongoing bloodbath of the record industry's stubborn refusal to accept digital formats, and even more-established local artists like Dan Wilson, Shannon Curfman, and Soul Asylum were searching fruitlessly for label deals. And Spymob's association with N.E.R.D., while beneficial on the balance, had its pitfalls. Because Spymob's music was so different from Pharrell and Chad's, fans of the latter were not likely to be fans of the former, and vice versa. This catch-22 was captured in *The Herald Scotland*'s review of a November show in Edinburgh Record: "Most notable are [N.E.R.D.'s] backing musicians, Spymob. Their own support set fails to register, but when they leave centre stage, they are able to produce the kind of grooves that are worthy of Funkadelic, The Revolution, or Cameo at their peak."

Ironically, the band weren't even still writing songs like the ones on *Sitting Around Keeping Score*. At this point, most of those tunes were three years old, and John's writing had gone completely in the direction of county and folk. The band were left trying to get a deal for and promote an album that didn't even accurately represent them. For Ostby, that was one of the most difficult parts of the whole experience. He says, "We kept trying to sell this thing that wasn't even what we currently were. It's kind of like if someone was really into a snapshot of you that was taken in the past, and you kept trying to make your appearance look like what you looked like five years ago, and kept trying to get your haircut in the exact same way, kept wearing the same clothes, smile the same way, you know."

Pharrell and Chad's prospects continued to rise as Spymob's stagnated. Pharrell's debut single "Frontin,'" which was featured on *Clones*, became a top ten hit, Clipse's album got a ton of critical praise, and Kelis's new song "Milkshake" was on its way to becoming a chart smash. The duo had also decided to make the next N.E.R.D. album on their own, still using live instruments but playing them themselves.

Spymob headed back home that early winter to regroup. They made the decision to start selling *Sitting Around Keeping Score* through their website. "There's been a demand for this record for well over a year," Fawcett told the *Star Tribune*. "We feel like we can't make people wait any longer." Meanwhile, they started working the proverbial phones, hoping for another miracle.

* * *

The release of *Dovetail* in late 2002 kickstarted Storyhill back into touring. Chris and John started with a Midwest jaunt in March and April of 2003, followed by shows in Saint Paul and Bozeman that summer, and another string of gigs in the Midwest and Montana in November and December. In between, Johnny kept up with his usual slate of projects. In late 2002 he and Fawcett had produced a set of songs for jMatt Keil's band Hi-Test, and the result was an EP called *World Class Loser*. Johnny also produced a new CD for Chris's old touring partner, Justin Roth. The record, *Shine*, features Eric on drums and Storyhill offering harmonies on "The Only Life" and "Pull." At the time, Justin said that working with Johnny and the musicians on the record resulted in "the most spontaneous, creative and fun process I've ever had in the studio."

Johnny also worked with Brenda Weiler at CityCabin on her new CD. Weiler had left Minneapolis for Portland, Oregon, but the record she made was clearly a product of the Twin Cities, starting with its title, *Cold Weather*. Brenda co-produced the record with Johnny, Darren, and Alex. Darren claimed at the time that rather than being too many cooks in the kitchen, the close relationship between the four fostered a lot of creative brainstorming. In addition to producing, both Johnny and Darren sang and played various instruments on the album. Appelwick came in to play bass and lap steel, and Fawcett played drums, marking the first time all four had appeared on record together.

The production and performance on *Cold Weather* takes Brenda's uneasy folk tunes and gives them a haunting, sonically-rich setting, what a review in *The Orgonian* called "cinematic moodiness." A couple of tunes—"Scatter" and "California"—stretch Brenda into indie rock territory. Darren sings with Brenda on his song "Honolulu, Minnesota" a duet with each singer expressing a contrasting point of view. Like a relaxed update of Johnny Cash and June Carter Cash's "Jackson," each singer is trying to convince the other to come to where they are (the two locations in the title) but it ends with no resolution, leading the listener to conclude that neither one ended up budging.

Finally, there was Alva Star. Johnny had revived the band in the summer of 2002 for a string of shows, including an every-Thursday residency at the 400 Bar in the month of June. Christopher McGuire was back on drums for some of these gigs, and Fawcett filled in on others when he was available. A third drummer, Ian Prince, also played with them sometimes. Around this time Johnny dropped a couple of mentions in the press about working on a new Alva Star record. They'd been using Friends Like These's studio space in Lowertown Saint Paul to do some recording, but so far there was nothing close to finished. Rather than bringing in songs he'd already written, Johnny was trying improvisational writing, using a loose musical framework and then making up lyrics on the spot.

Alva Star did travel to Chicago, however, to rerecord "Unhappily Yours" for a compilation of unsigned bands sponsored by Marlboro/Phillip Morris. It's unclear how sharing new music with their customers benefited the cigarette company, but for the bands it offered good money and exposure. The new version of "Unhappily Yours" is arguably better than the *Alligators in the Lobby* version, with the vocals (both lead and harmonies) more prominent, some fun new guitar interplay, and cool backing "hoo-hoo-hoo"s on the outro. Johnny had also collaborated with Appelwick to create a groovy cover of the Styx song "Lady" for a tribute CD called *Too Much Time On Our Hands* and they released it under the Alva Star name.

*   *   *

Kid Dakota weren't quite as active as a live band in the beginning of 2003 as they had been in late 2002, with recording taking precedent. In addition to ongoing work on the new album, they also recorded some songs for various compilations, including covers of tunes by Low ("Lullaby") and Madonna (a grinding "Into the Groove"). Additionally, both Kid Dakota and Vicious Vicious would land spots on *Stuck on AM 4*, a collection of live performances from Radio K.

The big Kid Dakota event of 2003, though, was their first major tour. In September and October, they hit the road opening for the Black Eyed Snakes, Alan Sparhawk's blues side project. The tour wound through 14 cities, including Chicago, New York, Philadelphia, Boston, Atlanta, Memphis, and Boston. For these shows, the band went back to its original form, just Christopher and Darren. A video interview early in the tour done by Brainwashed showcases their odd chemistry both onstage and off. Near the end of the interview, after taking the questions seriously for the most part, they start in on a strange inside joke that involves speaking in high-pitched voices and calling one another "lover." "Have you prepared the flesh suit?" Christopher asks. Darren answers, "I have knitted the flesh suit from seven Olympic hopefuls, lover." They end the exchange with a peck on the lips and a collapse into laughter.

Appelwick had been left at home, but wasn't at a loss for things to do. He played bass and other assorted instruments on a record Alex was producing and recording at Citycabin, Josh Aran's *Between Us There Arose Happiness*. During the summer of 2003 he began working with Caitlyn Smith, a 17-year-old Cannon Falls native, on her second album. He played various instruments on all but one of the songs (he's listed as "pretty much the one man band" in the liner notes on one of the songs), and co-wrote a farewell tune called "September." With hindsight, the groovy, funky intro is indication that Appelwick had developed the signature sound he'd be debuting more fully on the next Vicious Vicious record. (Smith is now a sought-after Nashville songwriter, having penned tunes for Megan Trainor, John Legend, Dolly Parton, and Garth Brooks; in January 2018 she released an album called *Starfire*, featuring the song "Saint Paul," a warm reminisence of her time spent in the city.)

Appelwick had also secured a deal with a tiny Florida record label called Twenty Seven Records to re-release *Blood and Clover* nationally in September. Vicious Vicious played a few shows here and there, but he didn't really tour to support the rerelease. The album did creep into the CMJ Top 200 for a handful of weeks, peaking at #108, but that was the extent of the national splash it made. Appelwick, as usual, was busy looking forward. He was writing new material for Vicious Vicious and working with Darren on revving up Camaro once again.

Darren had gotten a ProTools digital workstation, imported their original 8-track recordings, adding overdubs in the broom closet of his third floor attic apartment on Portland Avenue in South Minneapolis (the "studio" was so small, the lanky Erik had to duck to fit inside; they started referring to it as Shortman Studio). When Appelwick heard what Darren had done with the tracks he was ecstatic. He had basically left those songs for dead, but the pop sheen Darren had added through the miracle of unlimited tracks revived the tunes.

Erik ahold of a Juno 60 keyboard and added a bunch of keyboard parts. They also added in their beloved xylophone on several songs (Darren says that he and Appelwick made a pact to include the instrument on every record they were involved in). As they were working with the tracks, they built off Peter's drum parts. Appelwick recalls: "Peter really was amazing. He went off on some tangents on a couple songs that forced me to make some things more interesting, speaking of 'Motobike' in particular. That whole breakdown that happens there wasn't really like that at all when we played it before and what he did forced me to come up with all this other guitar stuff and made it a lot more compelling. His feel on 'Let's Go' was incredible. It pretty much made the song."

While working on the new versions of the songs, they did a couple more gigs with Camaro as a trio that spring and summer. One of them was the "Saint Olaf Post Campus Band Jam" at the 400 Bar, which had been organized by jMatt and featured eight Ole groups including Camaro, Hi-Test, Kid Dakota, and Johnny guesting on guitar with jMatt's newest group Kubla Khan. It was to be jMatt's last show with Camaro. Not long after, jMatt noticed Camaro on a concert calendar. "So I called Darren and was like 'Is Camaro playing a show?' And he was like, 'Yeah, this guy Sailor is going to play drums.'" And with that, jMatt was out of the band.

Instead of self-releasing the Camaro tunes, Appelwick and Darren began seeking out potential labels. They'd become aware of 2024 Records, a small local label that was just getting its start. Darren likely knew of them because Alex was recording with one of their artists, Romantica, an Americana group led by singer-songwriter Ben Kyle. 2024, started by friends Nate Roise and Todd Hansen, had been born of necessity. Hansen's band Standbye had recorded an album at Seedy Underbelly, but rather than seek out a label to release it, Todd instead decided to team with Nate and start their own.

Todd and Nate had met while attending Bethel College in the suburb Arden Hills, connecting over the fact that they were both drummers. Nate was a Mankato native that—like Matt O'Laughlin—was taken by the town's punk scene, first as a fan and then as a participant, drumming and/or singing in bands such as Align and Seconds Before. By the early 2000s he was working as a realtor. The housing market was strong, so Nate was able to put up the capital to get the label going. He did some deep research on the record industry and put what he'd learned into action to release Standbye's album *The Coping Mechanisms*. Standbye broke up, but 2024 next signed Fitzgerald, a folky duo comprised of married couple Nate and Mandy Tensen-Woolery. Romantica—Ben Kyle was one of their Bethel classmates—signed on soon after.

Through Alex, Darren and Appelwick both played on some of the songs on Romantica's debut, *It's Your Weakness that I Want*. They were impressed with the way 2024 were supporting the band, and with the roster of artists the label was assembling. To Darren, it was the fulfillment of a need. In a 2002 *Star Tribune* article about improving the Twin Cities music scene, Darren had said: "Seattle has their Barsuk and Sub-Pop. Chicago has Touch & Go, Drag City and Kranky. Even Omaha has Saddle Creek. Why doesn't Minneapolis have a label of this caliber?"

Nate, meanwhile, was a huge Kid Dakota fan, so a mutual admiration society was formed and the two set up a meeting to discuss the possibility of Camaro joining the label. In January 2004, Darren invited Nate over to his apartment and played the label owner a few of the Camaro tracks, singing along live to the ones they hadn't quite finished yet. Nate loved what he heard. Before long Darren and Appelwick had a deal with 2024 to put out not just the first batch of Camaro songs, but a follow-up album as well. One catch, however, was the name. Everyone was worried about getting sued by Chevrolet, so the search began for a new moniker. They briefly considered calling themselves Bows & Arrows, but then Darren had an inspiration. He was telling the guys about a friend who had a shot at making the Olympics in cross-country skiing. "And lights went off, buzzers, flashers. That was it." That's how they became Olympic Hopefuls.

9

A Holiday Until Tomorrow

In which Spymob's album is finally released and the band formerly known as Camaro takes over the Twin Cities.

Now that they had a deal to relase them, Darren and Appelwick needed to put the final touches on the songs. They recorded new vocals for the in the apartment's kitchen, which was so tiny that when Erik started rocking out during a vocal take of "Pretty Bigmouth" he knocked a plate off the dish rack (you can hear it shatter at approximately the 1:15 mark). They brought in their girlfriends, Erin Anderson and Genevive Christianson, to participate as well. Erin, a *Pulse of the Twin Cities* music writer and Saint Olaf grad who was dating Darren, played accordion and sang on "Trust Fund Junkie" while Genevive did the "it was once upon a time" line on "Let's Go."

2024 requested a 10-song album, so the guys needed one more track. Darren dusted off a tune called "Stoned Again" that dated back to his first stint living in Minneapolis, and he and Appelwick set up a recording session at CityCabin. Peter Anderson was too busy with his multiple commitments (he'd joined Kraig Johnson and the Program, was still playing with Iffy, and was also active again with Polara, who had recently come off hiatus), so instead they brought in Ian Prince to play drums on the track. Ian was a Michigan native who had moved to the Twin Cities halfway through his senior year so he could join his older brother Adam's band, Bump. The guys' father was a drummer who'd played in a "hard-hitting, MC-5 like band" when he was younger. He'd filled the house with rock music and the boys picked up instruments at a young age (both started on drums; Adam moved on to guitar and bass). They formed a hard rock cover band—Arson—when Ian was just 11 years old.

When Bump broke up Ian moved on to an "indie metal" power trio called Houston. In 2002, Houston did a show with Kid Dakota at the 400 Bar, and Ian became an instant fan: "I was completely floored by [Kid Dakota]. I really did fall in love with it right from the start."

In November of 2003, not long after Kid Dakota's tour with the Black Eyed Snakes, Christopher McGuire got an offer to join the Japanese indie rock band Quruli full time. Darren was down a drummer and began casting about for a replacement, with little success. A friend—Judd Hildreth, the drummer for a soon-to-be-2024 artist Valet—suggested Darren talk to Ian. So Ian went over to CityCabin, they began playing, and the musical chemistry was instant. Ian wasn't looking to leave Houston, but Kid Dakota was the one band that would tempt him. He began filling in at Kid Dakota gigs when and where he could. Through Darren, Ian began doing some Alva Star shows as well, and played on the new recording of "Unhappily Yours."

Ian recalls the "Stoned Again" session as being fun and collaborative. They recorded most of the track live, with he and Appelwick working out the construction and feel of the drums and bass within the song structure Darren had provided.

With ten songs recorded and the album finished, the next step was to put together a band. It was a stipulation of the deal with 2024 that Olympic Hopefuls be more than just a recording project, but also a group that performed live. Darren and Appelwick's first recruit was a familiar face from their home state. Erik had known bassist Heath Henjum since his days in the with the Harvesters (you may recall that Heath was in Violet, and that the two bands often performed together). Heath had left Sioux Falls in 1996 to head to Minneapolis, following a girl and better job opportunities in his chosen field of computer science. Not long after arriving in town he joined the Sycamores, a rootsy group in the same vein as Violet. Not to be typecast (Heath liked all kinds of music, and one of his heroes on the bass was Bruce Thomas of the Attractions), he started to venture into different territory with the Beatifics, a power pop group led by singer-songwriter Chris Dorn. Their 1996 album on Twin/Tone, *How I Learned to Stop Worrying*, had made a bit of a national splash, but the band had fractured after the album's release, and bassist Jacques Wait quit. Heath took his place. When Vicious Vicious opened a show for the Beatifics at the Dinketowner in 2002, Appelwick and Heath reconnected. Not long after, Appelwick drafted Heath into Vicious Vicious.

So it was a natural progression to playing bass for Olympic Hopefuls. Heath agreed, and before he knew it found himself in the midst of a photo shoot with Darren, Erik, and Peter Anderson. The four posed for what was intended to be a set of promo shots, but it was premature. Though he had played on most of the songs, Peter wasn't going to be in the group. Heath *was* going to be in the band, but hadn't played on the album, and hadn't even heard the final versions of the songs yet. After about a half hour on the couch, Peter recalls Appelwick saying, "'So we had this idea.'" Erik then reached into a plastic back and pulled out a red, white, and orange tracksuit. Peter's response? "That's funny. No way. I don't think that's a good ... gaaaahh.... I don't think I'm going to do that."

The tracksuit idea had come from Kii Arens, who the band had hired to design the CD artwork. Kii had formerly been a member of the Twin Cities cartoon glam-rock band Flipp, but with that group on hiatus had transitioned into full-time graphic design (he'd done the main logo for the ill-fated Woodstock '94). "I loved the band name," Kii says of Olympic Hopefuls, and doing promo shots in tracksuits was a natural extension. This was both a marketing idea and an expression of Kii's own sensibilities; Flipp were well known for their ostentatious outfits and accessories, as well as the KISS-inspired black and white face make-up occasionally worn by lead singer (and Kii's brother) Brynn.

But before any promo photos could be taken, the Olympic Hopefuls' line-up needed to be solidified. After a Vicious Vicious rehearsal one Tuesday, Appelwick and Heath headed over to the Triple Rock Social Club, a Dinkytown bar/restaurant/venue that featured two-for-one drinks on Tuesday nights. They ran into Friends Like These's Matt O'Laughlin, and as the three were talking, Appelwick offhandedly invited him to play drums for Vicious Vicious. Before Matt could even respond, Erik quickly changed course, "Or, you know what, maybe you should play drums for Olympic Hopefuls." Friends Like These, after a promising start, were not making money, and John Solomon had fallen hard into drug use, so Matt jumped at the new opportunity, and the chance to play with Erik. He didn't have an audition; Appelwick nonchalantly presented it to Matt as the band would do a show for the CD release party and then see where it went from there.

9. A Holiday Until Tomorrow

This ill-fated first Olympic Hopefuls photo shoot featured Peter Anderson but no Johnny, Matt, or tracksuits. From left to right: Erik Appelwick, Heath Henjum, Darren Jackson, Peter Anderson. Courtesy Nate Roise.

With Matt in place, the band was nearly set. But there was one more addition to come. Johnny had heard the record and knew Darren and Appelwick were putting a band together. He wanted in. The three had set a meeting with Nate Roise about the possibility of Alva Star putting out their upcoming second album on 2024, and Johnny asked that Darren and Appelwick arrive early so they could talk about the Olympic Hopefuls.

He said, "You guys, this record is going to do really well, and I want to be a part of it." He offered to play bass, not knowing they already had Heath in place. Both Appelwick and Darren were surprised at Johnny's interest, given all of his other commitments, but they weren't about to pass up having a musician of his caliber in the band. They offered him the opportunity to play keyboards instead. Johnny could play keyboard but he didn't really want to, so he decided to mull it over before giving an answer. He took the Olympic Hopefuls record with him on a Storyhill tour out west, and the more he listened, the more found his desire to be in the band outweighed his animus against being a keyboard player. He started to learn the key parts by listening to the album nonstop. Back in the Twin Cities, he told Darren and Appelwick he'd give it a try. And so the five-man group was in place. The group began rehearsing while the tracks went on to be mixed by Alex and then mastered.

Kii went to a trophy place down the street from his old apartment in the Saint Anthony Main area, and took the photos that ended up adorning the CD booklet, back cover, and inlay. As for the band portraits, which were shot in Kii's apartment, they wore red, orange, and white Puma tracksuits. Many of the photos found the band basking in the afterglow of a hard-fought competition: "Their approach to pretending they won the awards was pretty lifelike," Kii recalls wryly. Darren liked the look of the photos so much, he suggested they wear the suits at their first show. Johnny's reaction? "Aw, shit."

They called the album *The Fuses Refuse to Burn*, after a line in the song "Holiday." Listening to the full album in contrast to what had come before is striking. In the creative process there is always the danger of overworking something, of losing what was great about the first attempt to realize an idea, like a pencil sketch that has more life and movement than a finished painting. But there are other times where the extra time, thought, and labor produces something that far surpasses that first attempt. With the *Fuses* songs, it's clearly the latter. The Camaro takes of these songs have a raw, DIY charm, but Olympic Hopefuls weren't intended as an upstart indie band. They were a pop rock group, and the studio versions of their songs needed to be more ELO than the Eels.

Fittingly, the songs are filled with "yeah, yeah, yeah'"s and "la-la la-la la-la'"s and handclaps and sing/shout along moments like "You never thought that I was good enough!" on "Whisper." Peter's drums, especially on "Holiday" and "Shy," are epic. Appelwick and Darren more than fulfilled their goal of maximizing the xylophone usage. In an interview with *Pulse of the Twin Cities'* Rob Van Alstyne, the guys joked that they actually had to strip the xylophone off of some songs because it was just too much. "Erik took the xylophone away from me after awhile. He was like, 'I'm sorry Darren—you've abused your privileges.'"

With the addition of "Stoned Again" the album was divided neatly between Appelwick's and Darren's songs. This, combined with the fact that the guys didn't write together, created a situation where they both had to bring their "A" game. Ian Prince observed: "One thing that was important in making that first record as good as it was, was that there was some serious but friendly competition between Darren and Appelwick. I think they were both trying to rise to each other's levels, and it worked really well."

Though they didn't compose together, each of the guys' songs are stronger for the other's presence. Appelwick's guitar solo buoys up "Drain the Sea." Darren's distinctive guitar tone is a big part of "Imaginary" and "Shy" and his background vocals are all over Erik's songs. *Sponic Zine*, in their review of the album, pointed out just how complementary their vocals were, writing, "Really,

Promotional poster shot and designed by Kii Arens. Clockwise from lower left: Darren Jackson, Heath Henjum, Erik Appelwick, Matt O'Laughlin, John Hermanson. Courtesy Nate Roise.

though, these guys could be brothers, as they both have the same restrained discipline to their high-register crooning." The closest we get to some Lennon and McCartney sort of yin yang interplay is on "Let's Go" where Appelwick leads by telling us that "everything will be alright" and Darren follows not long after with "until the pills wear off." Whether it was down to complementary talents and sensibilities, or whether it developed through the sheer amount of time they spent together in various bands, the two had an undeniable musical chemistry.

Four of Appelwick's five songs are character pieces. Album opener "Imaginary" is a fine addition to the small-but-distinguished list of pop songs that feature narrators suffering from worrying mental health issues (See also: Rockwell's "Somebody's Watching Me," Talking Heads' "Psycho Killer," and Men At Work's "Who Can It Be Now?"). The imaginary in "Imaginary" is the narrator's girlfriend, and he seems vaguely aware that this isn't normal, but when she whispers in his ear ("Forget them dear and we'll disappear") his doubts are silenced.

The protagonist of the shimmering "Shy" just can't bring himself to approach the object of his admiration. "Motobike" is about a guy who likes to drive fast and tends to get in wrecks, despite the fact that it "breaks [his] girl's heart every time." "Pretty Bigmouth" takes the second person approach to address a woman with "a sense of style and a slightly upturned nose" who the narrator believes needs to "shut [her] mouth and listen" once in awhile. It walks right up to the line of misogyny, but everybody knows a person whose physical attractiveness has given them the false assumption that every thought they have is fascinating and must be uttered aloud.

Darren's songs can be read as documenting the stages of a romance, thanks largely to the fact that three of his five songs—"Holiday," "Whisper," and "Stoned Again" were about same relationship, the one with the girl who'd broken his heart in Providence (so were the Kid Dakota songs "Smokestack," "The Winter Without You," and "Crossin' Fingers," and a later OH song, "Idaho"). The romance starts in the energetic "Holiday," where the narrator gets wasted at an awkward party and misses out on something good: "I heard you tried to hit on me/such a pity I was too damn drunk to see." In "Drain the Sea," which Darren wrote during his Minnesota recovery stint in late 1999, the romance is in full bloom though not without turbulence: "I don't think your mother likes me/Your dad says my head is filled with rocks and sand."

That echoes in "Whisper," where the narrator is dating someone with very different background and sensibilities ("to you I was an experiment/let's try to make the bad boy better/see if he can eat organically/maybe wear a J. Crew sweater") and knows she's too embarrassed by him to fully commit. And that brings things to a conclusion in "Stoned Again" The two have parted not completely voluntarily (her lips quivered as they said goodbye on the driveway) and at first he's resolved to let her go completely. But by the song's powerful end he's done a 180 degree turn, vowing, "I'm gonna write you lots of love letters/and I'm gonna call you every day on the phone/and I'm gonna make you feel so much better/and I'm gonna make you regret you left me alone." A nearly psychedelic musical freakout ensues, with Darren repeating "All alone" over and over, undermining any message of hope.

An April 13 release date was backed by a robust marketing plan from 2024; the band had a website, interviews with local press, radio promotion with Vitriol, and hundreds of promo CDs sent to bloggers and college radio stations across the country. They were really going for it, but at the same time Darren and Appelwick weren't feeling overconfident. Johnny recalls "I told them the album was awesome, and they were just like, 'Pfeh, no it's not, it's a joke.'" Part of that may have been false modesty. Erik's approach was very much in line with how he had always faced putting his art into the world: "I tend to expect nothing and try to be gracious when good things happen." Darren was proud of the songs, but he and Appelwick were both the self-aware generation that couldn't do pure pop music without a bit of a wink and a nudge. In their minds, what they were doing in their other projects was artful and unique, whereas they viewed Olympic Hopefuls as uncomplicated and conventional.

Johnny had the right idea; the album hit the Twin Cities like a blizzard. First came the CD reviews. Molly Priesemeyer wrote in the *Pioneer Press* that the album was "a glorious, hook-filled, drunk-on-pleasure pop confection." The *Strib*'s Riemenschneider said, "Darren Jackson and Erik Appelwick managed to top their already well-liked individual acts with this charmed new group" and called the CD "clearly one of the must-hear local releases of the year." The burgeoning music blog world took notice as well, with the reactions typified by *Rift Magazine* assessment: "Olympic Hopefuls have a hit record on their hands, assuming they can get it in front of the right people."

The CD release show took place Saturday, April 10 at the 7th Street Entry. Pilot to Gunner, the Natural History, and Friends Like These (Matt pulled double duty) all served as warm-up acts. The show had been mentioned in *City Pages* as one of the "A List" events for the weekend, so the Entry was packed. The show went fantastically, though it started with what some might read as a bad omen: Heath recalls that as he was heading on stage he went to high five Vitriol Radio Promotions's Jesse Stensby and they both missed. The band wore their red, orange, and white Puma tracksuits and tore into the album's songs. Afterward, jMatt Keil approached Matt and said, "Great show, man. Good job."

"Thanks. It was fun. Those guys are fun to play with."

"Yeah," jMatt replied. "I had a lot of fun writing those drum parts."

For jMatt it was a complex mix of emotions to see the Olympic Hopefuls debut. Compared to years past, he had recently been busy with work and hadn't been following the day-to-day of what everyone was up to. He had heard the record and loved it, and was intrigued by the all-star quality of the live line-up. Seeing them that night, he says, "reengaged and reintrigued" him, though he was disappointed at the energy level from the audience during that first show. "The crowd didn't move, nothing happened, man. All that spirit and spunk that Camaro had, we played Carleton and everybody's dancing and going crazy." He didn't blame the band, but the audience's failure to match intensity and power of the songs left him wanting.

The Olympic Hopefuls didn't do more gigs right away. Johnny was already committed to a short tour with Storyhill from late April through mid–May, but while he was gone, *The Fuses Refuse to Burn* started climbing up the CMJ charts. It had debuted as the number four add on college radio the week of its release, just behind records by Modest Mouse, My Morning Jacket, and Bright Eyes (and ahead of Morrissey!), and after four weeks on the Top 200 chart had climbed to number 38. It would spend another six weeks beyond that on the chart, but never reached that high again. Heath found it to be both a major accomplishment and a bummer to get so near the top of the chart. "They always publish the CMJ top 20 in the back of *Rolling Stone*, and we didn't quite make it," he says. But he also notes also that most of the bands he's been in never even cracked the Top 200.

9. A Holiday Until Tomorrow 107

Olympic Hopefuls at Bar Lurcat, June 2004. This is the show where Eric Fawcett, Rob Stefaniak, and the author all first saw the band. From left to right: Erik Appelwick, Heath Henjum, Darren Jackson, John Hermanson. Courtesy Eric Fawcett.

And things were just getting started for the band. Once Johnny returned, they booked a slate of summer gigs, starting with a 2024 Records showcase at the Turf Club in Saint Paul, featuring Romantica, Valet, and another recent addition to the roster, a punk/ rap hybrid called the Plastic Constellations. These four showed off the diversity and quality of artists Nate and Todd had attracted to the label. The label was building itself a nice reputation, and they used the showcase as a fundraiser to purchase a red 2002 Dodge van for bands to take out on the road.

A review of OH's set that night on the now defunct website *How Was the Show* found writer Shawn Boyd won over a little more by each successive song the band played. "Laughing at the clever lines of 'Drain the Sea,' I turned to the other kids only to hear, 'We know: you like this song too.'" On the *Music Scene Network*, "rojicks" wrote of the show: "A keen pop sensibility, amazing vocal harmonies, and a presence on stage that made it obvious these guys are veterans of their craft. The Olympic Hopefuls have what it takes to deliver, and deliver on a very large level. I expect to hear nothing but bigger and better things coming from them in the upcoming months."

I'm guessing that he or she wasn't disappointed. As the gigs piled up over the summer of 2004, the accolades followed. When they played Peavey Plaza in downtown Minneapolis that July as part of the Marshall Field's Day of Music, long time *Star Tribune* music writer Jon Bream called OH "the Twin Cities' most promising and best pop band in ages." Bream had been intimately involved in the Minneapolis scene since 1974, and wasn't in the habit of tossing off hyperbole. Similarly, Jim Walsh wrote in *City Pages* about seeing that same show: "It was late, so my wife took the kids home. I stuck around for the rest of the night/morning, which was highlighted by a ridiculously buoyant set from Olympic

Hopefuls that, by its end, inspired street people, survivors of the old Duffy's scene, and indie rockers to waltz under the stars. It was as memorable a local music moment as I've ever witnessed."

This was coming from someone who had attended literally hundreds of local shows, including covering Prince's late night jams at Paisley Park throughout the 1990s. Chris Riemenschneider wrote around the same time that OH had "become a better band on stage even than on their well-received debut CD." He also pointed out that the band was threatening to overshadow Appelwick and Darren's solo projects.

Neither man intended for that to happen, but at the same time they were getting more attention and bigger crowds than they'd ever gotten before. They were also making more money than they ever had, and that especially made OH difficult to ignore. The guys in the band (Johnny notwithstanding) were flabbergasted by the intensity of the reaction, but their fellow musicians and contemporaries weren't, as typified by Ian's observations: "I wasn't surprised by it; it was a fun band and they were all really catchy songs; who doesn't love a good pop song? They were clever with the tracksuits; it was kind of like a party; they were clearly having fun and people gravitate towards that."

Sean McPhereson, bassist for the hip hop band Heiruspecs, went to OH shows too, but for a slightly different reason. He wrote in the *Pioneer Press*: "For a while in 2003 [sic] and 2004, the Olympic Hopefuls could fill the Uptown bar twice a month with late 20-somethings with real money who were outrageously good-looking. It was like an Edina High School reunion with extra tattoos and alcohol. So, I would make my way down there with the one button-down shirt I owned and try to tell the girls with the least hairspray that I played bass in Heiruspecs—and could I buy them a drink? It was just the youngish generation of Twin Cities music hitting their peak, playing great and making guys like me real jealous."

But Appelwick and Darren especially were baffled and a bit dismayed that something so transparently calculated, the pop hooks, the band uniforms, had connected so thoroughly. In an October *Star Tribune* article, Darren said, "Olympic Hopefuls make music for teenage girls," a comment he now says he regrets, and meant hyperbolically. They *did* make music for teenage girls, but also for everyone else. As Jim Walsh had described, their appeal was crazy-broad: The frat guys loved them, the punk girls loved them, the music geeks and indie kids and hipsters loved them, and so did the people who saw live music once or twice a year, or who normally went to a show and talked obnoxiously through the whole thing. Lindsey Thomas described an OH audience in *City Pages*: "There's the expected crowd of baby T-shirted young women who know all the words, but the glow of the stage lights also reveals a shuffling man in his sixties, a thuggish-looking guy in a wifebeater hopping from foot to foot, and a male poplocker sporting enough jelly bracelets to be a very fashionable seven-year-old girl circa 1985."

It's an understatement to say that Minnesota is not known for its demonstrative concert crowds. Matt Olson, the singer for Twin Cities band Smattering, said "most people [in Minnesota] are a little self-conscious, a little uncomfortable, wanting to be cool and progressive, but also stuck in this conservative anxiety." Nate Roise says OH broke through the typical disinterested, too cool shoegazer Minnesota crowd, "They were just so much fun to watch, and [it was] almost more fun to watch the crowd, because I haven't seen that level of enthusiasm." Likewise Chris Riemenschneider says, "This was still the era when indie rock bands weren't fun. The poppy peppy thing wasn't that cool in the late '90 and early '00s. It was a welcome contrast to that."

With the increased activity, the band decided to take on a manager. Rob Stefaniak was a Twin Cities native who'd just finished a MBA with a specialty in music industries at the University of Liverpool. He'd returned to his hometown to look for clients to start an artist management business. When he heard about the Olympic Hopefuls he was intrigued and decided to go see them at a June gig at Bar Lurcat in the Loring Park area of Minneapolis. He was impressed: "I thought they were destined for rock and roll glory, and that I had discovered lightning in a bottle," he recalls. "They had everything I was searching for ... the look, the sound, and the story ... they were an absolute spectacle to behold."

Manager Rob Stefaniak came up with the idea for the "I'm Hopeful" ringer shirts that helped build a sense of community around the band. Photo by Stacy Schwartz.

He set up a meeting with Darren and Appelwick at Sushi Tango in Uptown the following week, and outlined what he could do for them as a manager. They eventually agreed, on a handshake, to work together. Rob's initial vision was to help create a fan rapport and grassroots devotion to the band through accessibility and branding. He facilitated the recording and distribution of live shows, taken directly from the soundboard. He also came up with the idea for ringer t-shirts that said "I'm Hopeful," and hired a young illustrator named Adam Turman to produce concert flyers and posters with a uniform aesthetic (Turman has since gone on to become what the Star Tribune called "the state's most visible artist" with his prints, logos, posters, and murals adorning walls all over Minnesota and beyond). Rob often travelled with the band to out-of-town gigs in order to help out with anything that he could. As things accelerated at home, it was his job to help figure how to move the group to the next level.

With more shows came the need for more songs. Appelwick repurposed a couple of Vicious Vicious tracks—"Book of Love" and "Cavalier" for live performances. "Cavalier" ended up being the Olympic Hopefuls second appearance on CD, showing up on an August-released compilation called *The Audiophile's Guide to Music in the Twin Cities, Volume 1*. The song, which Erik recorded by himself, is a tribute to watching the Lynda Carter-starring *Wonder Woman* TV show as a child. He addresses her sexiness ("I'm in love with the Maybelline model on my TV/She wears star-spangled underwear") but also her toughness ("Check out those cheeks/They've never seen mascara streaks/She's a big girl/And big girls don't cry"). Darren brought in some tunes from his catalog of four-tracks for the band to arrange, too, a semi-humorous tale of lost love called "Idaho" and a shouty singalong called "Edge of Medicine."

That latter song's final section was a vibey rock-out with the repeated phrase "It was a long way back, and we almost made it," that was spontaneously added in rehearsals. These band practices, which took place at CitySound near University and Highway 280 in a "super small, stinky, sweaty room" according to Heath, were often revelatory. Matt O'Laughlin recalls: "Every single rehearsal, everyone would just start plugging in, not much conversation. And then someone would just start playing, and then another person would start playing with that person, and then all of the sudden the five of us would just have these jam sessions to start off and just warm up for like 8 to 10 minutes. They would have these epic arcs, and those guys would do shit that they thought was funny, but was also kinda good. That was some of the best playing I've ever been a part of. And it was just for us."

For Matt, this was the positive of being in the band. The negative came in the form of increasing guff from his Friends Like These bandmates, who couldn't understand why Matt had begun prioritizing OH and eventually asked him to choose between the two. Matt says, "It was like, okay, so these guys are not currently on drugs, they're better at their instruments, and I'm getting paid to play shows and people are coming to see us. If you want me to pick a band I'm gonna pick [OH]." They eventually let him just continue doing both.

The other downside was a near-constant air of disapproval from Darren. Matt says he understands it to a point; Darren was used to playing with very accomplished drummers, and here Matt was a 24-year-old with raw talent but not a lot of experience. "I always felt a lot of pressure to immediately improve," he says. "And that really fucked with my head." It got to the point that Darren recommended Matt take drum lessons with Christopher McGuire for $75 a pop. Matt wanted to get better, and he was a huge 12 Rods fan, so he did it. Before the first lesson, McGuire ceremoniously pulled a tiny table and placed it next to his drum set, with Matt wondering what kind of interesting lesson might result. Christopher then placed an ashtray on the table and lit up a joint. Despite the odd conditions, Matt says of Christopher, "He's an insanely talented musician and he had a very thoughtful approach."

As the year marched on, Olympic Hopefuls' momentum gained instead of slowing. In September, the annual Minnesota Music Awards ceremony was held in Saint Cloud. There were a whopping fourteen nominations tied to

Artist Adam Turman's first Olympic Hopefuls poster. The artist says when he did gig posters for OH he liked to pair something awesome with something going wrong. Courtesy Adam Turman (www.adamturman.com).

either the Olympic Hopefuls or one of its members, with another seven racked up by their 2024 labelmates Romantica and the Plastic Constellations (for comparison, Prince in his big comeback year got six nominations). Heath was nominated for Best Bassist, Appelwick for Male Vocalist, Darren for Best Songwriter, Ian Prince for Best Drummer, Johnny got a Best Producer nomination (likely for his work with Friends Like These, who got four nominations). Out of those fourteen nods, there were only two wins—*The Fuses Refuse to Burn* got Best Indie Label Recording, and Peter Anderson got a Best Drummer award—but the sheer number of nominations showed just how thoroughly Appelwick, Darren, and friends had taken over the Twin Cities scene.

As 2004 came to a close, the end-of-year lists continued the coronation. *Pioneer Press* placed *Fuses* at number six on their best local releases of the year list, and the CD made *City Pages*' unnumbered list as well. The Twin Cities Critics Tally named them as the second best live act in the state, right after Prince. And in a *Star Tribune* piece about the health of the local scene, OH were mentioned twice as exemplars.

Olympic Hopefuls' whirlwind year was crowned with an appearance on the cover of the November 24, 2004 City Pages. From left to right: Erik Appelwick, Heath Henjum, Marisa Collins (rear), Darren Jackson, John Hermanson, Matt O'Laughlin. Photo by Tony Nelson. Courtesy City Pages and Tony Nelson.

In November, the Olympic Hopefuls won the annual *City Pages* "Picked to Click" poll in landslide fashion, 41 points ahead of the nearest challenger (hip-hop collective Doomtree). Chis Dorn, the lead singer and songwriter of the Beatifics, said in the write-up that the band were "a perfect example of why great, fun pop songs—when written, sung, and played with intelligence, chops, and feel—can be transcendent and extraordinary." The paper did a cover story on the band in the very same issue, and for the photo the guys traded in their tracksuits for prom dresses and wigs. They brought their excellent reacting skills back to show the joy of being given the sash for "Best New Band."

The story itself is largely framed around the writer (Chuck Terhark) trying to gauge the guys' reaction to winning the poll while also discussing the reasons why they did. The latter, he says, is no surprise: "The Hopefuls were expected to perform well among the 16-to-21-year-old female demographic, thanks to their one-two-three combo of a sock-hopping debut, sexy uniforms, and five pairs of pink cheeks just ripe for the pinching."

And, "they're a cluster of musical vortices, five scenester mushrooms planting pop spores in countless bars, clubs, studios, and headphones across the state." At first he's baffled by the group's collective shrug upon hearing the news that they'd received "a citywide pat on the back" and then he postulates that "if you work as hard for as long as they have, you start expecting your dues." That was true, but so was Appelwick and Darren's ongoing ambivalence toward the whole experience. They had always had confidence in their ability to succeed, they just didn't expect it would happen like this.

10

Everyone Needs a New Soundtrack

In which Spymob, Alva Star and Kid Dakota put out their sophomore CDs.
In late 2003, Spymob got word that a label was interested in releasing *Sitting Around Keeping Score*. Ruthless Records, started by rapper Eazy-E in 1986, was a small-but-successful outfit, having released the early N.W.A. records and Bone Thugs-n-Harmony's smash *E. 1999 Eternal* album. Even before Eazy's death in 1995, the label had been sold to a larger company and shuffled around. By 2004, it was a Sony imprint headed by Tomica Wright, Eazy's widow. Before Spymob, the label had only dealt in hip-hop, but Wright decided to take a chance.

Besides the main storyline of the album finally getting its national release, there sits the fact that Spymob had now been paid three times for virtually the same record, once by Epic when it was called *On Pilot Mountain*, again by Arista, and now by Ruthless. And since Sony also owned Epic, that means that the company had now paid twice for an album it didn't previously want. That didn't make up for all the heartache along the way, but it was a bit of sweet poetic justice.

Since everything was basically ready to go, the CD was set for an April 6, 2004, drop date, amounting to a nine-month delay from the original Arista release date. *Sitting Around Keeping Score* was comprised of seven *On Pilot Mountain* tracks, three from the 2000 Spymob EP, and "I Still Live at Home," now gussied up with strings orchestrated by the legendary David Campbell (Beck's father). Unfortunately, Ruthless had nowhere near Arista's marketing budget, and a lot of press outlets had already covered the album before its aborted summer 2003 release date, so there wasn't a ton of attention given to the record. Also complicating matters was the fact that N.E.R.D.'s second album, *Fly or Die*, came out just two weeks earlier, so Spymob got caught up in the promotional efforts for that. Though that left little space for them to self-promote it did mean that they got to perform on the March 13, 2004, episode of Saturday Night Live with host Ben Affleck. N.E.R.D. performed "She Wants to Move" and "Maybe." They also did Letterman again, Regis and Kelly, and the Ellen DeGeneres show.

Spymob was commited to go on the road again with N.E.R.D., but did manage to get one brief tour of their own, sponsored by Ruthless. They played two weeks' worth of dates with Irish pop rock group the Thrills, whose Byrds-and-Beach Boys-indebted 2003 album *So Much For the City* had made a splash in the indie/alternative world. From there, though, it was right back to N.E.R.D. world, and shows in Japan, Australia, and Europe. Speaking of Japan, that was the one place where *Sitting Around Keeping Score* did make its mark. The album was released there with, as is typical for Japanese pop releases, two bonus tracks (and a green color scheme replacing the red on the U.S. release). The first was *Townhouse Stereo*'s "Give Us a Chance to Call" and the other was "Minneapolis Office of Tourism," a trancey, staticky piece of work with funny lines like "Walk out on the frozen lakes/It's the closest you will ever come to the moon/You can finally find out for yourself exactly what Neil Armstrong felt/He wore thick layers, too." The title track, meanwhile, was picked up by two Tokyo radio stations, InterFM 897 and J-Wave in the fall of 2004, getting as high as number ten on the latter.

Overall, though, the album was not a sales success. Instead, the guys had to settled for enjoying the ongoing surrealism of being on tour with Pharrell. In May they opened for Lionel Richie in Milan, Italy, and the artists flew out of the country together. Eric recalls the supreme strangeness of going through airport security with someone whose music had been such a big part of his formative years. "I grew up with the Commodores. I saw Lionel Richie in Ames, Iowa in 1978. It was one of my first concerts." At the after party for a Tommy Hilfiger fashion show N.E.R.D. played in New York, the guys found themselves sitting next to Jessica Simpson and Nick Lachey. Brent didn't recognize the latter, and thinking him one of the models said, "Hey, great job tonight. You guys were really good." Nick expressed his confusion and the two had some laughs over the misunderstanding.

Justin Timberlake would occasionally meet up with the band and come onstage for a mini-Justin set. During this period he was dating Cameron Diaz, and after one show she greeted Eric as he came off stage and said "Super job!" She then proceeded to take the towel from around his neck and dab his nose for him. "I was like, 'Great, Cameron Diaz just wiped snot from my face.'"

As the celebrity encounters piled up, it all started to seem commonplace. "What we found," Eric says, "Was that they were just totally normal people with normal insecurities. Most of them were super-impressive in many ways, some of them were really impressive in one way, and others we just couldn't believe they were successful."

Amid all the globe-hopping, Eric and Sarah welcomed a second son, Lewis, and John and Kristina had their first, Gus.

* * *

The Olympic Hopefuls had dominated the year, but somewhat lost in the hullabaloo over OH was the release of Alva Star's long-simmering second album, which Johnny had quietly put out in mid-July with a CD release show at the 400 Bar. There had been some initial talk of Alva Star joining the 2024 roster, but Johnny didn't like the publishing arrangement ("I did the smart thing and the Hopefuls didn't," he says). Instead placed the album with a small local outfit called Princess Records, which called itself "more of a consulting and support group than a traditional record label."

Escalator, by design, was not a logical follow-up to *Alligators in the Lobby*. Where the latter album's blueprint was mid-period Beatles, with hooky songs that shared a mood, *Escalator* was, in contrast, a meta-album created using a process that drew from the improvisational nature of jazz and hip-hop. Instead of bringing finished songs to his Lowertown studio to record, Johnny invented everything on the spot, including the lyrics, and recorded it all. He says it was an attempt to circumvent the creativity's greatest enemy, self-doubt, through spontaneity. He created the songs one by one, tracking each part before moving on to the next tune.

Once he had ten songs, Johnny brought in Darren, Applewick, and Ian to layer guitars, bass, keyboards and drums on top of the original tracks. Johnny was especially impressed with Ian's work: "Oh my god, that guy. What he did on that record is just mind-blowing because there was no click tracks, everything was recorded, and I had him come in in a night or two and he just played over the instruments and made sense of it."

As a result of this process, the album simultaneously is musically disparate and lyrically cohesive. Outside of the catchy, straightforward "Tornado Girl" there are only the barest hints of the buzzy power pop sound of *Alligators*, and when it does show up it's only in snippets, such as on the boppy keys and insistent guitar figure in the middle section of "Today." The other songs are a mash of pop genres: R & B, hushed acoustic, indie, psychedelia, lo-fi, glam rock, AOR, trip-hop.

Lyrically, though, it's a concept album about the uneasy relationships between creativity and commerce and criticism. Because Johnny wrote the lyrics on the spot and at virtually the same time, there are common themes and phrases throughout. Johnny drew on his experiences with Storyhill, his solo album, and the first Alva Star record, as well as his observations of other musicians' experiences, to deliver a multi-faceted portrait of the inner life of an independent musician: Wrestling with the question of going bigger ("let the record stand that you're unable to put on a face for the label"), the ardor of the scenesters ("way down in Uptown nobody wants to wait for the release date so they can talk it up"), what it's like to top out ("can you respect yourself that much more/king of a big small town"), self-doubt ("I won't be there for the curtain call/I don't believe that I deserve it/After all this time I don't believe it's really worth it"), and the lack of a clear blueprint for success ("You can't pretend to know the way/There's more than just burn out or fade").

It's almost shocking in its breadth of coverage of the topic. Adding to the complexity was the fact that Johnny's sing-it-as-it-occurs-to-you improvisation drew out thoughts he didn't even know he had. He told the *Pioneer Press* that, "The line between me and not me is totally blurred. I would sing thigs that I didn't necessarily know that I believe, and maybe don't, but it's kind of an internal dialogue. It forced me to either support or refute something I said." The lyrics are impressionistic enough that there's no clear story arc to be discerned, instead it's more of a thematic mood that's created.

In addition to the thematic connections, the record folds in on itself several times, becoming a meta-album. Songs refer to each other here and there, culminating in "Today," where Johnny incorporates the titles of all the other songs in one dizzying verse. The process of making the record comes up as well. In "The Messenger" he reveals "I may be writing this one out of order" and in "Downsides" he admits that he's "afraid of/what I make up/say too much." On closer "Get Behind Me" he claims, "the confessions I've poured out/every one of them is true/the truth is on the record now." Finally, in "The Level" he warns, "Careful what you think, Paige Turner," which is a reference to the fake CD review by the author of the same name that appears in the packaging inlay. The essay itself—written by Darren's girlfriend, Erin Anderson—is a brilliant parody of music criticism, mocking reviewers' faux academic comparisons to other pieces of entertainment (in this case to *Sesame Street*), inherent belief that older and familiar is always better, tortured metaphors ("harmonies tighter than pants my mom used to send me to school with"), and unwillingness to fully commit to an opinion ("I'm fully prepared to give *Escalator* two hearty thumbs up. Why? Because I don't get it. And I'm really hoping to get on the guest list for their CD release show.").

Incisive jokes aside, in rock critic parlance, *Escalator* is a "rewards repeat listens" record, a stark contrast to the instant pleasure of Olympic Hopefuls' *The Fuses Refuse to Burn,* despite having the same personnel (though the xylophone does show up briefly on "Cold Calculated" and "The Messenger"). *City Pages'* Lindsey Thomas called it "one of the more captivating local releases of the year" while also admitting it was "unexpectedly bizarre."

Escalator's marketing plan was also in direct opposition to that of *Fuses,* namely that it didn't have one. Johnny's weariness about the music business had reached the point where he had little interest in what happened to an album after he was finished making it. "The more you love a record the less you care," he says.

Johnny did some promotion for the record through Tinderbox, and that company ended up getting "Cold Calculated" in front of the music supervisors for the HBO show *Six Feet Under.* They chose the song to accompany a scene in the fourth episode of the fifth season, in which Claire Fisher (Lauren Ambrose) listens to new CDs in her car and checks her voicemail. The episode's writer was producer Craig Wright, who moved to Minnesota in high school and stayed there until his mid-30s when he headed to L.A. for a career in TV. As a former independent musician himself—in local bands the Tropicals and Kangaroo—Wright loved "Cold Calculated" and the whole *Escalator* album. He and Johnny eventually met and became friends, and Wright vowed to continue to look for places to use Johnny's music.

In the fall *Escalator* was nominated for Best Pop Recording at the Minnesota Music Awards (*Fuses* was nominated as well; both records lost to the Honeydogs' grandiose *10,000 Years*). *City Pages* brought the album back around for its "Best of 2005" issue, naming Johnny the Cities' best songwriter and calling *Escalator* "one of last year's smartest (if little-heard) pop-rock records." And in the *Star Tribune,* listed Alva Star as one of "25 Reasons the Scene is Now," saying that Johnny's songs on *Escalator* were exemplars of great art being born out of desperation. And Johnny had a fan in a former bandmate. Eric Fawcett got a copy of the album while on tour with N.E.R.D. and says, "I remember landing in Amsterdam and walking around the city listening to that record and crying. It's clear that Johnny went to a very real, honest place."

Besides Alva Star and Olympic Hopefuls, Johnny was also busy with Storyhill. After their spring tour, the guys spent some time in Johnny's studio working on their next album. Rather than a new collection of originals, he and Chris had decided to take Dave Weeks' advice and do interpretations of songs by famous duos of the 1970s. From September through December, Storyhill did shows at least a few shows every month in places like the Pacific Northwest, Colorado, Wisconsin, Chicago, North Dakota, Idaho, and Montana.

Johnny was also busy producing records for other artists. He spent part of the summer recording follow-ups from Panoramic Blue and Friends Like These, and the debut of a new band called the Glad Version. Recording with Friends Like These ended earlier than planned because the band ran out of money. They asked Johnny to front them the funds to mix four songs for an EP they called *Deliver Us From Evil,* promising to pay him back the $3000 after they went on tour. The songs on *Deliver Us From Evil* were a change of pace from the skewed pop of *I Love You,* more hard-hitting and blues-based, but still with those lovely harmonies. Opener "7th Street Queen" was a particular standout, and featured a song-ending guest appearance from Craig Finn, whose new band, the Hold Steady, had just released their first album. On "7th Street Queen" he reels off one of his trademark street corner rants about debauched behavior in various Twin Cities locales.

The tune picked up a nomination for Song of the Year at the Minnesota Music Awards, but lost to Prince's "Musicology."

The Glad Version were a group of friends who'd attended Luther College in Decorah, Iowa, and then moved to the Twin Cities together. The manner in which they came to work with Johnny as a producer was both unlikely and humorous. Upon moving to the Twin Cities in 2002, singer Adam Svec got a job at the call center for a law firm, Wagner, Falconer, & Wagner, where one of the new employees he had to train in was a job-hopping Erik Appelwick. Adam was a close follower of the Twin Cities music scene, and recognized Erik right away. Adam was embarrassed to be basically put in charge of someone whose music he admired, but the two formed a friendship, and Appelwick eventually hooked Adam up with Johnny, who produced the band's moody 2004 CD *Smile Pretty Make Nice*. The band's guitarist, Chris Salter, had been a Storyhill fan since junior high, and geeked out working with his idol. For Johnny this led to the somewhat discomfiting realization that not only was he serving as a mentor to slightly younger artists such as John Solomon and Friends Like These, he was now an elder statesmen in the scene.

* * *

A second Kid Dakota record had been a long time in the making, but *The West Is the Future* finally went out into the world in early October of 2004, right in the midst of Olympic Hopefulsmania. Released on Chairkicker's Union, the 9-song album features the full band Kid Dakota line-up on record for the first time, though it didn't start that way. Darren and Christopher had done quite a bit of recording all the way back in September of 2001, but ended up redoing most of the songs live with Zak Sally on bass and Appelwick on guitar. They then added layers of overdubs, with guests including Andrew Broder, once again on turntables (and piano on "Ten Thousand Lakes"), Brian Roessler playing upright bass on four songs, and Low's Alan Sparhawk and Mimi Parker offering backup vocals on "Homesteader." Alex Oana co-produced and recorded the record at CityCabin and Seedy Underbelly.

The album finds Darren looking outward in his songwriting. Whereas *So Pretty* was largely a record of confessional diary entries, *West* is more character-driven, though that doesn't make it any less bracing or dark. As Darren described it, the nine songs on the album were thematically connected by the false optimism offered by the promises of the future (technology and progress and revolution), and that's underscored by the opening and closing songs, "Pilgrim" and "Atomic Pilgrim," in which lines repeat: "The west is a promise/The west is a new land/The west is a lie/The west is a bad man." Darren's tendency to draw inspiration from philosophy and literature is prominent here, with the album serving almost as an aural short-story collection, albeit one where the stories' resolutions are all left to the readers' imaginations

Darren has also pointed out that all of the characters are facing harsh or unfamiliar conditions. There's "Ivan," in which the narrator is so fed up with the suffering and abuses of power he's seen that he has to act. The settlers in "Homesteader" face unmerciful weather, stillborn babies, and marauding drifters. In "Winterkill" the local lake is so thoroughly frozen that no light shines through and all the fish have died. "Pine Ridge" is a look at reservation life in Darren's native South Dakota, with "a lot of good people doing bad things to one another." In "2001" an astronaut flies untethered, trying to make a deal with God.

While most of the songs are from the perspectives of others, "Ten Thousand Lakes" is a notable exception. It's an account of his winter 1999 rehab stint in Minnesota, with Darren's confessional dark humor on full display: "I didn't come for ice fishin'/I didn't come for duck huntin'/I'm not Scandanavian/Or in search of Paul Bunyan/ I came for the taper, I came for the tapeworm, I came to get better."

Musically, the album is best described in Michael Metivier's *PopMatters* review, "a pummeling rock opera of contrasting dynamics ... anchored in the minor key" and containing "prog-rock accoutrements." It's a dense record, with all sorts of aural tricks, like Christopher's drums replicating a pow wow on "Pine Ridge" and the sci-fi laser effects on "2001." The country bar sounds underlying Darren's singing on "Starlite Motel," came from a recording Darren made of a local cover band playing "Tennessee Waltz" at the Pine Bowl and Cactus Lounge in Bison, SD (both are mentioned in the lyrics) "The animated man you hear in the recording is my uncle, Dan Jackson," Darren says.

William Schaff, founding member of Kid Dakota and the Tumble Weeds, created scratchboard illustrations for the CD booklet, as well as the cover. Will worked from a cassette of acoustic versions of the album's tracks to craft an image for each song. Darren says, "I think one night he listened to '2001' like eleven times in a row while making the scratchboard for it. That obsessiveness about the project is kind of what we brought to it as well." The drawings don't always literally depict the songs, instead capturing a mood or theme.

The powerful cover image was the result of a night Will spent with Darren while he was going through withdrawal symptoms. Darren had come to New York to play a show, counting on being able to score when he arrived. But he discovered that all of his old haunts had dried out. As Darren laid in a hotel bed shivering and sweating, Will drew the cover image as an emotional response to that moment they were in together.

There were two CD release shows—October 8 and 9 at the Triple Rock, with Low headlining both. Christopher flew in from Tokyo to play the shows (he was still with Quruli, but not for much longer; he'd leave the band over creative differences later in the month). At the show, the band played in various configurations, with the full band nearly overloading the speakers at the venue (a *How Was the Show* review of the second night said Kid Dakota had a low-end power "on par with what you might expect at a Pink Floyd arena show"). A week later, Darren and Christopher traveled to New York to play at the annual CMJ Music Marathon along with 977 other bands looking to make an impression on college radio stations. For *New York Times* music critic Jon Pareles, Kid Dakota rose above the noise. Pareles included the band as one of five standout acts, saying that Darren had "the kind of buoyant pop tenor that once carried Top 40 pop hits" and that the band succeeded by "blaring the songs with stark power chords and tolling drones while the drummer made hilarious faces."

Pareles was the most prominent to praise the band and its new album, but far from the only one. *Pitchfork* reviewed the record, giving it a 7.2 rating and called it "ample evidence of an ambitious, talented band just beginning to find its legs." Writer Matthew Murphy also wrote that that "Jackson's silvery voice flows through this parched scenery like water from a glacier-fed spring, making him sound like a Badlands version of Thom Yorke." Coming so near to the close of 2004, the record worked its way onto lots of end of the year lists. 30music put it at #14 on their Top 30 of 2004, calling it "masterfully executed and brilliantly produced." *Sponic* placed at #5 on their Top 10, saying that "huge clouds of delectable melodic dread make this as disturbing as it is accomplished."

The tandem releases of *The Fuses Refuse to Burn* and *The West Is the Future* had

The cover for Kid Dakota's *The West Is the Future,* **conceived by artist William Schaff. Courtesy Darren Jackson.**

established Darren as a rising indie star. His only trouble, really, was music writers constantly asking him about the stark contrast between the two groups. It was understandable; just as Darren's history of addiction had made an irresistible hook for journalists to use when writing about his first album, the tonal difference between his two musical projects was too interesting to not explore. As Chris Riemenschneider, who had been a big fan of Kid Dakota, said regarding OH: "That was part of the fun of it. Oh, wow, look at Darren being Mr. Sunshine!" Riemenschneider wrote the most direct and in-depth article about the dichotomy, a piece in the *Star Tribune* called "Dr. Hopeful and Mr. Kid." There, Darren says that the two bands were a way to give outlet to both sides of his songwriting, which tended to manifest as either light or heavy, rarely in between.

Around the same time, in *Pulse of the Twin Cities* he joked that he might just create a group for every genre: "We're working on a polka band now so I can finally get all of my polkas out into the world." In seriousness, though, he declared Olympic Hopefuls gave him a necessary injection of musical fun, but that he ultimately felt more connected to his original band. "Kid Dakota is more about fears and frustrations and grief and sadness. It's more about what's disconcerting in my life, which I think inevitably is the stuff you feel closer to." Darren's personality and tastes were more inclined toward the less accessible, more challenging, works of art like *The West Is the Future* that required focused attention and deeper thought to appreicate. "You might not like it very much unless you really dig into it," he said of the record. "I think a lot of people aren't going to get it."

Darren didn't feel any pressure to choose between his two personas, though, and was determined to prioritize both. The benefits were clear: He could be the popular crowd-drawing pop star and the challenging, dark cult-status singer-songwriter at the same time, and each might subsidize the other in various ways.

* * *

Two thousand four was without a doubt the year it all broke through for the musical collective that had formed around CityCabin and Alex Oana, so it's ironic that by the year's end, both were gone. Feeling he'd maxed out in the Twin Cities, Alex had decided to move to Los Angeles to pursue audio engineering there. The move was partly born of frustration. Alex had put so much of himself into the local records he recorded and produced (not just within the Saint Olaf circle, either; he had made albums with Three Minute Hero, Leep-27, Rude Ruby Ride, Bubblemath, and many more) and none of them—at least before *The Fuses Refuse to Burn*—had had the impact he'd hoped for or the attention he thought they deserved. And ten years of that same result took a toll on him. He says, "I just felt like, man, we we've been making great art. Why isn't this thing that we think is amazing being recognized by other people as amazing?" Speaking especially of Spymob and Storyhill, he says: "We felt like foreigners, we were speaking a different musical language than what was cool and what was okay in the Twin Cities. But what if we had been trying what we thought was cool in L.A.?"

So he decided to find out. It's ironic that Alex left Minneapolis when he did, but it's also fitting. He had come of musical age with Spymob and Storyhill, and then served as nurturer and mentor to Alva Star, Kid Dakota, and Vicious Vicious. He created the conditions for everyone to flourish creatively, the "rich, fertile" ground as Andy Carlson called it. CityCabin had given these wayward musicians a place to both live and forge lasting musical relationships. Alex provided expertise and guidance, and ensured that their albums had a sound to rival any expensive, professionally-produced major label record.

But by 2003 the baby birds had mostly flown away. CityCabin was no longer the bustling center of the scene. Peppermint had moved to Saint Paul, and Darren and John Solomon and jMatt had their own places. Appelwick was the only one left (when Alex sold CityCabin, Erik was forced to squat in his rehearsal space for awhile before moving in with Solomon, whose wife was attending grad school). And on recording level, Alex says, "I eventually taught myself out of a job." Appelwick, Darren, and Johnny had all essentially become their own engineers and producers. Darren and Johnny had set up their own studios. For a long time Alex was known as the "Pro Tools Hotline" the guys would call when they had an audio engineering question, and everyone adopted the motto "WWAD" (short for What Would Alex Do?, and pronounced "Wuhwad"). After awhile, the guys were more than facile at "using the recording studio as their instrument," as Alex puts it.

Alex knew the move was the right one for him, but he didn't fully consider the emotional ramifications. "I lost that day-to-day interaction with my best friends," he says. "I felt like I was 2500 miles away from my family." In L.A. Alex would continue to mix and master for the guys, working out of a home studio he playfully dubbed CityCabin West, and he would make frequent visits back, but that magical time when he was at the center of a genuine scene was gone forever.

Andy says that in their Northfield days Alex would often speak of his vision for a place called ARS (Alex Recording Studio; pronounced "ours"), which could serve as a base of operations for all of his friends to make music. For a decade, CityCabin was the fulfillment of that ambition.

11

Before They Interfere with a Beautiful Thing Somehow

In which Spymob breaks up and Olympic Hopefuls and Kid Dakota get shake-ups.

In early 2005, John Ostby gathered Twigg, Fawcett, and Brent together and broke the news to them: He was done with Spymob. "I can't do this and be a dad," he said, and added that he didn't know how Eric, who now had two boys, had done it.

Ostby says now impending fatherhood was certainly a factor in the decision to call it quits, though it wasn't the only one. Even after the amazing experiences traveling the world and appearing before millions of people on T.V., John had lost his confidence that Spymob was destined for wide popular acclaim. It seemed to him like they had plateaued. *Sitting Around Keeping Score* hadn't sold well, and he wasn't writing songs like the ones on the album anymore, instead moving toward country and folk. The other guys had gamely gone along with the new direction, but it wasn't where their interests or talents lay.

And even if it had been, and that had been a commercially viable way forward, it still would have required months on the road away from his wife and newborn son. The reality that had dawned on John was that he his current path wasn't going to lead him to "the middle class American Dream of home ownership and stable income" that he now desired. The odds had gotten even worse in March when Pharrell announced to the world, "N.E.R.D. is dead." This was largely due to irreconcilable disputes with their label, Virgin Records. It seems that even the world's biggest hitmaker wasn't immune to record company meddling.

Spymob's time with N.E.R.D., on balance, was good for everyone in the band. They got travel all over the world, play with amazingly talented people, and enter into a realm few others are allowed into. Having to consistently perform on that level and be able to witness Pharrell and Chad's creative process helped everyone grow exponentially as musicians. And for Ostby, Fawcett, and Brent especially, having such high-profile champions was validation of the years of hard work they'd put in. It was an assurance that they hadn't been crazy to believe so strongly in their music.

Yet at the same time, working with N.E.R.D. may have prematurely brought on the end of Spymob. Yes, it gave the group an amazing opportunity to appear before crowds of a size and diversity they never would have gotten otherwise, and two major label record contracts. But as much as they tried to cultivate it, there was little crossover between Spymob's potential audience and N.E.R.D.'s actual audience. And the fact that all of the interest in them was centered on older material, and so much of their time was devoted to N.E.R.D.'s music instead of their own, prevented them a natural creative progression. In an interview in early 2005, Fawcett told *Mpls St. Paul Magazine* that working with N.E.R.D. was "a liability, in terms of our own audience." But, he added, "we would make the exact same decision again."

Like that, Spymob's 12-year wild ride was over. Fawcett says the guys all reacted to Ostby's decision calmly and without anger or bitterness. There was sadness, yes, but also immediate acceptance of "Hey, okay, it's time for our next adventure." Brent started making plans to head to L.A. to get involved with engineering, producing, and guitar session work. John and Twigg would lay low for awhile before forming a new, lower-ambition group called Kentucky Air. Eric started casting about for opportunities that would keep him from having to go back to a day job. One of his first post–Spymob gigs was playing on former Soul Coughing frontman Mike Doughty's third solo album, *Haughty Melodic*, which Semisonic's Dan Wilson was producing. Eric's connection to that musical family, having played with Dan's brother Matt, led to him appearing on three songs on the record, including the hit "Looking at the World Through the Bottom of a Well." Around this same time, Eric also did some recording for songs that would end up on Dan's first solo album.

Fawcett also hooked back up with Johnny right away, which would lead him deeper into production work, and to taking on two high-profile new roles.

* * *

For Johnny, 2005 meant balancing his commitments to Storyhill and Olympic Hopefuls, and the contrast between the two types of shows were becoming clearer and clearer. He told an interviewer: "With the Hopefuls, it's obviously more energetic and, musically, it excites you. With Storyhill, I think it's more about the lyrical content, the intimacy and the connection you can have with the audience. After shows with Storyhill, we tend to talk to people a lot. The songs can spawn different types of conversations—thinking about the world and whatnot. But, with the Hopefuls, that really doesn't happen. All the action happens onstage, and you don't necessarily feel like you have the same connection you have in Storyhill. I love both, though, and I want to keep doing both."

The year started off Hopefuls-heavy, but March saw the official release of Storyhill's *Duotones: A Tribute to Duos of the '70s* and a supporting tour that would run through early May and hit some familiar spots as well as some new places for the guys, namely South Carolina and Colorado. They had begun working with a new booking agent, Renee Gebhardt, who was dogged about finding them new markets to break into. *Duotones* itself was a means to that end as well. When Dave Weeks had the idea, it was as a way to get the guys attention in places and avenues where they hadn't gotten it before, a way of showcasing their talent and sensibility.

The album features a fascinating collection of tunes, from the very familiar (the Carpenters' "We've Only Just Begun," Seals and Crofts' "Summer Breeze"), the nearly-forgotten (Brewer and Shipley's "One Toke Over the Line," England Dan and John Ford Cooley's "Love is the Answer") and the under-the-radar (Steely Dan's "Dirty Work," the Stills-Young Band's "Long May You Run"). And in what must have been a total eargasm for the music writers who'd been following the band for so many years, they took on the duo they'd been endlessly compared to, covering Simon and Garfunkel's "Cecilia" and "The Boxer."

As with *Dovetail*, Chris came to the Twin Cities long enough to complete his parts, and then left the rest to Johnny to work on at his studio in Lowertown. Johnny brought Appelwick as his primary partner in crime, and Erik serves again as "basically the one-man band," playing drums, bass, guitar, and keys. His touch is especially evident in the wah-wah guitar on "Summer Breeze" and the funky bass on "Love is the Answer" and "We've Only Just Begun." Fawcett and Ian also drummed on some of the tracks as well. It was the first and only Chris & Johnny/Storyhill album on which Chris didn't play guitar.

Ironically, given its origins and purpose, *Duotones* proved to be the end for Peppermint. In August 2005, the company celebrated eight years in business, but the very next month Dave Weeks made the decision to shut things down. He and Eric Tell had done an admirable job of keeping things going after their initial roster of artists had turned over and Andy Carlson had left in 2002 to pursue a career as a lawyer, but the economics of the music business were rapidly changing, shifting away from CD sales toward digital sales. Peppermint, which had never been a huge moneymaker even under the old model, found the new economics untenable. Dave says he remembers in the early days of Peppermint having an idea of a 1-800 number where you could call in and press different numbers to hear different Peppermint artists, which just illustrates how quickly things changed. The Internet and MP3s had made getting the music to people easier, but had also killed the profit margins. "I get it," Dave says, "Why would I pay $15 or even $10 for a CD when I can buy track by track and I only want four of them anyway?" The company had artists selling their music digitally, and 55 percent of the profits went to the digital distributor. As Dave put it, "The economics are quickly turned on their head."

Despite the fact that it ultimately wasn't sustainable, Dave and Andy are both proud of what they were able to accomplish with Peppermint. They had provided a vital service to over a dozen independent artists, reached tens of thousands of fans, and become a genuine presence in the Twin Cities scene. Andy says, "I remember one day after I had left Peppermint, I was on the bus and saw a college-aged woman with a Peppermint sticker on her water bottle. It made me reflect on Peppermint's impact—it felt to nice to realize that we had been a vehicle for thousands of people to connect with music that meant a lot to them."

Even with Peppermint defunct, there was always the possibility of Dave staying on as Storyhill's manager, but he decided against it. He says that interpersonal issues had started up again between Johnny and Chris, and both of them were beginning to view Storyhill as a burden again. From Dave's perspective, the guys needed to make the duo their number one priority to have the kind of success they wanted. But the rub was that Chris and Johnny's perceived freedom was a vital component of them continuing to be able to work together. By the end of 2005, Dave was tired of navigating the two personalities, and of trying and failing to get them more engaged in Storyhill. He left the music business completely, moving on to work in web/interactive strategy. And who would become Storyhill's new manager? Eric Fawcett.

* * *

In Febuary 2005, Kid Dakota went on their second tour, this time to Europe supporting Low. With an acclaimed new album and a high-profile touring partner, this was their biggest shot yet at breaking through on a national level. Once again the touring band was just Darren and Christopher, with the occasional appearance by Zak on bass

11. Before They Interfere with a Beautiful Thing Somehow   125

and Alan on guitar. Appelwick by this point was not in Kid Dakota anymore, nor was Darren in Vicious Vicious. With Alva Star playing sporadically, the friends had gone from being in four bands together to only sharing time in Olympic Hopefuls.

Kid Dakota did two European legs. The first covered several U.K. stops, Brussels, Amsterdam, and Dublin. In April they returned to play in Switzerland, Germany, Italy, Denmark, and Spain. The fans loved them. According to a report from concertgoer Alister on his blog, Kid Dakota "went down a storm with the audience" at the Edinburgh show. Of the London show, attendee Jane Rich wrote: "What a surprise treat. Pounding, spiraling rhythms search out the wide open plains of the Royal Festival Hall. Honey and gravel vocals deliver intelligent lyrics that upset my balance a little. Guitarist and frontman Darren Jackson's hypnotic riffs move in amongst the focused drumming of Christopher McGuire for the pregnant set like they were born to play together."

Thomas Hannan of *Rock Feedback* magazine wrote that the audience fell silent in reverence during Kid Dakota's set, and that "the two have such a grip on your emotions that it's as if they're holding your heart in the palms of their hand, squeezing and relaxing."

For all the acclaim, all was not well. In a late 2004 interview, Darren had promised another Kid Dakota album would be on its way in the fall of 2005. And indeed, the band played at least two brand new songs, "Long Odds" and "Fiber Optic Failure," on tour. But then came a shakeup. Specifics are hazy, but by the fall of 2005, McGuire would no long be in the band. With Houston having broken up in 2004, Ian Prince was now able to join Darren full-time in Kid Dakota. At the same time, Zak Sally had decided to retire from the music business and pursue cartooning, leaving both Low and Kid Dakota in October 2005. The new album would be delayed while Darren and Ian reconfigured as a duo.

It was one of those years of massive change. In May, Darren got married to Erin Anderson. Continuing the guys' tendency to marry accomplished women, Erin was a writer for *Pulse of the Twin Cities* (she got to interview Prince once, though the experience didn't go super well) and the respected literary magazine the *Utne Reader*. In 2005 she started working at Brain Traffic, a web content strategy consulting firm started by none other than Kristina Ostby, John's wife.

Around this time, Darren also made the decision to leave his job at the University of Minnesota and have a go at making music full time. This was a big deal. Most think of the pop musician's dream as being stardom, but it's really what John Ostby described: Being able to make a living without

The "new" Kid Dakota: Darren (left) and drummer Ian Prince (pictured here in a 2008 promo photo by Cameron Wittig). Courtesy Darren Jackson.

scraping by. In addition to the increased money from Olympic Hopefuls gigs, Darren had started to pick up some engineering, producing, and recording work both in and out of Shortman Studios. He engineered tracks on the Owls second album, *Daughters and Suns*, as well as the debut CD by teen '80s revivalists Melodious Owl. And, along with Appelwick, he recorded the second album by 2024 labelmates Fitzgerald, *Raised by Wolves* (according to the band, Erik worked with them during the day, while Darren took over at night, each offering their own specialties). Darren's interest and ability in engineering and producing had developed in his years working with Alex Oana. He told *Pulse* that "When I first worked with Alex I didn't have a lot of knowledge of why he used this mic or that compressor, it was all foreign to me. After working with him it started to rub off."

* * *

A band that comes out with instant appeal and acclaim is bound to lose momentum in its second year, but that didn't happen to Olympic Hopefuls. In fact, as they approached the one-year anniversary of *The Fuses Refuse to Burn* and their live debut, things only seemed to be growing. This was facilitated by a couple of developments.

First, 2024 had been aggressive about seeking licensing deals for their artists, and that led to them establishing relationships with agents in Hollywood. OH's first experience with this was the placement of a 10-second clip of "Imaginary" on the VH1 show Best Week Ever in October 2004. Not long after that, Alexandra Patsavas, music supervisor for the hit fox teen drama *The O.C.*, heard "Let's Go" on XM radio and got in touch with Nate Roise with a request to use the song on the show. This was a huge deal at the time. *The O.C.* debuted in 2003 and was an instant hit. The show quickly established a reputation for its use of music, serving as an expertly curated mixtape of new and established indie artists, and bands such as the Walkmen, the Killers, and Death Cab for Cutie all made appearances. The show also helped break new artists such as the Thrills, Rooney and Imogene Heap.

"Let's Go" ended up soundtracking one minute in the seventh episode of the show's second season. Starting up right after the opening credits, it plays under two conversation scenes involving main characters Marisa, Summer, and Seth. The episode aired January 6, 2005, and while the song's appearance didn't launch OH to stardom, it did result in a nice payday for 2024, Appelwick, and Darren. "Let's Go" would be used again later in the year, this time on the MTV reality series *Laguna Beach*, in an October episode titled "Our Last Prom."

The song also started getting local radio play. Modern rock station Drive 105 gave the song a few spins, which was significant since the station was not known as being particularly friendly to local bands (certainly nowhere near as much as its beloved and much-missed predecessor Rev 105). Outside of one-hour-a-week local shows on various stations and the AM-only Radio K, the vibrancy of the Twin Cities music scene was largely ignored on the radio waves.

That changed on January 24, 2005, with the debut of 89.3 the Current, a commercial-free FM station owned by Minnesota Public Radio (purchased, funnily enough, from St. Olaf, who had opereated it under a classical format since 1967). The station began with a mission of hiring respected local DJs such as Mark Wheat, Steve Seel, Bill DeVille, and Mary Lucia, and letting them share from their record collections, old or new. This utopian ambition was eventually reined in by more restrictive formatting, but in the early days

11. Before They Interfere with a Beautiful Thing Somehow

it really was like a pirate radio station with really good funding and marketing. And their motto "Great Music Lives Here" was a nod to the strength of the scene; in fact the station debuted with a local track, hip-hop group Atmosphere's Minnesota-upping "Shhh." Olympic Hopefuls were early favorites on the Current, with nearly every *Fuses* track getting airplay, and "Let's Go," "Holiday," and "Motobike" serving particularly as staples. The band played several Current-sponsored shows, and within the station's first couple of weeks appeared on Chris Roberts's Word of Mouth show.

Like OH, the station was an instant phenomenon, endearing itself to the locals both hipster and mainstream. It was all a part of the local scene getting its groove back. Instead of articles about how to revive local music, there suddenly were ones about the resurgence of the scene. *Pioneer Press* music writer Ross Raihala wrote a piece that spring that held both the Current and Olympic Hopefuls up as reasons that "it's almost starting to feel like the '80s, when Prince, Jimmy Jam & Terry Lewis, the Replacements, and Hüsker Dü earned the region national acclaim." Appelwick was interviewed for the article, and credited the Current for expanding their audience. "There are local shows that will sell out by 10 pm," he told Raihala. "I've never seen that before. And it's not just scenesters. There's all these new people at shows." It also drove up their CD sales in a time when nationally the trend was going down. Electric Fetus manager Bob Fuchs is quoted in the article saying that "The first month [of the Current] was amazing—we were getting hundreds of comments a week and getting caught short on a lot of titles." *The Fuses Refuse to Burn* was one of those CDs buyers were seeking out, and its overall sales soared toward the 4,000 mark, extraordinary for a local CD.

Their live shows continued to thrill. Long time scene veteran Cyn Collins wrote up a review of a January performance saying "The Olympic Hopefuls remind me of being a '60s child and listening to my first favorite groups: the Monkees, Bay City Rollers, the Beatles, the Association" because of their "brightness of sound and tongue-in-cheek lightness."

Another Adam Turman poster, this one for a show featuring three of the Twin Cities' hottest bands at the time. Courtesy Adam Turman.

But as well as things were going for OH's public profile, there was behind-the-scenes drama brewing. Spring brought several major changes to the band. In early March, the group decided to fire Matt O'Laughlin. Or, more accurately, Darren decided to replace Matt O'Laughlin with a drummer who was a longtime friend of the band's, who had recently returned to town, and whose band had broken up. That's how Eric Fawcett became an Olympic Hopeful. To Darren, it was a no-brainer. Where Matt was still raw and a full decade younger than the other guys, Fawcett was smooth and accomplished. Everyone knew him, and he could sing back up, giving the group 4-part harmonies. The firing was more of a "we found somebody perfect" situation than a "we don't like you" situation. To Matt that was cold comfort. Darren didn't even deliver the bad news himself. "Appelwick called me and said 'Darren and John want to bring in Fawcett.' He deflected a lot of the blame. That really sucked for me. I always felt like as a drummer I was at the mercy of whoever was the songwriter. I either need to put in a lot of time and effort to find people I respect and want to work with, or not. So when I finally got into the Hopefuls it was like validation, like, 'I can play with these guys!' Then I got fired, so I was like, 'I'm probably not that good.'"

Matt's exit required some tricky financial dealings. The previous fall, the band and label decided to make a video for the song "Motobike" and got together with photographer Darin Back to film the clip. Using a Super 8 camera, the concept was to follow the guys as they drove around Minneapolis on rented mopeds. Matt says initially they were going to drive across the Hennepin Avenue bridge swerving in and out of traffic, but when that proved too difficult they instead drove out ahead of traffic, holding up the cars behind them. They also shot some footage at DeLaSalle High School on Nicollet Island. As they were riding across the tennis courts, Matt decided it might be funny to lay down a skid mark. He revved up and then hit both brakes, and immediately started fishtailing before wiping out. He'd taken the song's lyrics ("every time I crash my motorbike") a bit too literally. And that brought everything to a screeching halt, so to speak. Matt was okay, but the moped was pretty beat up.

Turns out he'd done over one thousand dollars' damage to it. 2024 agreed to pay for half, but it basically ruined the bottom line for the video, which was never finished. At the time of his firing, Matt still hadn't paid it, but was owed $250 for a couple of shows. He reports Darren and Appelwick trading that, his tracksuit, and payment for his final show with the band to forgive his moped debt. A glamourous end, it wasn't.

On Fawcett's side of things, he says he never had designs to join the Olympic Hopefuls. The band had formed while he was away with N.E.R.D. and remembers being "psyched they were all playing together." He had managed to catch them at their Bar Lurcat gig when he was back in town briefly, and like so many others came away impressed. Once he was back in town and a free agent again, he says, "It just kind of became a logical thing to do, and making no comment on Matt's drumming because Matt is a great drummer. He was very much cutting it. I think it was just like, 'Yeah, Eric's in town now, and we all sort of grew up together, so it just kind of makes sense.'"

Fawcett's first show was a double-headlining gig at First Ave with the Honeydogs (whose new drummer was none other than *Fuses* and Alva Star stickman Peter Anderson) on March 26. It turned out to be a significant night for more than just the fact of Eric's debut. It was also the first appearance of the band's unofficial sixth member, Dancing Man, a.k.a. Rupert Matthew Pederson III.

How exactly this all happened is a matter of much controversy and rumor, legend

11. Before They Interfere with a Beautiful Thing Somehow

Ticket stub for the show that featured the debuts of Eric Fawcett and Rupert Pederson III. Author's collection.

and lore. It was the final Saturday night before a citywide bar and restaurant smoking ban went into effect, so the air was thick and hazy. The Olympic Hopefuls were just a few songs into their set, having just kicked into Darren's boppy "Drain the Sea," when it appeared that a drunken businessman had somehow wandered onto the stage. carrying a Pabst Blue Ribbon. He wore a black suit and tie, which drew a sharp contrast from the jeans and band t-shirts and beanie caps in the audience, not to mention the red and orange tracksuits on the stage. The crowd tensed. What was he doing up there? Was this a part of the show? Would the bouncers come get him? Was he going to fall off the stage?

And then he set down his PBR and started dancing, and it wasn't your typical head-nodding feet shuffling kind of dance, but the kind that's done with complete abandon: leg kicks, air punches, exaggerated clapping, scissor jumps, lip-syncing. He took off his suitcoat and spiked it. He accidentally kicked over his beer, and then, as the band went into "Let's Go," the dancing man somehow took it up a notch. He tore off his tie, twirled it around his head, and let go. He produced a white headband and red, white, and blue wristbands seemingly from nowhere and made a ceremony of putting them on. Somewhere between a cheerleader and a mascot, he got the audience clapping along, traversed the length of the stage, and fell to his knees as "Let's Go" came to its end. He left the stage after that, and the band proceeded directly into the next song as if nothing had happened. Those who were there were left baffled and exhilarated in equal parts, wondering just exactly what we had witnessed while at the same time basking in just how fantastic it was.

In the ensuing days and months, he appeared at more shows, including big gigs at the annual Basilica Block Party and Taste of Minnesota. Each time he danced a little bit longer and brought out new moves, such as playing the cowbell or miming guitar heroics with a towel. At the sweltering Basilica show, he cut open a large bag of Starburst and whipped it in a sideways motion so the tiny colorful squares sprayed out across the audience like water from a sprinkler. The fan community started to piece together details about the mysterious dancer. He was either a mortgage broker or accountant who had come to the show at First Ave directly from a disastrous client meeting. In his frustration he'd gotten drunk and let loose, unleashing a side to himself no one knew existed. Eventually we learned his name: Rupert.

That was the legend. The truth of it was that Rupert was jMatt Keil returning to the band and songs he loved. The day after his disappointment in the languorous crowd at the CD release show, he put on *The Fuses Refuse to Burn* while cleaning his bedroom and started dancing along, gaining steam as he went, playing it up in the mirror. "It was just like a lightning bolt," he says of the revelation that followed. "I need to show people how to dance and let it go."

It took him awhile to figure out exactly how he was going to do that, and Kubla Khan and his day job as a mortgage broker kept him busy, but it all started to come together that following spring. When the idea of dancing onstage occurred to him, he got in touch with his old roommate Fawcett first, who said he was fine with it but that it wasn't his decision to make, especially since he had *just* joined the band. Johnny was next and his response was similar: "Sure," he said, "If you can get Darren and Appelwick on board." From there he e-mailed the whole band, writing, "Let's throw your fans a curveball. You don't look at me, and I won't look at you, and that way if it falls flat then it's no big deal."

Darren thought the idea was ridiculous, and didn't respond. Appelwick did, with a typically terse: "I don't know. It sounds kinda cool." jMatt took that as a green light.

That night at First Ave he was hyped up but not terribly well-prepared. "I just thought, 'Once I get up there I'll totally know what to do.' Which was ridiculous." Though not completely. jMatt was both an athlete and a seasoned performer, and he knew how to work a crowd. He'd participated in lip sync contests back home in Beaver Dam, and his sister Jena was the captain of the dance squad at the University of Wisconsin–Eau Clair, which led to 10-year-old jMatt memorizing the team's routine to the Pointer Sisters' "Neutron Dance." But for Rupert's first appearance, there was no routine; jMatt didn't even know which song he was going to dance to. He was just going to let the spirit move him, and that's exactly what happened.

He says, "It wouldn't have happened if I hadn't have known people. I mean, Conrad [Sverkerson], the First Ave stage manager, had seen me so many times he was just like, 'What's up?' And I was like, 'I'm just gonna go on stage.' He just kind of waved me through." Once he started dancing, jMatt says he could feel a few things going on: The band was moving more; the crowd was throwing out a mix of emotions: hate, love, wonderment, bewilderment; and the temperature in the room was steadily rising. He got lost in the music around the time he kicked over his beer. "All I knew," he says, "was that I was in this euphoric state that was on another level of anything I'd ever done."

After he came off stage he walked through the crowd and ignored the audience members who were trying to get a grasp of what had happened: "Who are you? What was that? What's your name?" Feeling overwhelmed, he didn't even stay for the rest of the show. He'd known he'd accomplished his goal of injecting energy into the moment. Later that night he was at nearby Pizza Luce and ran into Darren. jMatt remembers him saying something along the lines of "That wasn't bad" or "Hey, that was pretty cool," nothing overly enthusiastic, but enough to validate what he'd done, to assure him that the risk had paid off.

From the band's perspective, there was mostly caution regarding Rupert. None of them were excited about adding what might be perceived as another gimmick on top of the tracksuits. Johnny had just recently begun to play a Moog Liberation synthesizer, also known as a "keytar." The instrument had a decidedly '80s look to it, having been invented in 1980 and quickly popularized by the likes of Jan Hammer, Devo and Kool and the Gang. It kept Johnny from being "a guy standing behind a keyboard" (though it weighed in the range of 30 pounds and gave him neck pains), but bordered on being another gimmick. Perhaps unsurprisingly, Darren was the most ambivalent about the whole thing initially, and this created a sort of protagonist/antagonist relationship, with Darren as the uptight perfectionist and Rupert as the devil-may-care insouciant. As if in illustration of that, there were at least a couple of times where jMatt got so lost in his dancing that he unplugged Darren's guitar.

The band eventually embraced it, all realizing that Rupert was providing a vital service to the band and its audience. Heath says, "The one thing I realized was that when people are watching four or five guys on stage play music it's not that interesting. But without Rupert, it would have been a lot different. I think he really energized the crowds, to the point that then you feed off that and it just builds. And when he was not there it would not be as energetic." Darren and Fawcett both agree. Eric says, "jMatt is a genius when it comes to understanding the energy in a room. There were many shows where it just took too long for the crowd to get over their Minnesota bashfulness. They wanted to dance, but no one wanted to start it. [Rupert's] presence, whenever he would come in, would just transform a room."

Even the vets of the scene thought the dancer took OH to another level. Brian Roessler says, "The first time the people in our circle were really like, 'Wow, this is something' was the first time that Rupert appeared with them." Chris Riemenschneider recalls: "You just couldn't take your eyes off that guy for whatever reason. That would normally be the kind of thing I hate, just real gimmicky, but it worked. It matched the unabashed joyfulness and playfulness of the band." Jon Bream wrote about Rupert in the *Star Tribune* after an August performance at the Minnesota Zoo, saying that he stole the show and was "worth the price of admission."

After the band played at the Cities 97-sponsored Basilica Block Party that July, which at that point was the biggest audience the band had played for, WCCO (the Twin Cities CBS affiliate) reporter Jason DeRusha interviewed not Darren or Appelwick, but Rupert. Dave Campbell acknowledges the corniness of a band having a dancer, but says nonetheless, "I love Rupert. When I see Rupert I'm like, 'Fuck yeah, let's have some fun!'"

Rupert also had an air of mystery. jMatt used half-truths about his own life to fill in the character's backstory, and Eric Fawcett had invented the name. Rupert became an essential outlet for jMatt, an extension of himself, and an alter ego. And it all came out of being moved by Appelwick and Darren's music. He'd loved the songs when they were Camaro songs, and nothing had changed, so if he couldn't be in the band he could at least be their superfan. "I got kicked out of a band I loved," he says, "and then I came back reincarnated."

With Rupert in their arsenal, the band would go on to slay several huge shows in 2005, but first there was a change in wardrobe. The tracksuits were never something the guys in Olympic Hopefuls loved—Appelwick says his never fit right; Matt made an earnest plea to ditch them—but they had played a significant part in the band's success. Darren says they decided to wear tracksuits more as a lark than as any sort of focused marketing plan. And the tracksuits wouldn't have made a difference if the music hadn't been good, but they did help people notice and actually listen to the music. Some fans found the suits campy but loved the band anyway, others thought the suits were sexy or funny. Pop music has a long history of bands dressing up to get attention: Appelwick and Fawcett's first musical love, KISS, are the most obvious example of a band using image to sell their

Olympic Hopefuls show off a new look at a summer 2005 gig. From left to right: Eric Fawcett, John Hermanson, Heath Henjum, Darren Jackson, Erik Appelwick. Courtesy Eric Fawcett.

music, but there's also Devo, Daft Punk, Village People, and countless others. In the Olympic Hopefuls' case, the tracksuits made them, as Ross Raihala put it, "instantly iconic."

In May, an opportunity came to make a change. The band had been invited to play the second annual Voltage: Fashion Amplified event, which combined local designers with local bands in a showcase for both. To mark the occasion, the guys hired designer Allison Nassif to create new tracksuits. These were a more rock-club-friendly dark navy blue, with white striping on the sleeves and legs, and the band's logo in white on the chest. The look was completed by white headbands and white Chuck Taylors. From that point forward, the band mostly retired their red, orange, and white suits.

The final major change of the spring of 2005 happened when Rob Stefaniak decided to step down as the band's manager. For Rob, his time working with Olympic Hopefuls had been the slow realization the band was more of a "happy accident" than a sincere attempt at building a sustainable musical entity. He decided that Darren and Appelwick weren't fully committed to do what it was going to take to escape the island of the Twin Cities scene. This came fully clear to Rob when he arranged the band to appear at two major festivals on the same weekend in early June—the CMJ/Rock Hall Fest in Cleveland and North by Northeast in Toronto—and they balked. Darren says they thought it would be a waste of time. Rob thought they didn't want to have to pay to travel and then play for free. At that point, Rob says, he decided to "gracefully and amicably resign, feeling strongly that working with them wasn't worth my time any longer."

12

Don't Look So Surprised

In which Vicious Vicious release their second album, the Olympic Hopefuls run afoul of the law, and music blogs go crazy for The Loon.

Amidst the Olympic Hopefuls' summer of big local gigs, Appelwick released a CD that would help cement the band's and his own dominance of the Twin Cities. He'd recorded the second Vicious Vicious record during the summer of 2004 at the original Shortman Studios, a.k.a. Darren's South Minneapolis attic, and at CityCabin before Alex sold it. Titled *Don't Look So Surprised*, the album marked an artistic leap for Erik.

Sonically, the record is a 180-degree turnaround from the lo-fi approach of *Cellophane/Lacerate* and *Blood and Clover*. Though Appelwick still played most of the instruments himself (Martin Dosh manned the drum kit and Alex played synth bass), the sound of *Don't Look So Surprised* is lush and cinematic, full and deep. He directed Alex to mix Dosh's drums big and fat, and to keep the low end really low, to evoke both pop rock and hip-hop.

Lyrically, Appelwick was not to be outdone by Johnny and Darren both creating concept albums, so *Don't Look So Surprised* is the story of an ill-fated romance, told in seven parts. In an interview with the *Pulse*, Erik revelard that the album was autobiographical: "There were a lot of things going on in my personal life at the time I was making the album that sort of ended up vomiting themselves onto the record. I wrote all of the songs really recently and at the same time and they were all being influenced by the same set of events." He added in a different interview, "One reason why I kept it at seven songs is because it's all cohesive. And it travels: from happy to sad, which is how life goes a lot of times."

The album is an impressive feat of storytelling, with lines and phrases and ideas bouncing between the songs, and the musical journey matching the emotional one. The album starts at the end of the story. "It's a Serious Thing" is a guitar-driven rocker that introduces the woman who serves as both heroine and antagonist: "Oh Jenny you're so vicious and Jenny you're so fine, but it's time that we forget about the days when you used to be mine." Then Appelwick goes ahead and spends the rest of the album remembering. The next song, slow-jamming "2 Much Time on My Hands," takes us back to their first meeting, at a pool party where her opening conversational gambit concerns the "hot sex" she had with her ex. "Here Come Tha Police," which finds Jenny and Appelwick on the run from the fuzz for unspecified infractions, is the fulfillment of Erik's goal to make "grooves and slamming bass funk shit." The song catches fire during a break-it-down-and-build-it-back-up at the two-and-a-half-minute mark that spotlights Alex's minisynth.

"Under California Skies" takes things down a notch musically but up a notch emotionally. It's a dreamy, sweeping pop song about the fantasy of escaping with the person you love. "Truth or Dare," another slow jam, highlights the stark differences in the couple's personalities. He wants to play spin the bottle, a game that ends in kissing. She wants to play truth or dare, a game with several possible outcomes, all of them risk-laden. The countrish shuffle of the title track and album closer, finds our narrator realizing the futility of trying to hold on to Jenny. The song features an audio clip inserted into the middle, in which a stentorian voice says, "You and I are doomed. Doomed to unimaginable despair. Or bliss! Unimaginable bliss." The line is from Tolstoy's tragic novel *Anna Karenina*, with the clip coming from the 1935 adaptation starring Greta Garbo and Fredric March. Like any good English major, Appelwick used a quote to emphasize his theme (and perhaps Darren's love of Russian literature was rubbing off).

Once the record was finished, with Alex mixing and mastering it out in L.A., Appelwick started looking for a label. He met with 2024, but Erik wanted more money for it than the label wanted to spend, and the label wanted him to add some songs and commit to an aggressive marketing/promotion plan, neither of which Erik was eager to do. In the meantime, Alex had given the album to Ryan Kuper, an L.A.-based music manager who also owned a small label, Redemption Record Company. Originally hailing from Omaha, Nebraska and that city's robust punk scene, Ryan had built both the label and his management company, Boundless Entertainment, from the ground up. His highest profile dealings up to that point involved getting major label deals for both Motion City Soundtrack and the All-American Rejects.

Alex and Ryan had met thanks to a Milwaukee Americana band called Ticklepenny Corner, whose 2004 album *Seven Years Bad Luck* Alex recorded and produced at City-Cabin. Ryan had inadvertently become a fan of the group when he ordered their CD instead of a similarly-named band's album. He loved what he heard, sought Alex out, and the two formed a friendship. One day, Ryan was visiting Alex in his new studio in L.A., and Alex said, "I'm gonna play you your new favorite band." He put on *Don't Look So Surprised*, which he had just finshed mixing. Ryan's reaction was exactly what Alex had hoped for:

"I was just blown away," Ryan says. "I thought it was fresh and fun, and I loved the lyrics, and it was clever amalgamation of musical styles. I've only had that feeling a couple of times in the whole time I've worked in the music industry, and that was definitely one of the strongest." After listening to the burned CD of the album in his car after leaving Alex's place, Ryan literally pulled over to call Alex and tell him that he had to work with Appelwick.

So Ryan became Vicious Vicious's manager, with the goal of securing a major label release for *Don't Look So Surprised*, and/or a multi-album deal for Appelwick. He put the CD out on Redmption to both lend it credibility and to take advantage of the mechanisms the label had in place, including digital distribution. He even set Appelwick up with his own imprint, Plexipuss, as an outlet to release albums by bands he worked with or admired.

The CD release show was at the 7th Street Entry on June 17. Heath played bass. Dosh moved over to keyboards to make room for new drummer Adrian Suarez. To set the tone for the new songs, Appelwick played Buddy Miles' 1970 funk masterpiece *A Message to the People* between sets. He revealed to *City Pages*' Lindsey Thomas that he stole the album from an abandoned car full of records when he was in college. "It's pretty much the dopest stuff ever," he told her.

12. Don't Look So Surprised

The Twin Cities fell hard for *Don't Look So Surprised*. "Here Come Tha Police" got significant airplay on the Current, and local journalists loved the album. *Pulse of the Twin Cities'* Rob van Alstyne praised the CD for being "immediately accessible, yet subtly intricate" and announced: "Appelwick's made a record that should rightfully go down in the annals of great Minnesota albums." Ross Raihala placed it at number six on his end of the year list of best local CDs." *City Pages* singled it out in their "Best of 2005" issue, and even the Wisconsin-based *Onion AV Club* got in on the action. In an article titled "2005: The Year in Music (Loon State Edition)," music editor Christopher Bahn placed the CD at number ten on his list top ten, writing that "bittersweet memories are still beautiful when they're given such a gloriously glossy pop sheen."

Ryan Kuper set up meetings with several major labels, and arranged for reps from ATO Records and a couple of other labels to attend a Vicious Vicious show in Minneapolis. Initial interest was strong, as *Don't Look So Surprised* got consistently positive reactions from the labels (especially "Here Come Tha Police"), but nothing ultimately materialized in terms of a deal. Ryan says he was up against the skittish constitutions of the big record labels: "They have always waited for and chased the sure thing ... that clear radio hit with the repetitive chorus. They wanted someone else to do all the work for them." As Spymob had discovered with Epic, gone were the days when a label invested in developing an artist's long-term potential.

As Ryan's work pushing the album ran its course, Appelwick kept moving forward, not banking on anything in particular happening. He kept writing and recording new Vicious Vicious songs and kept doing shows with Olympic Hopefuls. He wanted to have a career in music, but he wasn't the type to pursue a longshot. By this point Erik, like Darren, was attempting to make a living doing music. Circa 2004 he was working at a "soul-sucking" job at a bank. One beautiful and unseasonably warm April day, Erik went outside for lunch, and resolved that he wasn't going back inside. "I just said, 'Fuck this place,' walked out and never looked back."

Also like Darren, Erik had begun picking up recording and producing work, spreading the magic of what he'd learned over the last five years. In addition to working with Darren on Fitzgerald's *Raised By Wolves* and the Melodious Owl album (where he also sang backup on the track "Telephone"), Erik also ventured out on his own, producing debuts by two local bands.

The first was a group of four friends who'd met at suburban Armstrong High School, guitarist Joe Christenson, bassist Dan Larson, and brothers Mike (vocals) and Mark (drums) Schwandt. Calling themselves the Evening Glow, they were trying to make a go of it, but weren't able to get many gigs booked. They had saved some money and borrowed some more from their parents, and decided to do a professional recording of some of the songs they'd written. They sought out Appelwick as a producer after buying bought a bunch of local CDs and combing through the liner notes to see who worked on them. Erik's and Alex's names had both stood out for their balance of "really slick production with a little bit of that indie credibility," Joe says. The guys' songs were in the vein of new New Romantic bands of the mid '00s such as the Killers, with a bit of U2's anthemic style thrown in.

The band were completely inexperienced in the realm of professional recording, so Appelwick guided them through the whole process, even helping the band overhaul a couple of their songs before they started recording. "In the old seventies definition of the term he very much produced the record," Joe says. The album itself was recorded at

Shortman (Joe recalls that Darren—mindful of neighbors—had instilled "very rigid" 9:30 to 5 work hours: "As soon as 5 o'clock hits, amps gotta go off.") and the Terrarium during the summer of 2005. The result was a six-song EP called *The Dark Is Light Enough*. Erik exerted his influence in one last major way before the CD went out into the world. Joe recalls: "I think on the last night, Erik had brought a six pack and he was getting a little tipsy and that's when it came out, 'I hate your name, man.'" Arguing that it didn't fit their sound, Erik encouraged them to come up with something else.

Joe charged everyone to think up with fifteen options. One of his—White Night Riot—came from browsing through a Wikipedia entry on San Fransisco gay-rights activist Harvey Milk and the 1979 riots that ensued following the lenient sentence given the man who murdered him. The other guys liked that, but didn't want to be so tied to the political connotation, so Mike suggested that they change the "Night" to "Light." Later, they invented a different origin, telling journalists that they'd mashed up the Velvet Underground's *White Light/White Heat* with the Clash's "White Riot."

The strength of the EP (which was mixed and mastered by Alex) got the band rave local reviews—many of which singled out Appelwick's production work—and suddenly booking gigs was no longer a problem. Joe says there was a period where each successive show seemed to be bigger and better attended that the last. This culminated in a record contract with a Sony imprint.

White Light Riot had sought out Appelwick, but in the case of other band Erik worked with during the same period, he was the one who'd pursued. Tapes 'n Tapes were a group started at Carleton College by Josh Grier, Matt Kretzmann, Shawn Neary, and Karl Schewitz. When Josh was still in school, the student activities director at Carelton called jMatt and asked him to come talk to Josh about careers in music. jMatt says, "He was still making these whacked-out cassette tapes, recordings in his bedroom, and I met with him and he was super-sweet. But I didn't know how to help him." When the guys graduated in 2004, they headed north to Minneapolis.

Tapes 'n Tapes recorded a raw, genreless seven-song EP and played a handful of gigs around town at places like the Uptown Bar and the Turf Club. They wanted to do a full-length debut, but didn't make it a high priority. It was Appelwick's self-described pestering of Josh to let him record it that finally sent the band into action. With Erik and new drummer Jeremy Hanson, who had just graduated high school, the band convened in June 2005 at Shortman to record what would become *The Loon*. Appelwick produced, recorded, and mixed the album himself, and he brought just the right amount of pop polish and focus to the band's unpredictable, jittery sound. Josh says Erik wouldn't settle for anything less than a good take, which is not how the band had operated previously.

They put out *The Loon* in November 2005, and celebrated with a late October Turf Club release show. Ross Raihala called the album "hooky and dynamic," but TnT, unlike White Light Riot, were not an immediate hit with the locals. They did make it on to some end-of-the-year lists, but things were pretty low-key before band manager (and Josh's girlfriend) Keri Wiese sent MP3s to a few music blogs, including *Brooklyn Vegan* and *Pitchfork*. She had seen the way blogs had propped up first albums by Arcade Fire and Clap Your Hands Say Yeah, and didn't see any reason *The Loon*, with its indie-friendly sound, couldn't get a similar reaction. She was right. Blogs *EAR FARM* and *Music for Robots*, both of which posted MP3s for their readers, were the first to pick up on and praise the album, and it snowballed from there.

In February 2006 the album got a review in *Pitchfork*, earning an 8.3 rating and "Best New Music" tag. Writer Sam Ubl called *The Loon* "a rich, participatory, and eminently repeatable experience" and compared them to Wire, the Pixies, and Pavement. That was when the dam broke and Tapes 'n Tapes became the next big thing.

* * *

The Olympic Hopefuls had had a spring full of changes, and they only got a brief respite in early summer before the biggest change of the year occurred. In late June, Dave Campbell, who had come on earlier in the year as the Manager of Operations for 2024, got a letter from the United States Olympic Committee (USOC) threatening legal action for violation of trademark. Dave was dumbstruck, but quickly made a call to the organization to learn more. The USOC representative said, "We see that this record has gotten some press. How many records have you sold?" As the conversation unfolded, Dave panicked. "Holy shit," he remembers thinking, "We're up against a juggernaut."

Dave, Nate, and Todd were "terrified" upon learning that in 1950, Congress had passed a law—36 U.S.C. Section 220506—granting exclusive rights to the usage of the word "Olympic" to the USOC. It also included a prohibition on creating any variation of the Olympic rings, such as OH's upside down rings logo. This meant that Darren, Appelwick, and 2024 were in violation of federal law. Now, from 1974 to 1979 a British funk band called Olympic Runners released eight albums and charted several singles on both the U.S. R & B and UK charts. They appear to have never made it onto the USOC's radar.

The guys' initial reaction was "Can we fight it?" Heath was 100 percent in that camp. He says, "We were a small band from Minneapolis. We didn't really have much money. The number of CDs we had in stores was peanuts compared to bigger bands. What were [the USOC] going to take from us? I think we should have just laid low longer and ignored them."

"What if we offer to play every future Olympics for free?" Darren joked.

This is where the band's new manager, lawyer Dennis Pelowski, came in, and any hopes of ignoring or deal-making were quickly dashed. Dennis read up on the full code, discovering that there were a few exceptions to the law but none that remotely applied to OH. Even from this completely disadvantaged position, Dennis was able to negotiate that the band be allowed to keep selling their already-produced merchandise as long as the name was changed and no new merchandise was created with the Olympic Hopefuls name on it. It was, on the balance, the best possible outcome.

Everyone was bummed out. At the time, Darren said, "It was like someone telling me I couldn't live in my house anymore, that I would have to find a new house." For their new name, they first tried "endless adjectives" to replace "Olympic" in front of Hopefuls, but nothing worked. Appelwick remembers that all the discussions of completely new names were couched in a worry that they'd lose all the momentum they'd built.

In the end they went with the simplest solution, simply becoming the Hopefuls. The only real catch was that another band, a Christian rock group from Waynesfield, Ohio, was already using the name. The two bands connected and decided they likely wouldn't be stepping on each others' toes. Darren and company also vowed to continue to wear the tracksuits, non-sequitur as they were. They kept that going for a few months, though they would eventually set the suits aside permanently.

The one silver lining of the whole debacle was that the story—a compelling big guy vs. little guy narrative—got a ton of press, and not just locally. Naturally the *Star Tribune* and *Pioneer Press* reported on it, as did WCCO-TV, but Nate pushed the story out wider, resulting in an Associated Press article and a piece on MTV News' website. It was the most publicity, attention, and recognition the band had gotten yet, and just in time for a string of big summer shows.

When it rains it pours, however, so fans going to see the band at their gigs that July had to adjust to not only a band with a new name, but a different bassist. When Heath was sidelined by back surgery that June, a familiar face subbed in. Brian Roessler ended up playing bass in nearly ten shows that summer, including the Basilica Block Party, Taste of Minnesota, and Okoboji. He had to learn everything fast, but his years of playing with Fawcett helped a lot. "It was so much fun; I loved doing it. Their repertoire was so drenched with amazing songs." He especially enjoyed playing on one of the new songs, an epic Johnny-Appelwick collaboration called "Hold Your Own." He calls it "the kickass moment" of the shows.

Heath also missed the band's trip to Chicago to rerecord "Let's Go" for a Philip Morris-sponsored compilation called *The Latest*, just like Alva Star had done with "Unhappily Yours." *The Latest* included a video file featuring interviews and concert footage of four of the bands, including the Hopefuls, performing at the Metro in Chicago. The guys are shown onstage playing "Shy" and "Idaho" in their blue tracksuits. Backstage they answer questions about the rock lifestyle. When questioned about the worst part of their job, Fawcett says "putting a drum set together," Darren says "hauling amps around," and Johnny says, "the waiting." When the interviewer asks them to describe their sound, Appelwick deadpans, "Super happy number one fun time" while Johnny and Darren crack up.

What wasn't a super happy number one fun time was their relationship with 2024. After Rob Stefaniak left, Darren brought in lawyer Dennis Pelowski—a long time rock fan—as the band's manager. In hiring Dennis, they hoped to address two major problems they had with the label: money and marketing. The first issue stemmed directly from the contract Appelwick and Darren had signed. It was five pages long, simply written, and came down to a 50/50 split between artist and label, including publishing. Dennis says, "The 2024-Camaro contract was amongst one of the worst deals I've ever come across, and I've seen my share. I never faulted 2024 for that—Nate paid a lawyer to write something up and the lawyer slipped things in that I am sure he felt would be refused. You know, starting points to open negotiations. But Erik and Darren signed it, as was, without counsel. They admitted it."

Nate counters that the contract was taken directly from an entertainment law book, was five pages long and mostly free of legalese. He says that a 50/50 profit split (after the label recouped expenses), was common—if not standard—at the time for independent record label contract. "Why would we put forth an unfair contract and risk undermining goodwill from the start with an artist?" Nate asks rhetorically, "It would be unwise as well as unethical."

In the guys' view, they'd presented the label with a nearly-finished product. They'd received money to finish up the record, but 2024 had made that back and was now profiting, they felt, disproportionately. By Darren's estimate, Nate had made double what Darren and Erik had off the OH album. Dennis's mission, with Appelwick and Darren's full approval, was to tilt the monetary split toward the two writers. Dennis recalls, "Appelwick and Darren were more interested in the end, not the particular process. They understood the fact that there was a hardened battle ahead because, face it, Nate and 2024 held all the cards. Appelwick and Darren owed 2024 another full album and it was exclusive to 2024."

Dennis strategized with Darren, Appelwick, and Fawcett (who, having some experience with record deals, recognized how terrible this one was for the band) on attacking not just the money issue, but also pressing the label to step up their efforts in getting Olympic Hopefuls known beyond the Twin Cities. Dennis came at 2024 with a prosecutor's tenacity. The first meeting didn't go well, nor did the ones that followed. Nate and company were were taken aback and not a little pissed off. While Nate conceded that there was more the label could do for OH especially as it pertained to distribution and marketing, he dug in on the contract.

He countered that the label hadn't been given a finished product. They paid for the songs to be finished, mixed, and mastered, as well as graphic design and photography, none of which was inexpensive. He also insisted that 2024 had not made double what the band did, especially considering the expenses of running a business (personnel, office space, insurance, utilities, etc.), and if they had it would have been a clear violation of the contract.

Todd and Dave were confused and hurt. Todd says, "I really felt personally that this is a local band doing good. Why are we treating this like we're negotiating a multi-million, 360 deal? Why don't we all get over ourselves?" For Dave it was the beginning of the end of his tenure at 2024. A musician himself, he had considered the guys in the Hopefuls his peers, and he had promoted and supported them during his time in radio: "It got uncomfortable. It was hard to have these people who I thought of as friends go after, essentially, me and the business I was working for. I don't understand the grounds you have to do that."

With emotions running high on both sides, communication started to fail. Nate says, "When neither party is seeing what the other party is doing, there's a lot of opportunity for miscommunication and assumptions." He adds, "To his credit, Dennis did have some really good ideas, and I appreciated his hustle and tenacity. But trying to work with him was extremely difficult, and it changed the label's entire dynamic with the band."

Despite the behind-the-scenes drama, OH were ubiquitous in the second half of the year. In addition to their Basilica, Taste of Minnesota, and Minnesota Zoo shows, they sold out two consecutive nights at the Uptown in June. They also played the Green Man Festival in Duluth, along with the Violent Femmes, Mason Jennings, Alan Sparhawk, and several others. Duluth News Tribune writer Sarah Henning wrote that the band "brought out the first dance freakshow of the night, which is a true sign of greatness." They released a new song, "Book of Love," which was a repurposed Vicious Vicious tune performed by Erik, on a compilation called *Twin Town High: Music Yearbook Volume 07*.

In the fall, two major events shored up their status as the best band in the Cities. First came the 2005 Minnesota Music Awards. If they had flexed their muscles in the 2004 nominations, they completely hulked out in 2005. Members of the group nabbed seventeen nominations. Heath was up for Best Bass Player, Kid Dakota was nominated as Best Rock Artist, and the Hopefuls got a nod for Artist of the Year. Several categories found the guys competing against each other, or even themselves. Darren and Erik were both nominated for Best Songwriter. Darren, Erik, and Johnny all got nods for Best Male Vocalist. Both Vicious Vicious and the Hopefuls were nominated for Best Pop Group.

Rupert (front) works his magic at the 2006 Basilica Block Party in downtown Minneapolis. From left to right: John Hermanson, Eric Fawcett, Heath Henjum, Darren Jackson. Courtesy jMatt Keil.

And the *Don't Look So Surprised* track "Castaways" was in the running for Song of the Year.

The ceremony took place on September 21 at First Avenue. It was a rainy night, but that didn't ruin the parade of awards for the Hopefuls' guys. Vicious Vicious took home the Best Locally Released Recording statue (beating Kid Dakota's *The West Is the Future*). Johnny tied for Producer of the Year with Ed Ackerson. And the Hopefuls nabbed both Best Pop Group and Artist of the Year. The evening was the gold medal reward for their remarkable year and a half run.

The victory lap came the next month when the Hopefuls did a show at the Fitzgerald Theater on Exchange Street in downtown Saint Paul as part of the Current's Guest Session Sundays, a series of concerts where a local band would invite other musicians to join them and "extend the group's creativity and sound." The Hopefuls called on three fourths of Trip Shakespeare (or two thirds of Semisonic, if you prefer), asking Dan Wilson, Matt Wilson, and John Munson to perform with them. They also invited *Fuses* drummer Peter Anderson to sit in, and Rupert to dance. The end result was a wildly entertaining night of music.

After banging through a six-song set, the Hopefuls gave way to Dan Wilson, who did two songs—"Free Life" and "Sugar"—from the solo album he was then in the midst of recording (not coincidentally, with Johnny and Fawcett both participating). And then the Hopefuls picked it up for "Shy" and two new songs, Darren's "Red Stain" (a dramatic reworking of a four-track demo called "Stain on You") and "Swear to God." The former came out of a late night jam session with Johnny playing guitar and Erik on piano that also produced "Hold Your Own" (Johnny says, "While we were doing it we were laughing. It was just like, 'This is so awesome!'"). With its funky feel, Johnny singing in a Prince-like falsetto on the verses and Erik taking over on the chorus, it was a distinct departure from the typical Hopefuls sound, and an intriguing sign of the direction the band might be taking. In all the group performed six songs not on *Fuses*. One of the band's young superfans, Leo Vondracek was at the concert, and says, "Those new songs that made me really excited for the next record."

The second set opened cleverly with a song each from "guest" performers Kid Dakota ("Winterkill"), Alva Star ("Only Dreaming"), and Vicious Vicious ("It's a Serious Thing") before bringing on Matt and John, who were at that time performing as the Flops (they'd later change their name to the Twilight Hours), for three songs. From there it was an eight-song set of super-sized Hopefuls (with all guests on stage, including Peter doing double drums with Fawcett), highlighted by a barnstorming version of "Pretty Bigmouth" featuring John Munson on harmonica, and a cover of Semisonic's "Secret Smile" during which Rupert slow-danced with a chair. Heath calls the show one of the best moments of his Hopefuls experience. Leo found it to be a defining moment for the guys in the band: "That show you saw all the arms of everything they were involved with in the scene."

PART III: LOVE WITHOUT A FUTURE (2006–2012)

13

Blazing Out of Sight

In which the Hopefuls' loss is Tapes 'n Tapes' gain, Storyhill goes for the big time, and Eric and Johnny compete with Darren to see who can produce more records.

Kid Dakota sprang back into action in the beginning of 2006. In February, Ian did a marathon 16 tracks' worth of drums for the next record, then the duo went on a week's worth of tour dates with alt-country singer-songwriter Bobby Bare, Jr. The tour hit Chicago, Indianapolis, Cleveland, and New York with a couple of other cities in between. Ian was settling in well as the band's new full-time drummer. Replacing Christopher McGuire was a mammoth task, but he was up for it. "I had huge respect for the parts that Christopher wrote and how well it worked in those songs. I was a giant fan of that music. I didn't want to disturb that. I think I kind of put my own stamp on that." To honor McGuire he played with a similarly minimal kit and adjusted his style to give the songs space and make each hit have weight and importance. Jennifer Whigham's *How Was the Show* review of a gig with Cloud Cult later in 2006 perfectly captures the experience of seeing this version of Kid Dakota live: "The pair looks innocent enough, and then they start. Prince, in a primal, hair-swinging rage, smashes the drums so hard the set nearly topples off the stage, and Jackson, with his choir-boy tenor, sings beautiful epic melodies over the animalistic percussion, all the while inserting incredibly loud and dangerous guitar solos. The duo manages to sound like a full-on band, with energy alone."

Darren had barely any time to catch his breath after playing at the Mercury Lounge in New York before he was back out on the road with the Hopefuls.

Touring had been a source of contention with 2024. "They were always pressuring us to tour," Darren says. For decades, going out on the road and building an audience piece by piece is how a band paid its dues. It wasn't typically profitable, but was generally considered a long-term investment. But all of the guys had been playing music for audiences for a decade or more. They felt they had already paid their dues. They were all in their 30s. Everyone but Appelwick was married and had a mortgage; Fawcett, Heath, and Johnny all had kids. Heath was still working full time as a data analyst. None of them thought touring was the answer. "That was the old model," Darren says. "You have to have an audience built in; there's too much competition." The new model would turn out to be the Internet, but the infrastructure and mechanism for that was still a few years away.

"Leaving town for weeks on end, and coming home broke" is how Dennis puts the prospect of touring. Roessler backs that up, "It's a shitty life and there's no way to make money at it, especially in the U.S." Even so, the band booked a three-week tour, albeit without Johnny, who couldn't justify all that time spent away from home on something that wasn't a guaranteed moneymaker. So Appelwick, Darren, Eric, and Heath loaded up and kicked things off in a familiar place: The Cave at Carleton College. From there they headed east, playing Milwaukee, Chicago, Detroit, Philadelphia, New York, Indianapolis and several cities in between, doing a show every night.

Rupert came along for a few of the shows to liven things up, surprising the guys in Milwaukee, Madison, and Chicago. The latter gig, which took place at the Double Door, found him dancing on the venue's tables. He had expanded from dancing during one or two songs to dancing for a third of the show or more. Occasionally, he danced the entire set, though this wasn't without consequences. "I would just rip my body to shreds," jMatt reveals. By the summer of 2006 he'd was already dealing with tendonitis in his left knee, compartment syndrome in his leg, and a herniated disc in his lower back. And yet he endured. Dancing was a "natural drug" he wasn't about to quit.

Darren recalls the tour as being "really pointless." For all of the guys going from playing to ecstatic, sold out hometown crowds to indifferent, small ones was a shock. Darren felt especially bad for Fawcett. "He'd just gotten back from touring with N.E.R.D. Now you're playing Cleveland fucking Ohio with two people watching us in a place that smells like piss and beer." The tour had reaffirmed the guys' resolve that touring wasn't going to be the way to build the Hopefuls into something bigger. There was one positive effect, however. At their first show after the tour, Johnny was astonished by the precision of the other four: "Dammit," he said, "you guys are so fuckin' tight!"

Darren replied, "This is what happens when you play like twenty nights in a row."

The tour aside, things were not improving with 2024. The label had been named by *City Pages* as the Best Local Record Label in late 2005, with the paper saying their logo "bears the guarantee of smart pop," but that belied the drama going on behind the scenes. Dave Campbell left the label in January 2006, agonizing over the decision. He thought he had his dream job, one that combined all of his interests and talents, but the tremendous stress he felt constantly, along with the realization that the time management skills required were something he just didn't have, led him to quit. The Hopefuls' situation, and Nate's response to it, was certainly one of the main sources of his stress. He says, "Nate was stubborn. Darren was fucking stubborn. The lawyer was stubborn."

From Dave's perspective, the band were unrealistic about what they could expect from 2024, disinclined to do what it would take to expand beyond the Twin Cities, and churlish to challenge the contract they'd read and willingly signed. He says they saw Nate and the label as a cash machine. "Everyone was trying to monetize the situation before it was ready. Like when you put a pie in the oven you gotta let it cook until the pie is done. And then you take it out and you enjoy some delicious pie. But if you pull the pie out early, what are you eating? Raw dough and some gooey cold apple stuff."

Though the entire record industry was in upheaval at this time, with less-profitable digital sales outpacing physical ones, and vinyl having not yet made its resurgence, 2024 faced some unique problems on top of that. Namely the fact that the Twin Cities music scene's biggest strength—it's supportiveness—is also one of its biggest weaknesses if you have any long-term, grander ambitions. In an interview with the *Saint Paul Pioneer Press*,

Jeff Allen and Aaron Mader of 2024 band the Plastic Constellations discussed that very issue:

Jeff: Minneapolis is an amazing place if you're a creative person, whether it be music, visual arts, writing, whatever. There's so many opportunities and so many people doing amazing stuff. But because it's so encouraging, it can get kind of incubated.

Aaron: It's like the end of the world is the Turf Club, and the other end of the world is the Entry.

The Plastic Constellations and Romantica were the two 2024 bands fully committed to touring, and used the 2024 touring van extensively. Nate says, "You can get really comfortable here and have a good draw at your shows and sell lots of merch. But it's a long way to either coast." Johnny Solomon puts it even more bluntly, "This is the only place I know where you can be a star without anybody else knowing who you are."

So, in many ways, the Hopefuls' early success worked against them. They were doing well in the short term and it was hard to walk away from that. And logically it would seem to follow that if you conquer a scene as lively and diverse and strong as the Twin Cities scene, then surely the right person in the right place will notice. Chris Riemenschneider believes the Hopefuls were a victim of geography. "If the Hopefuls had been a band from Brooklyn, I'm pretty sure they would have been a very big deal," he says. But at the same time, he thinks the band didn't give themselves enough of a chance. "For a while anyway it did really seem like it could be a commercial breakthrough for all those guys. So it's kinda a big what if: What if they had stuck with it?"

Sticking with it would have meant putting out a second album while the attention and hunger for it was still there, but the sour relations with 2024 made that all but impossible. In slightly better times they'd asked the label for a $10,000 recording budget/advance for the second record, and the label had balked. This became one of the main points of contention between the two sides. In a late 2004, Darren had stated there'd be a second Hopefuls album out by the fall of 2005 ("most of the material is already in the bag," he said). In summer of 2005 Appelwick adjusted that prediction to early 2006, but by then, Darren says, they became resolved not to release any more material on 2024.

This is when both 2024 and Dennis Pelowski began searching for a larger label to take on the band's contract. 2024 already had experience with this. When New York label Frenchkiss (home to the Hold Steady, Passion Pit, and many others) expressed interest in the Plastic Constellations, 2024 worked out a deal that was beneficial to everyone. The band's 2006 album *Crusades* would feature the 2024 logo, but all the heavy lifting was done by Frenchkiss. This was totally in line with how Nate and Todd saw 2024: as a springboard for their artists. Everyone would have been happy to work out a similar situation for the Hopefuls, but it wasn't so easy.

Ross Raihala told the *Argus Leader* that the Hopefuls "sure seem like a band that a record label would want to snatch up" and he wasn't wrong from a musical or visual standpoint, but the reality was more complicated. Nate reveals that there were labels calling to express interest, but it didn't last once the reps heard more about the guys. "I'd get calls from A&R people and talent scouts from major labels or major label imprints, and once they found out, oh they're in other bands, and oh, they're how old, and, oh, they have marriage and mortgage and kids, [their interest died]. Labels are always really concerned that a band's going to tour, especially in the first couple of years when they're really getting established, 200, 250 days a year."

Dennis echoes this. He says the labels he spoke with about the band wanted solid answers to questions about their commitment to putting the Hopefuls before their other projects, their plan for touring, and their work to build relationships with other bands in the region. When none of these had acceptable or sufficient answers, the labels quickly lost interest. With no major label savior waiting in the wings, the second OH album went into limbo, and the relationship between the band and the label reached a stalemate.

Johnny says, "When it came time to do a record there was this legal stuff with the label that in retrospect was not something that we should have worried much about. We should have just been making music. Based on that deal, let's just do it."

Appelwick came to feel the same. "I chose to play music for a living, not get into a heated pissing contest." he says. He saw both Dennis and Nate as hot-headed and overly defensive. "The bottom line was, it became personal between them, and it stopped being about what's right or what's good and it became solely about winning. I found this all detestable."

Dennis saw it as necessary and advantageous: "Applewick had less stomach for the process, but then that's why artists are best advised to not enter contracts without legal counsel. Because once you contractually yield your rights, the money and exclusivity you signed away is not gifted back to you. You need to substantiate why the label has failed to honor the contract. That means exposing label deficiencies. No one at the label cares to hear about their flaws but it was my job. And the truth is, Applewick came out way ahead of where he was contractually entitled to be on account of the job I did."

Everyone was trying to do what they thought was best at the time, but the bad timing (that the guys were older and more tied down), bad circumstances (that they each had other musical priorities), and bad choices (signing a contract without consulting a lawyer; relying on the band for their livelihood) were insurmountable. If the Hopefuls had all collectively decided to make that band their number one priority, if they had banded together to move forward, it might have worked. But they weren't designed that way. Darren and Appelwick had ignored Rob Stefaniak's pleas to include the other band members in the business arrangement so they could all equally profit from the group. In many ways, those two were the architects of their own prison.

* * *

Contrasting the Hopefuls' troubles was Tapes 'n Tapes' situation, which was turning out like a high schooler's fantasy of what's going to happen to her garage band. In January they played three nights at three different venues in New York City, earning rave reviews. After their February *Pitchfork* review, other blogs started picking up on *The Loon*, and sales surged. They hit the 12,500 point in CDs with a few thousand more in digital sales (more than triple what the *Fuses Refuse to Burn* had sold). Drummer Jeremy Hanson, who was in his freshman year of college at the University of Minnesota, decided to drop out to devote his full time and energy to the band. In March, they played two shows per day for four days at South by Southwest, drawing the likes of Neil Young to the audience, and garnering an ecstatic review in the *New York Times*. In early April, *Rolling Stone* named them a "Band to Watch" and gave *The Loon* a 3.5 star review.

Labels had started their pursuit long before all of that; Keri Wiese told the *Pioneer Press* that Capitol Records called the day after the first blog write-up back in November. While in the midst of that courtship, and not long after a west coast mini-tour, TnT lost their bassist. It's unclear why and how Shawn Neary left the band. At the time, Keri put out a mixed message: "It's a bummer, Shawn is a great guy. It was just time for it to happen. It just didn't work out." Heath recalls Shawn being upset with the band signing on for a Phillip Morris compilation similar to what Alva Star and the Hopefuls had done, but if that's the case it was likely a symptom of a larger philosophical difference between him and the rest of the band.

Becasuse he played bass and knew the songs inside and out, TnT invited Appelwick to fill in during gigs while they figured out a permanent replacement. Erik still really dug what they'd made together: "Like three months after we finished the album, I went back and listened to it one night while I was getting ready to go out. I was like, 'Wow. This really stands up.'"

Meanwhile, TnT chose to sign with XL Recordings, a British label that counted the White Stripes and Radiohead among their roster. The band and friends had a quite a celebration with the five kegs of beer the label sent in congratulations. The label planned to rerelease *The Loon* that July, and booked the band a seven date U.K. tour in May, including two sold out shows in London, and a three-week cross country jaunt in June. Most notable on the U.S. tour were two sold out nights at New York City's legendary Bowery Ballroom (Matt Kretzmann said of the venue, "It was so pristine and professional. It's a gorgeous room with the best monitors we've ever had."). The shows went over like gangbusters, with the band getting tighter and more muscular along the way. Erik was there for all of it.

Appelwick was a perfect fit as bassist, so TnT offered him the gig full-time. Before that offer, Chris Riemenschneider wrote, "What a peculiar position Appelwick is in now. I'd have predicted success for [the Hopefuls or Vicious Vicious] before TnT—but isn't it funny to think that Erik could probably go farther playing bass with Tapes?"

Erik didn't want to have to choose. Even with all the drama surrounding the Hopefuls, he wanted to both join TnT and continue to play with the Hopefuls when he was able. That wouldn't be often at first—the XL contract had stipulations that Erik had to be available for all TnT activities—but it would mean Erik could play with the Hopefuls when he was back in town, and eventually make another record with them.

Darren didn't like the idea that Tapes 'n Tapes would always have first priority, as it would put the Hopefuls in the position of never quite knowing if Appelwick would be available or not. Darren says he brought these conditions to the band, and that no one was fully comfortable with them, so he told Erik that staying in Hopefuls wasn't an option if he took the TnT gig. To Erik this felt like getting fired from the band he'd co-founded. He genuninely wanted to do both, but there was no way he was choosing the Hopefuls over the chance to tour the world and play music for a living in a band that was on the rise.

"Honestly," he says now, "the Hopefuls had become a litigious hornet's nest breeding resentment and negativity. Getting thrown out was probably one of the better things that's happened to me" (though, that Erik was able to sign with XL at all was down to the fact Dennis had successfully challenged the 2024 contract; otherwise, XL would have had to buy Erik out, and would have sought to recoup that expense from Tapes 'n Tapes). Darren for his part, didn't understand why Appelwick would choose to be a "hired gun" in a band over staying in one he'd started and in which he had a large creative stake, but he also felt Erik wanted to be famous above all else. Erik's departure from the Hopefuls was not only the end of over five years of fruitful collaboration, it was essentially the end of his friendship with Darren.

13. Blazing Out of Sight

Maybe it was inevitable. Darren and Appelwick were similar in many ways. They shared ambition to be heard, a bottomless interest in the recording process, thoughtful approaches to their lyrics, mercurial personalities, and wickedly dry senses of humor. But in perhaps more fundamental ways, Erik and Darren were the most unlikely of partners, the clichéd odd couple. Darren's driven perfectionism contrasted greatly with Erik's smart-ass insouciance, and this produced a productive conflict that advanced both of them musically.

Certianly Olympic Hopefuls wouldn't never have existed without both men's specific sensibilities to bring it to life. While Darren kept things tight and moving forward, Appelwick brought a collaborative spirit that inspired the others. "Around 2005 Erik gave an interview that showed some hints of excitement about the Hopefuls' musical future: "We have written a pile of songs together with varying degrees of collaboration and it's really broadened the scope of what we are capable of doing." Songs like "Hold Your Own" and "Swear to God" were tangible evidence of that. What had started as a hermetic recording project had the potential to blossom into a true band. Without Erik, though, it wasn't to be. Even so, Darren was resolved to keep the Hopefuls going.

Johnny says, "I couldn't even believe we were going to continue. I was just like, 'What?!'" But he himself was a huge factor in the band being able to go on. If you lose a talented singer and songwriter, it's always nice when there's another one right there in the band. So instead of replacing Appelwick from outside, they'd do it from within, having Johnny step forward to sing and contribute songs.

This new status quo was something the band had to adjust to quickly, as they had a few big summer gigs (Taste of Minnesota, Basilica Block Party, the Minnesota State Fair) to get through before going they could take a break in the fall. The biggest adjustment was to the loss of Appelwick's songs. The only ones they continued to play were "Let's Go" (which Darren had co-written) and "Hold Your Own." To make up for the loss of such great tunes as "Shy," "Motobike," and "Cavalier," the band ended up incorporating some Alva Star songs—"Thing for Me," and "Tornado Girl," primarily—into their sets, even further blurring the lines between the two bands. By most accounts, the fans' enthusiasm wasn't dimmed by Erik's departure, though the musicians certainly noticed it.

Heath recalls listening back to a recording of a show at the 400 Bar when Appelwick was still with the band and thinking, "Wow, we were so much more powerful than we are now." Fawcett says he's proud of what the Hopefuls did post–Appelwick, but that it wasn't quite as special or rocking as what they'd had before: "There was something about the five of us coming together and doing that and just having a great time. Having two guitars that are just wailing away and Johnny on the keyboard, it was just wild. It was a fuller sound. When we were on point it was glorious." Johnny says of the new configuration: "It got to the point where it felt pretty good, but never like how it had felt. I mean Appelwick's the greatest guy to play with ever." Even Darren admits that he felt Erik's absence: "I missed playing with him a lot. I always loved to play the songs that Appelwick sang on because then I could just focus more on guitar and just rock out."

And the transition wasn't without its awkward moments. Both the *Pioneer Press* and *Star Tribune* reported that Appelwick would be back with the Hopefuls for their Taste of Minnesota gig that July when TnT returned from their U.K. tour, though that was never the plan. He did play a poorly-attended Vicious Vicious set at the festival, however. TnT and the Hopefuls even went head to head with dueling gigs on the night of July 22, with the former playing a sweltering sold out show at First Ave while the latter rocked out at the more modest O'Gara's Garage in Saint Paul.

Appelwick and the Tapes guys had entered an entirely different world. Just a few days after their First Ave show they were off to New York to play *The Late Show with David Letterman*, where they played "Insistor." After their performance, Jeremy got to experience Letterman's odd habit of complimenting drummers on their drumset and then asking if they own them ("Beautiful drumset. Are those yours, or are they rentals?"). Josh Grier called the whole experience so "surreal" that months after it seemed like it had never really happened. A few days after that they were in Chicago playing the Pitchfork Festival. The guys were first on the bill, so they decided to "get drunk and watch all these bands we've waited to see," as Josh put it, including the National, Spoon, Yo La Tengo, and Ted Leo.

In August, the band were featured in a sketch on the MTV show Human Giant that illustrated just how far they'd invaded the zeitgeist. In the sketch, Aziz Ansari plays an unhinged indie band marketer who bullies blogs into featuring MP3s of the bands he represents. "I've decided that if you don't post that Tapes 'n Tapes MP3," he says to one blogger, "I'm going to come back here tomorrow and give you a Colombian necktie."

The tour continued into late summer and fall, with repeat trips around the U.S. and U.K., including an appearance at the Reading/Leeds Festivals, and a southern U.S. tour in October that took them to Florida, North Carolina, and Georgia. At that October's Minnesota Music Awards, the band was nominated for Song of the Year ("Cowbell") and won Best Pop Group (beating, among others, the Hopefuls, though Eric Fawcett did win Best Drummer) and "Artist of the Year." Appelwick got a Producer of the Year nod and White Light Riot's EP got the Best Locally Released Recording award from the critics. In November, while the TnT were in the likes of France, Germany, and Sweden, none other than David Bowie wrote about "Insistor" on the Nokia Insight newsletter where he recommended new music. Here's what he said: "'Insistor' is the first single, and it's cracking. It was a slow grower, but once that chorus kicks in there's really no escape. If you find yourself trying to sing along, you best have access to the lyrics first. The band's songwriter … seems to inhabit a different place to most and he's not easy to second guess."

Tapes 'n Tapes had certainly lived the rock star lifestyle: making music videos, doing constant interviews, and hobnobbing with celebrities, but it wasn't all great. In December in Perth, Australia, on the last day of a tour that had taken them nearly all around the world, they stopped for a "frolic" at the beach and someone broke into their van. Minimal gear was stolen, but the thief took two laptops, all of Josh's clothes, two cell phones, keys, wallets, and glasses. Appelwick's passport was among the missing, and he ended up stranded there for several days while it all got worked out.

It was an ignominious ending to what had been a miraculous year. The band recovered and capped everything off with a headlining gig at First Ave. For Josh, despite all the amazing places he'd played in 2006, the best was the venerable hometown club. "Pretty much all of the best shows I've ever seen have been at First Avenue," he told Ross Raihala, "So getting to play there was amazing. Nothing really compares to playing a great show at home."

* * *

While Appelwick toured the world, Darren, Fawcett, and Johnny kept busy with their own pursuits, namely producing records for other artists, and, in Eric and Johnny's case, focusing on Storyhill. Between the three of them, they would be responsible for ten albums released in 2006 and 2007. In 2006, Darren's only release was the debut by Ian Prince's new band, Story of the Sea. Formed with Ian's brother Adam and bassist John McEwan, Story of the Sea had a pure melodic rock sound. Darren didn't fully produce the record, but at Shortman—which by this point had a new location built by Darren and his dad in the basement of Darren and Erin's Northeast Minneapolis home—helped engineer vocals and obverdubs that were added to the basic tracks that had been recorded in Illinois with producer Paul Malinowski. Applewick did some recording on the album, too, pre–Tapes 'n Tapes.

The album, *Enjoying Fire*, was the first release on Darren and Ian's new label, Speaker Phone. It's hard not to see the fact of Darren creating his own label as a thumbing of the nose to 2024, but the two were operated quite differently, primarily for the fact that Speaker Phone didn't do contracts. They had similar missions, though. Ian says the big appeal for him was "creating a community" within the scene, a place where bands could come to get guidance and assistance in making records. He also saw it as a curated label where he and Darren could release work by artists they truly believed in, though for Ian that was a smaller pool than it was for Darren. "Darren wanted to put out more records, but I was kind of a naysayer," Ian recalls. "I didn't want to just put everything out."

Meanwhile, Johnny and Fawcett were cooking with gasoline on their production work. 2006 saw five records with their names attached. First, Eric called on his N.E.R.D. experience to produce five tracks for hip-hop collective Leroy Smokes's album *Love Hustle Theater*. The songs Eric helmed are among the album's catchiest, including the bouncy "Kill the DJ." Johnny produced Andrew Benon's *Rock and Roll Moves*, a fun homage to mid-'80s David Bowie featuring Eric on drums, Applewick on bass, and Alex doing the mixing and mastering. Eric and Johnny also did a few albums as a production team at the Lowertown studio they'd taken over from John Solomon and Friends Like These—Lowertown Caves, they called it.

Fawcett says the duo had two main goals when producing: the artistic satisfaction of the band, and speed. On the latter they were inspired by having worked on too many records that took way too long, and by Eric watching Pharrell work. "We did whatever we could do to abandon sort of the Calvinist, diligent, you know, the-song-isn't-good-if-it-doesn't-take-a-long-time mentality, and to really trust our gut." Generally Eric would handle rhythm and arrangement and Johnny would take on the songwriting aspects. "We've always been a two-headed creative entity," Eric says, "Generally where I'm weak, Johnny strong, and where Johnny's weaker I'm strong."

Á la the Neptunes, Fawcett and Johnny invented a pseudonym for their joint work: Fiction. They created it as a brand name for a new commercial music production venture, but they also used it on albums they produced. The credit first appeared on Kubla Khan's second album, *Lowertown*. Kubla Khan had changed a bit since jMatt first pulled Andy Bast and Nate Eklund together to form the band as a piano pop trio. They'd added a horn section and guitar player, becoming a seven-piece monster wall of sound. jMatt sought out Eric and Johnny because he wanted them to bring a pop sensibility to Nate and Andy's jam-oriented songwriting styles. The band celebrated the release of the CD in July with a show at the 400 Bar. One of the opening acts was a surprise reunion set by Spymob. It'd been nearly two years since the guys had played together, and Brent had to fly in from Los Angeles. "I got them to do that," jMatt says proudly. He and Fawcett both pulled double duty that day, having danced and drummed at a Hopefuls performance at the Basilica Block Party earlier.

Girl/guy pop trio Mighty Fairly's album *Perfectly Good Airplanes* was another Fiction production. Fawcett played drums on the record, and they did all eleven drum tracks in a single day. As was becoming habit, hey also brought in Appelwick to play on the CD.

Around this same time, Friends Like These put out a follow-up to *Deliver Us from Evil*. Titled *I Hate You, Volume 1: The Greatest Generation*. The six-song EP was created during hard times. John Solomon had been living with Appelwick while his wife was away at grad school, but when Erik left to tour with Tapes 'n Tapes, Solomon fell harder into heavy drugs. He spent a couple of nights in jail. His wife had returned from grad school and, dismayed by his condition, kicked him out. He wasn't getting along with his bandmates, Adam and Matt, either. What's amazing is that it hardly shows in the songs. Solomon credits Johnny for keeping things together musically, calling him "the glue."

Unfortunately, not long after this, some people Solomon was associated with through his drug use found out where Fawcett and Johnny's studio was, broke in, and robbed the place. Though Solomon wasn't directly involved, it wouldn't have happened without him, and so Eric and Johnny cut off contact. It was the end of what had been both a fruitful musical collaboration and friendship.

As if all this producing and drama weren't enough, the guys were also working together to do more instrumental CDs for Lifescapes, titles such as *Yoga Flow* and *Quiet Christmas*, and they were starting to dabble in creating music for commercials and other marketing purposes.

And then there was Storyhill. Since taking over as manager of the duo, Fawcett's main priority was helping the guys find a way to maximize their earnings without maximizing their time spent on the band. It was no easy task. Eric's approach involved recording a new album with a high-profile producer, placing it with a label, and consolidating the band's reputation. On the first point, Eric had a plan. While working with Dan Wilson, he "announced" that the singer-songwriter was coming to a Storyhill show with him, much as Brian Roessler had forced Eric to go see a show many years before. Eric was convinced that, a) Dan would love it, and b) he would be a good creative match to produce Chris and Johnny.

Both hunches paid off. Dan says, "When I went to the show I was so incredibly moved by the songs. I think I wept four times. It was one of those eye-opening gigs. I was just blown away." Eric's response to Dan's reaction?

"On one hand I was like, 'Oh, that's very touching.' On the other hand I was like, 'Yes!'" Dan agreed to produce Storyhill's new album, and they set about recording the album in the summer of 2006. This was a big deal. Dan's co-write with the Dixie Chicks, "Not Ready to Make Nice" had just come out, and would eventually win three Grammys and transition Dan from guy-who-was-in-a-couple-of-great-bands to guy-who-writes-big-hit-songs-with-superstars.

Another way that the guys began to raise their profile around this time came about almost by accident. Chris's 2004 wedding was two-day affair at the Hyalite Youth Camp, located in the Gallatin National Forest 12 miles south of Bozman on the shore of the Hyalite Reservoir. They held the ceremony on the first day, followed by a gathering around the fire rings at the end of the day. The guests stayed in cabins and camped out that night, leading into a reception the next day, which included concerts by Johnny and Justin Roth. As indelible and beautiful as the experience was for Leslie and Chris, it also set off a light bulb.

He realized that he could take what he'd learned from arranging all the logistics for the wedding celebration and put it to use to organize a mini music festival. It would allow him and Johnny to connect with fans, and provide showcase for both Storyhill and the talented musicians they'd met in their travels. When Chris took the idea to his partner, Johnny's initial reaction was a firm "no way!" When Chris offered to take charge of the logistics (including picking artists to perform), Johnny's stance softened into a skeptical, "Let's try one and see how it goes."

It took awhile to come together, but over two days and two nights in late July 2006 the first Storyhill Fest took place. Performers included Stormy Creek, Justin Roth, Matt Coughlin, Barb Ryman, and Aaron Espe. Rhubarb Pie, the group that had inspired Johnny by covering Storyhill, also appeared. Around the music, the guys planned guitar workshops, hiking excursions, and yoga classes. Storyhill headlined the performances each night, which ended with a campfire singalong. Along to document it was filmmaker Andrew Zilch, a fan with Hollywood credentials. The end result was the documentary *Parallell Lives*, which traces the origins of the band and chronicles the first Storyhill Fest and the recording of the *Storyhill* album.

The poster for the first Storyhill Fest, which gave the guys another level of connection with both their fans and their fellow musicians. Courtesy Storyhill.

By all accounts, it was a rousing success. It turned a profit, something Fawcett says usually doesn't happen until five or so years into a festival, but more importantly it served as a reminder to Johnny and Chris of the power of what they'd created together.

With that positive mojo fueling them, the guys next flew to L.A. to open for Dan Wilson at the Largo. Fawcett had arranged for "business types, record label types, and rabid Storyhill fans" to attend. Johnny and Chris both were somewhat ambivalent about the whole thing. Chris was wary of what Storyhill hitting the big time would look like or mean, though he admitted that having a label to take care of all the business details would be nice. Johnny was intrigued by the idea of signing to a label, but also said, "part of me would lament not being able to do this on our own." Everyone was adamant that any label that expressed interest would have to want Storyhill as is. "You can't put a dance beat to it or anything," Johnny quipped.

As it was, none of the majors bit on what they saw. The duo instead immersed themselves in a fall tour of several of their favorite places, and in the creative process of recording. Working at the Ballroom in Minneapolis with Fawcett on drums and Roessler back on bass, Chris and Johnny found a groove working with Dan. Chris said he brought out the best in both singers, and Johnny agreed: "Dan is able to get performances out of people in a way that doesn't feel like you're being coached or anything." Everyone's goal was to make a Storyhill sound, in Dan's words, "elemental, simple, unproduced." The guys couldn't help but notice, when looking at their sales, that the live albums almost always sold better. They realized that their fans were most often reacting to the simplicity of the two of them and their guitars, with maybe light drums and bass. So they tried to do as much live as possible, which sometimes meant hitting record without a lot of rehearsal. "You can hear the musicians learning the song as it's going to tape," Johnny says. "There's sort of a window of opportunity where people know the song well enough to play it but not well enough to make it sterile and too good."

Chris added: "Nowadays anybody can make a great sounding record. You can move it around, you can make it groove if it doesn't groove, you can make it in tune if it's not in tune, we're at the point that we're just not really interested in making a perfect record anymore, we just wanna kind of capture a moment in time and the songs as they are."

With no major label takers, the band finished up the record, which they were calling *Storyhill* as a nod to its back-to-basics nature, and planned a September 9 CD release show at the Cedar Cultural Center. But, as it happened, just a few days before the show, a deal came together with Red House Records, the venerable Saint Paul folk label. Everyone recognized immediately it was a perfect fit. The label was not flashy; it was focused on the music and growing their artists. It was home to singer-songwriters Chris and Johnny both loved: John Gorka, Greg Brown, Lucy Kaplansky, and Peter Ostroushko, to name just a few. Better yet, the label wanted *Storyhill* as is, without any changes or additions, and signed the guys up for two more records after that. All plans to self-release the record were put on hold and Red House set a February 13 release date.

Chris calls the Red House deal a "crossroads" for the duo. As was typical, things weren't quite copacetic interpersonally. Chris admits that he and Johnny needed a third party to help out and mediate, but Chris had never been comfortable with Fawcett being that person. He loved Eric as a friend and collaborator, but the fact that Eric and Johnny were so close and seemingly like-minded made it feel like an "us against you" situation when there was a disagreement about the direction things were going. And there were lots of disagreements, as Chris was deeply dubious about any efforts to take Storyhill to a higher level, and Eric was aggressively pursuing that very thing. There was also the matter of Johnny and Eric working to find ad clients for Fiction, some of which was being done on the Storyhill dime and time.

By the point the Red House offer came along, Chris was at his end with Fawcett as the band's manager, and was even questioning whether their friendship would survive. Things improved once the band signed their deal. Chris was thankful for Eric's work to get Storyhill to that point, but also relieved. "Red House came along and would kind of cement Storyhill for awhile, give us some foundation to stand on, a fresh team and the resources to go forward." David Weeks says the Red House deal was bittersweet for him.

The Storyhill full band line-up from left to right: Brian Roessler, Chris Cunningham, Eric Fawcett, John Hermanson (pictured here in at Storyhill Fest in 2014). Courtesy Storyhill.

He was obviously happy for the guys, but sad he hadn't been part of it. "That was always our pipe dream during the Peppermint days."

On Valentine's Day 2007, Chris and Johnny gave a second try at having a CD release party for *Storyhill*, this time at the Varsity Theater in Dinkytown. But once again, luck wasn't with them. The city fire marshal showed up after receiving a complaint, quickly determined that the place was overcrowded, and ordered the show halted. Turns out there were 450 people in attendance at the 300-capacity venue. The Varsity apologized, and admitted they'd oversold when they realized the demand for tickets. They rescheduled for a month later, this time with two shows. At the second of those, Dan Wilson joined them on stage for a few songs. Katie Bratsch wrote on *How Was the Show* that, "About 10 songs into their set, the creative flow between these two musicians was powerfully apparent. With their instinctual strumming back and forth and trading off song lyrics mid-sentence, it was like they were playing a wild game of catch."

The album had come out the day before the ill-fated party, the first time a Storyhill CD was available in stores across the country. Though they hadn't necessarily intended it that way, the album was a good introduction to Chris and Johnny's music, a mix of ballads and mid-tempo shufflers with sticky melodies and those amazing harmonies.

Standouts on the record are many. Johnny wrote the pretty, contemplative "Give Up the Ghost" about a friend who had a pattern of completely committing herself to a new life philosophy every couple of weeks. "Highlight" is a gentle love song Johnny wrote for Chris and Leslie's wedding, and performed there for the first time. About halfway through that first perfomance, Chris found himself joining in on harmonies. He says, "It was like, 'I know this song, even though I didn't.'"

"Paradise Lost" is a sad rumination on the wilderness surrounding Bozeman being replaced by housing developments: "The hills above town used to be the best place for starry-eyed lovers and inspiration/Now it's all paved/Every street's a dead end/And empty summer houses stand along them." The chorus tells how it was a place for them to play and "run forever" when they were kids, but the soaring bridge laments, "Now there's no trespassing/There's no going back again/I only hope you remember the way it was/What we had back then." The tune serves as not only as an elegy for that specific area, but for anything fondly remembered that's been senselessly taken away.

The creation of "Paradise Lost" and another highlight of the record, "Blazing Out of Sight," illustrate the ups and downs of Chris and Johnny's creative partnership. On "Paradise Lost," Chris credits Johnny for taking his original tune and "tidying it up, making it hooky, and something people love." On "Blazing Out of Sight," though, the process wasn't as positive. In *Parallel Lives*, Johnny introduces the tune onstage at Storyhill Fest by saying that Chris wrote the song and then Johnny rewrote one verse, then another verse until it was a different song. He describes this process as "very collaborative," to which Chris swiftly and sardonically replies, "Very Storyhill." As it happened, Chris rarely rewrote any part of Johnny's songs, but the opposite often happened. "And I'll go along with it until it starts to feel like the song isn't mine anymore," Chris says. This was one of those ongoing issue personal issues between the guys. It was simmering during this time period, but would boil over later. Even despite this, Chris says of the *Storyhill* album, "God, that's my favorite record we've made."

The guys supported the album with a heavy slate of touring between February and June, including a showcase at South by Southwest in March, and an appearance at the Kerrville Folk Festival in May. At the latter they participated in the annual New Folk Competition along with over thirty other artists, ending up in the winner's circle of five. They played a four-song set at the Winner's Concert: "Give Up the Ghost," "Mary on the Mountain," "Paradise Lost," and a crowd-pleasing "Love Will Find You." Following that triumph, they both stayed close to home for the remainder of the year, largely because Johnny was expecting a third child (daughter Ella would be born that fall).

In October, Alva Star's "Beautiful" was used in the second episode of the ABC series *Dirty Sexy Money*, which was created by Craig Wright. Fiction were offered the chance to submit additional songs, so they created a couple, one sung by local singer Sophia Shorai and a cover of the 5th Dimension's "Let the Sunshine In." Neither were chosen, but the guys had built a relationship that would pay off later.

* * *

With Johnny gone for half the year, it's no surprise that the Hopefuls were not very active in 2007. They managed one show at the Triple Rock in March when Johnny was back for the Storyhill make-up dates, but it wasn't until summer that they put together a string of appearances. On July 13 they played at the downtown Minneapolis Aquatennial Block Party and then headed south to play Peavey Plaza for the Macy's Day of Music. Chris Riemenschneider wrote that the double-duty made them the winners of "this week's Bad-Ass Musicians trophy." They did mostly festivals that summer, including the St. John's Center Street Block Party, Lumberjack Days in Stillwater, and the McNally Smith Minnesota Music Festival.

National power pop distributor Not Lame started carrying *The Fuses Refuse to Burn*, but things were otherwise at a standstill business wise. 2024 weren't doing so hot themselves. After their 2004 explosion, they'd only put out one CD per year in 2005, 2006, and 2007. CD sales were trending down, and digital sales weren't making up the difference. Romantica, 2024's next highest-profile band after the Hopefuls and the Plastic Constellations, were starting to have trouble with the label as well. With the real estate market slowing down, Nate realized 2024 was going to have to start supporting itself. Dave Campbell says, "Nate needed money to come in, and the other bands weren't producing either. Nate's biggest problem was he had all these bands signed that didn't want to work. They just wanted to put out records."

* * *

With so little Hopefuls activity Darren kept busy in his studio, producing bands and continuing work on a new Kid Dakota album, tentatively titled *Long Odds*. There were four CDs produced by Darren released in 2007, spanning from chugging pop-rock (the Debut's *This Record is About Cars*) to glam metal revival (KWANG's For *What It's Worth...*), from quirky indie rock (Ice Palace's *Bright Leaf Left*) to stark folk (Brenda Weiler's *End the Rain*). That Darren could move so freely between diverse types of music was a result of his wide range of personal listening, as well as his time in the Blue Turks playing songs from across time periods and genres. Zak Sally put it like this: "Darren is kid of a pop slut. He works all over the pop-music idiom." Darren's philosophy of production was to let the artist lead the way, which sometimes meant just hitting record and other times meant going much deeper. Ian says, "I've seen Darren completely deconstruct other people's songs. He would chop it up and say why don't you do it like this. Give it more pop structure, trim off some of the fat. If that's what you're looking for, then he's great at it."

The Ice Palace and Brenda Weiler records were the second and third releases on the Speaker Phone imprint. Brenda's album was a harrowing one, the result of a cathartic songwriting jag following the suicide of her sister Jennifer. The songs are on the album in the order in which she wrote them, and Darren recorded the album simply, no other musicians, no overdubs. It was a stark contrast from the fullness of *Cold Weather*. In the album's liner notes, Brenda thanks Darren for "giving me room to laugh, and cry as needed and for believing in me when I truly didn't, both in studio and out."

Fawcett and Johnny's only 2007 production was a significant one, at least in terms of their shared history. Since putting Spymob on the shelf, John Ostby had continued to write songs, and decided to put a band together. He asked Twigg to play bass, and Twigg brought on drummer Bob Johnston (with whom he'd played in a band pre–Spymob) and guitarist Spencer Bernard. Both Bob and Spencer were veteran musicians, having done writing and studio work with Jimmy Jam and Terry Lewis (Spencer wrote "He Doesn't Know I'm Alive" on Janet Jackson's *Control* album). They were also part of a band called King's English that was signed to Flyte Tyme in the late '80s. They called the new venture Kentucky Air.

Johnny and Fawcett produced, engineered, and mixed Kentucky Air's self-titled album at Lowertown Caves. Ostby's songs are very much in the vein of the country songs that Spymob did, though with both Bob and Spencer singing harmony back-ups, the performances are more robust and more authentically country. And songs like "I Feel Low," are a touching portrait of his new domestic life. Kentucky Air self-released the CD, and gigged around town, but didn't have any grand ambitions for more than that. "Nobody was doing music anymore as their full-time profession," Ostby says. "But everyone had played professionally, so it was a professional level hobby band."

The other half of Spymob was on an opposite track, with Brent and Fawcett both involved in high-profile work beyond the Twin Cities. In L.A., Brent had started working with Pharrell again, and was doing engineering gigs with the likes of Clay Aiken and the Backstreet Boys. Pharrell and Chad asked Brent and Eric both to come back to play on a new N.E.R.D. album. Eric and Johnny had also played on Dan Wilson's 2007 album

Free Life, which came together over five years worth of recording sessions. Johnny played guitar on the song "Breathless," and Eric drummed on nine of the album's thirteen tracks, and threw in some harmony vocals on a couple of them. Dan tried to use the same approach he'd used for Storyhill, namely creating a chill, spontaneous recording situation. "I came into this project thinking it'd be a really high-pressure, professional situation," Eric says, "Here was the then-Grammy-nominated singer from Semisonic trying to capitalize on that success to catapult his solo career. But it was almost the exact opposite: Just a bunch of super-relaxed sessions at Dan's house."

* * *

After their whirlwind 2006, Appelwick and the other Tapes 'n Tapes guys started off 2007 with a much-needed break. Despite the hullabaloo, Josh Grier hadn't quit his job as a data analyst, so he went back to work. Erik picked back up on a project he'd started before everything went crazy: the next Vicious Vicious record. In 2006 he'd started recording on 4-track at Shortman with Darren engineering, then he took those tapes to It's a Secret Studio and put them in ProTools and did the drum tracks with Adrian Suarez. The TnT explosion had brought everything to a halt, though. So when he got back, he spent much of March with Heath and Adrian, banging out some new tunes and finishing up the old ones. The only TnT gigs during this time were an appearance on the Minnesota Public Radio program Wits (they were paired with pop culture philosopher Chuck Klosterman) and a show at the MX Beat Festival in Mexico City.

In April, the band started a six-week tour that included an appearance at Coachella. That summer they did a few gigs here and there while writing and rehearsing songs for their next album. In early September TnT, headed to Cassadaga, New York for one week to record with mega-producer Dave Fridmann, best known for his magic touch with the Flaming Lips on albums *The Soft Bulletin* and *Yoshimi Battles the Pink Robots*. If Appelwick was going to be passed over as producer, it least it was hard to argue with his replacement. "I expected Dave to be a dude with a pointy wizard hat and a robe, judging how out there the Flaming Lips records sound," Appelwick says. "But he wasn't flamboyant or eccentric. He was just a guy in jeans and a sweatshirt." The band worked fast, recording live. They would head back in October for another week to mix the record they'd made.

Appelwick had been using the in-between times to finish up the third Vicious Vicious' album, *Parade*. He unveiled it at a September 7 CD release show at the Varsity Theater, with Lateduster guitarist J.G. Everest joining the band's live line-up. The album was a logical extension of Appelwick's increased interest in bombastic production. "I would like the production to be as lush as possible without being ridiculous," he said in an interview for Whole Music. "It's a very fine line I've found where ridiculous starts and good stops." *Parade* walks that line admirably.

It's nearly uncategoriziable music. Appelwick's style had always drawn from many sources, but *Parade* takes that to the extreme. It's a 'roided up version of all of his earlier diverse influences with a healthy dose of E.L.O.-style grandiloquence. Perhaps Erik's acknowledgments in the liner notes explain it best. In part he gives special thanks to "Curtis Mayfield, Bali Shag, sunburn, broken hearts, disco, Motown, watermelon ... and John Phillip Sousa."

Lyrically, the songs after funky opener *Rain Parade* are concerned with romance. But unlike the doomy, sad heartbreak of *Don't Look So Surprised*, most of the *Parade* songs are more, well, hopeful. As Chris Riemenschneider put it in a profile of Appelwick and the record: "*Don't Look So Surprised* was something of a break-up album. This one sounds like its more about the hookup."

It's an album is full of pleas and pursuit. In the bobby "Beggars in the Rain" he wants to know "baby, what's your name?" and then he goes ahead and does a whole song called "Girl, What's Your Name?" (a lost '70s AM Gold hit featuring Darren on background vocals; he had engineered some songs at Shortman before Appelwick and Darren's friendship dissolved). "In "Ho Baby" he wakes in the middle of the night and sends out an S.O.S. (a.k.a. booty call) to his girl. "You should be next to me" he croons. In "Don't Let Me Down" he asks his girl to "kiss me, kiss me, kiss me, kiss me, kiss me right here where it hurts." And in the closing song, "We Don't Call It Love," he says, tongue-in-cheek and echoing the Beach Boys "Don't Talk (Put Your Head on My Shoulder)," "will you stay with me forever through the night?"

Appelwick had played the charming-but-vulnerable lothario before in "Shake That Ass on the Dancefloor" and he already had a reputation as local sex symbol (there were a couple of female DJs who regularly swooned over him, and the *Pioneer Press* included him in a Valentine's Day feature that asked readers to identify the lips of local celebrities), but *Parade* put this over the top. *City Pages*' review of the album found writer Sarah Askari said, Erik "sings with a shallow exhalation calibrated to breathing come-ons into might-be-willing ears" and that "when Erik Appelwick croons 'why don't you stay with me tonight?' ... all the reasons a girl could usually list on two hands are suddenly lost to her tongue."

Riemenschneider placed *Parade* at number three his best of 2007 list, saying that "the thematic lyrics read like a singles blog." And Ross Raihala had it at number two on his own list in the *Pioneer Press*, pointing out that the album shared a title with a 1986 Prince record: "But Appelwick has such a knack for breezy, instantly loveable pop songs, he makes it look every bit as effortless as the Purple One once did himself."

Appelwick didn't do a whole lot to promote the album outside of a few Vicious Vicious gigs here and there in the fall and winter. Part of that was down to his Tapes 'n' Tapes contract, which limited his solo ventures, but it was also Erik's style. He hadn't sought out a label for distribution, didn't promote to radio (the Current did play a few songs off the record, though). He just made the album and put it out there. Rather than spending his time on promotion and marketing, he was instead inclined to use it to make more music. He told *The Rake*'s Christy Desmith, "I'm not good at business. Talking about it sort of cheapens the experience for me. I'm much better at the process."

As it happens, Appelwick wouldn't have to worry about either for awhile. *Parade* would be the last Vicious Vicious album for five years.

14

Hold Your Own

In which Kid Dakota, Tapes 'n' Tapes, and the Hopefuls release long-awaited follow-up albums, and Fawcett goes to Vermont and China.

When Darren looked back on his 2007, he realized that the majority of his time had been spent recording. "At one point I did 100 days in a row in the studio," he recalls. He hadn't intended it to happen like that. When he initially got Shortman set up, he was so happy to have bands in there working that he didn't say no to anyone who wanted to work with him. It had snowballed from there, as bands noticed Darren's work with other artists and came calling. He'd even brought on an assistant, Will Johnston.

2008 saw the release of six albums that were at least in part created at Shortman. New Hopefuls and Kid Dakota CDs (more on these shortly), and four from other local bands. Unlike Darren's 2007 output, these four shared some musical DNA: full-sounding guitar pop. Zoo Animal's *Young Blood* is by turns moody and finger-snapping. Welcome to the Cinema's *Blocks and Hills* is a a herky-jerky, tightly played, melodic disc that in a just world would have gotten as much attention as Tapes 'n Tapes' *The Loon* (the record actually got quite a bit of airplay on the Current, but because the guys in the band still lived in South Dakota, they weren't able to capitalize on it). Aviette's *The Way We Met* is Darren's only production for another artist where he's listed as a band member and co-songwriter. Distinguished by singer/songwriter Holly Muñoz's supple voice, this album is the most downcast of the three, with "Say So" only a stone's throw from being a Kid Dakota song. Finally, there was the unabashed pop rock of Action Versus Action's *Sentimental City*. The band's lead singer, Ben Krueger, says: "Darren was a phenomenal producer. We got along really well, but at the same time he was very tough on certain things. He wouldn't let us be lazy or make bad choices. He'd tell us when something sucked or needed work and encouraged us when we thought something sucked and it didn't."

Darren was finally able to get out of the studio with the release of the third Kid Dakota record, *A Winner's Shadow*, the album he'd been promising for over two years. Part of the reason for the delay was Darren's composing process. He revealed to *City Pages*' Sarah Askari that his songs "get knocked together from scraps of bridges and choruses recorded then abandoned for months or even years." He also said, "It's really impossible for me to sit down and write a whole song. I think I've done it once. I think it drove Appelwick crazy that I wrote like that." This article also finds Askari—apparently unaware that Darren and Appelwick didn't work together at all anymore—postulating that their vastly different styles seemed to indicate that Erik had "somehow stolen Jackson's happiness." Darren, no doubt annoyed by the question, replied that Erik's "swinging bachelor shtick" was a ruse. "He's not really like that," he said.

14. Hold Your Own

A Winner's Shadow came out on Graveface Records, a Chicago indie label that started in 2004 as an outlet for releases by Ryan Manon's bands Black Moth Super Rainbow and Dreamend. It eventutally grew into a full-fledged label and retail shop, putting out records by the Appleseed Cast, Jason Molina, and dozens of others. Ryan first saw Kid Dakota in Chicago opening for Low at the Old Town School of Folk. A handful of years later, he came to see them again at another Chicago gig. While chatting after the show, Darren proposed that Graveface release the next Kid Dakota album on vinyl, a format that was then just starting to crackle back to life. Ryan loved the idea, and so began an artist-label relationship that would last over a decade.

Darren and Ian feted the album at a March 1 release party at the Turf Club, with Ice Palace and Jeremy Messersmith opening. Brian Roessler, who played on two songs on the record, joined the duo for a handful of tunes, as did Zak Sally. As different from *The West Is the Future* as that album was from *So Pretty*, *A Winner's Shadow* returns mostly to Darren's inner world while at the same time ranging further out musically. *West*'s songs weren't always easy to interpret, but they were all stories. The lyrics on *Shadow* are largely more imagistic and impressionistic, more like a journal. But there is a unifying theme, and a big clue to it comes in the cover art. Darren once again called on William Schaff, who created a diorama titled "Providence 1998." The album serves as a document of that place and time.

Many of the songs, such as opener "New York System," were even written at that time. Olneyville New York System is a restaurant in Providence famous for its "hot wieners," and where Talking Heads frontman David Byrne worked while he was a Rhode Island School of Design student. The restaurant is pictured in the bottom left corner of Schaff's diorama. There are other songs like this one that access the emotions, images, or moments of the time, tunes such as the expansive, hypnotic "Stars" or the keyboard-laden "Of Age" (a reworking of the old Headache tune from the mid–'90s). "Chutes and Ladders" and "Downhill" detail relationships in painful decline.

Specters of Darren's addiction appear on "Port Authority," "Fallout," and "Puffy Jackets," all of which feature narrators looking to score. On the latter Darren is overwhelmed by temptation to use, and the self-loathing that comes with giving into it: "I'm not in control," he wails, "I'm like an overthrown king." The lovely "Transfusion" is about rehab, or more accurately, the controversial practice called "rapid detox" in which a blood transfusion is performed to get the drug out of your system and accelerate or circumvent withdrawl symptoms. In the song, Darren imagines that undergoing the procedure will "take all the pain from my heart/and replace it with love," marking the tune as the flight of fancy of an addict who longs for an easy way to beat his habit (A persistent urban legend says that Keith Richards went through this process to quickly get clean for a 1973 Stones tour, though that has been proven false). In the upper middle section of the cover, Schaff included an illustration of Darren getting high with his trust fund junkie friend.

Alex Oana flew in to assist with recording Ian's drums, and he mastered the record at CityCabin West. Besides Ian on drums, Brain Roessler adding bass on two tracks, and Erin singing backup on one, Darren did everything else himself, including mixing. Stewart Mason's *AllMusic Guide* review of the record praises its "stark, bare-bones intimacy that's heightened by Jackson's clean, sparse production." But overall, reception to the album was muted. *Star Tribune* and *City Pages* both ran articles, and there were a couple of unenthusiastic blog reviews, but there was nothing like the onslaught of press and attention that had accompanied the previous two Kid Dakota records, no *Pitchfork* revew or appearances on end-of-the year album lists.

Not that the guys didn't bust ass to promote the record. Right before the album's release they traveled to South by Southwest, and a month later hit the road with Cloud Cult, who had just released their seventh album, *Feel Good Ghosts (Tea-Partying Through Tornadoes)*. The two Twin Cities bands went to the Pacific Northwest, California, and Colorado together. In a weird instance of worlds colliding, former Tapes 'n' Tapes/current Cloud Cult bassist Shawn Neary regularly joined Kid Dakota for a handful of songs during the tour. Since Appelwick had once been in Kid Dakota, it meant that, briefly, the two men had swapped bands.

Almost directly from there, Darren and Ian headed to Europe for a string of late May, early June shows. Darren had come to love touring overseas, enjoying the enthusiasm of the audiences and the fact that catered meals and hotel stays were included as part of their appearance. "It's safe to say that American bands get treated much better in Europe than they do in the States," he says. Ian agrees, adding, "In the States, you're lucky to get free beer, even in your home town."

But touring was tough. Ian says the crowds on the tour were "hit and miss" but adds "Houston had done so much touring that was mostly miss that any hits were a bonus for me." He says Kid Dakota would have the occasional show that would go over amazingly, and that kept them going. Nevertheless, the tour spelled the end of Kid Dakota 3.0. Ian is tight-lipped about exactly what happened, saying only that there was "a lot of drama" on the tour, and that he lost his love for being in Kid Dakota. Darren says he tired of Ian's split allegiance to Story of the Sea. They stopped playing together, their friendship and their joint venture label, Speaker Phone, also ended.

* * *

Appelwick and the other Tapes 'n' Tapes guys spent the beginning of 2008 gearing up for the April release of their much-anticipated follow-up to *The Loon*. There were publicity photo shoots, tours to plan, and interviews to give. They released the first single from the album, "Hang Them All," in February. Chris Cantalini at *Gorilla vs. Bear*—one of the first blogs to hype TnT—wrote: "Any worries fans had about Dave Fridmann possibly tinkering too much with the band's sound—I'll admit, I was *slightly* concerned—are erased upon first listen to the buzzing, anthemic 'Hang Them All.' Fans of *The Loon* are going to love this one."

He was wrong. The reaction to *Walk It Off* when it was relased that April was mixed. It didn't sell as well as *The Loon*, and critics were divided. Some reviewers, such as ones from *Spin* and the *Onion AV Club* thought he band was growing and improving. Other outlets, like *Pitchfork* and *Popmatters*, couldn't locate the charm they'd found in TnT's debut. Some critics blamed Fridmann, but Appelwick balked at that. He told the *Pioneer Press* that the producer would "make suggestions here and there, but he let us make the record we wanted to make." A Around the time of *Walk It Off*'s release, Josh told Minnesota Public Radio: "I love the record. I think it's great. And so, it's like, there it is, there's no more pressure because I'm happy with it. Beyond that, there's absolutely zero that we can control as to how much other people are going to like the record."

That attitude helped the band navigate what would eventually be labeled a "backlash" against their zero-to-eighty success. Getting out in front of their fans also helped. The band had previewed the record with three shows in three days at South By Southweast.

The day after *Walk It Off*'s release, April 9, TnT played a nervous version of "Hang Them All" on *Late Night with Conan O'Brien*. From there they headed home to kick-off a U.S. tour at First Ave. The band would be away from home pretty much until the middle of June, with a European tour following close on the heels of the U.S. shows. Appelwick, for one, was eager to get out on the road, telling Chris Riemenschneider that he hoped *Walk It Off* would inspire a year and a half of touring the same way *The Loon* had. The subtext of that hope is that Erik had come to enjoy the rhythm of life on the road. At home, with no day job and limited in his outside musical activities, he got bored.

Though they were still a healthy draw on tour, TnT didn't end up spending a year and a half on the road. After getting back from Germany that summer, they mostly stayed close to home. They did do a couple of festivals in August (Bumbershoot and Sound Fix), and a spot at McCarren's Pool in Brooklyn opening for the Black Keys. The band would pick up again for another tour in early 2009, but in the meantime, Appelwick had too much time on his hands.

* * *

While Appelwick and Darren spent early 2008 in the familiar routines of releasing and touring behind records, Fawcett and Johnny were exploring new and totally unexpected facets of being working musicians. One of those came together at the very beginning of the year. In late 2007, Eric had gotten a call from Stefan Lessard, the bassist of the Dave Matthews Band. Stefan had been asked to film a segment in one of filmmaker Warren Miller's ski films featuring amateur celebrity skiers and snowboarders in Killington, Vermont. Stefan had recruited his friends Ed Robertson from Barenaked Ladies and Adam Gardner from Guster. The film company then suggested that, with so many musicians, the guys do a show during the filming. They liked the idea, but needed a drummer, and that's where Eric came in.

Fawcett and Stefan had become buddies in 2004 when N.E.R.D. did six dates opening for Dave Matthews Band in Connecticut, New Jersey, and Virgina. Stefan, always seeking to expand the DMB fans' horizons, had been the one to bring N.E.R.D. on. It didn't quite work out. Eric says, the audience's response to N.E.R.D. was, "What the heck? This is so weird." But he and Stefan hit it off. Eric had been missing his kids, and spending time on Stefan's bus with his wife and two young daughters helped fill that hole a bit ("Every Dave Matthews Band member has his own bus," Eric reports). After the run of shows, Eric and Stefan kept in touch, and talked about collaborating, which Eric thought was mostly whistling in the dark. "I was like, in my head, 'According to every poll done for the last ten years you're already playing with the greatest drummer in the world, Carter Buford.' So, yeah, right."

When Fawcett got the call about the Warren Miller film he asked who else was in the band, and upon hearing the line-up immediately said yes. Then Stefan asked if he could snowboard or ski. Eric said, "Well.... I can kinda ski" and Stefan said, "Alright, you're in!"

The new "band" dubbed themselves Yukon Kornelius, after the gregarious prospector/Abominable Snowman fighter in Rankin/Bass's Christmas favorite *Rudolph the Red-Nosed Reindeer*. They set up a January 9 show at the Pickle Barrel Nightclub as a benefit for the local food shelter. It sold out immediately. Save two improvised tunes, the concert consisted solely of cover songs. Right away, the second song of the set in fact, they upped the surreality factor by bringing actor (and huge DMB fan) Jason Biggs on stage to play cowbell on Blue Oyster Cult's "Don't Fear the Reaper." Other tunes included Talking Heads' "Psycho Killer," the Clash's "Lost in the Supermarket," and the Rolling Stones' "Sympathy for the Devil." They kept it loose, switching instruments and bringing up sax player Steve Morell for their take on Wham's "Careless Whisper." Ed took over drums while Fawcett plunked the bass. Eric provided backing vocals, shining particularly on the "now that you're gone" falsetto bit.

But the show's clear highlight was when they brought Biggs back in on cowbell, and started in on Twisted Sister's "We're Not Gonna Take It" only to have Dee Snider himself come in on vocals, to the glee and shock of the audience. Snider stuck around for a rip-roaring closing take on what he calls "the rock 'n' roll national anthem," AC/DC's "Highway to Hell."

The cobbled-together quartet left the stage in triumph. Stephan Lessard said they'd all gone in treating it as an experiment since they didn't know each other well and hadn't rehearsed all that much. Adam Gardner said of the show, "All of us agreed it was the most fun we'd had in at least a decade in music, including in our own bands, because there was no pressure. It was purely for fun." Lessard says, "It was a massive party up there."

For Fawcett it was another strange and exhilarating moment that he never could have predicted. And the formation of Yukon Kornelius would end up being only the second strangest musical experience of Eric's year.

In 2007, he'd received a message via his MySpace page from a Taiwanese fan. It read, "Hey, my name is Wang Leehom and I'm an artist in Tawian. I want to work together long distance." Eric's first thought was, 'Oh, that's so charming. I have a Taiwanese fan!' Then Eric Googled the name, and discovered that Leehom was huge in China, a bonafide superstar in a country with very few pop idols. He was born in Rochester, New York to immigrant parents and lived in the United States until college, developing a strong interest in violin, piano, guitar, and drums. While visiting his grandmother in Taiwan the summer after his freshman year at Williams College he participated in a talent contest and was offered a record contract. He released two albums while in college that were not successful, but his third record in 1998 was a massive hit, and his star grew from there. *Goldsea Asian American Daily* named him one of the "80 Most Inspiring Asian Americans." Upon learning all this, Eric says, "It was like I opened a window on the side of my house that had been shuttered, and behind it was a completely different world."

Leehom had sought out Fawcett because he was a fan of N.E.R.D. and he wanted to explore that sort of sound in his own music. The two began collaborating, and Eric ended up drumming on half of the tracks on Leehom's 2007 CD *Change Me*, which sold one million copies in its first month of release. Eric also played on two songs on the 2008 chart-topping record *Heart Beat*, as well as "One World One Dream," Leehom's entry for the 2008 Olympic Games Theme Song Competition, (the tune didn't win, but it was selected as a participation song). From there, Leehom invited Eric to be the drummer for his fall MUSIC-MAN tour. The stage show was ambitious and expensive. All the band members and performers wore costumes, so Eric lived out his childhood Peter Criss fantasies, wearing a black vest adorned with silver stripes and a series of chains and stars.

Kicking off in Taipei in September, the tour would take Fawcett all over China and Southeast Asia playing in arenas to audiences of tens of thousands. The biggest, Eric says, was in Shanghai, where they played for 70,000 fans at the Shanghai Stadium (commonly known as the "80,000 People Stadium" because of its capacity). Eric had played at stadiums with N.E.R.D., but never to this many people. His impressions of the experience are not quite what you'd think. Here's what he wrote in his tour diary: "The sound of an amplified drum set in a stadium is so massive, it makes a drummer feel like some sort of god! And just the thought of playing in a stadium is mind blowing. But once the show begins, the experience of playing in a stadium is actually comparatively dull. When you play in a small room, or even in a theater, the audience is RIGHT THERE. You can see their faces, their eyes. You can clearly see the people you are performing for. In a stadium, the audience is so far away that it's actually difficult to feel their energy. No matter how loud the crowd screams, it's hard to feel a connection with a mass of anonymous dots!"

Eric's openness to the experience and his many years of professional drumming helped him find success in this high profile role. On her blog documenting the tour kickoff, backup singer Tay Kewai wrote that Eric's "energy and professionalism is astounding." She goes on, "He is the only drummer who makes me sit up and watch in awe."

While all this was going on, Fawcett was also somehow holding down a job at home. In the middle of 2008, Johnny and Eric folded Fiction Music into a larger Minneapolis agency, Modern Music, which described itself as a source of "original music, sound design, music licensing and supervision for advertising, film, television, gaming, and new media." jMatt had started working at the agency in 2004, and helped facilitate bringing on Eric and Johnny. One of their first efforts was to create various versions of the Beatles' "Hello Goodbye" for Target's ubiquitous Hello Goodbuy ad campaign.

Eric Fawcett (left) spent nearly four years off and on drumming with Wang Leehom, a mega star singer and actor in China. Courtesy Eric Fawcett.

Their new positions were thankfully flexible, because neither Fawcett nor Johnny was giving up their other music endeavors. They started at Modern in the summer, and not long after, Johnny was off on a Storyhill sojourn. In addition to the now-annual Storyhill Fest, he and Chris would sprinkle dates in the Midwest and Pacific Northwest throughout that fall and winter. Eric, meanwhile, was going a bit further away.

As if touring China and a brand-new job weren't enough, Eric and Brent reunited with Pharrell Williams and Chad Hugo to play on the majority of the tracks for N.E.R.D.'s third album, *Seeing Sounds*, which was considered a marked improvement over the Spymob-less *Fly or Die*. The feather in the cap of a crazy professional year was a personal triumph, the birth of Eric and Sarah's third child, a girl they named Cecilia.

* * *

Darren had started using again. He had fallen off the wagon before, but always got it back under control. This time was different. At first, at least, he was able to remain high-functioning. In October 2008 he took a trip with several other Twin Cities musicians, including the Glad Version, Sam Keenan, and the Bill Mike Band to take part in the Draw Fire Records showcase at the CMJ Music Marathon in New York City. Draw Fire had been started in part by Aviette's Holly Muñoz. Kid Dakota wasn't on the label, but since Darren was playing with Aviette, he did a solo set of KD tunes, which *City Pages*' Andrea Swensson described as "loud, aggressive interpretations." Keenan's drummer, Justin Korhonen surprised both the audience and Darren by jumping on stage to play a new song called "The Winter Without You." Swensson concluded that the show felt "like any other night at the Turf Club or Triple Rock—despite the fact that we were all over 1,200 miles from home."

Back home that early winter, Darren convened a new line-up of Kid Dakota, this time going with a full band. He gathered somewhat of a Minneapolis all-star group: Brian Roessler on bass, Al Weiers from Faux Jean on guitar, and Heiruspecs drummer Peter Leggett. The new configuration debuted at the Uptown Bar in November, and *How Was the Show*'s David de Young wrote that "one of the most important things to nail in these songs is the dynamics, and this well-versed 4 piece did it." Though he admitted he preferred Kid Dakota as a two-piece: "Like the 'Beatles or Stones?' question, I believe 'Kid Dakota as a 2 piece, 3 piece, or 4 piece?' is another question by which you can classify Twin Cities music fans."

Darren's most stunning accomplishment of 2008, however, was the shepherding of a new Hopefuls album into existence. Everyone's schedules what they were, the band had barely performed in 2008, doing a cancer research benefit in March with several other bands, a couple of summer shows (including headlining Welcome to the Cinema's CD release at the 400 Bar). No one considered the Hopefuls their main thing (even Heath had his work in the Beatifics and Little Man to keep him otherwise occupied, in addition to full time work and a young family), and the clamor had long since died down. They could have just as easily—more easily, even—faded away. But doing those summer shows had reminded everyone what the pure joy they got from playing together in that band. "Hopefuls shows were just fun from start to finish," Johnny says.

Everyone was excited about the creative challenge of creating a new Hopefuls record, so Darren and Johnny started doing demos, coming up with 30 songs between them. Their schedules made finding a time to record tricky, but the biggest impediment to a second album that the band were still contracted to 2024.

The guys had essentially gone ahead with recording, betting that the grim financial situation of the label would lead to a resolution in their favor. As of August that still wasn't the case. A *Star Tribune* article detailed the standoff between 2024 and both the Hopefuls and Romantica, and painted a dire portrait of the situation. Nate Roise told Chris Riemenschneider that he wanted "fair compensation" for the investment he'd made in both bands before he would let them move on. His other source of income—the real estate market—had entered a slump. "It's stay alive time," he told the paper.

In the end, both Romantica and the Hopefuls negotiated to buy out their contracts, and 2024 subsequently shuttered its operations. Nate was burned out, not only by the fighting, but by the business mindset toward music that he had been forced to develop. "I found it hard to go to shows and enjoy the music because I was analyzing the band's performance and how were people reacting to them." He had started the label out of a love for music, and now the love was gone. Nate says he didn't listen to anything but podcasts and audio books for a couple of years as a way of doing detox from his 2024 experience.

Nate is still proud of what he—and Todd Hansen, Dave Campbell, Jerry Steller (who replaced Dave), and many hardworking interns—were able to accomplish. Dave feels that the negative aspects of the experience were more than balanced out by the quality records 2024 helped bring into existence and the genuine excitement that enveloped the Minnesota scene at the time. "That was a great year of my life," he says now. Todd also takes pride in the work 2024 did, and says the label's failure was mostly down to poor timing. Much like Peppermint they got "caught on a sandbar somewhere" between CDs and the rise of digital music and resurgence of vinyl. "All we needed was two more years," he says. Dennis Pelowski, who's now the manager of the Meat Puppets, says that despite his issues with 2024, he admired several things about their operation, including their approach to licensing, Nate's eye for talent in both the bands he signed and the staff he hired, and the fact that they gave bands creative control. He says now he wishes he had gotten to know everyone and the situation better before charging in.

Nate says he wishes he'd been more humble and more willing to have conversations with the intent of clearing up misunderstandings. Everyone in the Hopefuls, to a man, regrets getting caught up in the drama instead of moving forward musically. Todd summarizes: "I wish it had been more party positive; if everyone could have gotten out of the way of themselves we could have made some really cool things."

For the Hopefuls the end of 2024 meant the freedom to release the second album that was already finished. They'd recorded the album in bits and pieces over the spring and summer. Because of their schedules, there was never a time during the recording process that all four Hopefuls were in the studio at once, and the album was even recorded in different studios. Darren did all of his parts, along with Heath's bass and Fawcett's drums, at Shortman. Johnny added his guitars, keytar parts, and vocals at Lowertown Caves. Eric did background vocals at his studio at Modern Music. "We had four hard drives flying around," Eric says. "For that record, I handed the hard drives to the guys and I said pick what you want, throw out what you want." It was a far cry from his ultra-controlled, ultra-precise Spymob recording days.

Once all the parts were recorded, Darren put everything together in the fall and handed it over to Alex Oana for mixing and mastering. The final result, titled *Now Playing at the One-Seat Theatre*, was released on Draw Fire Records in late December, just a few days before Christmas.

The record made a good story, with the band having been just inactive enough to create a "comeback" narrative. The *Star Tribune*, *Pioneer Press*, and *City Pages* all ran articles about the new album ahead of its release, and all were complimentary of it. Chris Riemenschneider wrote: "The sophomore effort is as infectious and candy-striped as the first incarnation of the band's blissful, Weezer-meets-Cheap Trick rock 'n' roll. But this one's also a lot more refined and ambitious, both lyrically and sonically. It's simply a bigger record all around."

The Current hyped the album, recalling how well the band had served them in their early days. A couple of weeks before the album's release, Current DJ Steve Seel hosted the guys for an interview and in-studio performance. They played "Virgin Wood," "Stacey," and "What She Wants," and Seel praised the band as not only being some of the "best players in town, but also the best vocal cords in town." He also labeled "Virgin Wood" an "instant earworm." Not surprisingly the track got some pretty heavy play on the station.

The CD featured four tracks that had been in the band's live repertoire since 2005: "Edge of Medicine," "Idaho," "Red Stain," and "Hold Your Own." The latter had been a long-time concert highlight thanks to its drum break-down and shift into the anthemic, fist-pumping climax: "It was a long way back," Johnny shout/sings over a fleet guitar figure and the trusty old xylophone, "and we almost made it."

A 2008 promo shot for Now Playing at the One-Seat Theater. From left to right: Eric Fawcett, Darren Jackson, John Hermanson, Heath Henjum. Courtesy Darren Jackson.

That same line appears in the thrilling final minute of Darren's "Edge of Medicine" as well, though with a different riff underneath. The guitar on the song was actually provided by Appelwick, done at Shortman a couple of years back when Erik was working on *Parade* there. The song's verses were completely rewritten from the version the Hopefuls had been performing live. The "on the edge of medicine I think I finally found a friend" hook remains, but where the older lyrics were addressed to an unspecified "you" who is disapproving of the narrator's newfound magic pills, the new version replaces that with a treatise on doping and steroid usage in sports. "Times are better than/than the times have ever been/we are fast and we are strong/and we won't be here for long/so let's set a record they could never break."

Many of the songs are concerned with romantic failure, which is no surprise since Darren's marriage was dissolving during the writing and recording of the album, largely due to his renewed drug use. The swirling, '60s-styled "Miss You" finds Darren begging his girl to come back, though he's clear-headed enough to know that even if she does return, she'll never love him the way she once did. The centerpiece of the record, both literally (it's smack in the middle) and figuratively (it gives the album its title) is "One-Seat Theatre." It uses a perfectly-executed metaphor of a broken relationship as a film. "Might as well have never happened/the scene distracted from the action," Darren sings. "Your version has all the edits/but I'm stuck with the director's cut." The music is as atmospheric and moody, owing a debt to Darren's youthful love of the Cure and the Smiths, at least until the cathartic final minute where it breaks out into a gloriously prog-pop keyboard line.

Johnny sang lead on two songs in addition to "Hold Your Own," and both touch on dysfunctional romances as well. The overcaffeinated "Stacey" finds the narrator breaking up with Stacey because he needs space. Darren's counterpoint backing vocals play the foil, asking him when he was ever there for her in the first place. "Only Dreaming," a dramatic reworking of the Alva Star tune, concerns a date that goes terribly wrong. The song's heroine embarrasses herself at a dressy outing by overindulging in drugs, alcohol, or both, and her date first cares for her, then leaves her to sleep it off under a table.

The band revealed the full album with a snowy December 20 CD release show at First Ave, with One for the Team and fellow Ole Chris Koza opening. *The Fuses Refuse to Burn* CD release show had been the debut of the tracksuits. At this one, the guys coordinated, but in a much dressier way. Darren wore a black button down shirt, white pants, and a white tie with pink and red vertical lines. Heath wore a white button down shirt, black jeans, a pink and maroon tie adorned with flowers, and a black sport coat. Johnny won the award for the night with his three-piece maroon suit. The coat had red lapels, and underneath was a black vest sporting pink polka dots. His tie was a complementary fuchsia. Fawcett, who normally played in a t-shirt, conceded to white jeans and a white short sleeve button down, with a red tie that he promptly shed. As a group they looked sharp. They sounded sharp too, and Rupert came out to cheer on a crowd that didn't need all that much encouragement to go nuts.

Heath remembers being surprised to see audience members mouthing the words to "Virgin Wood" and thinking, "How do you know the words to that? We just put that out!" For that song, the band brought a large group of women up on stage to perform a chorus of hand-clapping, much to everyone's delight. A *Star Tribune* blog report from the show stated that the band sounded "great, loud, brash, as the Hopefuls ought to."

Praise was all around. Thirteen-year-old blogger Max Timander (who would a few years later form the band Stereo Confession) wrote that "Edge of Medicine" was one of the songs of the year, and that "Stacey" could be the new big hit to carry the band outside of Minneapolis. Chris Riemenschneider agrees. "If they were going to try to use that record to get national exposure, they could have gotten radio play off of some of those songs, maybe attracted a bigger label." Pat O'Brian wrote in *City Pages* that "*Now Playing at the One-Seat Theatre* is catchier, tighter, and not as intentionally corny [as *Fuses*], elevating the song quality and lessening the guilty-pleasure factor. Song after song makes an attempt to be the one that really sticks in your brain, but they all are fighting a losing battle—much like a New Pornographers album, it's a lost cause trying to determine which one has the best hooks."

But the album didn't catch fire the same way *The Fuses Refuse to Burn* had. Part of this is the same we-already-got-excited-about-you mindset that Tapes 'n' Tapes had experienced, though without the backlash. As Tapes 'n' Tapes discovered fans and media are just not inclined to go nuts over an artist they've already pushed into the spotlight once. The response to *Fuses*, in so many ways, was an aberration, not because the album and band didn't deserve it, but because so much of it was about perfect timing.

Fuses and *Now Playing* had both been made in low stakes conditions. With the first album, Appelwick and Darren didn't have high expectations for its success. With the second, the band thought they'd made something great, but had made it mostly for the sake of making it. No one, barring landing a fluke national hit by going viral or via licensing, had any intention of pursuing the record after its release. They weren't even—as was the case for *Fuses*—all that open to chasing a surprise success, as everyone was even more firmly entrenched in their other musical lives than they were in 2004. Also Johnny, Fawcett, and Heath all had expanded their families in that time, so there was no chance for a tour. And as if all that weren't enough, the CD release show was the moment when Johnny, at least, realized Darren was using again, as he'd gotten high right before the band went on.

As it was, fans would be lucky after the release of *Now Playing at the One-Seat Theatre* to see any configuration of the band live. In the *Star Tribune* article about *Now Playing*'s release, Darren said of Fawcett, Johnny, and Heath, "It's still a lot of fun playing with those guys. If it wasn't, we probably would've already moved on." Unfortunately, the fun was about to run out. The band would play less than ten more shows.

15

Caught in a Mess

In which Tapes 'n' Tapes prepare to mount a "comeback," Storyhill release a new album and visit A Prairie Home Companion, the Hopefuls implode, and Darren heads west.

Tapes 'n Tapes continued to tour behind *Walk It Off* in early 2009, taking a nearly two-month sojurn across the U.S. in the first part of the year. Ever canny about keeping up a relationship with fans, they documented the tour through a series of YouTube videos that reveal, among other things, a lot of driving, the band's love for Phil Collins, and Matt Kretzmann's awesome dance moves. They did a sold out First Avenue show in February, the first time they'd played their hometown in the middle of a multi-city tour.

When they got home again in March, the band downshifted into home life, but kept surprisingly busy. TnT did a set at the Basilica Block Party in July, and in early October did a "Tour of the Twin Cities," where they performed three gigs in three days at the 7th Street Entry, Music Box Theater, and the Turf Club. From there, though, the band took a six-month break. After three years of steady touring, recording, and promotion everyone needed some purposeful time off to make sure the band kept feeling more like fun than work.

For Applewick the break was not necessarily welcome, but he did use the time to write and demo his own songs. What he was going to do with them, he didn't quite know yet.

* * *

Darren wanted desperately to get clean again. He'd kept things under control for the most part, but it was getting out of hand. As he prepared to take Kid Dakota (with Heath on bass and Peter Leggett on drums) on a January 2009 tour of Germany, Austria, Switzerland, and Denmark, Darren was determined to kick the habit. Rather than go to rehab, he weaned himself off of OxyContin just days before their departure. Heath says Darren "was totally going through withdrawal right when we got there, and he was sick all the time." The tour went well despite Darren's lowly state. Heath, like Ian before him, loved the experience of playing in Europe, namely the amenities and the engaged crowds. "I'd do that again in a heartbeat," he says.

When he got back, Darren did enter treatment, but it was too late to save his marriage. He and Erin would officially divorce that summer. As was his pattern, Darren threw himself into making music. He had been working up several new songs, many of them inspired by (or in the case of some of the older songs he reworked, echoing) the traumas he'd been mired in. They had titles like "Dawn Did Us Apart," "Torn in Two," "Phantom

Pain," and "The Winter Without You." He brought Alex in as engineer, and the two of them spent part of May recording the basics for nine songs at the Terrarium (it was another case of Darren and Appelwick just barely crossing musical paths, since Tapes 'n Tapes had just been there in March and April). Darren hoped to get the album out later in the year or early in 2010, which would have been by far the shortest wait between Kid Dakota albums thus far. But Darren had a history of promising his fans albums long before they'd actually appear, which was largely a function of his meticulous nature and his desire to group his songs thematically on albums, and this wasn't any different. Other projects started to pile up and get in the way, and the fourth Kid Dakota album was shuffled to the side.

* * *

The Hopefuls played a show right before Darren and Heath left for Europe, a Turf Club barnstormer that belied any sort of tumult going on with Darren. David de Young wrote about their set on *How Was the Show*, saying the audience and band were both so into it that he started to "wonder when the floor is going to give way under the strain of exuberance." jMatt came to the show intending only to be an audience member, but got carried away by the performance and brought out Rupert. He played cowbell, used a support pillar to do some pole dancing, and almost got thrown out by a bartender who somehow wasn't aware of Rupert's shtick (they sorted it out peacefully). With the Hopefuls' sporadic schedule, jMatt had brought Rupert to different bands, starting with the New Standards, a jazz pop super-group of sorts comprised of the Suburbs' Chan Poling, Semisonic's John Munson, and vibraphonist Steve Roehm. Beginning in 2006, the band put on an annual holiday show at the Fitzgerald Theater. Rupert would become a regular fixture of those shows, and would soon expand out to dancing with other local musicians,

Tapes 'n Tapes take a curtain call at a 2009 show at the Music Box Theater. From left to right: Matt Kretzman, Erik Appelwick, Jeremy Hanson, Josh Grier. Photo by and courtesy Stacy Schwartz.

such as Jeremy Messersmith and 4onthefloor. The other interesting bit about this particular show is that Peter Anderson sat in on drums for Fawcett, who was in China on another tour with Leehom. Peter's presence meant that the gig was just a Brian Roessler away from being an Alva Star reunion (they did play "Thing For Me," appropriately enough).

The Hopefuls wouldn't play another show until March, but in the meantime "Virgin Wood" climbed to number two on the Current chart, with only Lily Allen standing in the way of its domination. As if to build on that, the March show was one that featured another intriguing addition to the line-up. The gig was at First Ave, opening for the Honeydogs, and Dan Wilson came on stage with the band for roughly half of their set. It was much more than your typical guest appearance, it was more like he was a member of the band. In another timeline, he could have been. Dan had joined in on a couple of practices, and the guys made it very clear how much they would love him to join the group. Dan turned the idea over in his head a few times. His great respect for the guys, his love of their music, and the fun they had on stage made it tempting, but in the end it just didn't materialize. Instead it goes down as another fascinating "what if" in Hopefuls history. No one can say exactly what would have happened, but it's safe to assume that adding a Grammy-winning songwriter (whose highest-profile work was yet to come) would have completely altered the band's trajectory.

As it was, the Hopefuls did only two more shows that summer, followed by a late October three-day "tour" of Northeast Minneapolis called "The Hopefuls Haunt Nord'east," encompassing an in-store at now-closed Shuga Records, a show at the 331 Club, and one at the Ritz Theater with Romantica on Halloween. They didn't know it at the time, but the Ritz performance would be the Hopefuls' last show with Johnny and Fawcett in the band.

Fawcett was the first to go. He quit the Hopefuls in November 2009, feeling overwhelmed and overcommitted. He'd already stepped down as Storyhill's manager earlier in the year, but still had too much going on. There were shows with Leehom sprinkled throughout the year, each trip to China being a massive undertaking. And Yukon Kornelius had done a follow-up performance in January 2009 in Aspen, and briefly discussed mounting a short tour, though the guys simply couldn't make their schedules work. They played another show in Colorado at the end of the year, this time in Vail. Appropriately, one of the songs he did was KISS's "Shout It Out Loud," with Dee Snider on lead vocals.

At home, Fawcett was working with Matt Wilson and Jon Munson again, drumming on the Twilight Hours' debut album, *Stereo Night*, but did not join their live line-up because he didn't want to take on yet another musical obligation. He was working full time trying to learn the business of music in TV/film/advertising at Modern Music. And, after a divorce from Sarah, he was especially committed to devoting time and energy to his three children.

Something had to give, and that something was the Hopefuls. Eric had already been struggling to keep up with regular rehearsals and gigs, so when Darren started talking about a new album—they already had the basics for 20 new tracks—it was simply too much. He summarizes, "I can honestly say I was in the Hopefuls because it was fun, and I stayed in it as long as it was fun."

Without Fawcett, the band went on an unofficial hiatus.

* * *

Darren put his energies into the next Kid Dakota project, which surprisingly wasn't the studio album he'd worked on earlier in the year. Instead, it was a collaboration with Brian Roessler's improvisational jazz group, the Fantastic Merlins. The band was comprised of Roessler, saxophonist Nathan Hanson, and drummer Peter Hennig, with a rotating cast of cellists (at this time it was Matt Turner). They described their music as "a mysterious blend of jazz and chamber music." Darren mixed their second album, *A Handful of Earth*, which had been released earlier in 2009, and that along with his friendship with Roessler led to an ambitious collaboration called *How the Light Gets In*. The recording was to be comprised largely of interpretations of songs by Leonard Cohen, such as "Waiting for the Miracle" and "Heart with No Companion," with Darren providing both voice and guitar.

The project had its origins in a YouTube clip of 1989 appearance by Leonard Cohen on the short-lived NBC show *Sunday Night* (known as *Night Music* in its second, and final, season). The program typically brought together three or more musical artists and had them collaborate on each other's songs. The artists in this particular episode were Cohen, saxophonist Sonny Rollins, and the pop band Was (Not Was), and the musicians collaborated on a jazz-inflected version of "Who By Fire." The Merlins thought it might be cool to do a bunch of different Cohen songs in that manner, and invited Darren to sing. They tried it out on one of their regular Friday appearances at the Black Dog Café in Saint Paul, and they liked the results enough that they decided to make a recording.

The album was recorded by Steve Wiese at Creation Audio and was released by Hope Street Records, a French label, in a lavish package featuring 52 pages of illustrations by cartoonist Stéphane Levallois. Collaborating with writer Jean Simon, Levallois's loose, kinetic ink and watercolor pictures tell the story of the songs. Included are a couple of depictions of the band themselves, as well as Cohen. The band debuted the project officially at the Sons d'Hiver Festival in Paris in early February 2010.

When he got back from France, Darren dove back into recording projects. 2010 would turn out to be another year, like 2008, where several of his labors saw the light of day. It was a diverse collection of albums. There was the self-titled CD by Shape Then Shift, the alter ego of Brenda Weiler's brother Michael; Bella Koshka's *Deception Island*; and singer-songwriter Eliza Blue's *The Road Home*. A classically trained violinist, Eliza had been kicking around the Twin Cities scene since 2005 or so, playing her own songs and guesting with artists such as Charlie Parr, Dessa, and Roma di Luna. She'd gone to high school in Minnesota, but moved to New York before coming back in 2004. *The Road Home* was her third album, and having suffered from performance anxiety both on stage and in the studio, Eliza decided to record this one herself in her own attic. Once she had the basics recorded, she sought help from a number of producers to add overdubs. One of those was Darren, who recorded vocals and guitars for a couple of the album's songs. Like Darren, Eliza had recently gone through a divorce, and the two found themselves connecting on a level deeper than music. Soon, they were a couple.

Darren didn't produce it, but he played both guitar and keys on *Soundtrack to the End* by Communist Daughter, John Solomon's new band. Some of the material—about a third of the songs—on the album had been recorded at Shortman in 2007 or so, after Solomon's falling out with Johnny and Fawcett over the robbery at Lowertown Caves. This was just before the implosion of Friends Like These and John's month-long jail sentence for disorderly conduct. After that, Solomon had hit reset on his life by moving to nearby Prescott, Wisconsin and opening a restaurant, the Boxcar. It was there that he began to revisit the material he'd recorded at Shortman but Solomon decided that much of the results were too rocking to fit the muscular folk sound he was looking for (Appelwick and Ian Prince both played on these earlier, abandoned recordings). He kept some of it, but did a lot over, recording piecemeal in the basement of the Boxcar with musician friends who came by to eat and drink. When the band's drummer left, Christopher McGuire came in and finished the drum tracks. The resulting album was an instant local hit, with the song "Not the Kid" shooting to the top of the Current chart, and "Speed of Sound" and the title track landing on a season seven episode of *Grey's Anatomy*.

In early 2010, Darren was working with several artists, among them the Idle Hands, Golden Bubbles, and Inwood Radio. Around this time Darren became completely burned out. He'd spent so much time and energy ushering other people's albums into existence over the past four years that he was losing his love for it. Also, ends weren't meeting financially. With the divorce bringing him down to one income, and the money from Hopefuls gigs gone, he was struggling. This led him to do some casting about to try to make things work.

His first attempt was to get the Hopefuls up and running again. Darren had taken golf lessons at Columbia Golf Course in Minneapolis from the pro there, Mike Hinton. Darren discovered Mike was also a drummer, playing with local singer-songwriter Tim Mahoney. Considering Mike as a potential replacement for Fawcett, he e-mailed Johnny several times trying to get things restarted. Johnny, surprisingly, had been open to remaining in the Hopefuls without Eric. Darren's drug use was a huge concern for Johnny, but it was complicated. "Even despite all those issues, it was so much fun to play in the Hopefuls that I didn't want it to end and I didn't want to quit," Johnny says. Also, Darren rarely let his drug use affect his music. Heath says of Darren, "I always felt that despite issues he might have had going on that he always worked hard, was present, and contributed at a very professional level."

But the timing wasn't right. In addition to work at Modern Music, Johnny was consumed with Storyhill commitments. He and Chris had done shows in nine of 2009's twelve months, hitting their usual Pacific Northwest and Midwest cities, plus Colorado, Ohio, Texas, and Michigan. They had also started work on their ninth album. Ultimately, Johnny didn't so much quit the Hopefuls as Darren went on without him, marking the end of a decade of musical collaboration and friendship.

Darren had lined up a couple of gigs for the band that summer, primarily for the money. Replacing Johnny was keyboardist Leo Vondracek. Leo was a Hopefuls superfan from a small southern Minnesota town called Wells. Leo was still in high school when the band came on the scene and he fell in love. He went to every Hopefuls show he could that summer, even to the point of catching three identical sets in a row at the Minnesota State Fair. He would find a spot in the front row and "full body dance" as hard as he could. Eventually the guys in the band started to recognize him and he would have brief conversations with them before or after shows.

After graduating college, Leo moved to the Twin Cities along with his band the Golden Bubbles (which included his brother Christopher, drummer Jared Fette, and guitarist Brandon Mutschler) and the group hired Darren to help them make a record. The recording didn't go as well as they'd planned, but it did lead to Darren asking Leo to be in the makeshift version of the Hopefuls. "I was totally inexperienced," Leo says. "I had only played, like, nothing shows and then getting to play with them, I felt like I'd just jumped ahead."

With Darren's roommate, Jordan Cole, joining on guitar, the replacement Hopefuls only ended up playing three gigs. One was at Peavey Plaza, another was at a TCF corporate function held at the Varsity Theater, and the final gig was at the Ritz Theater as part of the Nordeast Music Festival. The Peavey Plaza show was the longest, and without Appelwick's or Johnny's songs there was a lot of space to fill, so the band did several covers, including the Church's "Under the Milky Way," "Lovesong" by the Cure, and the Replacements' "I Will Dare." Leo says the TCF crowd was mostly indifferent ("I don't think they even knew who we were"), and that the experience of being a new player in a band he'd loved brought up mixed emotions: "I feel like it was sort of awesome to be able to play with Darren, but at the same time it wasn't the same magic. I was just playing a role." Similarly, jMatt returned as to dance as Rupert for the Ritz show, but found the experience lacking. "They were the same songs I loved," he says, "but it definitely wasn't the same feeling."

Darren's other attempt to steady himself financially came when he joined the Honeydogs following the departure of lost their longtime guitarist, Brian Halverson. It was a choice gig with one of the most consistent, long-lasting, and highly-respected bands in the Twin Cities. They had a deep catalog of excellent tunes written by Adam Levy, and were a steady draw. They didn't tour often, but could put together a string of dates at places around the country when they felt like it. Darren began practicing with the group, and his first gig with them was set for August 6 in Rochester.

Then, in late July, just a week before the show, Darren revealed via Facebook that he'd accepted a job as a music teacher in hometown. Because Bison is so small it only has one school, so Darren would be working with students from ages 5 to 18. The drastic change in both career and scenery was the result of being completely burned out on life in the Twin Cities. The financial stress and unpredictability of being a full-time musician and producer had left him worn down and disillusioned. He says, "There's no infrastructure in music. In every other career you work hard, you do this, you get promoted, you get your 401K, your insurance, and you're always progressing toward something. In music there's no guarantee. It's dictated by consumer culture and taste. Not only can if feel very risky, but it can also be very discouraging. I felt both those things." He wrote to friends that hoped the change would simplify and streamline his daily life and help him "stay grounded and focused on what really matters."

Darren moved on August 17, and started teacher in-service the next day. He didn't leave the Twin Cities with any feeling of triumph or satisfaction for what he'd been able to accomplish in his nearly eleven years there. Instead, despite his voluminous musical accomplishments, he felt regret—that he'd spent more time other artists' music than his own—and an acute sense of failure. "When I moved away I looked back on my time in Minneapolis as being a big waste," he says.

* * *

Johnny was out of the Hopefuls, but Storyhill was keeping him plenty busy. He and Chris were working on their second album for Red House, and had brought on a new manager, Jim Kowitz. Jim started out as a fan, having been introduced to Storyhill by his older brother, Peter, when he was still in high school. Well, it didn't go quite as smoothly as all that. "My first impression of the guys was not favorable," Jim says, "I was growing up in the Twin Cities, listening to top 40 music, and the appeal of two guys playing guitars was lost on me." Like Fawcett and jMatt before him, Jim had to be won over by seeing Chris and Johnny in concert. He attended Luther College in Decorah, Iowa where he got involved with campus activities and booked Chris and Justin Roth, Alva Star, and Storyhill. Later, he sold merch for Storyhill at shows. In 2006, he got in touch with Fawcett to offer his services to the duo, and got hired on as a street team leader. His responsibilities grew over the next couple of years.

So it was a natural fit for Jim to take over as manager when Eric quit. Jim says, "I didn't have a lot of knowledge of the music industry, just a knack for planning and organizing people and events. The guys really gave me the opportunity to try new things and keep the Storyhill 'machine' going."

One of those new things was to expand on the continued success of Storyhill Fest. So Storyhill Fest Midwest was held in early September 2009 at Presbyterian Clearwater Forest Camp in Deerwood, Minnesota. The line-up included Cliff Eberhardt, Mother Banjo, Ben Kyle and Luke Jacobs from Romantica, Brenda Weiler, and Justin Roth. The format was consistent with the Montana version, even down to the late-night campfire jam.

Work on the new record, meanwhile, was laborious. "Over the years," Johnny says, "We've really tried to make sure that both of us are represented on the records, and that's led to a lot of difficult record-making." In the lead-up to their self-titled album, Chris and Johnny had cycled through 35 songs to settle on a final ten. This time around it was even worse. Johnny estimates that they considered 70 songs in the process of writing and deciding what to record.

"A sort of agreement we have is that we're not going to do songs that we're not both really excited about," he says, "We can't just kind of like them. They have to be like we really want them on the record." Once they made it through that process, Chris and Johnny once again called on Dan Wilson to produce. Dan's goal as producer was to try to capture the guys in the purest way possible: "I wanted this album to feel super-intimate and close-up to John and Chris, so I wanted a feeling of clarity and documentary realness." That meant going all the way back to the way it had been on the guys' earliest recordings: two guitars, and two voices in harmony.

Dan says, "I loved their blend, it was like a third guy with a really chorus-y voice. I brought that up as one of my favorite sounds of theirs—it could be a way to vary the vocal sounds we could get. Taking that idea to the maximum as is the tendency, Johnny announced that the two would sing together almost the whole time, either in unison or harmony." This approach gives the album a unified feel, and also puts a spotlight on the moments where they guys do sing solo, like the one in "Cover Your Tracks" where the guys trade off on lines in the final verse. The sudden break from harmony highlights the emotionality of those lines, with Johnny singing "I broke the silence because nothing hurts like nothing to say" and Chris following with "Wrote you a letter then wrote another and threw them away."

Much of the album was recorded live. There were edits, but no overdubs or punch-ins. You can even hear the creak of the floorboards on the recording of "Dangerous Weapon." Capturing simplicity is actually a very complex process, and one that Dan and engineer Brad Bivens took seriously. They recorded Chris and Johnny's vocals on one mic, keeping their voices on one track. Dan says, "John and Chris have a hair-raising blend live; they have it in the studio, too, and one great mic acts to unify the sound even more." Realizing that most recordings that audiophiles praise the highest have a dirtied-up sound, Dan used distortion "just under the threshold of hearing" when he mixed the album.

The album, *Shade of the Trees*, was relased in April 2010. The first three songs find Johnny reflecting on death through the eyes of others. The beautiful opener "Avalon," is about the mythical island where King Arthur was killed by his son Mordred, and Arthur's state of mind in the instant before his death. It's of a piece with "Better Angels," which depicts confederate general Thomas "Stonewall" Jackson's thoughts and words in his final moments. Jackson was shot three times by during the Battle of Chancellorsville by Confederate soldiers who mistook his party for Union men. He lost an arm, and contracted pneumonia. His final words were said to have been a delirious string of battle commands followed by a sudden calming and then, "Let us cross over the river, and rest under the shade of the trees." The third song, "Well of Sorrow," draws similarly on history and mythology, but is not focused on death as much as the sadness that sometimes arrives in and informs moments of festivity (in this case the December 13 celebration of Saint Lucia's Day).

As the album progresses, the talk of death recedes, but the mood doesn't quite lighten. Chris's raw, raspy "Caught in a Mess" tells of a relationship that has soured but is also inescapable. Lines like "Our good times are a curse" and "I need a new one now/a reconstruction of the way we feel somehow" could easily be about his struggles to make things work creatively and interpersonally with Johnny. Other songs follow along these lines of the battlefield of romance and relationships, from love being a "Dangerous Weapon" to "Town Talks," which serves as a warning to a loose-lipped philanderer. "Getaway" looks at a failing marriage through the eyes of a daughter during a final family vacation. Only the lovely "World Go Round" and closer "Pieces of Love" tip their balances toward happiness and optimism, but both still acknowledge the rougher side of relationships.

Chris Riemenschneider called *Shade of the Trees* "the darkest and weariest of the pair's releases." Ross Raihla wrote in the *Pioneer Press* that *Shade* it was "a collection of simple, elegant, and infectious tunes." *PopMatters* declared it was "the most timeless music of their career." Brian Roessler says he uses the album to turn people on to Storyhill. "That one is astoundingly good, just an unbelievably good record," he says. Dan Wilson wrote on his blog, "I love listening to the recently-released Storyhill album I produced, *Shade of the Trees*, as much as anything I've ever worked on. Maybe because it gives the impression of 'just happening,' and not being worked on at all."

The guys celebrated the record's release with a show at the Guthrie Theater's McGuire Proscenium, and with a clear capacity of 700, it wasn't overbooked like the Varsity show had been. That fell on the early side of what was near constant touring between March and May to promote the record. A day after the album's April 20 drop date, Chris and Leslie welcomed their own new addition, a son they named Caleb. It was a classic case of unavoidably bad timing, but Chris powered through the touring in May, and rushed back home to be with his new family.

The duo were on a break until the July Storyhill Fest, and then again until doing some shows in September in Kansas and Texas. With yet another reason to stick close to home, Chris held out hope for fewer shows in bigger venues. He told the *Duluth News Tribune* that he wanted to see Storyhill play more folk festivals in front of large crowds, establish themselves as a regular draw, and build something self-sustaining that way. One thing that definitely helped Storyhill's national name recognition was an October appearance on Garrison Keillor's *A Prairie Home Companion*. The show was recorded at the Fitzgerald Theater in Saint Paul, and featured special guest John Lithgow. When Storyhill came out to do their first song, Keillor introduced them by briefly telling about how they got started. He framed their reunion as them being compelled by fans to get back together, making them "prisoners of public approval." They played "Love Will Find You" and "Fallen" from *Storyhill*. After the latter song, the following exchange ensued:

Keillor: "Beautiful song. I don't want to tell you how hard I tried to learn that song. I listened to you sing that about twenty-five times. You're singing the hard part there."

CHRIS: "Yeah, yeah I am."
JOHNNY: "Let's switch around."
KEILLOR: "That was the part I couldn't get. I could not get that."
CHRIS: "I could give you lessons."

Later in the show they joined Keillor on the Christian hymn "For the Beauty of Our Earth" and then did "Better Angels" and "Paradise Lost." For Chris, who was a regular listener of *A Prairie Home Companion*, it didn't get much better. To be on the show and have Keillor so clearly enjoy their work, he says, "That was definitely the pinnacle."

16

Seven Shades of Blue

In which Johnny and Fawcett hatch a new plan, Vicious Vicious and Kid Dakota document their rough patches, and everyone says "so long" to the independent music scene.

If you happened to be at South By Southwest in 2011, you might have caught one of Tapes 'n Tapes' sets and then gone on to see Storyhill at the Driskill (the same place where Appelwick and the Harvesters had played 16 years earlier) at the Red House Records showcase. It was the start of a year of moderately heavy touring for Chris and Johnny. But the biggest story of the year for the duo was their new relationship with Garrison Keillor and *A Prairie Home Companion*. Keillor called the guys himself to personally invite them back not only on the show, but to the fifth A Prairie Home Companion at Sea, a week-long cruise from Boston to Montreal.

Storyhill's return to the show came on June 18 in Interlachen, Michigan. Keillor introduced them this time by saying, "Anybody who's ever tried duet singing admires these two right here, and that's why we asked them to come sing on our show. Out of envy, pure envy." He recounted their origin again, and then said, "They discovered that their voices merged in this beautiful weird way that you could work for years and never quite achieve." He asked when they first heard that overtone of their blend and Johnny replied that it was freshman year. Keillor wonders what they were singing, and suggests the Everly Brothers. Chris says dryly, "Stuff like that: John Denver and U2," to the audience's amusement. Chris and Johnny performed "Happy Man" and "Give Up the Ghost" from the *Storyhill* album. Their previous appearance had driven *Shade of the Trees* to the top of the Amazon folk albums chart, so perhaps they were trying to do the same with the earlier record.

As for the cruise, they traveled from Boston to Bar Harbor, Halifax, Sydney, the St. Lawrence Seaway, Quebec City, and finally to Montreal. Though they were both well-traveled individually, it was the first time Chris and Johnny had played outside of the United States together.

In the fall Chris and Johnny were back on *A Prairie Home Companion* at its usual home in Saint Paul at the Fitzgerald. They did "Blazing Out of Sight" and "Avalon" and joined Keillor and country music star Steve Wariner on the hymn "Will the Circle Be Unbroken" and a version of the folk tune "Goodnight Ladies" that segued into Simon and Garfunkel's "Cecilia."

There were sporadic shows and mini-tours sprinkled throughout the rest of the year, but Chris and Johnny kept otherwise occupied with projects at their respective homes. Chris had been steadily building his own studio facility, which he called Basecamp Recording, in Bozeman, and he had a healthy stream of artists joining him to record there. Johnny was still firmly ensconced with Fawcett at Modern Music. After running two Storyhill Fests again in 2010, the guys consolidated into one in 2011, choosing the Deerwood, Minnesota location because of its larger capacity. Performers included Carrie Elkin, Ray Bonneville, Grace Pettis, their former Peppermint compatriots Ellis and Peter Mayer.

* * *

For Fawcett, 2011 marked the end of his collaboration with Wang Leehom. The MUSIC-MAN tour had stretched over four calendar years and three albums, but with a new tour on the horizon it was time for Eric to step away. He made his fifteenth and final trip to China having played nearly forty shows. His biggest takeaway from his time with Leehom was the realization of the cultural relativism inherent in judging music, or as Eric puts it, the discovery that "the context of music is everything." While working at Modern Music, the conversations were constantly about what was cooler, fresher, better. In China Eric found himself playing music that "many American critics would criticize for being derivative, or as being cheesy, or schmaltzy." During shows, all of the lyrics to Leehom's songs would be shown on the Jumbotron and there would be tens of thousands of people singing along, a sort of mass karaoke. Eric says the goal of this was for Leehom to serve as a "big conductor of togetherness," in a culture that values the collective over the outstanding individual.

In the U.S., musicians are held up as exceptional, something to aspire to. And new and different are almost always better. But in China, Eric says, "What is derivative here is tradition there, what's schmaltzy here is an acknowledgement that there are certain things that we do in music that just work, and they're there because they just play with the heart in a certain way and just because reminds you because of how your heart felt when you were seventeen years old."

Fawcett also reunited with Yukon Kornelius that year for their first show in nearly two years. They played in December at the Gerald Ford Ampitheatre as part of the annual Vail Snow Daze event. Dee Snider was there again, but the number of guest musicians exploded to include more members of the Dave Matthews Band (Boyd Tinsley and Rashawn Ross), Mike McCready of Pearl Jam, and Olympic skier Lindsey Vonn (who came on stage for "Highway to Hell").

Even given all the big shows and travel, by far the biggest development for Fawcett and Johnny in 2011 was their decision to break off from Modern Music to create their own company. Joining them was fellow Modern employee Bryan Hanna (Hanna, you might remember, was the drummer, producer, engineer who had worked with Jay Hurley and Landing Gear). The trio scraped together savings, took out some loans, and burdened their credit cards, and by July had formed Egg Music, a one-stop shop for "original scores, music supervision, audio production and finishing for advertising, film, television, video games, and interactive media." They set themselves up with offices and a recording studio in a loft space in the Wyman Building in the Warehouse district in downtown Minneapolis, a seven-story structure built in 1896 and originally a home to a dry goods wholesaler.

It was quiet at first, "eerily, alarmingly quiet," as the *Pioneer Press* put it in a profile of the company. But then they started getting calls from their Modern Music clients. This was facilitated by the fact that, rather than try to replace nearly their whole team, Fischer Edit had dissolved Modern Music completely (and would itself only last another year). Egg Music was in business. In the division of labor, Fawcett took on the role of executive producer, taking on much of the communication with clients. Bryan and Johnny were co-creative directors and primary composers. They also brought over Brack Herfuth and Joanna Jahn from Modern to do production and licensing/business affairs, respectively. Singer-songwriter Lisa McGuire, who had interned for Eric and Johnny at Fiction back in 2007, also came on. Initially she was an intern again, but soon became a communications and social media manager, and then music supervisor as the client list grew.

In their first few months Egg did work for Target, Rimmel Italia, the University of Minnesota, and Cenex, among many others. The formation of Egg Music turned out to be a culmination of all the experience Fawcett and Johnny had been amassing in music for the previous two decades. They'd both performed in diverse corners of the pop milieu and could comfortably hop between generes. They'd spent thousands of hours in studios and knew recording and production inside and out. Even their work on the Lifescapes CDs were exercises in fulfilling a musical assignment based on a feeling or genre.

For Johnny, Egg was a perfect situation. "Creatively I'm in the best place I have ever been," he told the *Pioneer Press* in a 2014 article profiling the company. "I go in every day and make music that I want to make." After years of musical wandering, and of feeling confined by whichever path he chose, Johnny was finally free to roam. He was also somewhat liberated from the constant push and pull between the need for consistent income and the need to be there for his family.

For Fawcett the transition to working at Egg was slightly more complicated, even though working with clients was a natural fit for his outgoing personality. After spending over twenty years willing himself into becoming a world-class drummer, Eric was no longer focused on the instrument he'd grown up with. He loved drumming, but he realized looking back over his past endeavors that the thing that had always gotten him going was the collaborative aspect of making music. He would feel empty after session work where he basically just played what he was told and didn't have any part in the creative process. His conclusion, he says, is that "it's not the drumming, it's working with other people to make cool shit."

* * *

Appelwick had used the break from Tapes 'n Tapes to do what he always did, write and record songs. He didn't tend to compose on the road, finding the conditions nonideal, and settled only for texting himself lyrics. But whenever the band were back in the Twin Cities, Erik spent his time obsessively demoing songs in his small home studio (at this point he was sharing a place with his Tapes bandmate Matt Kretzmann). Money was tight off the road, but time wasn't. "He told Andrea Swensson, "As much as it sucks to be broke, it's also a really great thing to making music.... I was like a man possessed. I didn't have anything else to do besides just play music."

So in the three years since the release of *Parade*, he'd amassed a huge collection of demos, but hadn't been able to do anything with them under the contract with XL. He found himself just biding time before TnT could go back out on the road again. In the spring of 2010, the band came back with a blow-off-the-rust show at First Ave. The very next day they went to the Terrarium in Minneapolis to begin recording their third album. The release of *Walk It Off* meant the fulfillment of their contract with XL, and the band made the decision go back to their independent roots. Though relations with XL on the whole had been good, there had been some conflicts about things like radio edits, and the band didn't enjoy having a watchful eye on them in the studio. They'd saved enough money to finance a new record themselves, and they were able to score national distribution on their own, so there was no reason not to release the album on their own ibid label.

That meant no big-name producer this time. The band self-produced, hoping to capture the same sense of fun and spontaneity of *The Loon*. When it came time to mix the album, Josh went to Bridgeport, Connecticut to work with Peter Katis, who recorded and mixed Interpol's *Turn on the Bright Lights* and had worked on several albums with the National. By summer, the album—titled *Outside*—was done and the band went out for a few Midwest shows in June, and then on a longer tour in August.

The album came out in January 2011. This time around the critics were kinder to TnT. While no reveiw rushed to declare *Outside* superior to *The Loon*, most agreed that the band had gotten back to the core of their appeal. Tapes 'n Tapes hit the road a couple of weeks after the album's release on a U.S. tour that would take them through most of March and to another stint at South By Southwest, where they played five shows in two days. June saw TnT playing festivals in both Chicago (Ribfest) and Minneapolis (Rock the Garden). In August, they set off for another two months of touring, visiting cities in both the U.S. and Canada. In the midst of that they put out a video for "One in the World." A parody of the movie *Weekend at Bernie's* titled "Weekend at Bernice's," it features Appelwick in the titular role as a dead body. At a backyard party, the guys drag around Erik's lanky frame, providing him with a lit cigarette, taping a beer to his hand, feeding him ice cream, and putting floaties on his arms in the kiddie pool.

The band wrapped up the tour with an October 16 finale at the Turf Club and headed into another low activity phase. Within a week of getting back home, Appelwick was in the studio recording songs for the long-overdue fourth Vicious Vicious album.

He decided he needed some outside help to sort through the over 30 demos he'd amassed. He called his former Vicious Vicious drummer Martin Dosh and a new face, bassist James Buckley. Buckley had made his name as a versitile and ubiquitous player in bands such as Mystery Palace, the Pines, and his own jazz combo, the James Buckley Trio. Erik asked this distinguished rhythm section to sort through his demos and tell him what they thought.

James and Martin ended up making two piles, one of tunes that sounded like the pop-soul of Vicious Vicious past, and one of tunes that were a bit more world-weary and experimental. It was the latter group they were more interested in. James, for one, was pleasantly surprised. "Wow, Erik can write like this?" he said. "I want in." The other guys' interest and excitement were an impetus for Appelwick to put his full efforts into getting a new Vicious Vicious record out into the world quickly. The band began working out the songs together, in many cases streamlining Erik's layered demos, and quickly headed to Pachyderm Studio to put them to tape. Erik put out a for-fun appetizer for the album in late 2011, a hazy cover of "You're the One That I Want" from *Grease*.

The new album, self-titled, was released on January 10, 2012. So integral did Appelwick consider Martin and James' contributions to the record that listed the musicians' names next to his own on the album's front cover. The collaborative process resulted in a collection of songs that was dramatically different from any of Erik's other records. Its track selection gravitated toward the lyrically introspective, left-of-center songs, and the recording process leaned toward the experimental, with Martin especially bringing his background in electronic sound collaging to Erik's pop sensibility. Erik approached *Vicious Vicious* with a sense of gravity. He had been more than willing to play the clown for the press (to great effect), but he never wanted his music to seem glib or silly. He told *City Pages* that he purposefully gave the album a more solemn tone than his previous records: "I was tired of being misconstrued as kidding around," he said.

Sonically there's no true danger of that. The album has a gauzy feeling akin to the point at the end of a long night of drinking with friends where self-awareness is starting to creep back in. Sounds—swirling keyboards, ghostly vocalizations, staticky snaps—are heavily layered, with the vocals seeming two or three levels down in the mix. It takes repeated close listening to get to the melodies and songs beneath it all. Lyrically things are bit more varied. The band bio on their website circa the album's release accurately summarized them as "songs of stepping out and falling in love and getting all kinds of messed up."

There are come-ons (such as the R & B slow jam "Together," in which Appelwick promises, "I won't tell a soul/I won't tell your boyfriend") and ruminations (the syncopated "After Everything," which finds him, "Alone in my house/combing my hair/I stare in the mirror in my underwear/it's just another Friday night"). There are songs where he's mooning (*Get Ur Gunz*, where he tells a lady, "In your glasses I think you're the fucking shit/Tight black denim jeans on you they just can't quit.") and ones where he's sure to get hurt ("I Know U Know I Know" is about a guy who has discovered his girl is cheating but is waiting for her to confess).

Appelwick somewhat sheepishly admitted to Mary Lucia in an interview on the Current that the songs on *Vicious Vicious* all came from a personal place. Since they were written over a period of several years, they weren't all about the same woman. Appelwick

The final iteration of Vicious Vicious circa 2012. From left to right: Martin Dosh, Erik Appelwick, James Buckley. Photo by Graham Tolbert. Courtesy Erik Appelwick.

chalked a lot of the turmoil up to the transient lifestyle of a touring musician and not being able to give the proper time and energy to maintaining a romantic relationship when he was disappearing for months at a time.

His disinclination to confess that he'd lived a lot of his lyrics was a product of what he calls "crippling self-doubt" about his own work, and a desire for privacy. "As a songwriter you put your ass on the line," he told *City Pages*. "On all my records there are certain lyrics that when I first listened back to them I doubted I could actually let breathe out there in the world. I've slowly realized they become something else when you sing them enough times in the context of the music."

Despite its heaviness and significant shift in sound, local critics loved the record just as much as they had the previous Vicious Vicious albums. Rob Van Alstyne wrote in *City Pages* that "the songs beautifully blend shadowy atmospherics with pristine pop sensibilities." Andrea Swensson wrote on the 89.3 the Current blog that the album's "hints of psychedelia and experimentation are paired with an undercurrent of melancholy." Both Ross Raihala and Chris Riemenschneider placed the CD on their best of the year lists, with the not-typically-given-to-hyperbole Riemenschneider saying *Vicious Vicious* was "somewhere between a soft-grooving Prince album, an ambient techno-jazz jam and a Nick Drake bedroom-folk collection" and calling "Hangin On" a "bona fide masterpiece."

Tapes 'n Tapes were only sporadically active after finishing their *Outisde* touring. Between late 2011 and the middle of 2012 they released a cover of the Beatles "I Want You (She's So Heavy)," played at a set "The Current's 7th Birthday Party" at First Ave, and did a small handful of additional shows close to home. Just ahead of an appearance at the Caravan du Nord music showcase in Winona that summer, Josh Grier announced that it would be the band's last show for the foreseeable future.

In an interview with Andrea Swensson on the 89.3 the Current blog, Josh cited everyone's busy schedules as one reason for the break: "Now we're at a point where it's like, well, that last record went well and it was fun touring, but we all have jobs and lives and things, and so we're going to kind of do our thing for a while and we'll see what happens." He made a point to say that there was no band acrimony, and that they still all got together to watch football on Sundays.

When Swensson dug a little deeper on the TnT break, though, it was clear that this was going to go on a bit longer than the band's previous respites. She asked Josh whether or not he felt like the band needed an album to go out and tour behind. He admitted that was the expected cycle, and that the band had bought into that idea. And yet, it had worn them down. "Touring can be really hard on you. Not to sound like a fuddy duddy, but the older you get, the more you realize it's like, alright, well, do I want to be in a van with these four dudes for the next two and half months, and then do it again in six months? And then just kind of keep on doing it? I think sometimes you've just gotta be like, alright, well, let's not tour this year."

Talking to Mary Lucia, Appelwick shared his own mixed feelings toward life on the road: "The weird thing is that it's really exciting. It's a similar sort of grind every day, but at the same time you're in a different place every day, having new experiences, seeing people you've never met before. Then you get home and it's kind of like you just come down. And sometimes you come down pretty hard depending on where you're at with stuff in life. And the thing is, when you're gone, the rest of the world at home is still going, and you just find yourself like a ghost when you get back."

Though Josh and Erik were in agreement that touring was tough on a person, they came to separate conclusions about it. Josh was clearly done with the idea and ready to be closer to home more often, whereas Erik almost rather would have just stayed on tour and come home less frequently. As it was, he wouldn't have that option.

Appelwick did a couple more shows with Vicious Vicious that spring, a Turf Club appearance in May and a 331 Club gig in May that would turn out to be the final Vicious Vicious show. With TnT going on hiatus, Erik realized he needed a stable source of income.

Luckily, some old friends were hiring. That's how he joined Fawcett and Johnny as a composer at Egg Music. Appelwick enjoyed the work at Egg for the most part, though sometimes felt the twinge of guilt that came with using his music to sell things. But he tried to focus on the ways the work was challenging him to be flexible and explore different styles. It was the first time he'd had a steady workaday job making music, and an unexpected benefit of working at Egg was the way it allowed him the freedom to give up pursuing recognition for his work.

His Tapes 'n Tapes experience had also solidified this. "If people get excited about it, and great things happen, that would be awesome," he told *City Pages* regarding *Vicious Vicious*. "I understand that still means going out there and working your ass off." He'd learned, after being part of the ascent with TnT, that it didn't suddenly become a cakewalk once you got noticed and became a "rock star." There were no easy paths forward.

Ian Prince says that Erik falls into a special category of artist. "A lot of the truly talented guys aren't as ambitious as the less talented ones." In the end, like Johnny, most of Appelwick's pleasure and satisfaction comes from the creative process, not from the reaction to the final product. One gets the feeling he'll be in his 80s still recording complex demos in his home studio, the act of music just as natural as eating and breathing and sleeping.

* * *

Eliza eventually followed Darren to South Dakota. They moved into a house across the street from his parents' house and began the process of settling in to a completely different sort of lifestyle. Eliza had always been a city girl, but she embraced having chickens and sheep and other animals to care for. The couple started a large garden as well. Teaching full-time didn't slow Darren down in his own musical endeavors. Recording projects such as the Golden Bubbles record and Eliza's next album fell by the wayside, but Darren did manage to continue performing, making the 10-hour drive back to the Twin Cities on a surprisingly regular basis. In the early winter of 2010 he had taken a trip to France with the Fantastic Merlins, and immediately after performed with the Honeydogs at First Avenue's annual Replacements tribute show (the band covered "Unsatisfied" and "Alex Chilton"). It was only his second show as the band's new guitarist, but he and Adam Levy were already doing some writing for the band's next album.

In December Darren was back in the Twin Cities for another Honeydogs show at the Dakota Jazz Club. He was able to book some Kid Dakota shows as well, supporting Martin Devaney at the Turf Club, doing a solo set at Café Barbette in Uptown, and performing with Eliza at the Aster Café. They were back again both February and March. In June Darren did two nights at the Aster Café with the Honeydogs, in what would be his last gig with the band. It wasn't an acrimonious split, but the distance just wasn't feasible as the 'Dogs began to gear up for a new album. They'd already started recording without him, bringing back Brian Halverson to play on the tracks. Brian was at the Aster show as well, as the guitar torch was passed back.

With a summer off Darren was free to prep for the October release of the fourth Kid Dakota album, *Listen to the Crows as They Take Flight*, released on Graveface Records. The final version of the record showcased the live trio version of Kid Dakota, with Peter Leggett on drums and Brian Roessler on bass. The guest players on the album were a mix of Darren's collaborators old and new. Martin Dosh played Rhodes on "Fiber Optic Failure" and Andrew Broder sang and contributed turntables to "Phantom Pain" while Fantastic Merlins' cellist Matt Turner played on three songs. All but two of the album's ten songs feature prominent backing harmonies, split nearly evenly between Eliza and Minneapolis (by way of South Dakota) singer-songwriter Haley Bonar.

The harmonies and trio set-up make for a fuller, more traditional sound than the first three Kid Dakota records. You can hear Darren's classic country roots in many of the songs, as well as some of the poppier elements of his Hopefuls past. *City Pages*' Rob Van Alstyne put it best, saying, "With the Hopefuls now on ice, Jackson has been freed to finally unite the light and dark sides of his melodic mind." This is especially evident in the sparkly, swirling keyboard flourishes that show up here and there, and in the Heaven's Gate cult tale "Extra Ordinary," which in another timeline would have been a Hopefuls song.

Darren's divorce from Erin and his return to treatment, two events inextricably tied together, informed the records themes. Though many of the songs were written during his Providence days, Darren curated the tracklist to speak to what he was feeling in the present. Bracing opener "Dawn Did Us Apart" sets it all up. The song takes place post treatment, while Darren is still recovering, "I moved back in with my parents," he sings, "What else could I do?/I had lost everything that I'd loved except for you." Or so he thinks. He stays up all night every night waiting for her to call, to make plans for their future together, but the call doesn't come, leading to the final stab of a line "Dawn did us part/For better/For worse."

Much of the rest of the album details the fallout. "Dreaming of the City" details the end of a rehab stint in South Dakota and his desire to go back to the big city, even though he's returning to an empty house. In "Phantom Pain," featuring gorgeous harmony work by Haley, Darren compares missing his girl to phantom limb syndrome, in which a person still feels pain in an amputated arm or leg. "The Winter Without You" mixes up memories of Christmases past with the present, as Darren wonders how he's going to make it through the holiday season alone (the final line, "I could call you on the phone/But I'm pretty sure you're not home/I know it's New Year's Eve again/You're probably out with him," is an echo of *So Pretty*'s "Crossin' Fingers" and its opening lines, "It's late at night/I let the phone ring and ring/But no one picks up/I try to pretend you must be asleep/I try to convince myself/But I know where you are/I know you're with him"; the songs were written around the same time about the same woman). "Torn in Two" trades in the sadness and resignation for anger and self-pity, containing the teenagery line "No one knows what I'm going through." Closer "Fiber Optic Failure" serves as a bookend to the call that never came in "Dawn Did Us Apart," with Darren assuring his beloved that they no distance or inability to communicate can keep them apart because they are forever connected through what they shared together.

Critics certainly picked up on the record's themes. Chris Riemenschneider called the record "a light at the end of another long, dark tunnel." Ian Power-Luetscher wrote in *City Pages* that "it's an album concerned with the self, bouncing back and forth between seemingly adolescent feelings of angst, depression, and desire, and inherent frustration at being an adult and still feeling those same things." Musician Ryan Paul Plewacki, leader of Ryan Paul and the Ardent, and himself a former addict, wrote a glowing review of the record for *City Pages*, praising it musically ("every note and hook are carefully placed, arranged, and weaved together with precision") and lyrically ("Jackson's lyrics are vivid and transparent. If the images he's conjured are not directly about him or his experiences, it's clear that he's had an intimate relationship with the emotions behind them.")

The latter point was especially salient. With four Kid Dakota records and two Hopefuls albums to consider as a body of work, it's clear that trauma and tragedy are Darren's primary lyrical inspiration. He'd mentioned it all the way back after his second time in treatment, when he argued with his mother over whether the art that ensues from a bad experience is worth having to go through the bad experience.

Though it's there in subtext in a couple of places, drug use is less of an overt presence on *Listen to the Crows…* than on any other Kid Dakota record. Perhaps that's because Darren, though not ashamed of his past, was extremely wary of the view of creativity and drugs being natural bedfellows. He never bought into the fact that using heightened his creativity, and in fact almost never wrote when he was high. The trick was, however, that he did find his creativity in full bloom after coming out of a mess. And that's a psychological minefield, as one might start to throw themselves into horrible situations in the hopes of getting material out of it. Back in 2004 he'd told the *Pulse*, "I think a lot of people get used to being creative by putting themselves through different traumatic experiences and then they can't figure out how to do it without the trauma. I think it causes a lot of musicians to relapse. They don't know how to do what they used to do when they were in the mix."

In a *City Pages* feature story around the time of *Listen to the Crows…*'s release, Darren admitted to Rob Van Alstyne that he hadn't really written much of anything since moving to South Dakota. This was partially a function of his recording burn out. "I think at some point writing songs and working on music became less exciting and more of a job," Darren said. "I no longer loved doing it." Instead, he said, he was allowing his teaching experience to dictate his musical experience. Working with both primary and secondary grade levels meant Darren had to do it all: choir, band, orchestra, drum lessons, etc. Choosing pieces such as Offenbach's "Neighbors' Chorus" for his choir and playing the piano to accompany them causing him to stretch out and challenge the limits of his skills. He felt like he was growing as a musician, something that songwriting hadn't been allowing him to do. While this was all a factor in his songwriting lapse, there was also that factor of his personal life being in a calm place, perhaps not wanting to admit that without pain he was without inspiration.

But the inverse was also true. Darren says now, "It just took a lot of really difficult experiences to make me realize that writing music is one of the few things that makes me feel really happy." In a 2017 interview, he discussed Nietzsche's idea that humans have within them Appollonian (clarity, light, and form) and the Dionysian (drunkenness and ecstasy), and that much of the human struggle is in not going too far into either side of the dichotomy. Darren admitted that his lives as an academic and a musician had played out the two extremes. "When I'm interested in music, I feel very Dionysian. You know, I smoke, I drink, I do these things I probably shouldn't do. And when I'm in school and working on that I'm more rigid and less sort of spontaneous. I'm more calculative." The ultimate goal, he says, is "discipling of the two halves into a whole."

16. Seven Shades of Blue

Ironically, this is something he had figured out artistically long before. Nietzsche believed that an equilibrium those two elements in creative pursuits would lead to works of art that properly expressed the human condition. Darren's best and most affecting songs, both in Kid Dakota and the Hopefuls, take Dionysian content and express it in Appollonian form, telling small-scale tragic tales within carefully-considered structures. And while they're not on the level of ancient Greek tragedy or Wagner's operas (Neitzsche's preferred works of art), or a Dostevsky novel, they reveal the calamity and beauty and dark hilarity of the human condtion in similar ways.

* * *

The end of 2012 marked the first time that neither Appelwick nor Darren nor Fawcett were in an active band or immeniently releasing new music. Johnny had Storyhill, but even their touring pace had slowed considerably, and no new album was on the horizon. It was a stark contrast from just five years earlier, when you needed a scorecard to keep track of everything the four guys had their hands in. For all intents and purposes, they had all exited the independent music scene they'd called home for the previous two decades.

In some ways that exit seems like a defeat, and it may have felt like that at the time. But defeat isn't the same thing as failure. As "There are great artists and great musicians you'll never hear of," Brian Roessler says, "It's kind of a bummer, but that's the way it is. We hold on to the mistaken idea that, 'It must not have been that good because it was only local.' That's total nonsense. These were amazing bands that never became well known. And so what? They made great music."

Epilogue:
Enjoy the Ride (2013–2018)

"You can't pretend to know the way/There's more than just burn out or fade/You're working on your best mistake/You never have to rest your case/There's always something more to say"—Alva Star, "Today"

Darren's third year as a K-12 music teacher at Bison School would be his last. Though he found several aspects of teaching rewarding, and by many accounts was well-loved by his students, it was not something he saw himself doing forever. He applied to grad school at Virginia Tech with the plan of picking up on an old dream: getting his master's degree in philosophy. He was accepted, but would be heading east by himself. Darren and Eliza's relationship was at its end, and she surprisingly elected to stay in Bison rather than return to the Twin Cities. Eventually she would get married and have two kids, embracing life on the prairie.

In the summer of 2014, Darren was in a harrowing accident. He was visiting his parents in Spearfish, South Dakota, and was taking his new bike for a spin. While speeding down a steep hill at what he estimates to be 25 miles per hour he pulled the front hand brakes too hard and flipped over the handlebars, landing on his butt. The spill broke his pelvis in two places and resulted in severe nerve damage in his lower back. Doctors were initially unsure whether or not Darren would ever be able to walk again without a brace. After surgery and a three months of bedrest, he'd start an arduous regimen of physical therapy which would keep him bedridden and in near-constant pain for months. The whole situation sent Darren into a deep depression and despair. Near the end of his bedrest period, as his body began to recover, Darren picked his guitar back up and found he could play it without pain. "This was a welcome discovery," he wrote on the Kid Dakota Facebook page, "and with it came songs: sad songs, angry songs, playful songs, etc." He said, without hyperbole, that music was saving his life at that moment.

He rededicated himself to Kid Dakota, returning to Minneapolis that winter to perform his first Kid Dakota gig in a year and a half and first one in the Twin Cities in three. Due to his on-again-off-again relationship with Christopher McGuire, he brought in a new drummer, Matthew Kazama, who had played in a local group called the Birthday Suits. In early 2015 they went to Pachyderm Studio to lay down the basics for the new album, including, "Denervation," inspiration for which had come directly from his accident. They planned to finish the album in spring of 2016.

Unfortunately, Pachyderm owner John Kuker died suddenly in February 2016. Kuker had been extremely influential and supportive in Darren's early days in Minneapolis (he had provided free studio time for Camaro to record their demo and to Kid Dakota for *The West Is the Future*, among many other kindnesses), and Darren took his death very hard. He put aside work on the new record.

In the meantime, Darren had landed an unexpected gig. Director/screenwriter Ken Sanzel, most known for being the showrunner on the CBS drama *Numb3rs*, was working on a feature film called *Blunt Force Trauma*, starring Mickey Rourke and Freida Pinto. Sanzel was a New York cop who moonlighted as a screenwriter until fully switching careers. He was also well known as an indie music enthusiast with a knack for finding the perfect song to match a scene. Back in 2008 he'd used Kid Dakota's "Stars" on a 5th season episode of *Numb3rs*. For *Blunt Force Trauma* he wanted to use all Kid Dakota tunes, as well as have Darren score the film. Darren readily agreed, composing seven instrumental tracks to serve as the score, and allowing many of his other songs to be used as well, five tracks from *The West Is the Future*, "Phantom Pain," and "Denervation." The latter song notwithstanding, the new Kid Dakota album was still missing in action as Darren headed back to Virginia Tech to continue his studies.

In early 2017, Darren married Brieanna Watters, a University of Minnesota graduate teaching assistant in sociology. He moved back to Minneapolis, with plans to remotely pursue a PhD at Virginia Tech through an interdisciplinary course of study combining art and philosophy. At the same time, he reopened Shortman Studio. He started recording other artists again, and decided to finish work on the tracks he did with John Kuker, bringing in new friends (singer-songwriter Jeremy Messersmith, Trampled By Turtles' Dave Simonett, and Todd Trainer from Shellac) and old (Martin Dosh, Andrew Broder, Alan Sparhawk, Johnny and Molly Solomon). The resulting album, *Denervation*, was released February 2018 on Graveface Records. Darren says it's "an intensely personal record that addresses the subject of loss from diverse perspectives." Despite a fitful reunion with Darren that started in late 2015, Christopher McGuire does not play on the new record, nor is he performing regularly with Darren. Their working relationship seems destined to be tumultuous. In early 2018, Darren ran a successful Pledgemusic campaign to release *So Pretty* on vinyl, and he has ambitious plans for the future, including three new studio albums and a vinyl reissue of *The West Is the Future*. He also released a new Hopefuls song, "The Gift," though none of the other guys are involved.

* * *

Johnny's career as a pop musician since 2010 has been limited to his work for Egg, for the most part. In 2014 he teamed up with Appelwick and Lisa McGuire to record four songs as Fort in the Forest. The "band" didn't do any shows, but they did put their EP on Soundcloud. Around the same time, Johnny posted five new vibey and vibrant Alva Star tunes on Soundcloud as well. He'd been talking about a third record for awhile, and this was the first (and so far only) evidence of what that might have been like. Since *Escalator* was so different from *Alligators in the Lobby*, Johnny said in a 2009 interview with the *Duluth Budgeteer*, he'd reached the point where he considered Alva Star as a "catchall" outlet for whatever he felt most like doing at the time. The five new songs notwithstanding, it seems his time in the Hopefuls and then at Modern and Egg had mostly satisfied his need to rock.

In 2015 he provided music and songs for *Dragonfly*, an independent movie filmed in Minneapolis by writer/actress/director Cara Greene. In the fall of 2015, Bettine Hermanson was diagnosed with breast cancer. To help with their medical bills, Johnny digitally released all 33 tracks from his *Dragonfly* score as a benefit. The collection is largely instrumental, but does feature the Fort in the Forest song "Awake" and the keyboard-laden "Healing," which sounds like it could have been on the next Hopefuls album that never was. Bettine had successful surgery to remove the tumor, and entered chemo and radiation therapy that lasted into the following summer. At that point she was declared cancer free.

Johnny's music in recent years has seen turn toward the theological and spiritual. In 2009 he set ten different Biblical psalms to music for the Oak Knoll Lutheran Church (making them available on Bandcamp as an album, *Psalms*). In 2010 he wrote a liturgy called "Is This the Feast of Victory?" In 2016 he recorded an album, *Isaiah*, based on the Old Testament book of the same name. To "promote" the album, Johnny streamed himself doing a live performance of all ten of its songs nightly for the duration of the advent season (which amounted to nearly 30 consecutive performances). In an interview with WCCO, Johnny said the repeated performances had become a ritual and a time to meditate upon the meaning of the words he'd adapted to song: "It feels like I've stumbled upon this new way of looking at the text," he said. In many ways, Johnny had come back around to where he started, playing guitar at Christikon and writing songs about his faith on the original Chris & Johnny tape.

Egg Music rode the waves of a "highly, sometimes-frustratingly unpredictable industry," (as Fawcett described it) always turning a profit but to varying degrees. Craig Wright hired Egg to do the music for his MTV series called *Underemployed*, which ran for one season. On top of that, Egg continued to land work with big names such as Nike, Microsoft, Chevorlet, and Tommy Hilfiger, while contributing to less conventional projects such as the sounds coming from Totem Light Garden at the Target Field light rail station and the Lucy Light Forest in Boston, which features motion-triggered lights and music along a running path. They also collaborated with local poet Todd Boss to turn published work by a variety of poets into short films called "Motionpoems" that allowed everybody to indulge their creativity even more than usual. Their clients consistently praise their commitment to every project no matter how small it might seem, and their versatility. Wright told the *Pioneer Press*, "So if you need them to execute a Bobby Short-like jazz track complete with dusky vocal, they can do that; or a radio-worthy pop song; or something ambient; they can do it all," Wright said. "And when you want someone to really go way out to left field and bring back something no one else ever would have thought of, they can do that, too. That's a rare combination."

Though busy with Egg, Johnny continued to tour with Storyhill and put on Storyhill Fest, though the 2014 edition—which included Grace and Pierce Pettis, Lucy Kaplansky, and Johnny Solmon and Molly Moore—would turn out to be the last. Jim Kowitz says, "The three of us loved the festival and the experience we had with the fans, but in the end, because of not making enough money, Storyhill was essentially paying to put on a festival. The model was not sustainable." In the summer of 2014 the guys got together in Montana to rehearse new songs, and posted some clips on YouTube. "Heart of the City," "Spring Snow," and "Venice Beach" are all gorgeous, delicate, classically Storyhill tunes. "What Terrifies Me" and "Wide Jordan" both fit in with their jauntier work. They'd been promising a new record for awhile, first hoping to have it out first in 2014 and then 2015, but the process of compiling a list of songs both of them could agree upon—songs that had "mutual resonance" as Chris put it—was laborious, just as it had been for the previous two albums. Chris admits that his creative output had diminished while Johnny's had stayed the same or even grown. Without at least a 60/40 balance ("It's never really been a 50/50 thing," Chris says) they couldn't move forward. His own were becoming more personal, less suitable for a duo to sing. Related to that was the sometimes-contentious process of Johnny reworking Chris's songs. Chris says, "I'll go with it to the point that sometimes it gets reworked too much and I feel like I lose my song and my story." He says that was starting to happen a bit too much, causing things to feel forced.

Interpersonally, things had essentially gone back to the way they were before the first break in 1997, with the guys rarely talking to one another outside of Jim Kowitz's regularly scheduled conference calls and onstage. He also found himself in the middle of lots of negotiations between Chris and Johnny. "Like the other managers before me," Jim explains, "My role as band manager also included occasionally being a referee, counselor, and therapist."

As if the creative and personal loggerheads weren't enough, the group was struggling to maintain profitability, and in fact were barely breaking even. Most importantly, Chris had been partially absent for some of the hardest and most rewarding years of parenting, and that had taken its emotional toll. He realized he needed to be home way more often than he had been for Caleb's first four years: "There's so much to be said for nurturing your nest when there's a young one there, and not be flying off," he says.

So, just as he had in 1996, Chris told Johnny he needed to stop being in Storyhill. Once Chris explained his reasoning, especially as it related to his family, Johnny completely understood. This time, though, the guys learned their lesson and didn't declare a break-up. Instead, they called it a hiatus. "Like two professors taking a sabbatical," Chris says, "Or a farmer letting a field lie fallow for a year." In the spring of 2015 Storyhill went a brief "Hiatus Tour," starting with another appearance on A Prairie Home Companion at Sea that March, this time cruising the Caribbean, leaving from Fort Lauderdale and calling at Grand Turk, San Juan, St. Maarten, and Half Moon Cay. They were joined by Leslie and Caleb, Bettine, and both Johnny and Chris's parents. The Storyhill progenitors had always been friends, and so the two families happily shared a dinner table every night for a week while enjoying all of the other aspects of the cruise. "It was just dreamy, man," Chris summarizes.

After that there were just three more shows in Minnesota, one in Stillwater, and one in Zumbrota. Ironically, as Jim points out, they played four or five new songs at each show. The final gig was held at the Great American History Theatre in Saint Paul, the place where their reunion had been ignited 15 years prior. They'd come full circle.

Chris (left) and Johnny (right) share a moment during the final show of their 2015 "Hiatus Tour." Courtesy Storyhill.

In late August 2018, Chris and Johnny launched a Kickstarter campaign for a new live album—*Stages*—drawn from those "Hiatus Tour" performances. The campaign fully funded in two days, and by the end nearly doubled its goal. The guys also announced their first set of concert dates in three years, with shows scheduled in both Minnesota and Montana.

Whether or not this means Storyhill is fully active again, Chris and Johnny's nearly 30-year partnership is evidence of the value of sticking it out, even if it takes 1,000 miles of distance and several lengthy breaks. They have a bond that will be there as long as both of them live. During the 2013 Storyhill Fest, at one of the evening campfires, Johnny's daughter Ella (then six years old) asked, with everyone listening, "Daddy, is Chris your best friend?" This put Johnny in the awkward position of having to answer in front of an audience that included Chris. He had what Chris calls the perfect response, "Um, no," he said. "We're friends, dear, but actually we're more like brothers."

* * *

In the mid-'00s, Fawcett's dedication to the creative pursuit had gotten him a gig as a columnist for the U.K.-based *Drummer Magazine*. He used the opportunity to explore the ins and outs of living a creative life. In 2014, as an extension of those columns, Eric started a website called DumbDrummer.com, dedicated to what he calls "artrepeneurship," the intersection of money and art. The site includes deep-dive essays from his own experience, as well as a podcast where Eric interviews other people working in the arts.

Fawcett's only dabbling in the pop world from this point forward was sporadic gigs with Yukon Kornelius. In March 2013, the band played in Ludlow, Vermont at the Okemo Mountain Resort. Members of O.A.R. and Fuel joined them again, as did Dee Snider. The new face this time was another '80s pop metal frontman, Skid Row's Sebastian Bach, who joined the group for versions of his band's "I Remember You" and "Youth Gone Wild" and a cover of Guns 'N Roses' "Sweet Child 'O Mine." Yukon Kornelius did a brief set in February 2015 in Park City, Utah with "Black Horse and the Cherry Tree" singer KT Tunstall on several songs. Not long after that the band went into the studio and recorded some original tunes, though to this point they haven't seen the light of day.

On the topic of long unreleased recordings, Fawcett and Spymob shocked their fans in late 2013 by announcing they would be digitally releasing a new album—*Memphis*—in January 2014. The trick was that the band hadn't reunited, and that the record was only "new" in the sense that fans hadn't heard it. It was the set of country songs the band had recorded at Seedy Underbelly with John Kuker circa 2004, not long before they called it quits. Several of the songs—"Making a Killing," "Dream About Her," Sugar Free," "Sundays," and "I Feel Like I Let You Down"—had been part of their shows circa 2002 and 2003, often as a mini country set. On the album, Ken Wilson played pedal steel as he had on so many Storyhill records, and a few other guests came on, including Johnny on guitar and fiddle. The genre sets it apart from the other Spymob stuff, obviously, but so do John's relatively straightforward lyrics. However, when included with the entire Spymob oeuvre it reveals an astoundingly versatile band.

"The biggest model for Spymob is the *White Album*, just random kooky, goofy songs and just not caring whether it's going to be appealing to anyone," John says. He clarified that he didn't mean the analogy as a musical one, but that works as well, since the *White Album* finds the Beatles genre-hopping effortlessly between folk, pop, country, avant garde, and hard rock. John goes on to say that what made Spymob special was their chemistry, "It was so intuitive how we played together." Eric agrees, saying that when they played together it was like different parts of the same body: "It's not like I'm playing the drums, I'm influencing everyone, and reciprocally what John's doing on the piano or what Twigg or Brian are doing on the bass or what Brent is doing on the guitar is influencing me; we were playing each other."

Spymob didn't play any shows to promote *Memphis*, but they did briefly reunite in 2014 to perform at jMatt Keil's 40th birthday party. Brent was touring with Pharrell, so Egg's Joey Verskotzi filled in on guitar on the band's *Memphis*-heavy five-song set. Everyone by that point had pretty firmly gone their own ways. Brent's producing, engineering, and playing career has only gotten more impressive, and he continues to play with Pharrell and work with artists such as Katy Perry, Snoop Dogg, and Rob Thomas. He even got to work with Nick Lachey, whom he'd mistaken years before for a male model, on the 98 Degrees song "Microphone." Twigg and Ostby have both moved out of the world of professional music, with the latter having gone back to school to get a counseling degree to become a practicing therapist.

In January 2018 the band announced they'd gotten the masters for *Sitting Around Keeping Score* back from Ruthless. In March they digitially re-released the record with three bonus tracks and a new song order.

* * *

In late 2013 and early 2014 Appelwick began using the Egg studios after hours to work on his own songs, starting with electronic beats and then layering guitars and synths. The sound of his new songs was playful, but in a different way than the early Vicious Vicious tunes had been. The layered, synth-heavy approach was very much akin to the last Vicious Vicious album but the construction and content of the songs was more loose and pop-oriented, even veering toward hip-hop in a few places. One thing Erik didn't want to do was replicate the hazy, world-weary sound of the previous record, a sound he said had in retrospect made him feel "creatively-strangled."

Another aspect of that was the personal nature of the lyrics, so for these new songs he decided to create some distance via storytelling. He imagined himself as a famous billionaire traveling on a yacht called the Avtomatik and having various adventures. It was literal yacht rock. As he wrote on Facebook, "The album is mostly an autobiographical account of the travels and tribulations, wanderings and meanderings, islands and beaches, party people, and paparazzi I encountered along the way from the Tropic of Capricorn to the Cape of Good Hope, Straits of Magellan to Micronesia."

Appelwick said the album was "a laugh at wealth culture. It's hedonistic spray-tan absurdism." And he's right that songs such as "I Got U with My Camera," "Avtomatik," and "Moneyshake" have great fun with the concept, mimicking hip-hop's obsession touting one's assets (Erik even raps on "Avtomatik," which he called "fucking ridiculous because I don't have any business doing that"). Other songs though, get into the same soulful, thoughtful realm as a lot Erik's Vicious Vicious songs, tunes like the hypnotic "Staring at Pictures" and gorgeous "Over the Ocean."

He called the new project Tropical Depression, and initially intended to put the album out without his name attached, and to take any interview requests in character, making outrageous claims such as he'd recorded the songs in the yacht itself. But when he played the tunes for Martin Dosh and James Buckley they both wanted to play the album live, and Appelwick decided to give it a bit more of a traditional push. Johnny and

Eric were both big fans of what their old friend had done, too, and offered to release the record via Egg.

Appelwick had fun with promotion, not completely abandoning the myth-making behind its creation. In a *City Pages* interview he answered a question about his goal for the album thusly: "Our goal for Tropical Depression is to have as much fun as possible, play a lot of shows, star in a made for daytime TV special on a cable channel, win a handful of Grammy's and have our names in the Hollywood Walk of Fame. Those of us that aren't yet married are hoping to find trophy wives based on the merits and successes of this album."

The real plan was very similar to the one Erik had followed with his previous couple of albums. Put out an album, do a few local shows, and then move on to the next thing. Egg didn't have a ton of money for promotion, but they did send it out to dozens of blogs, and a couple of the songs got play on the Current. The press for the album was fantastic, with *L'Etoile Magazine* writing that the album was "the best Indie-rock-take ever on 80s cocaine-induced yacht music, and I mean that in the best way imaginable." *City Pages'* Youa Vang called it "sunny, blissed-out guitar synth-pop that has plenty of neat, slo-mo hooks." Chris Riemenschneider put it on his "Best of 2014" list.

Fawcett is baffled that the album didn't catch on in a major way. Calling it "one of my favorite records ever" he says, "This sounds like hyperbole, but I can't believe that all those songs are on one record, and I cannot fucking believe that that record isn't super well-known."

In 2014 and 2015, Egg Music endured some major changes. Original partner Bryan Hanna left the company in the spring of 2014 to focus on his own freelance audio engineering and producing business. Brack Herfuth left at the end of the 2014, and a tough year financially led Eric and Johnny to the awkward position of having to lay off both Lisa and Appelwick in 2015. Without hard feelings, the latter decided to go freelance and devote the extra time to his own projects.

Since leaving Egg he's gotten back into producing (his first project was Totally Awesome Summer's *Adventure* record, eleven songs inspired by the film *Pee Wee's Big Adventure*). He digitally released three albums worth of ambient instrumental music created in collaboration with his former TnT bandmate Matt Kretzmann under the name Monolux. In 2016 Erik put out a follow-up to the first Tropical Depression album, the digital only *Islands*. The 10-song collection is a logical extension of the first record, but without any of the yacht talk. Drawing on his experience at Egg, Erik made a video collage to accompany the entire album using mostly clips from '70s and '80s B movies and stock footage. *Islands* contains some of the strongest songs and recordings of Erik's career, particularly "The Words," "Cherry Blossom," and "Big Talk," which all manage to perfectly toe the line of evoking '80s synth nostalgia while also feeling completely new and contemporary.

In early 2018, Appelwick, Fawcett, and Johnny teamed with singer/multi-instrumentalist Todd Caspar (the Great Depression) and recorded an album's worth of songs as Intl Falls. They describe the music as "an otherworldly blend of dreamy guitars, lavish synths, and cathedral harmonies." In many ways the record feels like the fulfillment of the creative collaboration—embodied by co-writes like "Swear to God" and "Hold Your Own"—that might have continued in the Hopefuls had Appelwick remained in the band.

* * *

Here's where some of the rest ended up:

Epilogue: Enjoy the Ride (2013–2018) 195

Jay Hurley and Landing Gear took four years to make *Break-Up Songs for Relationships that Never Happened*, which they released in 2004. The band fell apart during the making of a second album and broke up in 2008. After a couple of other forays, Jay is now semi-retired from music, though he teaches guitar at Blue Tree Music in South Minneapolis. He says, "I had some decent opportunities to succeed. You just have to kind of scratch your head and go, 'Obviously the universe was saying it isn't meant to be.' The amount of talented people I've played with, that in and of itself is worth all the time and energy."

jMatt Keil continued to play with Kubla Khan and bring Rupert to dance for various bands, most notably becoming a fixture at the New Standards' annual holiday show. He discovered that not every artist he tried was suitable for Rupert. jMatt says, "Originally I thought I could just dance with anybody, but it didn't work. I learned quickly that I have to really like them personally, and be genuinely moved by the music or I literally felt like maybe how a stripper might feel. I was on stage moving around and I was like, 'This is awful.'"

He's proud of Rupert's longevity. "Even the haters have come around on me," he says, "I out-enduranced the haters." Kubla Khan continued to play for their own enjoyment, eventually morphing into a country flavored iteration, Virginia Circle. The group recorded one album before its members went their separate ways. jMatt moved to Boston in 2016 with his wife, Kristy, and the couple had a son, Emmett, in 2017. The family moved back to Minneapolis in 2018. jMatt says Rupert still emerges whenever he hears the Hopefuls: "To this day I hear it I dance to it. It completely genuinely moves me. If I hear 'Drain the Sea,' I will dance. If I hear 'Let's Go,' my theme song, my body moves. My heart starts thumping, my stomach churns. It's like a weird Incredible Hulk reaction to the music. It's very very very visceral."

Matt O'Laughlin continued to play with Friends Like These for another year or so after he left Olympic Hopefuls. But the band continued to struggle forward due to John Solomon's drug addiction. Not long after a gig at CBGB's opening for the Plastic Constellations and the Hold Steady, John Solomon got arrested, missed a gig, and went into rehab, effectively ending Friends Like These. Matt got married and gave up the music biz, focusing instead on a career in advertising. "I played so much and made so many sacrifices that I was done," he says. But he'd do it again: "Anyone should pursue art. It's awesome."

Tapes 'n Tapes' hiatus has now stretched into its seventh year, almost as long as the band was active. After releasing an album under the name Gingko album, Josh Grier has stayed away from music for the most part, and one wonders if he'll come back. Drummer Jeremy Hanson plays with alt-country singer-songwriter Frankie Lee, as well as Haley Bonar. Besides his work with Applewick on Monolux, Matt Kretzmann has a general contracting business, Grey Duck, doing new construction and home remodeling. Even if the hiatus never ends, TnT's achievements are impressive. In 2010, *Complex Magazine* named *The Loon* their number 53 album of the '00s, and the group is one of the few native Twin Cities acts to have their name on a star at First Ave.

Chris Cunningham has used the Storyhill hiatus to put his focus on his home life and on nurturing his Basecamp studio past the ten-year mark. He still regularly records musicians there and plays both locally and on small solo tours. There was a time when he was doubtful if he'd stick with making music for himself, but more recently has been feeling renewed and hopeful. In 2016 Chris released his first solo work in nearly 13 years, an EP called *If You Knew All Along*. It features seven warm, folky tunes in Chris's signature style, including "Spanish Dove," which he wrote all the way back in his year in Spain. After so long searching for his voice, at one time feeling supremely uncomfortable presenting himself solo, he finally feels fully confident in who he is as a songwriter and performer: "Give me an upright bass player who can hold it down and a decent fiddle player who can switch over to mando or banjo," he says, "And I'm ready to do three hours now, or five."

After leaving Kid Dakota, Ian Prince made a couple more albums with Story of the Sea before joining Casey Virock's band Porcupine, which currently features Hüsker Dü bassist Greg Norton as well. Ian has few regrets about not hitting the big time, saying "I'd rather work my day job and make the kind of music or art that I want to make on my own terms." The one experience that caused him to question that was witnessing what Johnny and Fawcett are doing. They hired him to paint the Egg studios, and Ian says, "I was jealous that's that what they were doing for work."

After the success of the first Communist Daughter record, Johnny Solomon shut down his restaurant, entered rehab again, and came out better for the wear. He married his bandmate Molly Moore and the group released a couple of EPs and a follow-up full-length *The Cracks That Built the Walls* (2016) to rave reviews. They have a national following and continue to tour the country and make new music. He looks back bemusedly at his younger self who wanted to "make it big" beyond the Twin Cities. He says, "Getting big back then meant touring, getting my music out to a lot of people, and making a living writing and playing music. I've done all that. I had to find my own way for a long time, but I'm one of the lucky ones. There's a lot of great bands that never get to do that."

Alex Oana quickly discovered that things in Los Angeles didn't work the way they had in Minneapolis. He'd hoped to build word-of-mouth about his engineering skills the way he had in the Twin Cities, but found that the music scene in L.A. didn't have the sort of interconnectedness that would allow for that. So after working a while as a freelance audio engineer, and doing pro audio retail sales for Vintage King Audio, he moved on to become the Vice President of Creative Operations at Slate Media Technology where created the Raven multi-touch production console, an innovative touchscreen workstation for audio mixing. Now, following a brief return to marketing and sales for Vintage King, he made the leap into the world of tech startups with two others to form his own company. Called Audio Test Kitchen, it will provide recording artists a better way to compare various pro audio gear online. It's yet another step in Alex's ongoing mission of, as he puts it, "making the world a better-sounding place." He looks back fondly and wistfully at his time in Minnesota and "the freedom, the feeling and reality that there was nothing to lose but the opportunity to prove to ourselves we could become who we dreamed."

Discography

John Hermanson

As primary performer

- Chris & Johnny—*Chris and Johnny* (1989), cassette only, digital download
- Chris & Johnny—*Shapeshifting* (1991), cassette + CD
- Chris & Johnny—*Different Waters* (1992), cassette + CD
- Chris & Johnny—*Live at the Grand* (1993), cassette + CD
- Chris & Johnny—*Miles and Means* (1994), cassette + CD (also released under the name Chris Cunningham John Hermanson)
- Chris Cunningham John Hermanson—*Clearing* (1995), cassette + CD
- Storyhill—*This Side of Lost* (1996), CD
- Storyhill—*Collage* EP (1996), promo CD
- Storyhill—*Live* (1997), CD
- Storyhill—*Echoes: The Final Show* (1997), two-CD
- John Hermanson—*John Hermanson* (1998), Parachute Adams, CD
- John Hermanson—*John Hermanson* EP (2000), CD
- Alva Star—*Alligators in the Lobby* (2001), Parachute Adams, CD
- Storyhill—*Reunion* (2001), two-CD
- Storyhill—*Dovetail* (2002), CD
- Alva Star—*Escalator* (2004), Princess, CD
- Storyhill—*Duotunes: A Tribute to Duos of the '70s* (2005), CD
- Storyhill—*Storyhill* (2007), Red House Records, CD
- John Hermanson—*Psalms* (2009), digital download
- Storyhill—*Shade of the Trees* (2010), Red House Records, CD
- Storyhill—*Stages* (2018), CD + vinyl
- Fort in the Forest—*Maybe We Should Get Together Someday* EP (2014), streaming
- John Hermanson—*Dragonfly* (2015), digital download
- John Hermanson—*Isaiah* (2016), CD
- INTL Falls—self-titled (2018), digital download

Compilations

- *Sam Goody Samples Minnesota* (1997), CD (Storyhill—"White Roses")
- *Peppermint Sampler '97* (1997), Peppermint, CD (Storyhill—"White Roses" and "Steady On")

- *Peppermint Sampler, Vol. 2* (1999), Peppermint, CD (John Hermanson—"Outdone" and "Sensational + Storyhill—"If I Could")
- *Minnesota Homegrown: A Showcase of the Best Acoustic Singer/Songwriters of 1999* (1999), Pulse of the Twin Cities, CD (John Hermanson—"Letter of the Law")
- *Peppermint Sampler, Vol. 3* (2002), Peppermint, CD (Storyhill—"What Was Wrong," + Alva Star—"Girlfriend")
- *Silage: Live Recordings from Studio B* (2003), KQ92 Homegrown, (Alva Star—"Girlfriend")
- *Too Much Time on Our Hands: A Styx Tribute Album*, 2003, (Alva Star—"Lady")
- *Copper Label* (2003), Philip Morris, promo CD, (Alva Star—"Unhappily Yours")
- *For New Orleans: A Benefit for the Musicians' Village Habitat for Humanity* (2006), two-disc CD, Sugarfoot Music, (Storyhill—"Give Up the Ghost")
- *Live Current Volume 3* (2007) (Storyhill—"The Ballad of Joe Snowboard")
- *Our side of Town–A Red House Records 25th Year Collection* (2008), Red House Records, CD (Storyhill—"Blazing Out of Sight")
- *Red House 25: A Silver Retrospective* (2008), Red House Records, CD (Storyhill—"Paradise Lost")
- *Road Trip: American Singer Songwriters* (2008), Feed Them with Music, 2008 (Storyhill—"Blazing Out of Sight")
- *A Nod to Bob 2: An Artists' Tribute to Bob Dylan on His 70th Birthday* (2011), Red House Records, CD (Storyhill—"Lay Down Your Weary Tune")
- *Bird Songs* (2013), House of Mercy, CD (John Hermanson—"Awake")
- *A Prairie Home Companion: Duets 2* (2014), Highbridge, CD (Storyhill—"Fallen")
- *Voice: Songs for Those Who are Silenced* (2015), House of Mercy, CD, (John Hermanson—"Calling Your Name")
- *Devil Music* (2016), House of Mercy, CD, (John Hermanson—"Halleluia")

As John August

(All CDs released by Lifescapes)
- *'Tis the Season: Christmas Lullabies* (1999) (Fawcett drums, Alex mixes)
- *Meditations: Native American Flute* (2000)
- *Lifescapes: Sleep, The Wellness Seeker* (2001)
- *Lifescapes: Peace* (2002) (John August—"How Can I Keep from Singing?")
- *Lifescapes: Inner Peace* (2003)
- *Music for Mind and Body* (2005)
- *Massage: Zen Garden* (2006)

As Fiction

(All CDs released by Lifescapes)
- *Yoga Flow* (2006)
- *Lifescapes: Quiet Christmas* (2007)
- *Sunday Morning Blend: Relaxing Guitar* (2007)
- *Lakeside Escape* (2007)
- *Arizona Spa* (2007)
- *Lifescapes Kids' Playlist* (2014) (with Rick Mayer)

As producer and/or secondary performer

- Ride Ruby Ride—*Brothers* (1996), CD (played on)
- Justin Roth—*Up Until Now* (1997), CD (played on)
- Brenda Weiler—*Fly Me Back* (2000), CD (produced, played on)

- Panoramic Blue—*More than Just a Lady* (2002), CD (produced, played on)
- Brenda Weiler—Cold Weather (2003), Virt, CD (co-produced, played on)
- Justin Roth—*Shine* (2003), CD (produced, played on)
- Rex Haberman—*Monte Rio* (2003), CD (string arrangements)
- Friends Like These—*I Love You* (2003), CD (produced, played on)
- Hi-Test—*World Class Loser* (2003), CD (string arrangement on "World Class Loser")
- Bryan Burnett—*Two and Out* (2003), CD (produced, played on)
- The Glad Version—*Smile Pretty, Make Nice* (2004), CD (produced, played on)
- Friends Like These—*Deliver Us From Evil* (2004), CD (produced)
- Mighty Fairly—*Perfectly Good Airplanes* (2006), CD (produced, played on)
- Andrew Benon—*Rock N Roll Moves* (2006), CD (produced), 2006
- Kubla Khan—*Lowertown* (2006), CD (co-produced)
- Fuller Still—*Color & Feeling* (2006), CD (produced, played on)
- Panoramic Blue—Sessions (2006), CD (produced)
- Friends Like These—*I Hate You* EP (2006), CD (produced, played on)
- Kentucky Air—*Kentucky Air* (2007), CD (produced, played on)
- Dan Wilson—*Free Life* (2007), CD (guitar on "Baby Doll")
- Mother Banjo, *The Sad and Found* (2008), CD (co-produced, played on)
- Annabelle Chvostek—*Resilience* (2008), Borealis Records, CD (played on)
- Mother Banjo—*Stray Songs* (2011), CD (sang on "New")
- Carrie Elkin—*Call it My Garden* (2010), CD (sang on)
- Spymob—*Memphis* (2014), digital download (played on)
- Holly—*#2 Record* (2015), CD + vinyl (sings on "For Ever Times Nine" + "Two Person Canoes")

Darren Jackson

As primary performer

- Headache—*Headache* (1995), self-released, cassette
- Kid Dakota—*So Pretty* EP (2000), self-released, CD-R
- Alva Star—*Alligators in the Lobby* (2001), Parachute Adams, CD
- Kid Dakota—*So Pretty* (2002), Chairkicker's Union, CD
- Kid Dakota—"Get Her Out of My Heart"/"Two Fronts" (2003), La Verdad Recrods, 7" vinyl
- Kid Dakota—*The West is the Future* (2004), Chairkicker's Union, CD
- Alva Star—*Escalator* (2004), Princess, CD
- Kid Dakota—*A Winner's Shadow* (2008), Graveface, CD + vinyl
- Kid Dakota and Fantastic Merlins—*How the Light Gets In* (2009), Hope Street, CD
- Kid Dakota—*Listen to the Crows as They Take Flight* (2011), Graveface, CD + vinyl
- Kid Dakota—*Denervation* (2018), Graveface, vinyl + cassette

Compilations

- *Apartment Music* (2002), Free Election, CD (Kid Dakota—"Get Her Out of My Heart," "Two Fronts")
- *Silage: Live Recordings from Studio B* (2003), KQ92 Homegrown, CD (Darren Jackson w/ Brenda Weiler, "Honolulu, Minnesota")
- *Stuck on AM 4: Live Performances from Radio K* (2003), CD (Kid Dakota—"Negative Kid")
- *Hit the Hay, Vol. 7* (2004), Sound Asleep Records, CD (Kid Dakota—"Pairin' Off")
- *We Could Live in Hope: A Tribute to Low* (2004), Fractured Discs, CD (Appelwick on bass, Prince on Drums, Paschke on guitar) (Kid Dakota—"Lullaby")

- *More Than a Woman: Female Artists Covered by 19 Male Bands* (2004), My First Sonny Weissmuller Recordings, CD (Kid Dakota—"Into the Groove")
- *About Songs Volume 1* (2006) DevilDuck Records, CD (Kid Dakota—"Ten Thousand Lakes")
- *Label WG* (2008), Label WG, CD (Kid Dakota—"Stars")
- *Absolutely Cuckoo: Minnesota Covers "The 69 Love Songs"* (2012), free digital download (Kid Dakota—"No One Will Ever Love You")
- *Weary Engine Blues: A Tribute to Jason Molina* (2013), Graveface, two-disc CD (Kid Dakota—"Crab Orchard")
- *Till the Dirt, Plant the Home, Watch it Grow* (2014), 75 or Less Records, charity giveaway CD (Kid Dakota—"Phantom Pain"–Alternate Acoustic Version)

As producer and/or secondary performer

- Brenda Weiler—*Live* (2001), CD (sings and plays) (Alex Oana engineered)
- Dosh—*Dosh* (2002), Anticon, CD (plays on "DJ DJ")
- Brenda Weiler—*Cold Weather* (2003), Virt, CD (co-produced, played on)
- Melodious Owl—*Melodious Owl* (2005), CD (engineered)
- Story of the Sea—*Enjoying Fire* (2006), Speaker Phone, CD (engineered)
- Fitzgerald—*Raised By Wolves* (2005), 2024 Records, CD (co-produced, played on)
- Ice Palace—*Bright Leaf Left* (2006) Speaker Phone, CD (produced, recorded, mixed) (Alex mastered)
- Brenda Weiler—*End the Rain*, Speaker Phone, CD (2007)
- Kwang—*For What It's Worth* (2007), CD (produced)
- The Owls—*Daughters and Suns* (2007), CD (recorded)
- Cinema Eyes—*Three Song EP* (2007), digital download (recorded)
- The Debut—*This Record is About Cars* (2007), CD (recorded)
- Aviette—*The Way We Met* (2008), Draw Fire, CD (produced and played on)
- Welcome to the Cinema—*Blocks and Hills* (2008), CD (produced)
- Zoo Animal—*Young Blood* (2008), CD, (produced)
- Action Versus Action—*Sentimental City* (2008), CD (produced)
- The Idle Hands—*The Hearts We Broke on the Way to the Show* (2009), CD (engineered)
- Fantastic Merlins—*A Handful of Earth* (2009), CD, (engineered)
- Story of the Sea—*Lunar Co.* (2009), The Cultural Society, CD + vinyl, (Darren engineered)
- Mother Banjo, *The Sad and Found* (2008), CD (co-produced, played on)
- Communist Daughter—*Soundtrack to the End* (2010), Grain Belt, CD + vinyl (played on)
- Eliza Blue—*The Road Home* (2010), CD (recorded, played on)
- Bella Koshka—*Deception Island* (2010), CD (produced)
- Shape Then Shift—*Shape Then Shift* (2010), CD (produced)
- The Idle Hands—*Life is Beautiful* EP (2011), CD (engineered)
- Inwood Radio—*The Loneliness of Champions* (2012), digital download (produced)

Erik Appelwick

As primary performer

- The Harvesters—*The Harvesters* (1995), CD
- Erik Appelwick—*Excerpts from Floodgate Days* (1999), CD
- Erik Appelwick—*Cellophane* (2000), CD
- Erik Appelwick—*Lacerate* (2000), CD

- Vicious Vicious—*Blood and Clover* (2002), CD, re-released by Twenty-Seven Records in 2003
- Vicious Vicious—*Don't Look So Surprised* (2005), Redemption Record Company, CD
- Vicious Vicious—*Parade* (2007), CD
- Tapes 'n Tapes—*Walk It Off* (2008), XL, CD + vinyl
- Tapes 'n Tapes—*Outside* (2011), ibid, CD + vinyl + cassette
- Vicious Vicious—*Vicious Vicious* (2012), CD
- Tropical Depression—*Tropical Depression* (2014), Egg Music, CD
- Fort in the Forest—*Maybe We Should Get Together Someday* EP (2014), streaming on Soundcloud
- Monolux, *Elements* (2014), streaming
- Monolux, *II* (2015), digital download
- Tropical Depression—*Islands* (2016), digital download
- Monolux—*Kurami* (2017), digital download
- INTL Falls—self-titled (2018), digital download

Compilations

- *Stuck on AM 4: Live Performances from Radio K* (2003) (Vicious Vicious—"Shake That Ass On the Dance Floor")

As producer and/or secondary performer

- Josh Aran—*Between Us There Arose Happiness* (2003), CD (played bass)
- Kid Dakota—"Get Her Out of My Heart"/"Two Fronts" (2003), La Verdad Recrods, 7" vinyl (played on)
- Alva Star—"Lady" on *Too Much Time on Our Hands: A Styx Tribute Album*, 2003, (played on)
- Kid Dakota—*The West is the Future* (2004), Chairkicker's Union, CD (played on)
- Alva Star—*Escalator* (2004), Princess, CD (played bass)
- Caitlyn Smith—*Silence* (2004), CD (production, multiple instruments, co-write and vocals on "September")
- Kid Dakota—"Lullaby" on *We Could Live in Hope: A Tribute to Low* (2004)
- Tapes 'n Tapes—*The Loon* (2005), ibid, CD + vinyl, re-released by XL Records in 2006 (produced)
- Shaan Sharma—*The All New End* (2005), CD (played bass)
- Shadow Box—*Lonely City* (2005), CD (played bass)
- Storyhill—*Duotunes: A Tribute to Duos of the '70s* (2005), CD
- White Light Riot—*The Dark is Light Enough* (2005), CD (produced)
- Melodious Owl—*Melodious Owl* (2005), CD (engineered, sang on 'Telephone")
- Fitzgerald—*Raised By Wolves* (2005), 2024 Records (co-produced, played percussion and bass)
- Josh Aran—*Water to Wash Water Away* (2006), CD (played bass)
- Story of the Sea—*Enjoying Fire* (2006), Speaker Phone, CD (engineered, played on)
- Dosh—*The Lost Take* (2006), Anticon, CD + vinyl (plays guitar on "Mpls Rock and Roll," "O Mexico," and "Bottom of a Well")
- Mighty Fairly—*Something About Airplanes* (2006), CD (played on)
- Andrew Benon—*Rock N Roll Moves* (2006), CD (played bass)
- Idle Hands—*The Hearts We Broke on the Way to the Show* (2009), CD (engineered)
- Totally Awesome Summer—*Adventure* (2016), digital download (mixed, co-produced, and played on)

Eric Fawcett

As primary performer

- Shark Sandwich—*Shark Sandwich* EP (1990), cassette
- Reno—*Reno* EP (1994), cassette
- Spymob—*Townhouse Stereo* (1996), CD
- Spymob—*Spymob* EP (1999), CD
- Spymob—*On Pilot Mountain* (2000), CD (self-released version of Epic album)
- Spymob—*Basement Tapes* (2001), CD + digital download
- N.E.R.D.—*In Search Of...* (2002), Virgin Records, CD + vinyl
- Spymob—"Walking Under Green Leaves"/"It Gets Me Going" (2003), Arista, 7" + 12" vinyl
- Spymob—*Sitting Around Keeping Score* (2004), Ruthless Records, CD
- Spymob—*Memphis* (2014), digital download
- Spymob—Sitting Around Keeping Score (2018), remastered with bonus tracks, self-released, digital download
- INTL Falls—self-titled (2018), digital download

Compilations

- *Sam Goody Samples Minnesota* (1997), CD (Spymob—"Half-Steering, Half-Eating Ice Cream")
- *The Cornerstone Player 040* (2003), Cornerstone Promotions, CD (Spymob—"It Gets Me Going")
- *MTV Presents Advance Warning 5/03: Word of Mouth* (2003), MTV, CD
- *Neptunes Presents.... Clones* (2003), Arista, CD (Spymob—"Half-Steering, Half-Eating Ice Cream")

As producer and/or secondary performer

- Chris Cunningham John Hermanson—*Miles and Means* (1994), cassette and CD
- Chris Cunningham John Hermanson—*Clearing* (1995), cassette and CD
- Storyhill—*This Side of Lost* (1996), CD
- Storyhill—*Collage* EP (1996), promo CD
- Storyhill—*Live* (1997), CD
- John Hermanson—*John Hermanson* (1998), Parachute Adams, CD
- John Hermanson—*John Hermanson* EP (2000), CD
- Brenda Weiler—*Fly Me Back* (2000), CD (played on)
- Bryan Burnett—*Two and Out* (2003), CD (played on)
- Alva Star—*Alligators in the Lobby* (2001), Parachute Adams, CD
- Panoramic Blue, *More than Just a Lady* (2002), CD (played on)
- Storyhill—*Dovetail* (2002), CD (played on)
- Brenda Weiler—*Cold Weather* (2003), Virt, CD (co-produced, played on)
- Justin Roth—*Shine* (2003), CD (played on)
- Kubla Khan—*The Things That You Lack* (2003), CD, played on
- Hi-Test—*World Class Loser* (2003), CD (played on)
- Friends Like These, *I Love You* (2003), CD (played on)
- The Glad Version—*Smile Pretty, Make Nice* (2004), CD (played on)
- Storyhill—*Duotunes: A Tribute to Duos of the '70s* (2005), CD (played on)
- Joe Rogness—*Retrospect* (2005), Two Fish Records, CD (played on)
- Mike Doughty—*Haughty Melodic* (2005), ATO Records, CD + vinyl (played on)
- The Twilight Hours—*Stereo Night* (2006), CD + vinyl (played on)
- Mighty Fairly—*Perfectly Good Airplanes* (2006), CD (produced, played on)

- Andrew Benon—*Rock N Roll Moves* (2006), CD (played on), 2006
- Kubla Khan—*Lowertown* (2006), CD (co-produced)
- Fuller Still—*Color & Feeling* (2006), CD (co-produced, played on)
- Kentucky Air—*Kentucky Air* (2007), CD (produced)
- Dan Wilson—*Free Life* (2007), CD (played on)
- Wang Leehom—*Change Me* (2007), Sony, CD (played on)
- Annabelle Chvostek—*Resilience* (2008), Borealis Records, CD (played on)
- Storyhill—*Storyhill* (2008), Red House Records, CD (played on)
- N.E.R.D.—*Seeing Sounds* (2008), Interscope, CD + vinyl (played on)
- Wang Leehom—*Heartbeat* (2009), Sony, CD (played on)
- *Fast and Furious: Original Motion Picture Soundtrack* (2009), Star Track, CD + vinyl (played on selected tracks)
- Griffen House—*The Learner* (2010), CD (played on)
- Tropical Depression—*Tropical Depression* (2014), Egg Music, CD (played on)

Camaro / Olympic Hopefuls / The Hopefuls

- Camaro—*El Demo* (2001), CD
- *The Fuses Refuse to Burn* (2004), 2024 Records, CD
- *The Audiophile's Guide to the Twin Cities* (2004), Pioneer Press, (Olympic Hopefuls—"Cavalier")
- *Twin Town High: Music Yearbook Volume 07* (2005), Pulse of the Twin Cities (Olympic Hopefuls—"Book of Love")
- *The Latest* (2005), Philip Morris, promo CD (The Hopefuls—"Let's Go")
- *Voltage 05: Fashion Amplified* (2005), CD (Olympic Hopefuls—"Let's Go," "Holiday")
- *For New Orleans: A Benefit for the Musicians' Village Habitat for Humanity* (2006), two-disc CD, Sugarfoot Music, (The Hopefuls—"Drain the Sea")
- *Now Playing at the One-Seat Theatre* (2008), Draw Fire, CD
- "The Gift" (2018), digital download

jMatt Keil

- Ellis—*Soft Day* (1996), CD
- Bobby Llama—*Bobby Llama* (1997), CD
- Bobby Llama, *Dyskonesia EP* (1999), CD
- Brenda Weiler—*Crazy Happy* (1999), CD
- Justin Roth—In Between (2000), CD
- Camaro—*El Demo* (2001), CD
- Hi-Test—*World Class Loser* (2003), CD
- Kubla Khan—*The Things that You Lack* (2003), CD
- Stuart Davis—*Between the Music: Volume One and Volume Two* (2006), DVD
- Kubla Khan—*Lowertown* (2006), CD
- *Absolutely Cuckoo: Minnesota Covers "The 69 Love Songs"* (2012), digital download (Rupert—"How Fucking Romantic")
- Virginia Circle—*Virginia Circle* (2014), CD (limited) + digital download

Jay Hurley

- The Sedgwicks—*The Sedgwicks* EP (1989), cassette
- The Sedgwicks—"Up Till Now"/ "Sorry Soul" (1990), Susstones, 7" vinyl

- Jay Hurley—*Thee Jay Hurley* (1992), demo cassette
- Hovercraft—*Been Brained* (1994), Noiseland, CD
- Shatterproof—*Slip It Under the Door* (1995), MCA/Fort Apache, CD
- Shatterproof—*Signal Flare* EP (1996), Fort Apache, CD
- Landing Gear—*Landing Gear* EP (2000), CD
- Shatterproof—*Splinter Queen* (2007), Catlick, CD (limited) + digital download
- Landing Gear—*Break-Up Songs for Relationships That Never Happened* (2004), Catlick, CD

2024 Records

- Standbye—*The Coping Mechanisms* (2002), CD
- Fitzgerald—*Light a Match and Burn It Slowly* (2003), CD
- Romantica—*It's Your Weakness That I Want* (2004), CD
- Olympic Hopefuls—*The Fuses Refuse to Burn* (2004), CD
- The Plastic Constellations—*Mazatlan* (2004), CD
- Valet—*Life on the Installment Plan* (2004), CD
- Fitzgerald—*Raised by Wolves* (2005), CD
- Duplomacy—*All These Long Drives* (2006), CD
- The Plastic Constellations—*Crusades* (2006), Frenchkiss/2024, CD
- Romantica—*America* (2007), CD

Bibliography

Sources—Part I

INTERVIEWS WITH Peter Anderson, Erik Appelwick, Andy Carlson, Chris Cunningham, Bill DeVille, Erik Fawcett, Heath Henjum, John Hermanson, Darren Jackson, Alex Oana, John Ostby, Chris Riemenschneider, Doan Roessler, Dave Scarbrough, William Schaff, Justin Seim, and David Weeks

"About." Spymob.com. December 24, 2002. (https://web.archive.org/web/20021224020057/http://spymob.com:80/about2.html)

Apold, Dallas. "Keepin' it on the down-low: Spymob is Minnesota's best kept musical secret." *Pulse of the Twin Cities*, vol. 4, issue 39. December 27, 2000.

Appelwick, Erik. "IUMA: Erik Appelwick" Internet Underground Music Archive. December 11, 2000. (https://archive.org/details/iuma-erik_appelwick)

Baumgarten, Mark. "Darren Jackson Leads Indie Rock Duo Kid Dakota Through the American Psyche." Minnesota Daily. August 13, 2001. (http://www.mndaily.com/2001/08/13/darren-jackson-leads-indie-rock-duo-kid-dakota-through-american-psyche)

"Bio." Kiddakota.com. June 2, 2002. (https://web.archive.org/web/20020602030023/http://www.kiddakota.com:80/bio.htm)

Bream, Jon. "Fresh Crop of CDs Sprouts at Seedy Underbelly" *Star Tribune*. June 5, 1998.

Bream, Jon, Vickie Gilmer, and Tom Surowicz. "Mill City Music Festival Highlights." *Star Tribune*. September 2, 1999.

Campbell, Dave. "Artist of the Month: 12 Rods." Local Current. March 5, 2013. http://blog.thecurrent.org/2013/03/artist-of-the-month-12-rods/

Carbone, T. "LA music producer Paschke heads back to his roots." *Grand Forks Herald*. February 1, 2013. (http://www.grandforksherald.com/entertainment/2187698-la-music-producer-paschke-heads-back-his-roots)

Carlson, Amy. "Six Questions with John Hermanson." *St. Paul Pioneer Press*. June 7, 2002.

Carlson, Andy. "Biting Rock from Across the Cannon." *The Carletonian*. February 9, 1990.

Child, Elizabeth. "Chris and Johnny are back—and bigger than ever." *St. Olaf College News*. August 25, 2007. (http://www.stolaf.edu/news/index.cfm?fuseaction=NewsDetails&id=4009)

Cunningham, Chris and John Hermanson. "Storyhill's Parting Message." Peppermintcdswww. (https://web.archive.org/web/20010429060815/http://www.peppermintcds.com:80/archive/cjmsg.html)

Desmith, Christy. "Local Music: Wanted Man." *The Rake*. September 25, 2006. www.rakemag.com/2006/09/local-music-wanted-man

Doane, Donny. "Kid Dakota, High Plains Lifter." *Pulse of the Twin Cities*, vol. 5, issue 3. April 18, 2001.

Ellis, Andrew. "Interview with Alva Star's John Hermanson." GloryDazeMusic.com January 31, 2002. (http://glorydazemusic.com/articles.php?article_id=1427)

"Episode 79: Eric Fawcett." *10,000 Hours* (podcast), December 14, 2015. http://www.10khrs.co/ep79/

Everest, JG. "Erik Appelwick" (filmed interview). Whole Music Club. September 27, 2007.

Everest, JG. "Darren Jackson" (filmed interview). Whole Music Club. March 27, 2008.

Fawcett, Eric. "Bravery" (speech). Dumbdrummerwww.

Gilmer, Vickie. "Out for a Spin." *St. Paul Pioneer Press*. October 20, 1996.

Green, Alex. "Kid Dakota: Go West Young Man." *Amplifier*, no. 46. December 12, 2004.

Harris, Keith. "Closing Time." *City Pages*. September 13, 2000. http://www.citypages.com/music/closing-time-6705472

Keyes, Bob. "Harvesters Clinging to Roots." *Argus-Leader*. February 29, 1996.

Mayer, Jim. "Now Hear This." *Star Tribune*. January 24, 1997.

Milner, Greg. "Olaf's Live Bait: Shark Sandwich Attack." *The Carletonian*. March 1, 1991.

Musser, Jim. "Three Quick Fixes for the Winter Listening Blues." *Iowa City Press-Citizen*. December 17, 1998.

Peterson, Erin. "Ole's Rock." *St. Olaf Magazine*. Fall 2013.

Priesmeyer, Molly. "Alva Star." *St. Paul Pioneer Press*. July 16, 2004.

Riemenschneider, Chris. "Dr. Hopeful and Mr. Kid." *Star Tribune*. October 8, 2004

Riemenschneider, Chris. "A New Day Rising at Old Blackberry Way." *Star Tribune*. May 1, 2008.

Shefchik, Rick. *Everybody's Heard About the Bird: The True Story of 1960s Rock N Roll in Minnesota*. University of Minnesota Press, Minneapolis, 2015.

Silver, Kate. "Action Jackson." *City Pages*. April 25, 2001. (http://www.citypages.com/music/action-jackson-6704273)

Skeppstadt, Matthais. "Minnesota's Brave New Rockers?" *Minnesota Daily*. May 21, 2001. (http://www.mndaily.com/2001/05/21/minnesotas-brave-new-rockers)

Storyhill—Parallel Lives (2008). Documentary film directed by Andrew Zilch.

"Studio for Sale: Citycabin, Minneapolis, Minn." Mix. July 6, 2004. (http://www.mixonline.com/news/mixline/studio-sale-citycabin-minneapolis-minn/419417)/

Surowicz, Tom. "Now Hear This." *Star Tribune*. November 27, 1998.
Undem, Kyle. "The West is the Future." 30musicwww. January 30, 2005. (https://web.archive.org/web/20051219201107/http://kiddakota.com/press/articles&interviews/TheWestistheFuture_30music.htm)
Walsh, Jim. "Best of August." *St. Paul Pioneer Press*. August 30, 2000.
Wenzel, John. "Subtle Crusher: 13 Questions with Kid Dakota." Sponic. January 15, 2001. (https://web.archive.org/web/20051219025334/http://kiddakota.com/press/articles&interviews/SoPrettyep_Sponic.html)

Sources—Part II

INTERVIEWS WITH Peter Anderson, Erik Appelwick, Kii Arens, David Campbell, Andy Carlson, Joe Christenson, Chris Cunningham, Bill DeVille, Eric Fawcett, Todd Hansen, Heath Henjum, John Hermanson, Jay Hurley, Darren Jackson, jMatt Keil, Ryan Kuper, Alex Oana, Matt O'Laughlin, John Ostby, Dennis Pelowski, Ian Prince, Chris Riemenschneider, Doan Roessler, Nathan Roise, Johnny Solomon, Rob Stefaniak, Leo Vondracek, and David Weeks.

"About." Spymob.com. December 24, 2002. (https://web.archive.org/web/20021224020057/http://spymob.com:80/about2.html)
"About." Spymob.com. April 22, 2003. (https://web.archive.org/web/20030224173428/http://spymob.com/about2.html)
Appelwick, Erik. "Lover's Rock." *City Pages*. September 18, 2002. (http://www.citypages.com/music/lovers-rock-6700273)
Baumgarten, Mark. "Darren Jackson Leads Indie Rock Duo Kid Dakota Through the American Psyche." Minnesota Daily. August 13, 2001. http://www.mndaily.com/2001/08/13/darren-jackson-leads-indie-rock-duo-kid-dakota-through-american-psyche
Boyd, Shawn. "Olympic Hopefuls (Friday, May 7, 2004, Turf Club, St.Paul)." *How was the Show*. May 8, 2004. (http://www.howwastheshow.com/reviews-2004/olympic_hopefuls-05-07-04.html)
Bream, Jon. "Pick Six." *Star Tribune*. July 18, 2004.
Bream, Jon. "Pick Six." *Star Tribune*. September 4, 2005.
Bernstein, Michael. "NERD—'In Search of...'" Pitchfork. *Pitchfork*. March 25, 2002. (http://pitchfork.com/reviews/albums/5748-in-search-of/)
Browne, David. "NERD—'In Search of...'" *Entertainment Weekly*. March 11, 2002. https://web.archive.org/web/20020414173420/http://ew.com/ew/article/review/music/0,6115,216215~4~0~insearchof,00.html
Caramanica, Jon. "Spymob—Sitting Around Keeping Score." *Spin*. August 2003.
Carlson, Amy. "Six Questions with John Hermanson." *St. Paul Pioneer Press*, June 7, 2002.
City Pages Staff, "Picked to Click." *City Pages*. May 9, 2001. (http://www.citypages.com/news/picked-to-click-6704301)
City Pages Staff. "Best of 2005: Best Songwriter." *City Pages*. April 27, 2005. http://www.citypages.com/best-of/2005/people-and-places/best songwriter-7362986
Collins, Cyn. "Radio K's Best New Bands of 2004 Showcase (Wednesday, January 19, 2005, First Avenue, Minneapolis)." *How Was the Show*. January 20, 2005. (https://web.archive.org/web/20050306062609/http://www.howwastheshow.com/reviews-2005/best_new_bands-01-19-05.html)

Crigler, Pete. *Majorlabelland and Assorted Oddities*. iUniverse. 2013
De Young, David. "Kid Dakota CD Release Party (Saturday, October 9th, 2004, Triple Rock Social Club, Minneapolis)." *How was the Show*. October 10, 2004. https://web.archive.org/web/20041213042705/http://www.howwastheshow.com/reviews-2004/kid_dakota-10-09-04.html
De Young, David. "Voltage: Fashion Amplified 2005 (Wednesday, May 25, First Avenue, Minneapolis)." *How Was the Show*. May 26, 2005. (https://web.archive.org/web/20060510014031/http://www.howwastheshow.com/reviews-2005/voltage_05-25-05.html)
Dorn, Chris. "Picked to Click." *City Pages*. Novemeber 24, 2004. http://www.citypages.com/news/picked-to-click-6694536
Ellis, Andrew. "Interview with Alva Star's John Hermanson." GloryDazeMusic.com January 31, 2002. (http://glorydazemusic.com/articles.php?article_id=1427)
"The Eye—Kid Dakota and Black Eyes Snakes." Brainwashed. June 5, 2013. https://www.youtube.com/watch?v=XYM1d1mm7FA
"From folk to rock, Johnny Hermanson's mastered it all." *Duluth Budgeteer*. April 3, 2009.
Green, Alex. "Kid Dakota: Go West Young Man." *Amplifier*, no. 46. December 12, 2004.
Greenblatt, Leah. "So Pretty LP." *Time Out New York*. September 18, 2003.
Gross, Jason. "Old-school boogie-pop minus the pet rocks and mood rings." *Blender*. Undated. https://web.archive.org/web/20040420142118/http://www.blender.com/reviews/review_1748.html
Hall, Adam. "Speak No Evil." *City Pages*. May 16, 2001.
Hall, Nathan. "So Pretty LP Review." *Minnesota Daily*. March 27, 2003.
Hannan, Tom. "Low / Kid Dakota / The London Dirthole Company—London Royal Festival Hall - 18/2/05." *Rock Feedback*. February 18, 2005.
Harris, Keith. "Married to the Mob." *City Pages*. June 5, 2002. http://www.citypages.com/music/married-to-the-mob-6700894
Heater, Rob and John Wenzel. "Sponic's Top Ten Rawk Albums of 2004." *Sponic*, issue 20. January 2005. https://web.archive.org/web/20050305170350/http://www.sponiczine.com/main.htm
Henning, Sarah. "Real-Time Reviews From the Green Man" *Duluth News Tribune*. July 16, 2005.
Hill, Marcie. "Tears of a Clown." *City Pages*. Aug 21, 2002. (http://www.citypages.com/music/tears-of-a-clown-6700783)
Hill, Marcie, "Picked to Click XII." *City Pages*. September 18, 2002. (http://www.citypages.com/news/picked-to-click-xii-6700261)
Jordan, Chris. "N.E.R.D., Sans Chad Hugo, Get Ribald and Funky in Philly." MTVwww. June 3, 2002. http://www.mtv.com:80/news/articles/1454947/06032002/nerd.jhtml
Justin, Neal. "Music Rocks TV Even If Ratings Don't Roll." *Star Tribune*. December 21, 2003.
"Kid Dakota." *Perspective*. February 28, 2005. http://alister.blogspot.com/2005/02/kid-dakota.html
"Kid Dakota, 'So Pretty.'" *Brainwashed*. undated. http://www.brainwashed.com/index.php?option=com_content&view=article&id=2143%3Akid-dakota-qso-prettyq&catid=13%3Aalbums-and-singles&Itemid=1
Klein, Andrew. "4.7.03." *Storyhill.info*. April 7, 2003. http://www.storyhill.info/journal.html.
Lenzmeier, Losi. "Alex Oana: Back on top again." *Pulse of the Twin Cities*, October 10, 2002.

Marsh, Steve. "Big in Japan, Anonymous in Minny." *Mpls.St.Paul Magazine.* March 2005.
Matos, Michaelangelo. "An Oral History of the Foxfire." *City Pages.* February 27, 2017. http://www.citypages.com/music/an-oral-history-of-the-foxfire-minneapolis-fleeting-and-beloved-all-ages-rock-club/414412323
McGuire, Matt. "Hired Guns." *Chicago Tribune.* April 7, 2004.
Metivier, Michael. "Kid Dakota: The West is the Future." PopMatters. November 23, 2004.
Meyer, Jim. "Listen Up." *Star Tribune.* February 11, 2001.
Montgomery, James. "Olympic Hopefuls Forced to Change Their Name." *MTV News.* August 5, 2005. http://www.mtv.com/news/1507047/olympic-hopefuls-forced-to-change-their-name/
Moritz, Lenore. "Ellis." *Mom Culture.* October 23, 2009. http://momcultureonline.com/2009/10/23/ellis-musician/
Morel, Paul, "So Pretty." *Pulse of the Twin Cities.* October 16, 2002.
Murphy, Matthew. "Kid Dakota, 'The West is the Future.'" *Pitchfork.* October 31, 2004 http://www.pitchfork.com/reviews/albums/4587-the-west-is-the-future/
Nemo, John. "Performers Save Show from Down Time." *St. Paul Pioneer Press.* September 19, 2002.
Ohmart, Ben. "Alva Star—Alligators in the Lobby." Music Dish. May 3, 2001. http://www.musicdish.com/mag/index.php3?id=3728
Pareles, Jon. "Feeling Hyper, Indie Rock Casts Off Its Slacker Image." *New York Times.* October 16, 2004.
Priesmeyer, Molly. "Hear Now: Olympic Hopefuls." *St. Paul Pioneer Press.* April 9, 2004.
Priesmeyer, Molly. "Are You There God? It's Us, the Rockers." *City Pages.* May 26, 2004.
Rabin, Nathan. "NERD—'In Search of…'" *AV Club.* March 12, 2002. (http://www.avclub.com/review/nerd-emin-search-ofem-22082)
Raihala, Ross. "Rocker on the Fast Track." *St. Paul Pioneer Press.* December 26, 2004.
Raihala, Ross. "Sound Recovery—It's in the Air: Signs are the Twin Cities could be in for another heyday" Pioneer Press. May 14, 2005.
Raihala, Ross. "Monday Holiday Means You Can Hit All Your Favorite Haunts This Week." *St. Paul Pioneer Press.* October 27, 2005.
Raihala, Ross. "Lo and Behold, the (Olympic) Hopefuls are Back in the Game." *St. Paul Pioneer Press.* February 19, 2008.
Riemenschneider, Chris. "Ol' Yeller, other local bands learn new tricks at SXSW." *Star Tribune.* March 22, 2002.
Riemenschneider, Chris. "Saved by the N.E.R.D.s." *Star Tribune.* June 7, 2002.
Riemenschneider, Chris. "So Pretty LP." *Star Tribune.* November 10, 2002.
Riemenschneider, Chris. "Happy Apple CD is still baking in major label oven." *Star Tribune.* November 11, 2002.
Riemenschneider, Chris. "Minnesotans Do Texas Right." Star Tribune. March 21, 2003.
Riemenschneider, Chris. "Local Acts Face Record-Label Blues." *Star Tribune.* April 4, 2003.
Riemenschneider, Chris. "Liberty Won" *Star Tribune.* April 20, 2003.
Riemenschneider, Chris. "Weiler Returns for 'Cold Weather.'" *Star Tribune.* November 7, 2003.
Riemenschneider, Chris. "New 2024 Label is Full of Hopefuls." *Star Tribune.* May 7, 2004
Riemenschneider, Chris. "First Ave Dances to a New Tune." *Star Tribune.* July 2, 2004
Riemenschneider, Chris. "Best Local CDs of 2004…So Far." *Star Tribune.* July 23, 2004.
Riemenschneider, Chris. "Dr. Hopeful and Mr. Kid." *Star Tribune.* October 8, 2004
Riemenschneider, Chris. "Between the Turf and a Hard Place." *Star Tribune.* April 15, 2005.
Riemenschneider, Chris. "A Bloody Valentine, by Fitzgerald" *Star Tribune.* April 22, 2005.
Riemenschneider, Chris. "Down for the upbeat." *Star Tribune.* June 17, 2005
Riemenschneider, Chris. "Trademark trips up band that's making name for itself." *Star Tribune.* July 28, 2005
Riemenschneider, Chris. "A Vicious Vicious Circle," *Star Tribune.* September 7, 2007.
Rich, Jane. "Low, Kid Dakota." *Cellular Fever.* February 18, 2005. http://cellularfever.blogspot.com/2005/02/low-kid-dakota.html
Rojiks. "May 7, 2024 Records Showcase at Turf Club." Music Scene Network. May 8, 2004. (https://web.archive.org/web/20050509175815/http://www.musicscenenetwork.com/portalpak/forumdetail.asp?frid=181754)
Silver, Kate. "Action Jackson." *City Pages.* April 25, 2001. http://www.citypages.com/music/action-jackson-6704273
Spano, Charles. "Vicious Vicious—Blood and Clover." All Music Guide. http://www.allmusic.com/album/blood-amp-clover-mw0000996566
Spoto, Cara. "Minnesota's Brave New Rockers?" *Minnesota Daily.* May 21, 2001. (http://www.mndaily.com/2001/05/21/minnesotas-brave-new-rockers)
Taylor, Luke. "Bassist Francois Rabbath loves to share the 'beautiful sound.'" Classical MPR. July 8, 2014. http://www.classicalmpr.org/story/2014/07/08/bassist-francois-rabbath-loves-to-share-the-beautiful-sound
Terhark, Chuck. "Talk of the Town." *City Pages.* November 24, 2004. (http://www.citypages.com/news/talk-of-the-town-6693864)
Thomas, Lindsey. "Skating rink soul from Erik Appelwick." *Minnesota Daily.* September 12, 2002.
Thomas, Lindsey. "Olympian Heights." *City Pages.* July 21, 2004. (http://www.citypages.com/music/olympian-heights-6695444)
Thomas, Lindsey. "Hot and Bothered." *City Pages.* June 29, 2005. (http://www.citypages.com/music/hot-and-bothered-6691961)
Thomas, Lindsey. "Rupert Pederson." *City Pages.* June 21, 2006. http://www.citypages.com/unknown/rupert-pederson-freak-out-dancing-is-his-profession-refinancing-your-mortgage-at-a-low-low-rate-is-his-passion-6724447J
Ubl, Sam. "Tapes 'n' Tapes, 'The Loon.'" *Pitchfork.* February 27, 2006. www.pitchfork.com/reviews/albums/8314-the-loon
Undem, Kyle. "The West is the Future." 30musicwww. January 30, 2005. (https://web.archive.org/web/20051219201107/http://kiddakota.com/press/articles&interviews/TheWestistheFuture_30music.htm)
Van Alstyne, Rob. "Friends Like These." *Pulse of the Twin Cities.* December 23 2002.
Van Alstyne, Rob. "The Olympic Hopefuls: Going for the Gold." Pulse of the Twin Cities. April 8, 2004. (http://www.pulsetc.com/article363b.html?sid=1007)
Van Alstyne, Rob. "Kid Dakota: Atomic Pilgrim." *Pulse of the Twin Cities.* December 15, 2004 (http://www.pulsetc.com/article1fd2.html?op=Print&sid=1541)

Van Alstyne, Rob. "Vicious Vicious: Mr. Soul." *Pulse of the Twin Cities*. January 5, 2005.
Van Alstyne, Rob. "Hot Tickets for June 15—June 21, 2005." Pulse of the Twin Cities. June 14, 2005. http://www.southsidepride.com/pulsetc/article53d7.html?sid=1890
Walsh, Jim. "Rock of Ages." *City Pages*. July 28, 2004 (http://www.citypages.com/columns/rock-of-ages-6695473)
Walsh, Jim. "25 Reasons the Scene is Now." *City Pages*. June 8, 2005.
Walters, Barry. "NERD—'In Search of...'" *Rolling Stone*. March 28, 2002. https://web.archive.org/web/20020826150846/http://www.rollingstone.com/recordings/review.asp?aid=2042790
Williamson, John. "Music: NERD, Corn Exchange, Edinburgh." *The Herald*. November 10, 2003.

Sources—Part III

INTERVIEWS WITH Erik Appelwick, David Campbell, Andy Carlson, Chris Cunningham, Bill DeVille, Eric Fawcett, Todd Hansen, Heath Henjum, John Hermanson, Darren Jackson, jMatt Keil, Jim Kowitz, Ben Krueger, Ryan Kuper, Matt O'Laughlin, John Ostby, Dennis Pelowski, Ian Prince, Doan Roessler, Nathan Roise, Chris Riemenschneider, William Schaff, Johnny Solomon, Rob Stefaniak, and Leo Vondracek.

Alexis, Nadeska. "Holiday Music Reviews." *Blackbook*. December 16, 2010.
Askari, Sara. "Vicious Vicious, 'Parade.'" *City Pages*. September 26, 2007, http://www.citypages.com/music/vicious-vicious-parade-6685828
Askari, Sarah. "The Year in Music 2007." *City Pages*. December 19, 2007.
Askari, Sarah. "Kid Dakota Visit the Depressionitorium." *City Pages*. February 20, 2008,.
Avard, Christian. "Yukon Kornelius returns to Vermont." *Rutland Herald*, March 14, 2013
Bahn, Christopher. "Tapes 'n' Tapes—Outside." *AV Club*. January 11, 2011.
Bajrami, Mike and Nicole Slater. "Episode 001: Alex Oana—Music Industry to Mindful Entrepreneur." January 25, 2018. http://mentalnotespodcast.com/episode-001-alex-oana/
Bowie, David. "David Bowie on Insight." *Nokia Insight*. November 14, 2006. http://www.bowiewonderworld.com/press/00/061114insight.htm
Boyd, Betsy. "Mood shifts set music on 'Numbers.'" *Variety*. April 30, 2009.
Bratsch, Katie. "Storyhill, March 20, 2007." *How Was the Show*. March 21, 2007. https://web.archive.org/web/20100326201956/http://www.howwastheshow.com/index.cfm/action/reviews.view/reviewKey/626
Calder, Simon. "Kid Dakota on Back to the City: A Mpls Music Conversation" (interview). July 29, 2017. 7/29/17 wwwyoutube.com/watch?v=JSx4SD
Cantalini, Chris. "New Tapes 'n' Tapes mp3: 'hang them all.'" *Bear Vs. Gorilla*. February 15, 2008.
City Pages Staff. "Best Local Record Label: 2024 Records." *City Pages*. April 27, 2005. http://www.citypages.com/best-of/2005/people-and-places/best-local-record-label-7362079
Cole, Matthew. "Tapes 'n' Tapes—Outside." *Slant Magazine*. January 7, 2011. http://www.slantmagazine.com/music/review/tapes-n-tapes-outside
Curran, Grayson. "Tapes 'n' Tapes—Outside." *Pitchfork*. January 10, 2011.
Curtin, Kevin. "Tyler, the Creator Returns to Austin." *Austin Chronicle*. June 3, 2015. http://www.austinchronicle.com/daily/music/2015-06-03/tyler-the-creator-returns-to-austin/
Desmith, Christy. "Local Music: Wanted Man." *The Rake*. September 25, 2006. www.rakemag.com/2006/09/local-music-wanted-man
De Young, David. "Kid Dakota CD Release Party at the Turf Club on 3/1/08." How Was the Show. March 2, 2008. (http://web.archive.org/web/20081222155713/http://www.howwastheshow.com/index.cfm/action/reviews.view/reviewKey/895)
De Young, David. "Western Fifth CD Release Party with Kid Dakota at Uptown Bar and Cafe on 11/21/08." *How Was the Show*. November 22, 2008. (http://web.archive.org/web/20081217161802/http://www.howwastheshow.com/index.cfm/action/reviews.view/reviewKey/1064)
De Young, David. "The Hopefuls at The Turf Club on 1/9/09." How Was the Show. January 10, 2009. http://www.howwastheshow.com/index.cfm/action/reviews.view/reviewKey/1094)
Elgoodnews. "Live Music Will Cheer You Up" *Star Tribune*. December 20, 2008. http://www.startribune.com/live-music-will-cheer-you-up/36517129/
Everhart, John. "Tapes 'n' Tapes—Outside." *Under the Radar*. January 7, 2011. http://www.undertheradarmag.com/reviews/outside
Frederickson, Erika. "Same old Storyhill? Acoustic duo recommits, prepares to launch." Missoula News. September 28, 2006. http://missoulanews.bigskypress.com/missoula/same-old-storyhill/Content?oid=1137544
Hoenack, Dave. "Communist Daughter's Lions and Lambs EP Explores Johnny Solomon's Recovery from Addiction." *City Pages*. July 4, 2012. http://www.citypages.com/music/communist-daughters-lions-and-lambs-ep-explores-johnny-solomons-recovery-from-addiction-6760134
Jarnstrom, David. "Ellis Drum Shop—Shop Talk with Ian Prince" (filmed interview). (https://vimeo.com/2497028)
"John Hermanson" (interview). March 12, 2010. http://www.nemercy.org/category/liturgy/john-hermanson
"John Hermanson Scores MTV's 'Underemployed.'" lbbonline.com. October 13, 2012. https://lbbonline.com/news/john-hermanson-scores-mtvs-underemployed http://www.slate.com/blogs/browbeat/2014/10/08/weezer_s_new_album_everything_will_be_alright_in_the_end_a_history_of_weezer.html
Kewei, Tay. "Leehom Music Man Tour in Teipei." Say What? September 24, 2008. (http://taykewei.blogspot.com/2008/09/19-200908-leehom-music-man-tour-in.html)
The Know Staff. "WTF: Should Yukon Kornelius really be considered a super group?" *Denver Post*. December 8, 2011. http://theknow.denverpost.com/2011/12/08/yukon-kornelius-vail/42475/
Lawler, Christa. "Storyhill Masters Give-and-take to Create Albums." *Duluth News Tribune*. November 18, 2010.
Lenser, Barry. "Tapes 'n' Tapes, Walk It Off." *PopMatters*. April 8, 2008.
Lucia, Ali. "WCCO Minneaosotan to Meet: John Hermanson." *WCCO*. December 20, 2016. http://minnesota.cbslocal.com/2016/12/20/m2m-john-hermanson/
Lucia, Mary. "Vicious Vicious performs in The Current Studio 1/31/12" (interview). *89.3 The Current*. January 3, 2012.

Mason, Stewart. "Kid Dakota, 'A Winner's Shadow.'" *AllMusic Guide*. Undated. http://www.allmusic.com/album/a-winners-shadow-mw0000496556

McGlynn, Matthew. "Storyhill 'Shade of the Trees' Sessions." *Recording Hacks*. July 20, 2010. http://recordinghacks.com/2010/07/20/dan-wilson-brad-bivens-interview/

Micallef, Ken. "N.E.R.D, Old Money, New Money." *Electronic Musician*. June 1, 2008.

"MOKB Premiere: Vicious Vicious: I Know U Know I Know." My Old Kentucky Blog. January 9, 2012. http://www.myoldkentuckyblog.com/?p=25547

Morast, Robert. "Popular band Olympic Hopefuls have S.D. pedigree." *Argus-Leader*. February 20, 2005.

O'Brien, Pat. "The Hopefuls CD-Release Show." *City Pages*. December 17, 2008. http://www.citypages.com/calendar/the-hopefuls-cd-release-show-6736043

Ojeda-Zapata, Julio. "Minneapolis' Egg Music Cracks a Market Wide Open." *Saint Paul Pioneer Press*. September 6, 2014.

Perpetua, Matthew. "Tapes 'n' Tapes, 'Walk It Off.'" *Spin*. April 15, 2008. http://www.spin.com/2008/04/tapes-n-tapes-walk-it-xl/

Perrine, Matthew R. "Despite recorded evidence, Mother Banjo is happy." *Duluth Budgeteer News*. June 12, 2009.

Phares, Heather. "Tapes 'n' Tapes, 'Walk It Off.'" *AllMusic Guide*. Undated. http://www.allmusic.com/album/walk-it-off-mw0000783377

Plewacki, Ryan Paul. "Kid Dakota's Listen to the Crows as they Take Flight, First Listen." *City Pages*. September 16, 2011. (http://www.citypages.com/music/kid-dakotas-listen-to-the-crows-as-they-take-flight-first-listen-6644483)

Power-Luetscher, Ian. "Kid Dakota and Marketa Irglova top October 11 Releases." *City Pages*. October 11, 2011.

Raihala, Ross. "Track Meet." *St. Paul Pioneer Press*. April 6, 2008.

Raihala, Ross. "Tapes 'N Tapes signs with record label." *Pioneer Press*. April 26, 2006.

Raihala, Ross. "Two bands, two hot career arcs, two incredible tours." *St. Paul Pioneer Press*. July 20, 2006.

Raihala, Ross. "This was the Year for Quietdrive to Gun its Engines while Tapes 'n' Tapes Reeled in the Glory." *St. Paul Pioneer Press*. December 21, 2006.

Raihala, Ross. "Rocker on the Fast Track" Pioneer Press. December 26, 2004.

Raihala, Ross. "Nationally, it was the Trip, Locally, It was the Tunes." *St. Paul Pioneer Press*. December 28, 2007.

Raihala, Ross. "Lo and Behold, the (Olympic) Hopefuls are Back in the Game." *St. Paul Pioneer Press*. December 19, 2008.

Raihala, Ross. "Record Store Day Puts a New Spin on Clever Marketing." *St. Paul Pioneer Press*. April 16, 2010.

Reller, Mary. "A Nautical Tale by Erik Appelwick." *Minnesota Daily*. March 31, 2015. http://www.mndaily.com/ae/music/2015/03/31/nautical-tale-erik-appelwick

Riemenschneider, Chris. "A rewind on Tapes." *Star Tribune*. May 12, 2006.

Riemenschneider, Chris. "Local News and Views." *Star Tribune*. June 1, 2007.

Riemenschneider, Chris. "Get Ups Stand Up on CD." *Star Tribune*. July 14, 2006.

Riemenschneider, Chris. "Down for the upbeat." *Star Tribune*. June 17, 2005

Riemenschneider, Chris. "Fast forward—Indie-rock sensations Tapes 'N Tapes are ready to take on the world." *Star Tribune*. July 21, 2006.

Riemenschneider, Chris. "A Vicious Vicious Circle." *Star Tribune*. September 7, 2007.

Riemenschneider, Chris. "The Devil Pays off for Mallman." *Star Tribune*. September 8, 2006.

Riemenschneider, Chris. "Item World—Local News and Views." *Star Tribune*. October 5, 2007.

Riemenschneider, Chris. "The Kid Stays in the Pictutre." *Star Tribune*. February 29, 2008.

Riemenschneider, Chris. "With New CD, Tapes 'N Tapes Quell Backlash Over Their Sudden Fame." *PopMatters*. April 9, 2008. www.popmatters.com/article/with-new-cd-tapes-n-tapes-quell-backlash-over-their-sudden-fame

Riemenschneider, Chris. "Local Bands Rock in Europe" *Star Tribune*. May 26, 2008.

Riemenschneider, Chris. "Hard times Spawn Hard Feelings at Local Label" *Star Tribune*. August 25, 2008.

Riemenschneider, Chris. "Refusing to Burn." *Star Tribune*. December 19, 2008.

Riemenschneider, Chris. "Solomon's Kingdom." *Star Tribune*. April 2, 2010.

Riemenschneider, Chris. "Stop, Shop and Rock 'n' Roll." *Star Tribune*. April 16, 2010.

Riemenschneider, Chris. "The Rumble in Lowertown." *Star Tribune*. July 30, 2010.

Riemenschneider, Chris. "Communist Daughter ready for Fall Rush." *Star Tribune*. September 22, 2011.

Riemenschneider, Chris. "Kid Dakota and Eliza Blue at Cedar Cultural Center." *Star Tribune*. December 30, 2011.

Riemenschneider, Chris. "Best local albums of the year (so far)." *Star Tribune*. June 29, 2012.

Riemenschneider, Chris. "Best of 2014: Twin Cities Critics Tally." *Star Tribune*. December 26, 2014.

Rietmulder, Michael. "Tapes 'n' Tapes talks about the band's self-released third album." *Vita.mn*. February 24, 2011. http://www.vita.mn/story.php?id=116774679

Rizov, Vadim. "Tapes 'n' Tapes, 'Walk It Off.'" *AV Club*. April 7, 2008. http://www.avclub.com/review/tapes-n-tapes-emwalk-it-offem-7162

Roberts, Chris. "Tapes 'n' Tapes roll again." *MPR News*. April 10, 2008. https://www.mprnews.org/story/2008/04/10/tapesntapes

Seel, Steve. "Current in Studio, interview w/ the Hopefuls." *89.3 The Current*. December16, 2008. (http://www.thecurrent.org/feature/2008/12/16/the_hopefuls)

Spevak, Jeff, "Area Native a Star—In China." *Democrat and Chronicle* (Rochester, NY). November 8, 2007.

"Storyhill Fest 2014, Sept 2, 2014," *Cherry & Spoon*. September 2014. http://www.cherryandspoon.com/2014/09/storyhill-fest-2014.html\

Swensson, Andrea. "Kid Dakota, Aviette, The Glad Version, and Others Travel to CMJ." City Pages. November 5, 2008. http://www.citypages.com/music/kid-dakota-aviette-the-glad-version-and-others-travel-to-cmj-6683311

Swensson, Andrea. "Erik Appelwick opens up on new Vicious Vicious album." *Local Current*. February 6, 2012. http://blog.thecurrent.org/2012/02/erik-appelwick-opens-up-on-new-vicious-vicious-album/

Swensson, Andrea. "Tapes 'n' Tapes frontman Josh Grier on the band's impending hiatus and his new solo project." *Local Current*. September 27, 2012. http://blog.thecurrent.org/2012/09/tapes-n-tapes-frontman-josh-grier-on-the-bands-impending-hiatus-and-his-new-solo-project/

Storyhill—Parallel Lives (2008). Documentary film directed by Andrew Zilch.
Timander, Max. "The Hopefuls, 'Now Playing at the One-Seat Theatre." *Are You Rockin.'* December 2008. http://areyourockin.blogspot.com/2008/12/hopefuls-now-playing-at-one-seat.html
Timander, Max. "Honeydogs CD Release Show." Are You Rockin.' March 22, 2009.
Unterberger, Andrew. "Review: Blink-182 Guess What Growing Up Is on 'California.'" Spin. June 30, 2016. www.spin.com/2016/06/review-blink-182-California/
Van Alstyne, Rob. "Kid Dakota transforms on Listen to the Crows..." *City Pages*. December 28, 2011.
Van Alstyne, Rob. "Vicious Vicious Bringing Sincere Sexy Back." *City Pages*. February 8, 2012. (http://www.citypages.com/music/vicious-vicious-bringing-sincere-sexy-back-6757643)
Thomas, Lindsey. "Rupert Pederson." *City Pages*. June 21, 2006. http://www.citypages.com/unknown/rupert-pederson-freak-out-dancing-is-his-profession-refinancing-your-mortgage-at-a-low-low-rate-is-his-passion-6724447J
Van Alstyne, Rob. "Friends Like These: Call it a comeback." *Pulse of the Twin Cities*. April 27, 2006.
Thompson, Erik. "The Current's 7th Birthday Party at First Ave, 1/27/12.," City Pages. January 30, 2012.
Thompson, Erik. "Billy Idol's Acoustic Foray at Turf Club was a Quick One." *City Pages*. January 20, 2015. http://www.citypages.com/music/billy-idols-acoustic-foray-at-turf-club-was-a-quick-one-6652328
Van Alstyne, Rob. "Story of the Sea Change Things Up." *City Pages*. November 7, 2012. http://www.citypages.com/music/story-of-the-sea-change-things-up-6763467
Vang, Youa. "Tropical Depression: I recorded a bunch of songs because I was on a yacht." *City Pages*. July 18, 2014. http://www.citypages.com/music/tropical-depression-i-recorded-a-bunch-of-songs-because-i-was-on-a-yacht-6630885
Warner, Ryan. "The First Non-Depressing Kid Dakota Article? Sorta!" *City Pages*. December 30, 2015.
"Weekend What's What: 7/17–7/20." *L'etoile*. July 17, 2014. http://www.letoilemagazine.com/2014/07/17/weekend-whats-what-717-720/
Whigham, Jennifer. "Kid Dakota and Cloud Cult (Monday, November 21st, Coffman Union, University of Minnesota)." How Was the Show. November 21, 2005. (https://web.archive.org/web/20060217065820/http://howwastheshow.com/reviews-2005/cloud_cult_kid_dakota-11-21-05.html)
Wilson, Dan. "Storyhill Album Shade of the Trees." *Dan Wilson's Blog Thing*. May 7, 2010. http://danwilsonblog.blogspot.com/2010/05/storyhill-album-shade-of-trees.html
Wood, Arthur. "Kerrville Folk Festival 2007." Folkville. Undated. http://myweb.tiscali.co.uk/pawtrait/folkville/biographies/feature-Kerrville2007.html
Wood, Mikael. "Three Questions for Tapes 'n' Tapes." *City Pages*. December 28, 2006. http://www.citypages.com/music/three-questions-for-tapes-n-tapes-6631333

Index

Ackerson, Ed 57, 69, 71, 140
Action Versus Action 158
Alligators in the Lobby 76–78, 98, 115
Alva Star 68, 77–79, 89, 98, 101, 114–116, 125, 141, 147, 154, 167, 171, 189
Anderson, Erin 101, 115, 125, 159, 169
Anderson, Peter 6, 37, 68, 77–78, 88, 101–103, 111, 128, 171
Appelwick, Erik: childhood 8, 9; early bands 9; influences 9, 156; as producer 126, 135–137, 194
Askari, Sarah 157, 158
Aviette 158

Basement Tapes 81, 94
Basilica Block Party 129, 131, 138, 140, 147, 149, 169
The Beach Boys 85, 157
The Beatles 4, 29, 48, 65, 77, 105, 127, 163, 164, 183, 192
Blackberry Way 30
Blood and Clover 86, 99
Blue, Eliza 172, 184–185, 188
Blunt Force Trauma 189
Bobby Llama 72–74, 90
Bonar, Haley 185, 195
Bowie, David 93, 95, 148
Buckley, James 181–182, 193

Camaro 6, 63, 71, 74–75, 87, 88, 99, 100, 104, 106, 109; *see also* Olympic Hopefuls
Campbell, David 78, 131, 137, 165
Carlson, Andy 23–25, 30, 32, 38–39, 43, 60, 79, 81, 120, 124
Cellophane 56, 63, 75
Chris & Johnny 10, 12–17, 23–26, 31–32, 38–40, 72; *see also* Storyhill
Chris & Johnny 15–16, 190
City Pages 51, 54, 69, 70, 78, 83, 86, 87, 90, 94, 106–108, 111, 116, 134, 135, 157–159, 166, 168, 182–186, 194
CityCabin 30, 37–38, 41, 50, 51, 60, 62, 63, 67, 68, 73, 74, 77, 79, 86–88, 90, 97, 98, 101, 117, 120, 121, 133

Clearing 38–40, 44
Cloud Cult 142
Communist Daughter 172, 196
Cunningham, Chris 75–76, 195–196

Davis, Stuart 74
Day, Brent 26, 31, 32, 73
Day, Meleia 31, 32, 73
Denervation 189
DeVille, Bill 5, 54
Different Waters 24–25
Diggins, Billy 59, 64
Don't Look So Surprised 133–135, 157
Dosh, Martin 6, 86, 87, 133, 134, 181–182, 185, 189, 193
Doughty, Mike 123
Dovetail 91, 97
Dragonfly 189, 190
Duotones: A Tribute to Duos of the '70s 123–124

Echoes—The Final Show 48
Egg Music 179–180, 184, 189, 190, 193–194, 196
89.3 The Current 1, 5, 126–127, 135, 140, 157, 158, 166, 171, 173, 183, 194
Ellis 73, 74, 79, 179
Escalator 114–116

Fantastic Merlins 172
Fawcett, Eric: childhood 10–11; early bands 11; influences 10, 11, 28; as producer 149–150, 155; as session player 90, 123, 150, 155, 156, 162, 180
Fine Line Music Café 29, 30, 50, 54, 67, 68, 75
First Avenue 2, 79, 85, 128–130, 140, 148, 161, 167, 169, 171, 180, 183, 184, 195
Fitzgerald 100, 126, 135
Fitzgerald Theater 140, 170, 176, 178
Flag with Hank 33
400 Bar 2, 19, 67, 75, 78–80, 83, 98, 99, 101, 114, 147, 149, 164
Foxfire Coffee Lounge 51
Friends Like These 90–91, 106, 110, 111, 116, 117, 149, 150, 172, 195

The Fuses Refuse to Burn 104–106, 111, 116, 127, 130, 154

Gardner, Adam 161, 162
The Glad Version 116, 117
Graveface Records 159, 185, 189

Hansen, Todd 99–100, 137, 139, 165
The Harvesters 6, 32, 33–37, 44, 54, 178
Hauss, Sarah 41, 57, 74, 83, 114
Hay, Phil 28, 40
Henjum, Heath 1, 6, 33, 36, 102, 103, 106, 110, 111, 131, 134, 137–139, 141, 142, 156, 164, 165, 167–169, 170, 173
Hermanson, John: childhood 13; early bands 14; influences 13, 14; as producer 67, 97–98, 111, 116–117, 149, 150
Hi-Test 90, 97, 99
The Honeydogs 116, 128, 174, 184
The Hopefuls 138–141, 142–149, 154, 164–168, 170–171, 173–174, 185, 189, 190, 194; *see also* Olympic Hopefuls
Hovercraft 69–70
How the Light Gets In 172
Hugo, Chad 81, 82, 93
Hurley, Jay 63, 69–71, 75, 87–88, 195
Hüsker Dü 2, 30, 196

Intl Falls 194
Islands 194

Jackson, Darren: childhood 7; early bands 7–8; influences 7, 21, 37; as producer 97–98, 126, 155, 158, 172–173
Jackson, Janet 19, 94, 155
John Hermanson 60–62
Jones, Scotty 12, 18, 28, 29

Keil, JMatt 6, 63, 42, 71–75, 87–88, 90, 97, 99, 106, 120, 130–131, 136, 143, 149, 163, 193, 195
Kentucky Air 123, 155
Kid Dakota 4, 49, 50–54, 62–63, 75, 79, 83–85, 89, 98, 101, 117–

120, 124–125, 139–142, 155, 158–160, 164, 169–170, 172, 184–189
KISS 8, 10, 102, 131, 171
Kowitz, Jim 174–175, 190, 191
Kubla Khan 99, 130, 149, 195
Kuker, John 50, 61, 75, 85, 188–189, 192
Kuper, Ryan 5, 134, 145

Lacerate 62–63, 75
Landing Gear 70–71, 75, 87–88, 195
The Late Show with David Letterman 93, 96, 148
Leehom, Wang 162–163, 171, 179
The Lefty Devils 54–55
Lessard, Stefan 161–162
Lironi, Steve 63, 64
Listen to the Crows as They Take Flight 185–186
Live at the Grand 26
The Loon 3, 136–137, 145–146, 195
Low 54, 84, 98, 117, 118, 124, 125, 159

Mandelbaum, Tim 59, 81, 82
McGuire, Christopher 6, 50, 51, 53, 62, 63, 68, 77, 79, 85, 86, 98, 101, 110, 125, 152, 173, 188, 189
McKinstry, Steve 18, 26, 31, 32
Messersmith, Jeremy 159, 171, 189
Miles & Means 31–32
Modern Music 163, 165, 171, 173, 179
Munson, John 2, 57–58, 140–141, 171

Neistat, Van 95
N.E.R.D. 5, 82–83, 92–97, 113–114, 122–123, 155, 161, 164
The New Standards 170, 195
Now Playing at the One-Seat Theater 165, 166–168

Oana, Alex 6, 17–23, 26, 30, 38, 39, 41–44, 47–52, 58–61, 63, 67, 73, 79, 85–89, 94, 95, 96, 97–100, 103, 117, 120, 121, 126, 133–136, 149, 159, 165, 170, 196
The O.C. 126
Okoboji 33, 138
Olympic Hopefuls 1–5, 98, 100, 102–112, 119, 126–132; *see also* The Hopefuls
On Pilot Mountain 63, 64, 67, 81, 93, 113
Ostby, John 6, 12, 17–21, 23, 26–29, 40–42, 44, 57, 61, 63–67, 81–83, 93–97, 122–123, 125, 155, 193
Outside 181

Panoramic Blue 90, 116
Parade 156, 157, 167
Paschke, Brent 28–29, 42, 58, 64, 66, 83, 85, 93, 114, 123, 149, 155, 156, 164
The Pause 10, 17, 18, 28, 72, 73

Pearl Jam 14, 70, 179
Pelowski, Dennis 137–139, 143–145, 165
Peppermint 60, 61, 67, 74, 76, 78, 120, 124, 153
The Plastic Constellations 107, 111, 144
Polara 57, 58, 68, 88, 101
A Prairie Home Companion 176–178, 181
Prince 2, 33, 93, 108, 111, 117, 125
Prince, Ian 6, 98, 101, 102, 104, 111, 125, 142, 149, 160, 173, 184, 196
Pulse of the Twin Cities 52, 53, 66, 89, 101, 104, 119, 125, 126, 133, 139, 186

Quruli 101, 118

Radio K 54, 86, 98, 126
Raihala, Ross 127, 132, 135, 136, 144, 148, 157, 183
Reno 28–29, 40; *see also* Spymob
The Replacements 2, 30, 63, 184
Reunion 80
Rhubarb Pie 92, 151
Riemenschneider, Chris 4, 85, 86, 89, 106, 108, 119, 131, 146, 154, 156, 157, 161, 165, 166, 168, 176, 183, 185, 194
Roessler, Brian (Doan) 6, 22–24, 26, 28, 29, 31, 38–41, 44, 47, 57–59, 61, 62, 64, 65, 67, 78, 79, 91, 117, 131, 138, 143
Roise, Nate 99–100, 107–108, 126, 137–139, 143–145, 154–155, 165, 185, 187
The Rolling Stones 4, 65, 159, 162, 164
Romantica 99–100, 107, 111, 144, 154, 165, 171, 175
Roth, Justin 60, 76, 97, 150, 175
Round Trip 21–22
Rundgren, Todd 12, 51
Rupert 128–131, 140–141, 143, 167, 170, 174, 195

Saint Olaf College 8 – 10, 16, 17, 25, 26, 72, 73, 99
Saint Paul Pioneer Press 46, 66, 67, 79, 106, 108, 111, 138, 143, 145, 147, 157, 160, 166, 176, 179, 180, 190
Sally, Zak 54, 62, 84–85, 117, 125, 155, 159
Salmagundi Studio 18, 26, 31, 32, 41
Saturday Night Live 113
Scarbrough, Dave 6, 33–36, 55
Schaff, William 5, 49, 118, 119, 159
The Sedgwicks 69
Seedy Underbelly 58, 73, 75, 79, 85, 89, 99, 117, 192
Seim, Justin 6–8, 32–37, 49, 54, 86
Semisonic 45, 50, 58, 73, 140, 141
7th Street Entry 19, 58, 79, 106, 134, 144

Shade of the Trees 175, 176, 178
Shapeshifting 23, 24, 48
Shark Sandwich 10, 12, 13, 17–20, 22, 26, 28
Shatterproof 70
Shortman Studio 99, 126, 133, 136, 149, 156–158, 165, 167, 172, 173, 189
Show, Rich 33, 34
Sitting Around Keeping Score 58, 94–97, 113, 114, 122, 193
Six Feet Under 116
Skaboom 19, 20
Smith, Caitlin 99
Snider, Dee 162, 171
Solomon, Johnny 5, 90, 91, 102, 144, 150, 172, 189, 195
Spymob 5, 40–43, 57–59, 62–67, 80–83, 92–97, 113, 114, 122, 123, 149, 155, 192, 193; *see also* Reno
Spymob EP 58, 59, 82, 94, 113
Stages 192
Star Tribune 2, 4, 42, 78, 85, 86, 87, 90, 94, 106–108, 111, 116, 134, 135, 145, 157–159, 166, 168, 182–186, 194
Stefaniak, Rob 107, 109, 132, 145
Story of the Sea 149, 160
Storyhill 5, 43–48, 60, 61, 73, 76, 77, 79–81, 89, 91, 92, 97, 106, 116, 117, 120, 123, 124, 150–154, 171, 173–179, 187, 190–192; *see also* Chris & Johnny
Storyhill 152–154
Storyhill Fest 5, 150, 151, 153, 175, 176, 179, 190, 192

Tapes 'n Tapes 3, 136, 137, 145–148, 156, 160, 161, 169, 180, 181, 183, 184, 195
Taste of Minnesota 129, 138, 139, 147
This Side of Lost 44–46, 61, 73
Thomas, Lindsey 86, 108, 116, 134
Timander, Max 167, 168
Townhouse Stereo 41, 42, 57, 58, 65, 114
Tread Water 22–24
Trip Shakespeare 57, 68, 140
Tropical Depression 193, 194
Turf Club 88, 107, 136, 144, 157, 164, 169, 181, 184
12 Rods 50, 51, 80
2024 Records 99–101, 103, 105, 107, 111, 114, 126, 128, 134, 137–139, 142–145, 149, 154
Twigg, Christian 6, 65, 66, 83, 93, 123, 155, 193
The Twilight Hours 141, 171

Underemployed 190
United States Olympic Committee 137
Uptown Bar 2, 79, 108, 136, 164

Van Alstyne, Rob 104, 135, 183, 185, 186

Vicious Vicious 5, 86–87, 94, 98, 99, 102, 109, 133–135, 139–141, 147, 156, 157, 181–184
Vicious Vicious 181–183
Violet 33–34, 36, 54, 56, 102
Vondracek, Leo 141, 173, 174

Walk It Off 156, 160, 161, 169, 180
Walsh, Jim 67, 107, 108
Weeks, David 25, 30, 32, 38, 43, 60, 81, 92, 116, 123, 124, 152, 153
Weiler, Brenda 60, 67, 74, 78, 79, 83, 90, 97–98, 155
Welcome to the Cinema 158, 164
The West Is the Future 117–120, 189
White Light Riot 135, 136, 148
Williams, Pharrell 81–83, 92–97, 114, 122, 149, 155, 164, 193

Wilson, Dan 57, 58, 96, 123, 140, 150, 153, 155–156, 171, 175–176
Wilson, Matt 57–58, 68, 141, 171
A Winner's Shadow 158–160
Wright, Craig 116, 154, 190

XTC 11, 12

Yukon Kornelius 161–162, 171, 179, 192

www.ingramcontent.com/pod-product-compliance
Lightning Source LLC
Chambersburg PA
CBHW081555300426
44116CB00015B/2892